Web3 Development with Angular

Building Web Applications with Blockchain and Web3 Technologies

Soumaya Erradi

Apress®

Web3 Development with Angular: Building Web Applications with Blockchain and Web3 Technologies

Soumaya Erradi
Concesio, Brescia, Italy

ISBN-13 (pbk): 979-8-8688-1885-1				ISBN-13 (electronic): 979-8-8688-1886-8
https://doi.org/10.1007/979-8-8688-1886-8

Copyright © 2025 by Soumaya Erradi

This work is subject to copyright. All rights are reserved by the Publisher, whether the whole or part of the material is concerned, specifically the rights of translation, reprinting, reuse of illustrations, recitation, broadcasting, reproduction on microfilms or in any other physical way, and transmission or information storage and retrieval, electronic adaptation, computer software, or by similar or dissimilar methodology now known or hereafter developed.

Trademarked names, logos, and images may appear in this book. Rather than use a trademark symbol with every occurrence of a trademarked name, logo, or image we use the names, logos, and images only in an editorial fashion and to the benefit of the trademark owner, with no intention of infringement of the trademark.

The use in this publication of trade names, trademarks, service marks, and similar terms, even if they are not identified as such, is not to be taken as an expression of opinion as to whether or not they are subject to proprietary rights.

While the advice and information in this book are believed to be true and accurate at the date of publication, neither the authors nor the editors nor the publisher can accept any legal responsibility for any errors or omissions that may be made. The publisher makes no warranty, express or implied, with respect to the material contained herein.

Managing Director, Apress Media LLC: Welmoed Spahr
Acquisitions Editor: Anandadeep Roy
Coordinating Editor: Jessica Vakili

Cover image by Pixabay.com

Distributed to the book trade worldwide by Springer Science+Business Media New York, 1 New York Plaza, New York, NY 10004. Phone 1-800-SPRINGER, fax (201) 348-4505, e-mail orders-ny@springer-sbm.com, or visit www.springeronline.com. Apress Media, LLC is a Delaware LLC and the sole member (owner) is Springer Science + Business Media Finance Inc (SSBM Finance Inc). SSBM Finance Inc is a **Delaware** corporation.

For information on translations, please e-mail booktranslations@springernature.com; for reprint, paperback, or audio rights, please e-mail bookpermissions@springernature.com.

Apress titles may be purchased in bulk for academic, corporate, or promotional use. eBook versions and licenses are also available for most titles. For more information, reference our Print and eBook Bulk Sales web page at http://www.apress.com/bulk-sales.

Any source code or other supplementary material referenced by the author in this book is available to readers on GitHub (https://github.com/Apress). For more detailed information, please visit https://www.apress.com/gp/services/source-code.

If disposing of this product, please recycle the paper

*To everyone who writes code not just
to solve problems, but to open possibilities.*

Table of Contents

About the Author xxv

About the Technical Reviewer xxvii

Preface xxix

Introduction xxxi

Chapter 1: Web3 1

    Introduction 1

    Introduction to Web3 2

        Definition and Scope of Web3 2

        Evolution from Web1 and Web2 3

        Web1: The Static Web 4

        Web2: The Social and Interactive Web 4

        The Need for Web3 4

        Key Characteristics of Web3 5

        The Broader Implications of Web3 8

    Security 9

        Cryptographic Principles 9

        Decentralized Security Mechanisms 12

        Security Challenges and Solutions 15

    Ownership 19

        Concept of Digital Ownership 19

        Non-Fungible Tokens (NFTs) 21

        Implications for Content Creators and Consumers 24

    Native Payments 26

        Integration of Cryptocurrency 26

TABLE OF CONTENTS

- Benefits over Traditional Payment Systems 30
- Case Studies and Examples 33
- Transparency 36
  - Open-Source Nature of Web3 36
  - Transparent Transaction Records 38
  - Benefits for Users and Developers 41
- Driving Technologies 43
  - Blockchain Technology 43
  - Smart Contracts 46
  - Decentralized Storage and Computing 49
- Application Types 53
  - Decentralized Applications (DApps) 54
  - Decentralized Finance (DeFi) Platforms 58
- Conclusion 64
- Chapter Summary 64

Chapter 2: Blockchain 65

- Introduction 65
- Introduction to Blockchain 66
  - Definitions and Basic Concepts 66
  - Historical Background and Evolution 67
  - Blockchain 1.0: Bitcoin and Cryptocurrencies 68
  - Blockchain 2.0: Smart Contracts and Ethereum 68
  - Blockchain 3.0: Scalability and Interoperability 68
  - Key Players and Projects 69
  - Technology Overview 71
  - Blockchain Architecture 72
  - Consensus Mechanisms 74
  - Nodes and Network Structure 77
  - Understanding Blockchain Transactions 80
  - Transaction Lifecycle 81
  - Transaction Fees and Incentives 83

TABLE OF CONTENTS

    The Principle of Decentralization 86
    Definition and Importance 86
    Benefits over Centralized Systems 88
    Challenges and Trade-Offs 91
    Blockchain Security 94
    Cryptographic Security 94
    Network Security Mechanisms 96
    Case Studies of Security Breaches and Solutions 100
Conclusion 102
Chapter Summary 102

Chapter 3: Use Cases 103

Introduction 103
Blockchain Applications 103
    Finance 105
    Currency 110
    Property Records 118
    Smart Contracts 124
    Supply Chains 130
    Voting 136
Conclusion 143
Chapter Summary 144

Chapter 4: Pros and Cons of Blockchain 145

Introduction 145
The Benefit of Decentralization 146
    Reduced Single Points of Failure 146
    Enhanced Security and Resilience 147
    Real-World Examples of Decentralization Benefits 148
    Challenges of Decentralization 148
Efficient Transactions 149
    Speed and Cost Benefits 150

vii

TABLE OF CONTENTS

- Comparisons with Traditional Systems 151
- Reliability and Accessibility 152
- Examples of Efficient Transactions in Practice 152
- Innovative Use Cases for Transaction Efficiency 153
- Challenges to Achieving Efficiency 154
- Future Trends in Blockchain Efficiency 154

Transparency in Blockchain 155
- Public Ledger Benefits 155
- Applications in Various Sectors 156
- Innovative Use Cases 157
- Challenges of Blockchain Transparency 157
- Future Trends in Blockchain Transparency 158

Cost Considerations 159
- Initial Setup and Operational Costs 160
- Cost Savings Through Efficiency 162
- Balancing Costs and Benefits 162
- Environmental Costs 163
- Case Studies of Cost-Saving Implementations 164
- Future Trends in Cost Management 164

Transaction Speed 165
- Factors Affecting Speed 165
- Comparisons with Traditional Systems 167
- Examples of High-Speed Blockchains 167
- Challenges in Achieving High Speed 168
- Innovations in Driving Transaction Speed 168
- Future Trends in Transaction Speed 169

Regulatory Challenges 169
- Legal and Compliance Issues 170
- Case Studies of Regulatory Responses 171
- Challenges in Regulatory Implementation 172
- Opportunities for Regulatory Advancement 173

Future Trends in Regulation 173
Expanded Regulatory Applications 174
Conclusion 174
Chapter Summary 175

Chapter 5: Blockchain Applications 177
Introduction 177
Differences Between Web2 and Web3 177
Architectural Differences 177
User Experience Changes 179
Identity and Access 179
Financial Interactions 180
Content Ownership 180
Case Studies of Transition 181
Choosing the Right Blockchain 183
Factors to Consider 184
Scalability 184
Security 185
Decentralization 186
Developer Ecosystem 186
Costs 187
Regulatory Environment 187
Interoperability 188
Comparisons of Popular Blockchains 188
Decision-Making Framework 189
Introduction to Ethereum 190
Overview of the Ethereum Platform 191
Ethereum's Vision 192
Key Features and Functionalities 193
Smart Contracts 194
Ethereum Virtual Machine (EVM) 195
Ether (ETH) 197

Proof of Stake (PoS) 198
Layer 2 Scaling Solutions 199
Token Standards 200
Ethereum Ecosystem and Community 201
DeFi on Ethereum 202
NFTs and the Creator Economy 203
DAOs and Decentralized Governance 204
Developer Ecosystem 205
Ethereum's Future 205
Conclusion 206
Chapter Summary 207

Chapter 6: Wallet 209

Introduction 209
Understanding Cryptocurrency Wallets 209
What Is a Cryptocurrency Wallet? 210
Definition 210
Purpose 210
How Wallets Work 211
Asymmetric Cryptography 211
Transaction Process 212
Types of Wallets 213
Custodial vs. Non-custodial Wallets 214
Importance of Wallet Security 215
Common Misconceptions About Wallets 215
Real-World Examples 216
Mnemonic Phrases and Their Importance 216
What Is a Mnemonic Phrase? 216
Why Is It Important? 218
Best Practices for Mnemonic Phrase Security 218
Real-World Lessons: Horror Stories 223
Advanced Security Techniques 224

Encrypting Your Mnemonic 225
Multi-signature Wallets 225
Hidden Wallets 225
Cold Storage Solutions 225
Keys: Public and Private 226
Definition and Differences 226
What Is a Private Key? 226
What Is a Public Key? 227
Key Differences: Private vs. Public 228
Why Is This System Brilliant? 228
Importance of Key Management 229
Common Key Management Strategies 230
Real-World Key Management Failures 230
Advanced Key Management Strategies 231
Wallet Setup Process 232
Step-by-Step Guide to Setting Up a Wallet 233
Common Pitfalls and Solutions 237
Types of Wallets 238
Hardware Wallets 239
What Is a Hardware Wallet? 239
How Hardware Wallets Work 239
Advantages of Hardware Wallets 239
Disadvantages of Hardware Wallets 240
When to Use a Hardware Wallet 240
Real-World Example 241
Software Wallets 241
What Is a Software Wallet? 241
How Software Wallets Work 241
Advantages of Software Wallets 242
Disadvantages of Software Wallets 242
When to Use a Software Wallet 243

TABLE OF CONTENTS

    Real-World Example 243
    Paper Wallets 243
    What Is a Paper Wallet? 243
    How Paper Wallets Work 244
    Advantages of Paper Wallets 244
    Disadvantages of Paper Wallets 244
    When to Use a Paper Wallet 245
    Real-World Example 245
    Comparing Wallet Types 245
  Conclusion 246
  Chapter Summary 247

Chapter 7: Provider 249
  Introduction 249
  Role of Providers in Blockchain 249
    What Is a Provider? 250
    Why Providers Are Needed 251
    Historical Evolution of Providers 251
    Types of Providers 252
    Full Node Providers 252
    RPC Providers (Remote Procedure Call Providers) 253
    Wallet Providers 254
    Gateway Providers 256
    Indexing and Querying Providers 256
    Hybrid Providers 257
    Why Providers Are Critical to Blockchain Growth 257
  Network Considerations for Providers 258
    Performance Metrics 258
    Latency 258
    Throughput 260
    Uptime 261
    Global Geographic Coverage 262

TABLE OF CONTENTS

Reliability and Failover Strategies 263
Multi-region Redundancy 264
Automatic Retries and Circuit Breakers 264
Provider Fallback Mechanisms 265
Security Implications 266
Man-in-the-Middle (MITM) Risks 267
Data Injection Attacks 267
Key Management 268
Privacy Considerations 268
IP Address Exposure 268
Transaction Metadata Leakage 268
Techniques to Preserve Privacy 269
Comparing Wallet Providers vs. RPC Providers 269
Wallet Providers 270
Key Responsibilities of Wallet Providers 270
Private Key Management 270
Transaction Construction and Signing 271
Session Management and Permissions 272
Categories of Wallet Providers 273
Real-World Case Study: MetaMask 273
RPC Providers 274
Key Responsibilities of RPC Providers 274
API Exposure 274
Node Management and Scaling 275
Real-World Case Study: Infura 275
Key Differences: A Deeper Comparison 276
Choosing the Right Provider(s) 276
Provider Selection Criteria 277
Speed and Performance 277
Key Performance Indicators (KPIs) 278
Importance of Regional Distribution 278

xiii

- Case Study: NFT Minting Stress Test 278
- Decentralization and Trust Models 279
- Levels of Decentralization 279
- Why Trust Models Matter 279
- Case Study: Infura Outage (2020) 280
- Security and Compliance 280
- Security Factors to Evaluate 280
- Regulatory and Legal Compliance 281
- Case Study: Tornado Cash Sanctions (2022) 281
- Cost and Pricing Structures 281
- Cost Factors to Compare 282
- Optimizing Costs 282
- Developer Experience (DX) 282
- Multichain and Scalability Support 283
- Future-Readiness: Emerging Technologies 283

Advanced Provider Topics 284
- Self-Hosting RPC Endpoints 284
- Requirements for Running Full Nodes 284
- Operational Challenges 285
- When Self-Hosting Makes Sense 286
- Hybrid Architectures 286
- Decentralized RPC Networks 287
- Case Study: Pocket Network Growth 288
- Provider Aggregators and Fallback Systems 288
- Example Strategies 289
- Libraries Supporting Provider Aggregation 289
- Multichain Application Design 290

Evolving Responsibilities of Providers 290
- Best Practices for Working with Providers 290
- The Future of Providers 291

Conclusion 293

Chapter Summary 293

Chapter 8: Smart Contracts and Decentralized Applications 295

Introduction.. 295
Deep Dive into Smart Contracts 296
    What Are Smart Contracts? 296
    Core Properties.. 296
    How Smart Contracts Differ from Traditional Contracts 297
    How Smart Contracts Work (Under the Hood)... 298
    The Ethereum Virtual Machine (EVM) 299
    Limitations and Design Constraints 300
    Real-World Examples of Simple Contracts 301
    Why Smart Contracts Matter 302
    Smart Contract Architecture 302
    On-Chain vs. Off-Chain Logic 302
    Contract Interfaces and ABIs 303
    Storage and State Design.. 304
    Modularity and Contract Composition 305
    Inheritance 305
    Delegation (Proxy Pattern)... 306
    Events and Logs 306
    Reentrancy and Call Context 307
    Composability and Interoperability 308
    Popular Use Cases for Smart Contracts 308
    Decentralized Finance (DeFi).. 308
    Non-Fungible Tokens (NFTs)... 310
    Marketplace Contracts (e.g., OpenSea and Blur)... 311
    Decentralized Autonomous Organizations (DAOs) 311
    Escrow and Conditional Payments 312
    Identity and Reputation Systems... 312
    Gaming and Virtual Economies 313
    Supply Chain and Real-World Asset Tracking 313
    The Smart Contract Lifecycle 314

xv

TABLE OF CONTENTS

 Drafting the Contract Logic 314
 Writing the Contract (Solidity) 315
 Compiling the Contract 316
 Deploying the Contract 316
 Verifying the Contract 317
 Interacting with the Contract 317
 Monitoring and Maintaining 318
 Gas, Costs, and Efficiency 318
 What Is Gas? 318
 Why Gas Efficiency Matters 319
 Common Gas Costs for Operations 320
 Optimizing Contract Design for Gas Efficiency 320
 Testing and Profiling Gas Usage 322
 Tools for Gas Profiling 322
 Gas Limits and Out-of-Gas Errors 322
 Gas Optimization Tradeoffs 323
Implementation of Smart Contracts and dApps 323
 Development Tools Overview 323
 Hardhat 324
 Foundry 325
 Truffle 326
 Remix IDE 327
 Tool Comparison Table 327
 Plugin Ecosystem and Extensions 328
 Workflow Recommendation by Use Case 328
 Writing Your First Contract (Line by Line) 328
 Contract Goals 329
 Full Code (Solidity 0.8+) 329
 Walkthrough by Section 331
 Pragma and License 331
 State Variables 331

Events	331
Modifiers	332
Constructor	332
Vote Functions	332
Close Voting (Owner Only)	333
Testing Your Contract	333
Compiling and Deploying Your Contract	334
Understanding the Compilation Process	334
Deployment Best Practices	338
Testing and Security Best Practices	339
The Role of Testing in Smart Contract Development	339
Types of Smart Contract Tests	340
Writing Unit Tests with Hardhat	340
Writing Tests in Foundry	341
Fuzz Testing and Invariant Checks	341
Common Smart Contract Vulnerabilities	342
Using Static Analysis Tools	343
Slither	343
MythX	343
Foundry Coverage	343
Auditing Basics	343
Real-World Testing Strategy	344
Integrating Smart Contracts into Decentralized Applications (dApps)	344
dApp Architecture Overview	345
Connecting to Wallets	345
Using ethers.js to Call Contracts	346
Calling View Functions (No Gas)	346
Sending Transactions (Costs Gas)	346
Displaying Events and Real-Time Feedback	346
Handling Gas, Errors, and Confirmations	346
Network Management and Testnets	347
Using Frontend Libraries and Frameworks	348

UI/UX Patterns for Web3 348
Conclusion 349
Chapter Summary 349

Chapter 9: Web Development with Angular 351

Introduction 351
Introduction to Angular 351
    A Brief History 352
    From Rewrite to Reinvention 352
    Core Design Principles 352
    Who Uses Angular Today? 353
    Staying Current 353
Angular Architecture and Core Concepts 354
    Components, Services, and Modules 354
    Routing and Navigation 354
    Change Detection 355
    Forms: Template-Driven vs. Reactive 355
    Directives and Pipes 356
    Component Lifecycle Hooks 356
    Putting It All Together 356
Angular CLI and Project Setup 357
    Installing the Angular CLI 357
    Creating a New Project 358
    Project Structure 358
    Standalone vs. Module-Based Structure 359
    Environmental Management 360
    Modern Build System 360
    Extending the Project with Schematics 361
    Putting It into Practice 361
State Management in Angular 361
    Why State Management Matters 362
    Local State with Components 362

Reactive State with RxJS	363
Global State with Store Patterns	364
Fine-Grained Reactivity with Signals	364
When to Avoid Overengineering	365
Putting It into Practice	365
Working with HTTP and APIs	**366**
The HttpClient	366
Creating a Service for API Calls	367
Consuming Data in a Component	368
Handling Errors and Retries	369
Working with REST and GraphQL APIs	369
Real-Time Data with WebSockets	369
Example: API Service with Pagination	370
Putting It into Practice	371
Building Reusable UI with Angular Material	**371**
What Is Angular Material?	371
Adding Angular Material to a Project	372
Theming and Customization	372
Commonly Used Components	372
Creating Custom Components with the CDK	373
Combining Components into a Layout	374
Putting It into Practice	375
Routing, Guards, and Lazy Loading	**375**
Angular Router Fundamentals	376
Nested Routes and Route Parameters	376
Route Guards	377
Lazy Loading	378
Advanced Routing Features	378
Putting It into Practice	379
Testing Angular Applications	**379**
Why Test?	380

TABLE OF CONTENTS

    Unit Testing Components and Services 380

    Testing Components with TestBed.. 381

    Modern Test Runners.. 382

    Mocking HTTP Requests... 382

    End-to-End (E2E) Testing 383

    A Balanced Testing Strategy 384

  Performance Optimization 385

    Tree-Shaking and Ahead-of-Time (AOT) Compilation 386

    Change Detection Strategies 386

    Fine-Grained Reactivity and Zoneless Change Detection 387

    Component-Level Optimizations... 387

    Lazy Loading and Route-Level Code Splitting 387

    Server-Side Rendering (SSR) and Hydration 388

    Putting It into Practice 388

  Angular in the Real World... 389

    Angular vs. Other Frontend Approaches 389

    Best Practices from Large Projects 389

    Preparing for Modern Integrations 390

    Case Study: Evolving an Enterprise Dashboard 390

    Putting It All Together 391

  Conclusion 391

  Chapter Summary.. 392

Chapter 10: Web3 Development with Angular 393

  Introduction.. 393

  Introduction to Decentralized Applications (dApps) 393

    What Defines a dApp? 394

    The Role of the Frontend 394

    Typical dApp Architecture... 395

    Why Use Angular for dApps? 396

    What Comes Next 397

Connecting Angular with Blockchain Networks 397
Setting Up the Development Environment 397
Required Tools and Versions 397
Creating the Project Structure 398
Running a Local Blockchain 398
Compiling and Deploying 398
Connecting the Angular App 399
Using a Wallet 399
Understanding Blockchain RPC Providers 399
Using Libraries for Blockchain Access 400
Managing Provider Connections in Angular Services 400
Network Switching and Fallbacks 401
Security Considerations 402
Putting It into Practice 402

Managing Wallet Integration 403
What Is a Wallet? 403
Connecting to a Wallet in an Angular App 403
Handling Wallet State Reactively 404
Requesting Permissions and Signing 405
Security Best Practices 406
Putting It into Practice 406

Smart Contracts: Reading and Writing Data 407
Interacting with Smart Contracts in Angular 407
Reading Contract State 407
Writing Data and Sending Transactions 408
Handling Gas and Fees 409
Handling Errors and Edge Cases 409
Putting It into Practice 410
Full Smart Contract Example with Hardhat 410
Writing the Contract 411
Compiling the Contract 411

TABLE OF CONTENTS

- Deploying the Contract Locally 412
- Copy the ABI 412
- Creating the Angular Contract Service 412
- Using the Service in a Component 414
- Recap 415
- Handling Real Errors and Gas Estimation Problems 415
- Why "Cannot Estimate Gas" Happens 415
- Practical Strategies to Handle It 416
- Defensive Patterns 417
- Putting It into Practice 418
- Real-World Patterns for Web3 Frontends 418
- Protecting Routes and Features 419
- Listening for Blockchain Events 419
- Keeping UX Responsive 420
- Security Best Practices 420
- Handling Network Changes 421
- Resilient Error Handling 421
- Putting It into Practice 422

Putting It All Together: A Mini Angular dApp 422
- A Practical Example: Decentralized Voting App 422
- Project Structure 422
- Connecting the Wallet 423
- Reading On-Chain Data 424
- Writing a Transaction 424
- Protecting Voting Routes 425
- Reactive Feedback 425
- Full Example: Combining It All 425
- Final Tips 425

Testing and Deployment Strategies for Angular dApps 426
- Testing Smart Contracts 426
- Testing Angular Wallet Logic 427

Using Testnets	428
Deployment Best Practices	428
Maintainability	429
Conclusion	**429**
Chapter Summary	**430**
Final Words and Further Learning	**431**
Suggested Resources for Continued Learning	431
Keep Building	432
Index	**433**

About the Author

Soumaya Erradi is an experienced web developer and passionate IT and electronics trainer, specializing in frontend development and enterprise applications built with Angular. She spends most of her time exploring new advancements in the tech world and helping other developers enhance their skills. As a conference speaker, she covers advanced Angular topics, provides tips for integrating smart contracts, and shares the best solutions for Web3 applications.

About the Technical Reviewer

Serena Sensini is an Italian computer engineer specializing in Artificial Intelligence (AI) and Natural Language Processing (NLP). She has extensive experience in designing and developing web and stand-alone software solutions from scratch, with skills spanning mobile cross-platform development, web design, data-driven solutions, and software architecture. Serena is also an author of five technical books on topics such as Docker, Kubernetes, and NLP, and she runs a popular tech blog called TheRedCode.it where she shares insights and fosters tech culture. She currently serves as an Innovation & Emerging Technologies Leader at Dedalus, and beyond her professional roles, Serena is a tech content creator, speaker, and educator, regularly conducting courses and seminars with nonprofit organizations, contributing significantly to the tech community in Italy.

Preface

This book is the result of years of exploration and study of the Web3 ecosystem. I wanted to bring together everything I've learned into one place to support those who find themselves in the same position I was when I first started, unsure where to look and with very few resources available. At that time, there was a lack of documentation and practical examples, and as someone used to building applications with Angular, I often had to figure things out on my own.

I'm proud of the path I've taken and of everything I've learned along the way. The Web3 community, although still small, has been a source of energy, encouragement, and inspiration, giving me the strength to keep moving forward and achieve this goal.

As I often like to say, *"If it doesn't exist, build it yourself."* That's exactly what I did, and now, I'm sharing it with you.

Introduction

Web3 has become one of the most transformative movements in modern software development. By shifting from centralized platforms to decentralized applications, it introduces new possibilities for ownership, trust, and innovation on the web. At the same time, Web3 development brings its own challenges: learning how blockchains work, writing and deploying smart contracts, and connecting them to user-friendly applications.

This book is written to guide you through that journey. It combines the worlds of **blockchain and smart contracts** with **modern Angular development**, showing you how to move from theory to practice with clear explanations, code examples, and real-world use cases. Whether you're a web developer curious about blockchain or a blockchain enthusiast looking to build accessible frontends, this book will give you the tools and confidence to create complete decentralized applications.

Who This Book Is For

This book is aimed at developers with some experience in web technologies, especially JavaScript or TypeScript, who want to understand how to build decentralized applications. If you are comfortable with Angular basics, that will help, but the chapters are structured to provide step-by-step guidance. Even if you are new to blockchain, you will find foundational chapters that introduce the core concepts before moving to more advanced topics.

How This Book Is Structured

The book is organized into three parts that build on one another:

- **Part I – Foundations of Web3 and Blockchain**

    These chapters introduce blockchain architecture, consensus mechanisms, and the evolution of the web from Web1 to Web3. You'll also learn about decentralization, smart contracts, and the advantages and challenges of blockchain.

INTRODUCTION

- **Part II – Building Blocks of Web3 Applications**

    Here, we explore practical use cases across industries, examine the strengths and weaknesses of blockchain technology, and dive deeper into applications such as finance, property records, and supply chains. This section also includes a detailed discussion of Ethereum and its ecosystem.

- **Part III – Developing Web3 Applications with Angular**

    The final chapters bring everything together. You'll see how to integrate Angular with Web3 libraries, design and implement decentralized frontends, manage state, and test your applications effectively. The book concludes with a full dApp example, complete with smart contract deployment and Angular integration, to help you put theory into practice.

What You Will Learn

By the end of this book, you will

- Understand the core principles of blockchain and decentralized applications.

- Write and deploy smart contracts to Ethereum-compatible networks.

- Build modern dApps with Angular, integrating them seamlessly with blockchain backends.

- Explore best practices for state management, testing, and performance in Web3 projects.

- Gain a clear picture of where Web3 is today and where it is heading.

This book is not only about code but also about context. Web3 is evolving rapidly, and developers need to grasp both the technical details and the broader ecosystem. My hope is that this book will help you join the conversation, contribute to the community, and build applications that make a real impact.

CHAPTER 1

Web3

Introduction

This chapter introduces Web3 as a foundational transformation in the way the internet is built, accessed, and experienced. Moving beyond its blockchain roots, Web3 encompasses a broader shift toward decentralization, transparency, and user empowerment. Through this chapter, readers will

- Understand the historical evolution from Web1 to Web3
- Discover the technologies and principles that define Web3 (e.g., decentralization, trustless systems, and digital ownership)
- Learn about key application areas, including decentralized finance (DeFi), native payments, and NFTs
- Examine the security challenges and solutions within decentralized systems
- Explore how transparency, governance, and user control are embedded into Web3
- Analyze real-world case studies to understand practical adoption

This chapter sets the stage for more advanced topics on smart contracts, DApps, and blockchain integration in the following chapters.

CHAPTER 1   WEB3

Introduction to Web3

Definition and Scope of Web3

When we talk about Web3, the first thing that often comes to mind is blockchain technology. While blockchain is a crucial component, Web3 represents a much broader paradigm shift in how the internet is structured and operates. Web3 is the third generation of the web, moving beyond the centralized, server-client model of Web1 and the more interactive, but still centralized, Web2. Figure 1-1 illustrates the transition from Web1 to Web3. At its core, Web3 envisions an internet where data, applications, and services are decentralized, providing more control, privacy, and opportunities to users.

Figure 1-1. *Evolution of the Web*

In this new era, Web3 aims to decentralize not just data storage and processing but also governance and decision-making. Through technologies like blockchain, distributed ledgers, smart contracts, and decentralized applications (DApps), Web3 introduces a trustless and permissionless environment. This means users no longer need to rely on centralized entities or intermediaries for online transactions, communications, or access to services. Instead, these processes are automated and secured by cryptographic algorithms and consensus mechanisms. This distinction is visually represented in Figure 1-2.

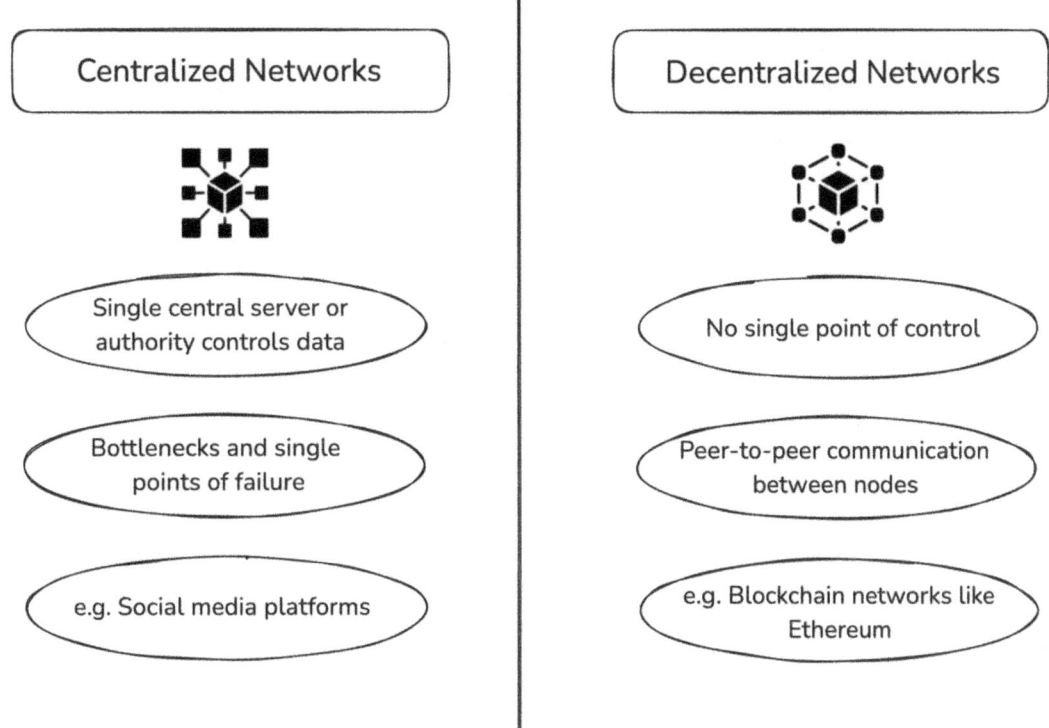

Figure 1-2. Centralized vs. Decentralized Web

Web3's scope extends far beyond finance and cryptocurrencies, impacting areas such as social media, content creation, governance, and even the future of work. It seeks to redefine how we interact with the digital world, promoting concepts like digital ownership, privacy, and transparency. In this chapter, we will explore these key aspects, investigating how Web3 represents a transformative shift in the foundation of the internet's architecture and the profound implications it has on individuals and society.

Evolution from Web1 and Web2

To fully understand the significance of Web3, it's essential to comprehend its evolution from the earlier stages of the internet: Web1 and Web2.

CHAPTER 1　WEB3

Web1: The Static Web

Web1, also known as the "read-only" web, marked the beginning of the internet era in the late 1980s and early 1990s. During this period, the web was primarily composed of static web pages. Users could consume content, but interaction was minimal, if not nonexistent. Websites were essentially digital brochures, and information flowed in one direction, from the publisher to the consumer. The web was a decentralized network in terms of hosting, but the experience was limited, as it lacked user interaction and dynamic content.

Web2: The Social and Interactive Web

The transition to Web2, starting in the early 2000s, brought a more dynamic, interactive, and social web. Web2 is characterized by the rise of user-generated content, social media platforms, and the centralization of services. Major tech companies like Google, Facebook, and Amazon became gatekeepers of data and information. While Web2 made the internet more accessible and interactive, it also led to issues such as data privacy concerns, monopolistic control, and the exploitation of user data for profit.

In Web2, users could not only consume content but also create, share, and interact with it. However, this increased interactivity came with a trade-off: users had to surrender control over their data to centralized platforms, which could manipulate, monetize, or censor content at their discretion. This centralization also led to significant power imbalances, where a few corporations have a huge influence on the digital lives of billions of people.

The Need for Web3

The limitations of Web2, particularly regarding data privacy, ownership, and centralization, laid the foundation for Web3. Users and developers alike began to seek alternatives that would restore control, transparency, and trust in the digital realm. Web3 addresses these issues by decentralizing the web, giving power back to the users through technologies that enable peer-to-peer interactions without the need for intermediaries. The Web2 to Web3 transition is shown in Figure 1-3.

Web3 envisions a web where users own their data, identity, and content. They can interact, transact, and collaborate directly with others in a secure and trustless environment. This shift is not just technical but also ideological, advocating for an internet that is more fair and inclusive, where users have more control and autonomy.

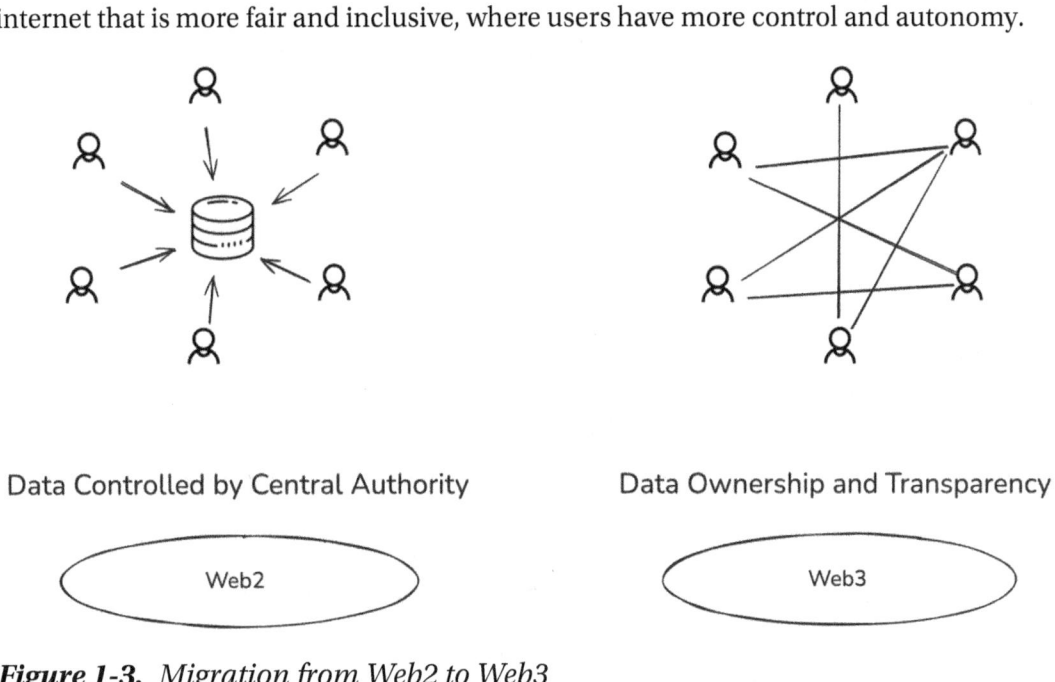

Figure 1-3. Migration from Web2 to Web3

Key Characteristics of Web3

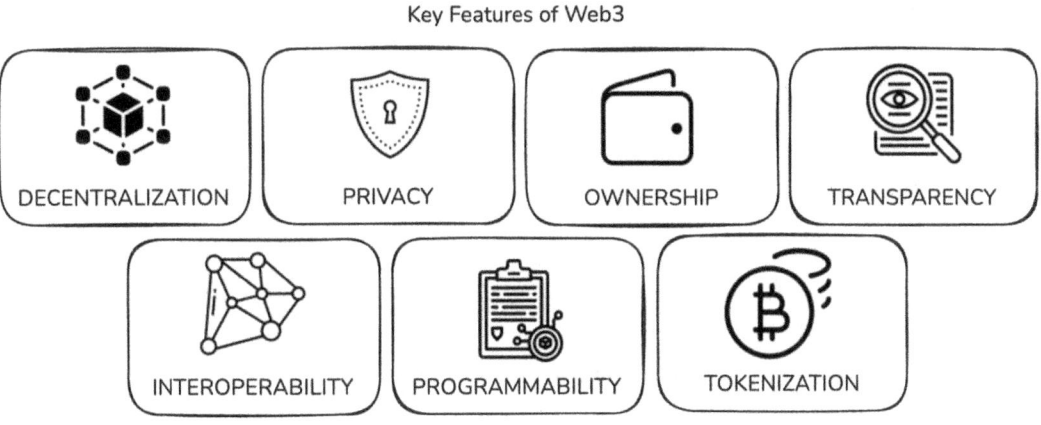

Figure 1-4. Benefits and Features of Web3

CHAPTER 1 WEB3

As we move forward into the Web3 era, several defining characteristics set it apart from its predecessors (Figure 1-4 summarizes the core features of Web3):

1. **Decentralization:**

    One of the foundational principles of Web3 is decentralization. Unlike Web2, where data and services are controlled by centralized entities, Web3 relies on distributed networks. Blockchain and other decentralized technologies ensure that data is stored across a network of nodes, reducing the risk of censorship, data breaches, and single points of failure.

2. **Trustless and Permissionless:**

    Web3 operates on a trustless model, meaning that participants do not need to trust a central authority or intermediary to engage in transactions or interactions. Smart contracts, self-executing contracts with the terms of the agreement directly written into code, play a crucial role in this trustless environment. Additionally, Web3 is permissionless, allowing anyone to participate in the network without needing approval from a central authority.

3. **Digital Ownership and Identity:**

    In Web3, users have full ownership of their digital assets and identities. Through technologies like NFTs (non-fungible tokens), users can prove ownership of digital items, such as art, music, and virtual real estate. Moreover, decentralized identity solutions empower users to control their online identities without relying on centralized platforms.

4. **Interoperability:**

    Web3's interoperability makes it possible for different networks, platforms, and applications to work seamlessly together. This interoperability is enabled by open standards and protocols, which facilitate the easy exchange of data and assets across various decentralized systems.

5. **Enhanced Security and Privacy:**

   Security and privacy are central to Web3's design. Cryptographic techniques ensure that data is secure and private, while decentralized architectures reduce the risks associated with centralized data storage. Users have greater control over their personal information, with the ability to share data on a need-to-know basis.

6. **Incentivization and Tokenomics:**

   Web3 introduces new economic models through tokenomics, the use of tokens to incentivize and reward network participants. Tokens can represent ownership, governance rights, or access to services. This creates a more participatory economy where users are not just consumers but also stakeholders in the networks they use.

7. **Transparency and Open Source:**

   Web3 is known for its transparency. Most Web3 projects are open-source, allowing anyone to audit the code and verify the integrity of the system. Users and developers are able to trust each other when a network is open because they can see exactly how it operates and where potential vulnerabilities may lie.

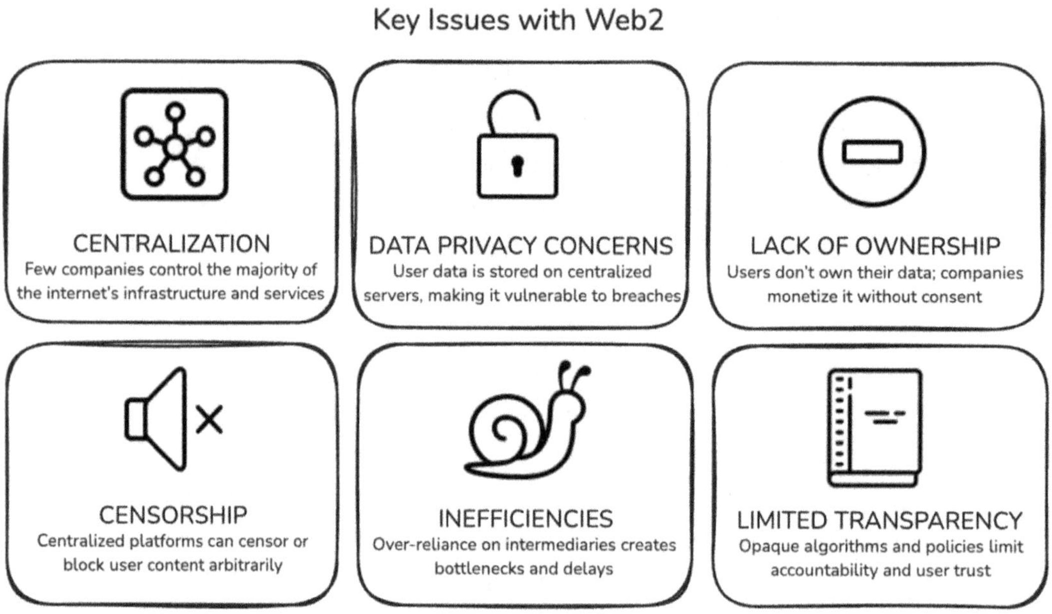

Key Issues with Web2

CENTRALIZATION
Few companies control the majority of the internet's infrastructure and services

DATA PRIVACY CONCERNS
User data is stored on centralized servers, making it vulnerable to breaches

LACK OF OWNERSHIP
Users don't own their data; companies monetize it without consent

CENSORSHIP
Centralized platforms can censor or block user content arbitrarily

INEFFICIENCIES
Over-reliance on intermediaries creates bottlenecks and delays

LIMITED TRANSPARENCY
Opaque algorithms and policies limit accountability and user trust

Figure 1-5. Problems with Web2 Architecture

The Broader Implications of Web3

The rise of Web3 is not just a technological evolution but also a social and economic revolution. By decentralizing the web, Web3 challenges existing power structures, giving more agency to individuals and communities. It has the ability to make access to information, financial services, and digital assets more accessible, reducing the digital divide and promoting greater inclusion. These societal implications are shown in Figure 1-6.

For content creators, Web3 offers new ways to monetize their work and engage with their audiences directly. For consumers, it provides greater control over their data and interactions online. For developers, Web3 opens up a new frontier of innovation, where they can build decentralized applications that operate independently of any central authority.

Figure 1-6. Social Impact of Web3

Security

Security is a fundamental aspect of Web3, essential for maintaining trust and ensuring the integrity of decentralized networks. In this section, we will explore how security is managed in Web3, focusing on the unique challenges and solutions that emerge in a decentralized environment. We will look at the role of cryptography, decentralized identity, and how security is enforced in a permissionless world.

Cryptographic Principles

Web3's architecture relies heavily on cryptography to secure data, transactions, and user identities. The cryptographic principles that make up Web3 are essential to its operation as a decentralized and trustworthy system. These principles ensure that data is protected and that transactions are managed securely across the network.

CHAPTER 1   WEB3

1. **Public and Private Key Cryptography:**

   Public and private key cryptography is the foundation of secure communication and transactions on Web3. See Figure 1-7 for how public/private key pairs function. Each participant in a Web3 network holds a pair of keys: a public key that can be shared with others and a private key that must be kept secure. This system allows for the encryption of messages and transactions, ensuring that only the intended recipient can decrypt and access the information.

   The use of digital signatures, enabled by private keys, is crucial in Web3. When a user initiates a transaction or interaction, they sign it with their private key. This signature can be verified by others using the corresponding public key, confirming the authenticity and integrity of the transaction without the need for a central authority.

   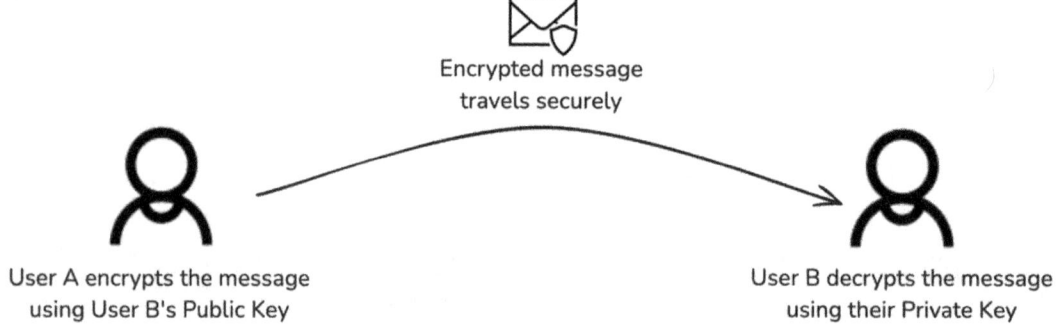

   Figure 1-7. Public vs. Private Key Encryption

2. **Zero-Knowledge Proofs (ZKPs):**

   Zero-knowledge proofs are a fascinating cryptographic technique that allows one party to prove to another that they know a value without revealing the value itself. ZKPs are increasingly important in Web3, particularly for enhancing privacy and security in decentralized applications. Figure 1-8 illustrates the principle behind ZKPs.

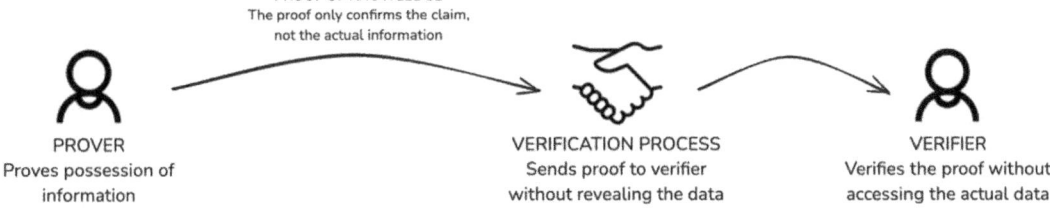

Figure 1-8. How Zero-Knowledge Proofs Work

For example, in a transaction, a zero-knowledge proof might allow a user to prove they have enough funds to complete a transaction without revealing their entire balance. This protects user privacy while still ensuring the transaction's validity. ZKPs are being used in various Web3 applications, including decentralized finance (DeFi) platforms, where privacy and security are essential.

3. **Decentralized Identity (DID):**

   Decentralized identity is an emerging area in Web3 that addresses the issue of identity management in a decentralized environment. In traditional systems, identity is often tied to centralized entities like governments, corporations, or platforms, which can lead to security risks, including identity theft and data breaches.

   In contrast, DID systems give users control over their digital identities. These identities are stored on a blockchain or decentralized ledger, allowing users to prove their identity or credentials without relying on a central authority. This reduces the risk of identity theft and provides a more secure way to manage personal information.

   Users in a DID system can also control what information they share and with whom, enhancing privacy. For instance, a user could prove they are over 18 without disclosing their exact birthdate. This selective disclosure is particularly valuable in Web3, where privacy and user control are key priorities. The concept is summarized in Figure 1-9.

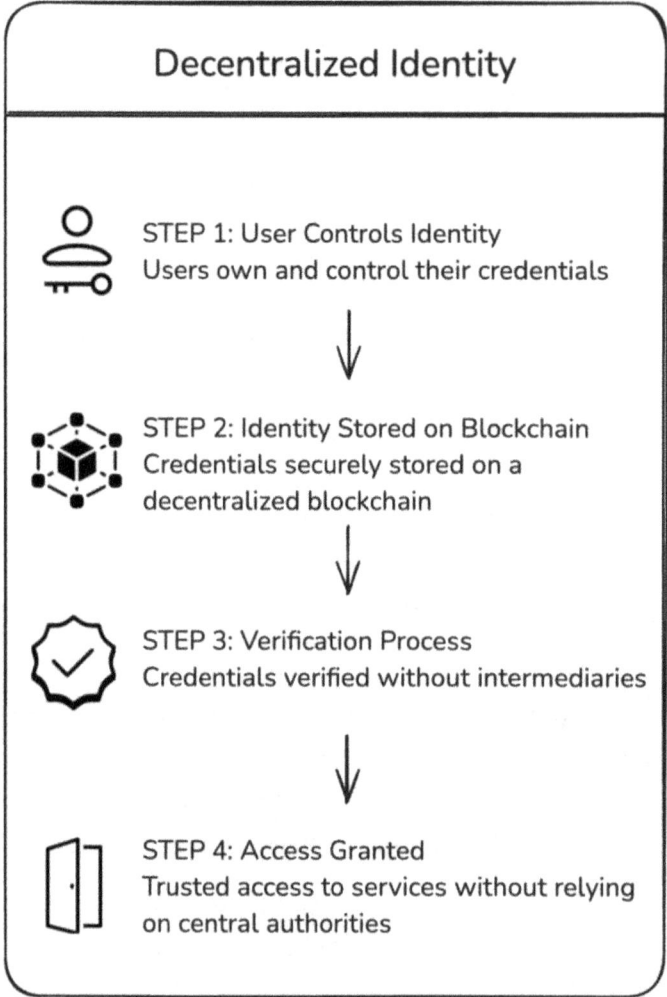

Figure 1-9. *Decentralized Identity Structure*

Decentralized Security Mechanisms

Web3's security architecture is different from traditional centralized systems. In Web3, security is distributed across the network and uses various mechanisms to secure the system's integrity, prevent malicious actors, and maintain trust without central supervision.

CHAPTER 1 WEB3

1. **Peer-to-Peer Networks:**

   In Web3, peer-to-peer (P2P) networks are the foundation for decentralized communication and data sharing. These networks operate without a central server, distributing data across numerous nodes. Each node in the network communicates directly with others, sharing information and resources. Figure 1-10 shows a typical P2P structure.

   This decentralized approach enhances security by eliminating central points of failure. In a traditional centralized system, if the central server is compromised, the entire system can be affected. However, in a P2P network, even if some nodes are compromised, the network as a whole can continue to function securely. This resilience is a key security advantage of Web3.

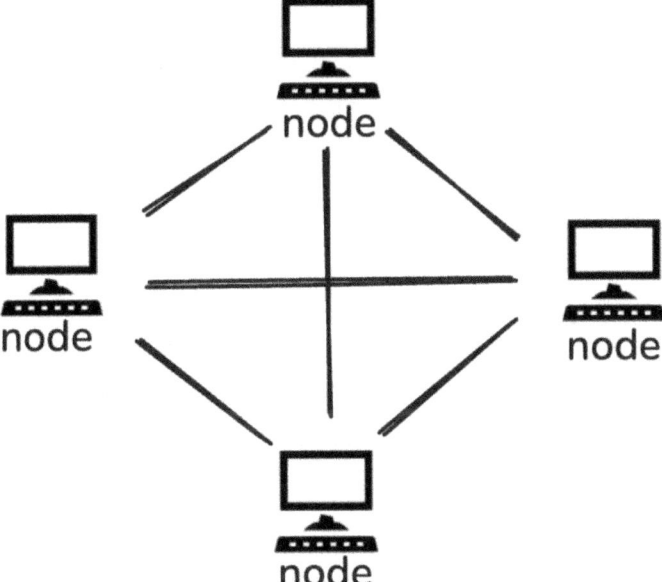

Figure 1-10. Peer-to-Peer Architecture

2. **Decentralized Governance:**

   Decentralized governance plays a crucial role in the security of Web3 networks. Unlike traditional systems where a central authority makes decisions, decentralized networks often use decentralized autonomous organizations (DAOs) to govern the network. Refer to Figure 1-11 for a DAO governance process.

In a DAO, decisions are made collectively by the community, often through a voting process where token holders can vote on proposals. This decentralized approach to governance reduces the risk of corruption and central points of control, which are common vulnerabilities in traditional systems. It also ensures that security measures can be updated and improved through a transparent, community-driven process.

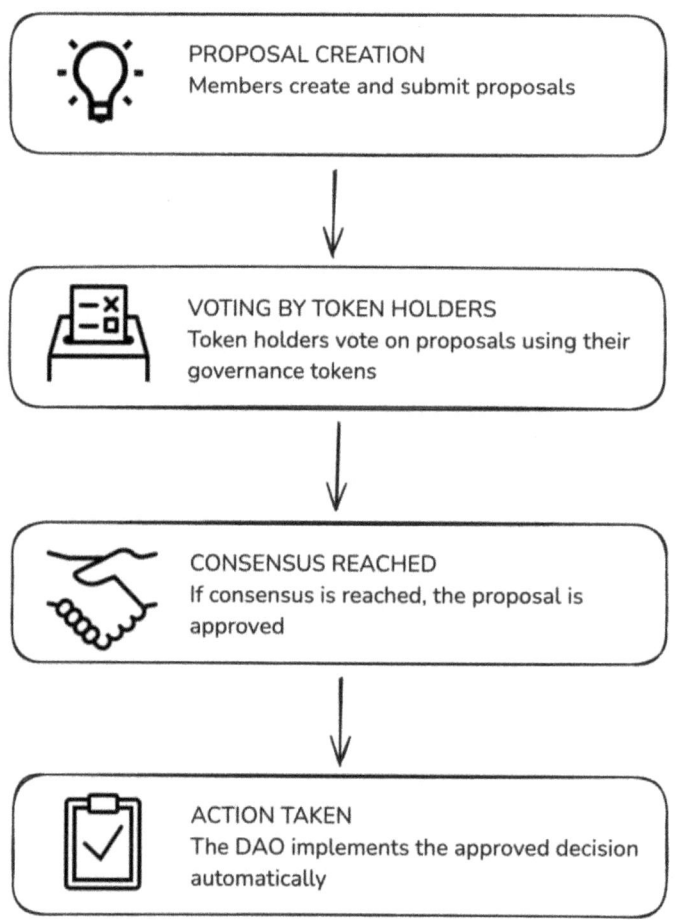

Figure 1-11. *DAO Governance Model*

CHAPTER 1 WEB3

3. **Privacy-Enhancing Technologies:**

   In addition to ZKPs, Web3 incorporates various privacy-enhancing technologies that contribute to its security framework. These technologies help protect user data and ensure that sensitive information is not exposed during transactions or interactions.

   As an example, mixing services, also known as tumblers, are used in some Web3 applications to enhance transaction privacy. These services mix the cryptocurrency transactions of many users to obfuscate the origin of funds, making it difficult to trace a transaction back to its source. This is particularly useful in scenarios where users wish to maintain anonymity. See Figure 1-12 for how mixing services work.

   Another example is the use of homomorphic encryption, which allows data to be encrypted and processed in its encrypted form. This means that sensitive data can be analyzed and used without ever being decrypted, protecting user privacy and enhancing security.

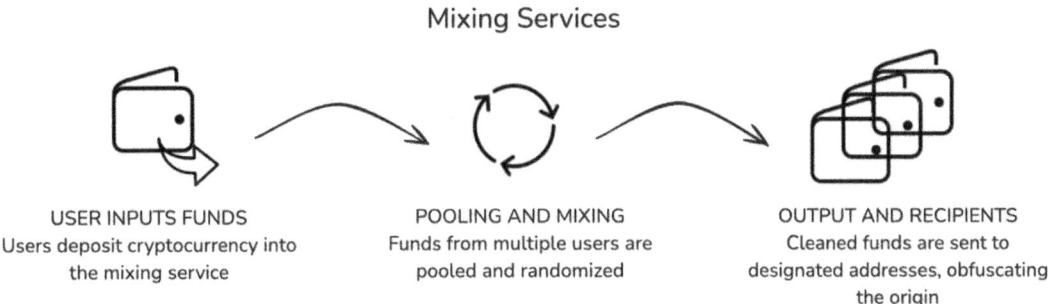

Figure 1-12. Privacy via Mixing Services

Security Challenges and Solutions

While Web3 offers significant advancements in security, it also presents unique challenges. These challenges arise from the decentralized nature of Web3, the early stages of its technologies, and the need for large adoption of best practices.

1. **User Responsibility and Education:**

   One of the primary challenges in Web3 security is the shift in responsibility from centralized entities to individual users. In Web3, users are responsible for managing their private keys, securing their wallets, and understanding the implications of their actions on the network.

   This increased responsibility can lead to security risks, particularly for users who lack expertise in the complexities of cryptography and decentralized systems. Phishing attacks, loss of private keys, and user errors are common issues that can result in the loss of funds or data.

   To address these challenges, education is crucial. Users must be informed about best practices for securing their assets, including the use of hardware wallets, multi-factor authentication, and the importance of safeguarding private keys. Key management strategies are shown in Figure 1-13. Developers and platforms can help reduce user errors by creating interfaces that are more intuitive and user-friendly.

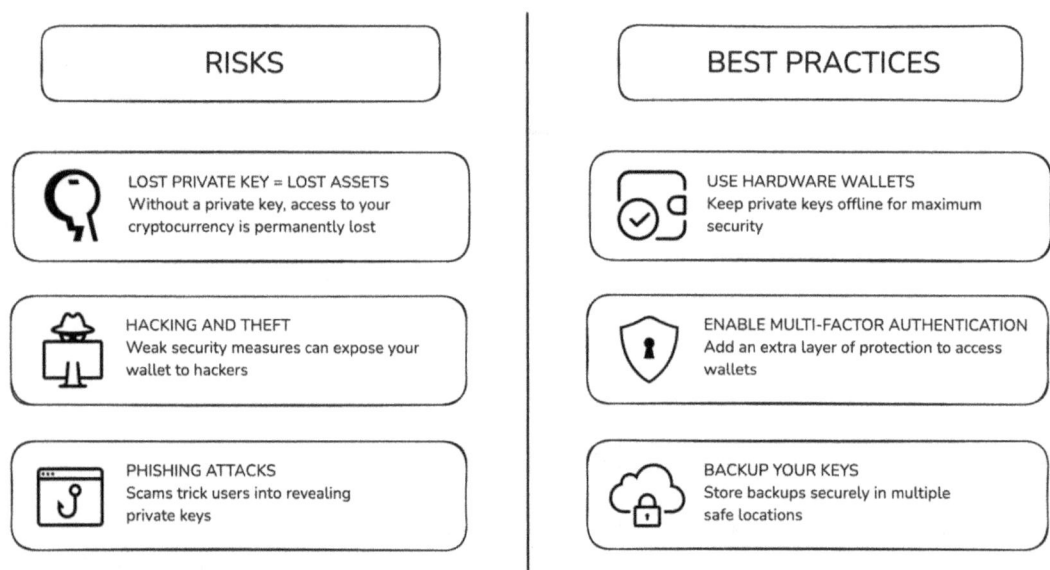

Figure 1-13. Key Management Best Practices

2. **Social Engineering and Phishing Attacks:**

   Social engineering and phishing attacks are significant threats in Web3 because they focus on the human element instead of technical vulnerabilities. In these attacks, malicious actors attempt to trick users into revealing their private keys, passwords, or other sensitive information. Common attack vectors are illustrated in

   In the decentralized world of Web3, where transactions are irreversible and there is no central authority to appeal to, falling victim to such attacks can have severe consequences. To deal with these threats, Web3 platforms must implement robust anti-phishing measures, such as warning users of potential risks, educating them about common attack vectors, and using technologies like domain verification to ensure the legitimacy of websites and services.

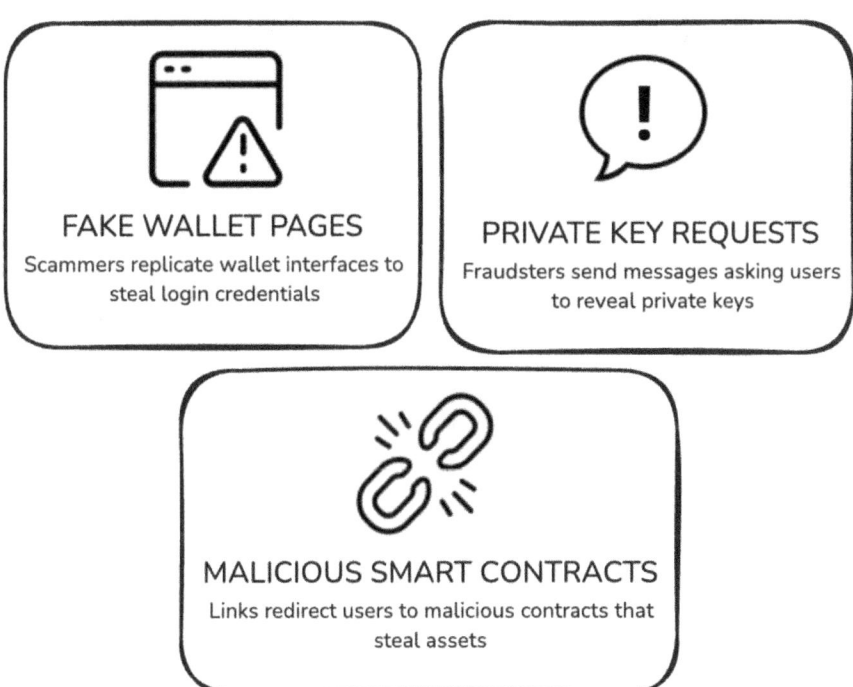

Figure 1-14. *Phishing Attack Vectors*

3. **Legal and Regulatory Challenges:**

   Web3 operates in a largely unregulated environment, which can lead to legal and regulatory challenges. The decentralized nature of Web3 makes it difficult to enforce traditional laws and regulations, which are typically designed for centralized entities.

   As governments and regulatory bodies begin to focus more on Web3, there will be an increasing need for legal frameworks that balance innovation with security and compliance. This includes addressing issues such as the legality of DAOs, the taxation of cryptocurrency transactions, and the enforcement of data protection laws in decentralized networks. Figure 1-15 maps global regulatory challenges.

   Web3 developers and stakeholders should be vigilant in working with regulators to make sure that new laws and regulations are fair, effective, and supportive of the decentralized ethic of Web3. This might involve the creation of self-regulatory organizations or industry standards that can help guide the development of secure and compliant Web3 technologies.

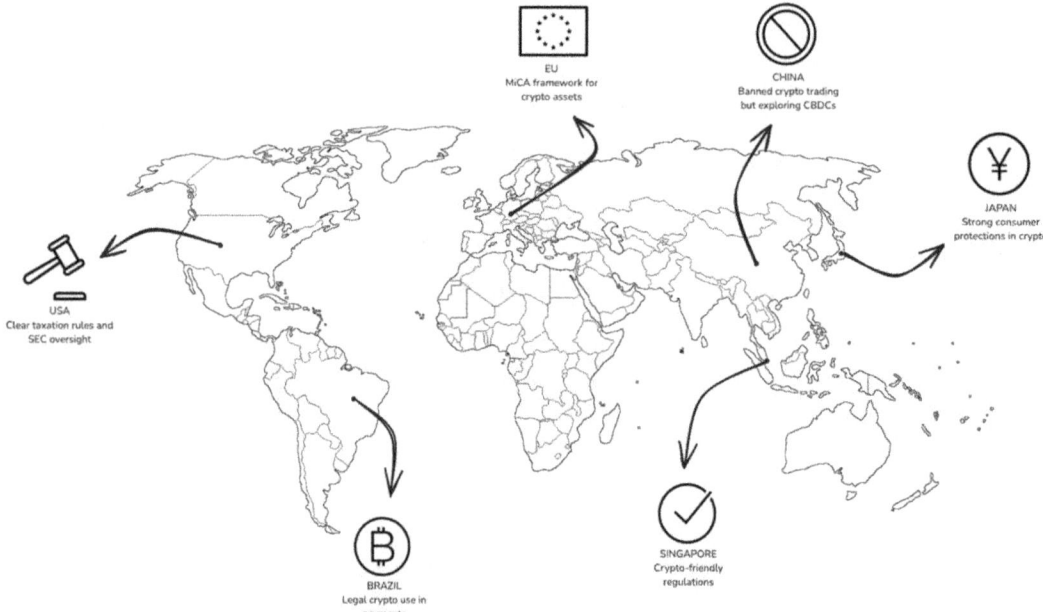

Figure 1-15. Global Regulatory Considerations

Ownership

Ownership is a central concept in Web3, primarily changing how we perceive, manage, and transfer digital assets. In contrast to the traditional web, where centralized entities often control and monetize user data and content, Web3 empowers individuals with true ownership of their digital assets, identity, and interactions. This section will explore the concept of digital ownership, the role of non-fungible tokens (NFTs), and the implications for content creators and consumers.

Concept of Digital Ownership

In the Web2 era, digital ownership is often a vague concept. While users may believe they own the content they create or the data they generate, the reality is that this "ownership" is often controlled by centralized platforms. These platforms can modify, delete, or monetize user content without the user's direct consent, leading to significant questions about who truly owns digital assets in the modern internet.

1. **Centralized vs. Decentralized Ownership:**

    In centralized systems, digital ownership is typically governed by the terms of service of a platform. For example, when you upload a photo to a social media site, the platform often retains certain rights to use, distribute, or even sell that content. Similarly, in the case of digital goods, such as eBooks or music, users often only purchase a license to use the content, not the content itself. This centralized model limits user control and creates a dependency on the platform's continued existence and terms. See Figure 1-16 for a comparison of ownership models.

    Web3 changes this dynamic by leveraging decentralized technologies, such as blockchain, to give users direct control over their digital assets. In a Web3 environment, ownership is verified and managed through cryptographic keys, ensuring that only the owner of a private key can access or transfer the associated digital assets. This shift from platform-controlled ownership to user-controlled ownership is one of the most significant advancements of Web3.

CHAPTER 1   WEB3

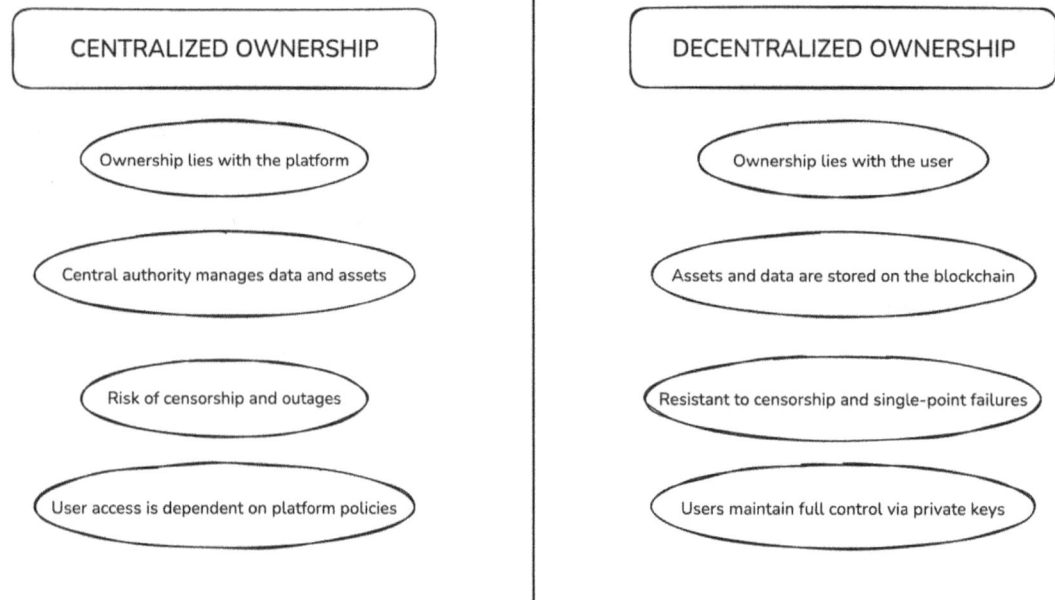

Figure 1-16. *Centralized vs. Decentralized Ownership*

2. **True Ownership in Web3:**

    In Web3, true ownership means having direct and exclusive control over digital assets. This is made possible through decentralized networks where ownership records are stored immutably on a blockchain. Once you own a digital asset, it cannot be taken away or altered without your permission, and you can transfer or sell it independently of any centralized platform.

    This form of ownership extends beyond simple digital goods to include a wide range of assets, including cryptocurrencies, domain names, virtual real estate, and even digital identities. An illustrative case is having a cryptocurrency wallet in Web3, which gives you complete control over its funds, with no one being able to freeze or take your assets. Ownership verification is shown in Figure 1-17.

True Ownership via Blockchain

USER WITH PRIVATE KEY
User secures access to assets or data with their private key

BLOCKCHAIN VERIFIES OWNERSHIP
The blockchain cross-checks the private key to authenticate ownership

OWNERSHIP STORED IMMUTABLY
The ownership is recorded on the blockchain and cannot be altered

Figure 1-17. Verifying Ownership via Blockchain

Non-Fungible Tokens (NFTs)

One of the most visible manifestations of digital ownership in Web3 is the rise of non-fungible tokens (NFTs). NFTs represent unique digital assets that can be owned, traded, and verified on a blockchain, providing a new way to establish and prove ownership of digital content.

1. **What Are NFTs?**

    Non-fungible tokens (NFTs) are cryptographic assets that represent something unique and cannot be exchanged on a one-to-one basis like cryptocurrencies. The distinction is shown in Figure 1-18. Each NFT has a distinct value and identity, often associated with digital art, music, videos, virtual real estate, collectibles, and more. Unlike cryptocurrencies such as Bitcoin or Ethereum, which are fungible (each unit is identical and can be exchanged), NFTs are indivisible and unique.

    NFTs are stored on a blockchain, where they can be bought, sold, or traded. The blockchain ensures the provenance and authenticity of the NFT, meaning that the ownership history of the digital asset is transparent and cannot be tampered with. This makes NFTs particularly valuable for artists, creators, and collectors, as they can prove ownership of their work or collection in a way that was not possible before.

CHAPTER 1 WEB3

Interchangeable and identical units (e.g., Bitcoin, USD)   Unique assets with individual value (e.g., digital art, collectibles)

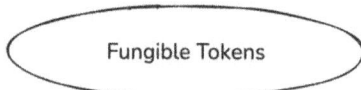 

Figure 1-18. *Fungible vs. Non-Fungible Tokens*

2. **The Role of NFTs in Digital Ownership:**

    NFTs have revolutionized the concept of digital ownership by allowing creators to tokenize their work, thereby turning digital files into unique, tradeable assets. For example, an artist can create a digital painting, mint it as an NFT, and sell it to a buyer who will then have verifiable ownership of that digital painting. The NFT can include metadata that links to the artwork, as well as information about its creator, its purchase history, and any royalties owed to the artist on future sales. Figure 1-19 illustrates the lifecycle of an NFT.

    This innovation has significant implications for the digital economy. For one, it allows content creators to directly monetize their work without relying on intermediaries like galleries, record labels, or streaming platforms. Moreover, NFTs can be programmed with smart contracts that automatically pay royalties to creators each time the NFT is resold, providing a continuous revenue stream and ensuring that creators benefit from the increasing value of their work.

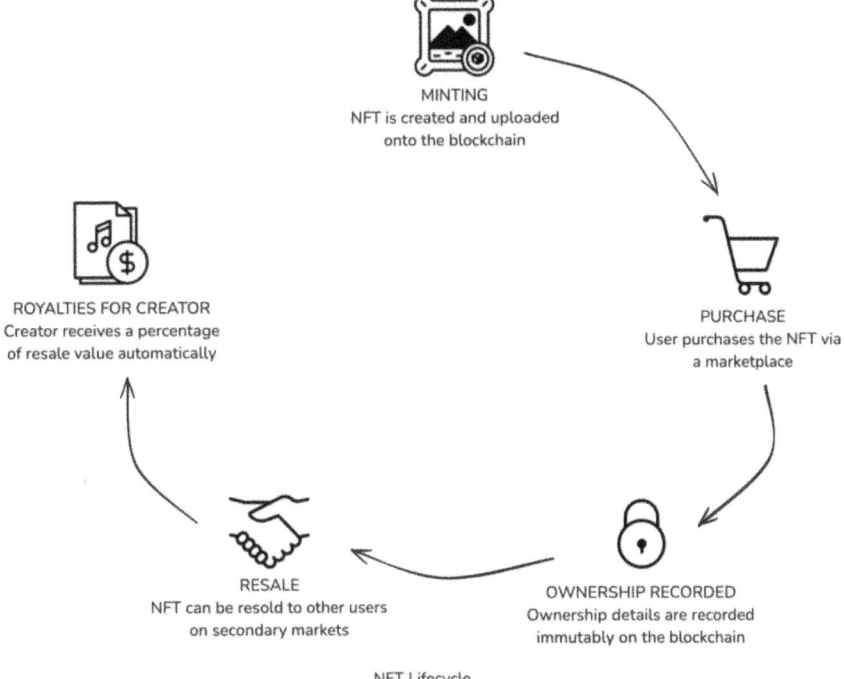

Figure 1-19. *NFT Lifecycle Overview*

3. **Use Cases and Examples:**

    The impact of NFTs is already being felt across various industries. In the art world, digital artists like Beeple have sold NFT artworks for millions of dollars, highlighting the demand for verifiable digital ownership. NFT use cases across industries are shown in Figure 1-20. Musicians are also exploring NFTs as a way to release limited edition albums, concert tickets, or exclusive content, directly connecting with their fans without the need for traditional music distribution channels.

    In the gaming industry, NFTs are being used to create and trade in-game items, skins, and virtual land. Players can own and trade these digital assets independently of the game developer, ensuring that their investments in time and money remain theirs, even if the game or platform changes. Virtual worlds like Decentraland and The Sandbox have embraced NFTs to enable users to buy, sell, and develop virtual real estate, creating entirely new economies within digital environments.

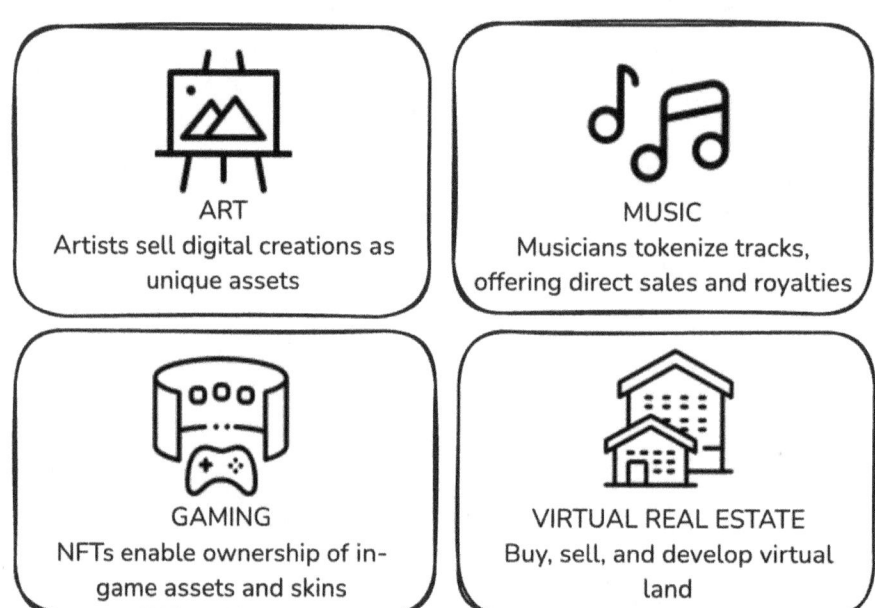

Figure 1-20. *NFT Use Cases*

Implications for Content Creators and Consumers

The transition to true digital ownership in Web3 has significant repercussions for both content creators and consumers. It changes the power dynamics of the internet, opens new avenues for monetization, and alters the process of creating and distributing value in the digital world. This contrast is visualized in Figure 1-21.

1. **Empowering Content Creators:**

    Web3 gives content creators more control over their work and how it is distributed. By minting their creations as NFTs, artists, musicians, writers, and other creators can directly sell their work to consumers without intermediaries taking a significant cut of the profits. This democratization of the creative economy allows more creators to earn a living from their work, regardless of their geographic location or access to traditional distribution channels.

Furthermore, the ability to program smart contracts into NFTs means that creators can ensure they continue to receive royalties on secondary sales. This is a significant shift from traditional models, where creators often only profit from the initial sale of their work, with little to no control over how it is used or resold in the future.

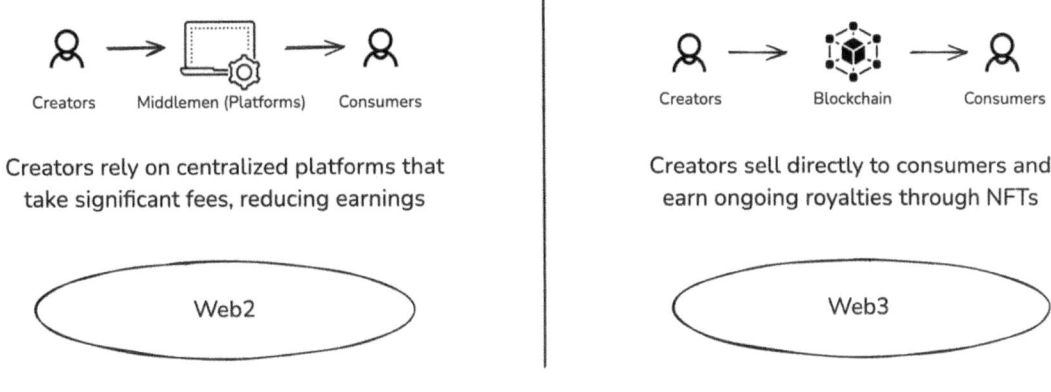

Content Creators

Figure 1-21. Web2 vs. Web3 Creator Rights

2. **Consumer Benefits and Challenges:**

    For consumers, Web3 and the advent of NFTs offer the opportunity to own unique digital assets that can appreciate in value over time. This is in contrast to the current model in Web2, where users typically do not own the digital content they purchase but merely have a license to access it.

    However, with this new model also come challenges. The value of NFTs can be highly speculative, with prices fluctuating dramatically based on market trends, demand, and the perceived value of digital assets. Additionally, the decentralized nature of Web3 means that consumers must take greater responsibility for securing their digital assets, as there are no central authorities to assist in recovering lost or stolen NFTs.

3. **The Future of Digital Ownership:**

    As Web3 continues to evolve, the concept of digital ownership will likely expand to include new forms of assets and interactions. For example, decentralized social media platforms could allow users to own their data and content, choosing how and where it is shared and even monetizing it through microtransactions or data marketplaces.

    Additionally, the integration of NFTs with virtual and augmented reality could create immersive digital experiences where ownership of virtual goods and spaces plays a central role. This could lead to the development of entirely new digital economies, where value is created, exchanged, and owned in ways that are currently unimaginable.

Native Payments

One of the most transformative aspects of Web3 is the integration of native payments directly into the structure of the internet. Unlike traditional payment systems that rely on banks and payment processors as intermediaries, Web3 enables peer-to-peer transactions using cryptocurrencies and decentralized financial technologies. This section explores the role of native payments in Web3, the benefits they offer over traditional systems, and real-world examples of their application.

Integration of Cryptocurrency

At the heart of Web3's native payments is the use of cryptocurrency. Cryptocurrencies, such as Bitcoin, Ethereum, and a multitude of other digital currencies, serve as the primary medium of exchange within the Web3 ecosystem. These currencies are designed to operate on decentralized networks, enabling secure, trustless, and borderless transactions.

CHAPTER 1 WEB3

1. **What Are Native Payments?**

   Native payments in Web3 refer to the use of cryptocurrencies for transactions directly within decentralized applications (DApps) and platforms. Unlike traditional online payments that require a third-party processor like PayPal or Visa, native payments occur directly between users via blockchain technology. Smart contracts make it possible to exchange directly without the need for an intermediary, as they automatically enforce transaction terms. See Figure 1-22 for a comparison of payment models.

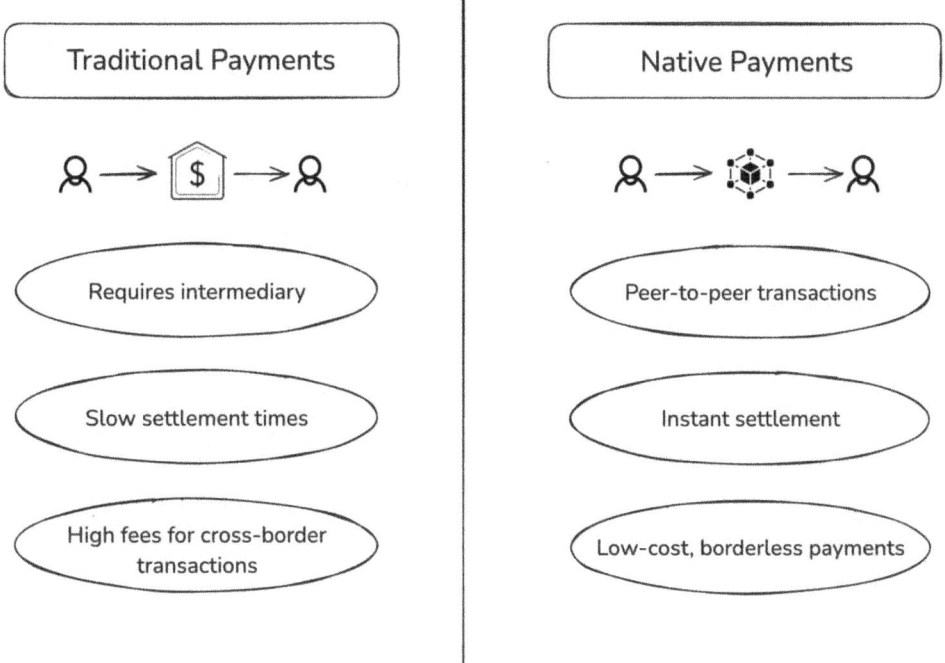

Figure 1-22. Native vs. Traditional Payments

   This can be seen in a decentralized marketplace; a buyer can pay for goods or services using cryptocurrency, with the payment being processed and recorded on the blockchain. The seller receives the payment directly in their digital wallet, often within minutes, with minimal transaction fees compared to traditional payment systems.

27

2. **Types of Cryptocurrencies Used:**

   There are various types of cryptocurrencies used in Web3 (Figure 1-23), each serving different purposes:

   - **Bitcoin (BTC):** The first and most well-known cryptocurrency, Bitcoin is often used as a store of value and medium of exchange in Web3 transactions. Its decentralized nature makes it a popular choice for payments in the digital economy.

   - **Ethereum (ETH):** Ethereum is not only a cryptocurrency but also a platform for building decentralized applications. Ether (ETH), its native currency, is widely used in Web3 for transactions, paying for gas fees and participating in decentralized finance (DeFi) activities.

   - **Stablecoins:** Stablecoins, such as USDT (Tether) and USDC (USD Coin), are cryptocurrencies pegged to the value of a fiat currency, typically the US dollar. These are used in Web3 for transactions that require price stability, making them a preferred choice for everyday payments and remittances.

   - **Altcoins and Tokens:** Beyond Bitcoin and Ethereum, there are numerous other cryptocurrencies and tokens that serve specific functions within their respective ecosystems. Governance tokens allow holders to participate in the decision-making processes of a DAO, while utility tokens provide access to specific services within a DApp.

CHAPTER 1 WEB3

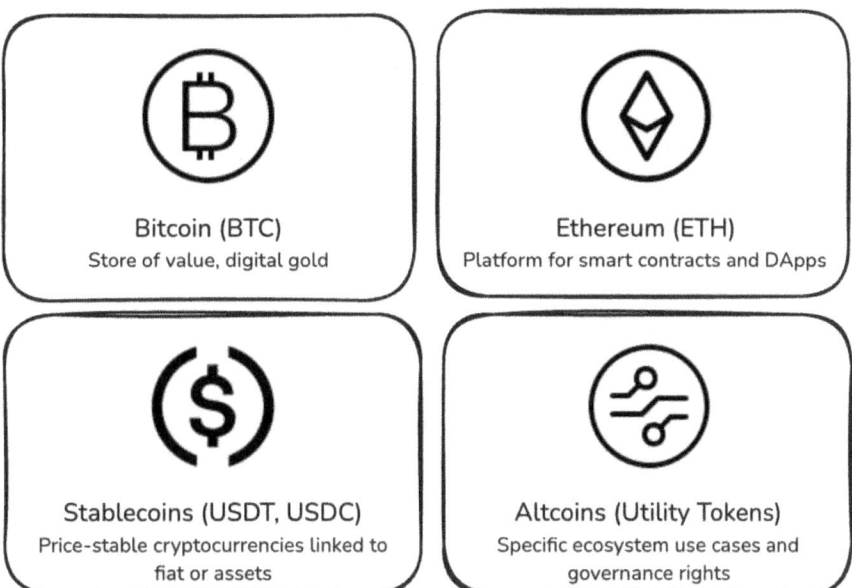

Figure 1-23. *Types of Cryptocurrencies*

3. **The Role of Smart Contracts:**

    Smart contracts are self-executing contracts with the terms of the agreement directly written into code. They are integral to native payments in Web3, as they automate and secure transactions without the need for intermediaries. When a transaction is initiated, the smart contract verifies the conditions of the exchange and automatically transfers the funds once those conditions are met. See Figure 1-24 for how payments work with contracts.

    For instance, in a decentralized lending platform, a smart contract might automatically transfer collateral to the lender if the borrower fails to repay the loan on time. This trustless mechanism reduces the need for third-party arbitration and ensures that transactions are completed according to predefined rules.

    [IMAGE] payments-smart-contract

29

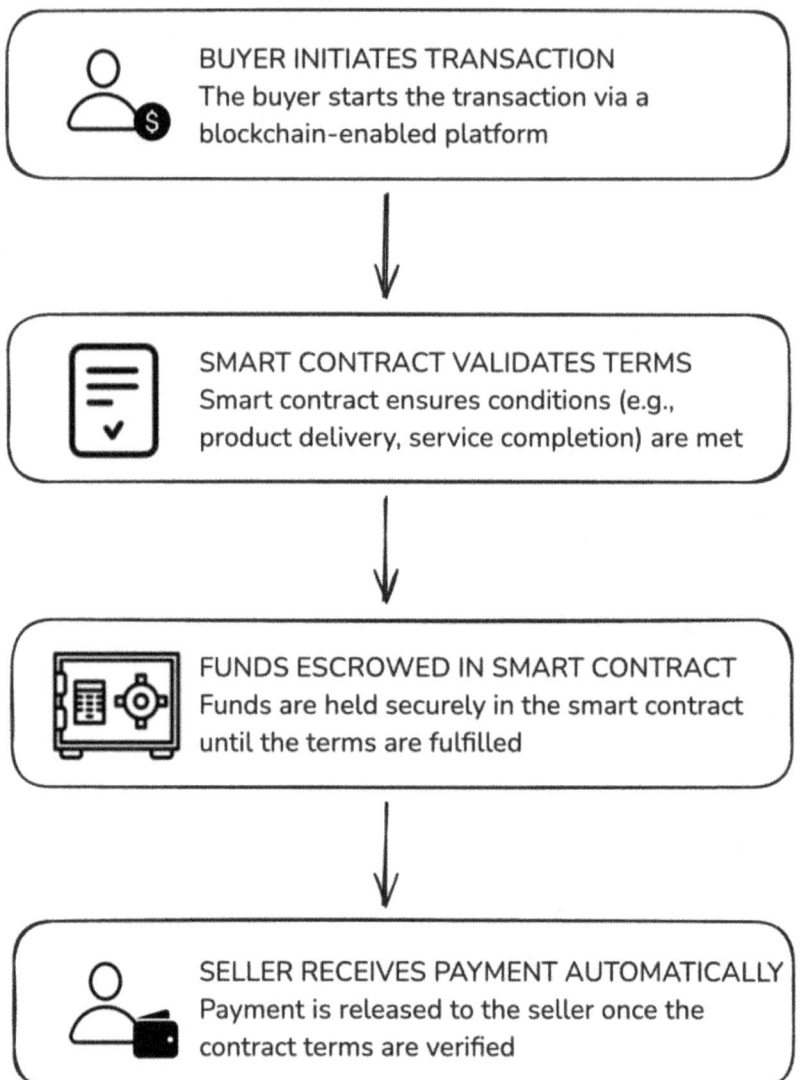

Figure 1-24. Smart Contracts in Payments

Benefits over Traditional Payment Systems

Native payments in Web3 offer several advantages over traditional payment systems, particularly in terms of speed, cost, security, and accessibility. Table 1-1 compares traditional systems and native Web3 payment features.

Table 1-1. Benefits over Traditional Payment Systems

Feature	Traditional Payment Systems	Native Web3 Payments
Intermediaries	It involves banks, payment processors, and other third parties.	Peer-to-peer transactions directly on the blockchain.
Transaction Speed	Can take several days, especially for cross-border payments.	Transactions settle within minutes, regardless of location.
Fees	High fees, including transaction, processing, and currency conversion fees.	Lower fees due to the elimination of intermediaries.
Accessibility	Limited access for the unbanked or underbanked populations.	Accessible to anyone with an internet connection.
Security	Centralized databases are vulnerable to cyberattacks and breaches.	Secured by cryptography and decentralized networks.
Privacy	Requires sharing personal data with intermediaries.	Privacy-preserving, with minimal personal data exposure.
Global Reach	Subject to local banking regulations and time zones.	Borderless and operates 24/7 globally.
Financial Inclusion	Limited to users with access to banks or financial institutions.	Provides financial services to unbanked and underbanked populations.
Transparency	Transactions are not publicly visible; there is limited transparency.	Transactions are recorded on a public blockchain, ensuring transparency.
Fraud Prevention	Relies on intermediaries to detect and resolve fraud cases.	Blockchain immutability reduces risk, but users must secure private keys.

1. **Speed and Efficiency:**

    Traditional payment systems often involve multiple intermediaries, such as banks and payment processors, which can slow down the transaction process. Cross-border payments, in particular, can take days to settle due to the involvement of various financial institutions.

In contrast, native payments using cryptocurrencies are processed directly on the blockchain, often settling within minutes, regardless of the transaction's value or the participants' locations. This speed is especially beneficial for global commerce, where time zones and banking hours can otherwise delay payments.

2. **Lower Transaction Costs:**

The fees associated with traditional payment systems typically include transaction fees, currency conversion fees, and service charges imposed by intermediaries. Small businesses and individuals who make frequent transactions can be especially hit by these fees.

Native payments in Web3 significantly reduce these costs by eliminating intermediaries. While there are still network fees (e.g., gas fees on the Ethereum network), these are generally lower than the combined fees of traditional systems, especially for international transactions. Additionally, new Layer 2 solutions and alternative blockchains are further reducing these fees, making native payments even more cost-effective.

3. **Increased Security and Privacy:**

Security is a major concern in traditional payment systems, where centralized databases holding sensitive information are prime targets for cyberattacks. Breaches can lead to significant financial losses and identity theft.

In Web3, native payments are secured through the decentralized nature of blockchain technology and cryptographic protocols. The immutability of transaction records makes it impossible for malicious actors to alter or manipulate them. Furthermore, since transactions do not require sharing personal information with intermediaries, users' privacy is better protected.

4. **Financial Inclusion:**

    One of the most profound benefits of native payments in Web3 is their potential to increase financial inclusion. Traditional banking services are inaccessible to billions of people worldwide due to factors such as geographical location, lack of documentation, or high fees.

    Cryptocurrencies, on the other hand, are accessible to anyone with an internet connection. Native payments enable unbanked and underbanked populations to participate in the global economy, providing access to financial services that were previously out of reach. This democratization of finance is one of Web3's most transformative promises.

Case Studies and Examples

The practical application of native payments in Web3 is already visible across various industries, showcasing the potential of this technology to revolutionize the way we handle transactions.

1. **Decentralized Finance (DeFi):**

    DeFi platforms are leading the way in using native payments in Web3. These platforms allow users to lend, borrow, trade, and earn interest on cryptocurrencies without relying on traditional banks or financial institutions. For example, platforms like Aave and Compound enable users to deposit cryptocurrencies and earn interest, with the entire process governed by smart contracts. Figure 1-25 gives an overview of the DeFi ecosystem.

    DeFi platforms often use stablecoins for transactions, providing a stable medium of exchange within the ecosystem. The transparency and efficiency of DeFi have attracted billions of dollars in value, demonstrating the viability of native payments as an alternative to traditional financial systems.

CHAPTER 1   WEB3

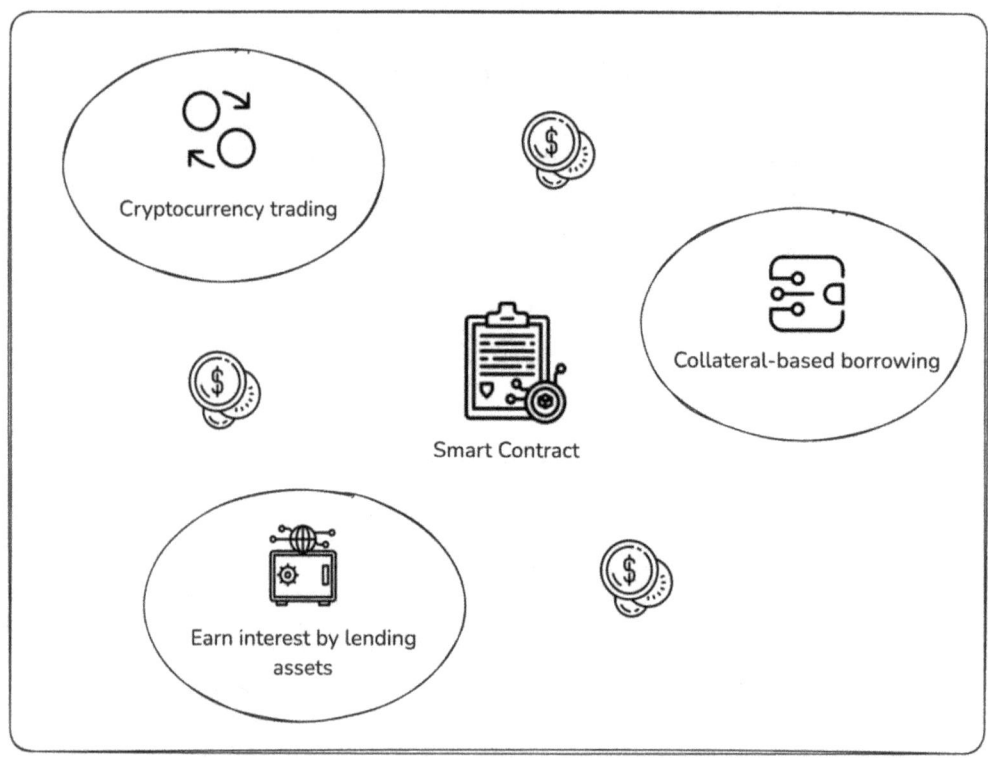

Figure 1-25. *Overview of DeFi Ecosystem*

2. **E-Commerce and Digital Goods:**

    Several e-commerce platforms and marketplaces are beginning to accept cryptocurrencies as a form of payment, leveraging the benefits of native payments. For instance, OpenSea, one of the largest NFT marketplaces, allows users to buy, sell, and trade digital assets using Ethereum. An example is shown in Figure 1-26 with OpenSea.

    This integration of native payments enables seamless transactions in the digital goods economy, where users can purchase virtual real estate, digital art, and other unique assets with cryptocurrencies. The use of native payments simplifies the process and provides a secure way to verify and transfer

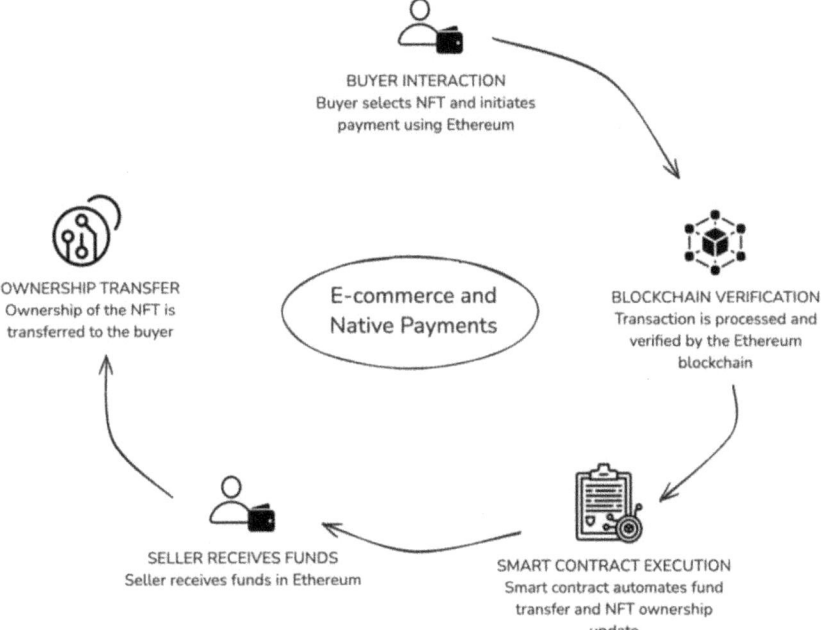

Figure 1-26. *OpenSea Payment Flow*

3. **Cross-Border Remittances:**

    Cross-border remittances are another area where native payments are making a significant impact. Traditional remittance services often involve high fees and long processing times, especially for transfers to developing countries.

    Cryptocurrencies offer a faster and cheaper alternative for sending money across borders. For example, platforms like Ripple and Stellar focus on facilitating cross-border payments with minimal fees and near-instant settlement times. These solutions are particularly valuable for migrant workers sending money home, as they can save on fees and ensure their families receive funds quickly. Remittance comparison is shown in Figure 1-27.

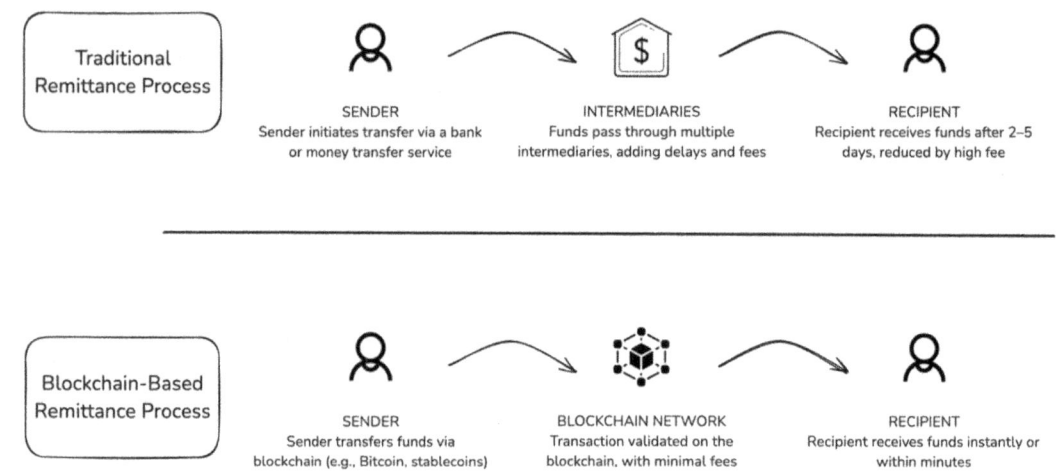

Figure 1-27. Traditional vs. Crypto Remittance

Transparency

Transparency is a fundamental principle of Web3, driving toward a more open, accountable, and fair digital ecosystem. Unlike the systems of Web2, where data is often controlled by centralized entities with minimal control, Web3 leverages decentralized technologies to ensure that transactions, code, and processes are visible and verifiable by all participants. In this section, we will discuss the significance of transparency in Web3, the importance of open-source development, and the advantages of transparent transaction records for both users and developers.

Open-Source Nature of Web3

One of the most important aspects of transparency in Web3 is the open-source nature of its development. Open-source software (OSS) is software with source code that anyone can inspect, modify, and improve. In the context of Web3, this approach is not just a best practice but a necessity, as it allows communities to build, maintain, and trust decentralized systems.

1. **Community-Driven Development:**

    In Web3, many protocols, platforms, and applications are developed in the open, with source code made publicly available on platforms like GitHub. This transparency allows developers from around the world to contribute to the codebase, identify bugs, suggest improvements, and ensure that the software behaves as intended. The decentralized nature of Web3 means that these contributions are often driven by the community, rather than by a single entity or corporation.

    This approach has many advantages. First, it leads to more robust and secure code, as a diverse group of contributors can inspect and evaluate the software. Second, it fosters innovation, as developers can build on each other's work, creating new applications and features that might not have been possible within a closed, proprietary system. Finally, it enhances trust among users, who can verify that the software they are using is free from malicious code or hidden functions.

2. **Governance and Transparency:**

    Many Web3 projects are governed through decentralized autonomous organizations (DAOs), where decision-making is transparent and participatory. In a DAO, governance decisions, such as changes to protocol parameters or the allocation of resources, are made collectively by token holders, with votes recorded on the blockchain.

    This transparent governance model ensures that no single entity has unilateral control over the project and all stakeholders can see how decisions are made and implemented. This is in contrast to traditional corporations or platforms, which often have centralized decision-making systems, limiting users' understanding of how policies are established or enforced.

3. **Open Audits and Security:**

    The open-source nature of Web3 also extends to security, where transparency plays a crucial role in maintaining trust. In traditional systems, security audits are often conducted by internal teams or external firms, with the results shared only with select stakeholders. In Web3, however, security audits are typically conducted in the open, with audit reports made publicly available.

    This transparency allows anyone to review the security posture of a project, providing an additional layer of accountability. It also enables the community to quickly identify and respond to potential vulnerabilities, making Web3 platforms more resilient and secure over time.

Transparent Transaction Records

One of the defining features of Web3 is the transparency of transaction records. In a decentralized network, every transaction is recorded on a public ledger, such as a blockchain, where it can be viewed and verified by anyone. This level of transparency offers significant advantages over traditional financial systems, where transaction data is often hidden from public view.

1. **Immutable Ledgers:**

    In Web3, transactions are recorded on blockchain ledgers that are immutable (Figure 1-28), meaning once a transaction is confirmed, it cannot be altered or deleted. This creates a permanent and transparent record of all transactions that have occurred on the network.

    The immutability and transparency of blockchain ledgers provide several benefits. For one, they ensure accountability, as all actions are publicly recorded and can be traced back to their origin. This makes it much harder to commit fraud or engage in corrupt practices, as any illicit activity would be immediately visible to the network.

Additionally, transparent ledgers enhance trust between parties who may not know or trust each other. In traditional systems, intermediaries like banks or escrow services are often needed to ensure that both sides of a transaction fulfill their obligations. In Web3, however, the public nature of the blockchain allows participants to independently verify that a transaction has been completed as agreed, reducing the need for intermediaries.

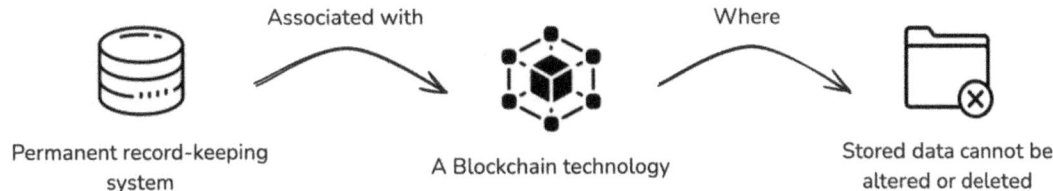

Figure 1-28. Immutable Ledger in Blockchain

2. **Transparent Supply Chains:**

    One of the most promising applications of transparent transaction records is in supply chain management. In traditional supply chains, it can be difficult to trace the origin and movement of goods, leading to issues like fraud, falsification, and inefficiency.

    Web3 enables fully transparent supply chains by recording every step of the process on a public ledger. From the sourcing of raw materials to the final delivery of a product, each transaction can be tracked and verified on the blockchain (Figure 1-29). This transparency helps ensure that goods are authentic, ethically sourced, and handled according to agreed-upon standards.

    For example, a consumer purchasing a luxury item could verify its authenticity by tracing its history on the blockchain, from the manufacturer to the retailer. Similarly, companies could ensure that their suppliers are adhering to ethical labor practices by auditing the supply chain records. Traditional systems do not allow for this level of transparency because supply chain data is often hard to access.

CHAPTER 1 WEB3

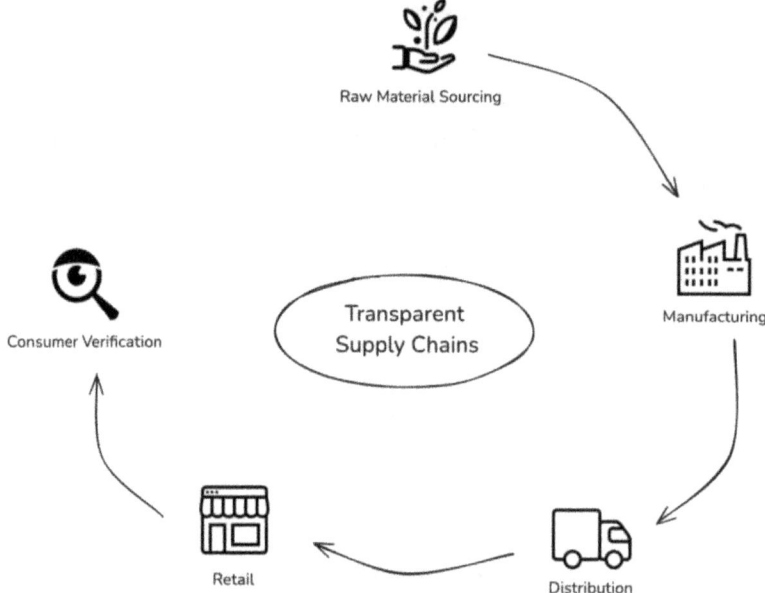

Figure 1-29. *Blockchain in Supply Chain*

3. **Transparent Financial Systems:**

    Web3 also has the potential to create more transparent financial systems. In traditional finance, the flow of money is often not transparent because intermediaries control the movement of funds and take a cut at every step. This can lead to a lack of transparency, high fees, and potential conflicts of interest.

    With Web3, all financial transactions are recorded on a public blockchain, where they can be audited by anyone. This transparency reduces the risk of corruption and fraud, as every transaction is visible and traceable. It also lowers costs by eliminating the need for intermediaries, making financial services more accessible to a broader range of people.

    Namely, decentralized finance (DeFi) platforms enable users to lend, borrow, and trade assets without the need for banks or brokers. All transactions are conducted transparently on the blockchain, allowing users to see exactly how their funds are being used and managed. This openness fosters trust and encourages more people to participate in the financial system.

Benefits for Users and Developers

The transparency inherent in Web3 offers significant benefits for both users and developers, fostering a more open and accountable digital ecosystem.

1. **User Empowerment:**

   For users, transparency in Web3 means greater control over their data, assets, and interactions. They can see how their information is being used, how transactions are being processed, and how decisions are being made within the platforms they use. This contrasts with Web2, where users often have little visibility into how their data is handled or how platforms operate.

   This empowerment extends to financial transactions, where users can independently verify the integrity of the systems they are using. For instance, when using a DeFi platform, users can audit the smart contracts that govern the platform to ensure that their funds are secure and that the platform is operating as intended.

2. **Developer Accountability:**

   For developers, the transparency of Web3 encourages higher standards of accountability and security. Since code and transactions are visible to the public, developers are incentivized to write secure, efficient, and trustworthy code. Any vulnerabilities or malicious behavior can be quickly identified and exposed by the community, which holds developers to a higher standard than in traditional closed-source environments.

   Moreover, transparency fosters collaboration and innovation among developers. Open-source projects allow developers to build on each other's work, share knowledge, and contribute to the improvement of the ecosystem as a whole. This collaborative environment is a key driver of innovation in Web3, leading to the rapid development of new tools, platforms, and applications.

CHAPTER 1   WEB3

3. **Building Trust:**

    Finally, transparency is essential for building trust in Web3. In a decentralized environment where there is no central authority to enforce rules or guarantee outcomes, trust is established through transparency. Trust mechanisms are summarized in Figure 1-30. Users and developers alike can see how systems operate, how decisions are made, and how assets are managed, which creates confidence in the integrity and fairness of the platform.

    This trust is especially crucial in emerging markets and communities where traditional institutions may be absent or unreliable. Web3's transparency can help bridge the trust gap, providing a reliable and open alternative to traditional systems.

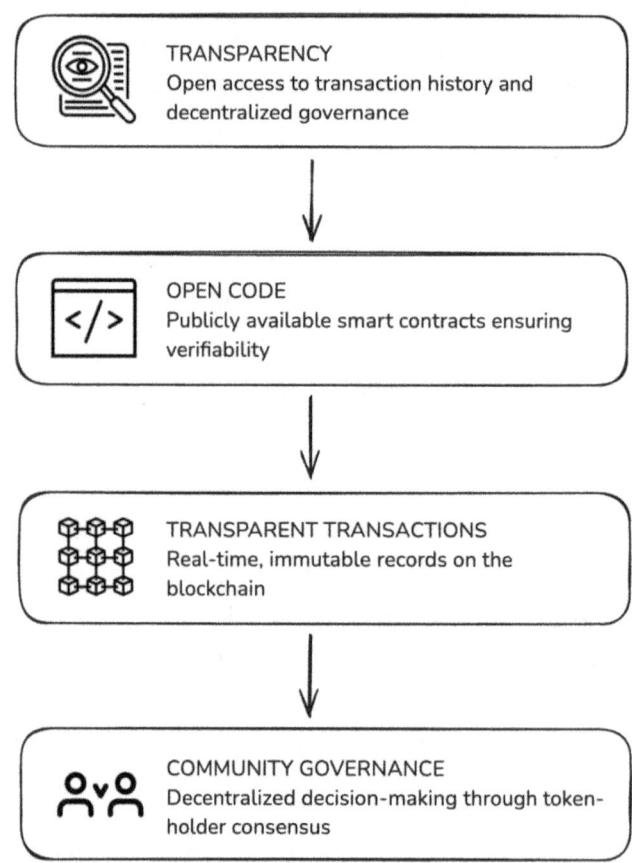

Figure 1-30. Building Trust in Decentralized Systems

Driving Technologies

Web3 represents the next evolution of the internet, with decentralization, transparency, and user control taking center stage. This transformation is driven by a set of innovative technologies that fundamentally alter how data is stored, processed, and exchanged across the internet. In this section, we will explore the key driving technologies behind Web3, including blockchain, smart contracts, and decentralized storage and computing.

Blockchain Technology

Blockchain is the foundational technology upon which Web3 is built. A basic architecture is illustrated in Figure 1-31. It is a decentralized, distributed ledger that records transactions across a network of computers, ensuring transparency, security, and immutability.

1. **Decentralized Ledger:**

    At its core, a blockchain is a chain of blocks, each containing a list of transactions. These blocks are linked together in chronological order and secured using cryptographic techniques. The ledger is decentralized, meaning it is maintained by a network of nodes (computers) rather than a single central authority. Each node in the network has a copy of the blockchain, and all copies are synchronized and updated through a consensus mechanism.

    This decentralization is crucial for Web3 because it removes the need for a central authority to validate transactions or control data. Instead, trust is established through the collective agreement of the network participants, making the system resistant to censorship, fraud, and manipulation.

CHAPTER 1   WEB3

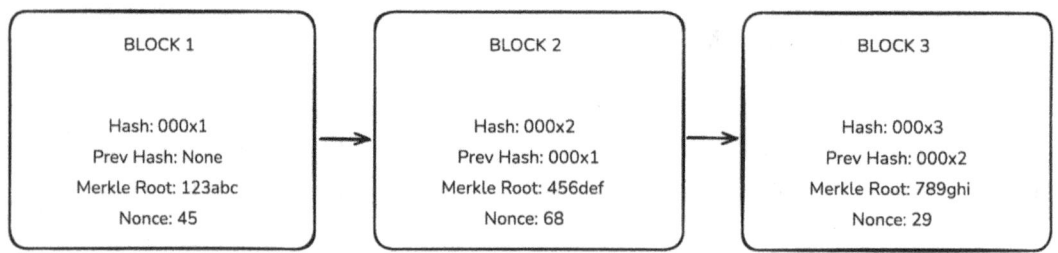

Figure 1-31. Blockchain Technical Architecture

2. **Consensus Mechanisms:**

    Consensus mechanisms are algorithms used to achieve agreement among the nodes in a blockchain network about the state of the ledger. The most common consensus mechanisms in Web3 are Proof of Work (PoW) and Proof of Stake (PoS), each with its own strengths and trade-offs. Comparison is shown in Figure 1-32.

    - **Proof of Work (PoW):** PoW is the original consensus mechanism used by Bitcoin and several other cryptocurrencies. In PoW, nodes (called miners) compete to solve complex mathematical puzzles. The first node to solve the puzzle gets to add a new block to the blockchain and is rewarded with cryptocurrency. PoW is secure but energy-intensive, as it requires significant computational power.

    - **Proof of Stake (PoS):** PoS is a more energy-efficient alternative to PoW. In PoS, nodes (called validators) are chosen to add new blocks based on the number of tokens they hold and are willing to "stake" as collateral. Validators are incentivized to act honestly, as they stand to lose their staked tokens if they attempt to cheat the system. PoS reduces the energy consumption associated with mining and allows for faster transaction processing.

    In addition to PoW and PoS, other consensus mechanisms, such as Delegated Proof of Stake (DPoS), Proof of Authority (PoA), and Byzantine Fault Tolerance (BFT), are also being explored and implemented within various Web3 platforms, each offering different balances of security, scalability, and decentralization.

CHAPTER 1 WEB3

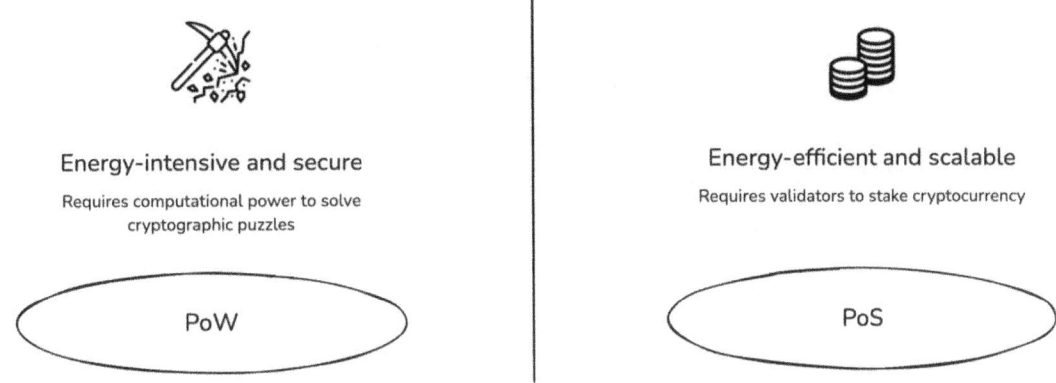

Figure 1-32. PoW vs. PoS

3. **Layer 2 Solutions:**

   As blockchain technology evolves, Layer 2 solutions have emerged to address some of the scalability and speed issues associated with traditional blockchain networks. Layer 2 refers to secondary frameworks or protocols that are built on top of the existing blockchain, enabling faster and cheaper transactions without compromising security. Figure 1-33 shows examples of Layer 2 scaling.

   Examples of Layer 2 solutions include:

   - **State Channels:** State channels allow two parties to conduct multiple transactions off-chain while only recording the final state of the transactions on the blockchain. This reduces the load on the main chain and significantly speeds up transaction processing.

   - **Sidechains:** Sidechains are independent blockchains that run parallel to the main chain. They can process transactions and smart contracts independently, reducing congestion on the main network while still being able to interact with it.

- **Rollups:** Rollups bundle multiple transactions into a single transaction that is then recorded on the main blockchain. This allows for higher efficiency and lower costs, making blockchain applications more scalable and effective.

Layer 2 solutions are essential for enabling Web3 to scale and handle the increasing number of users and transactions without sacrificing the principles of decentralization and security.

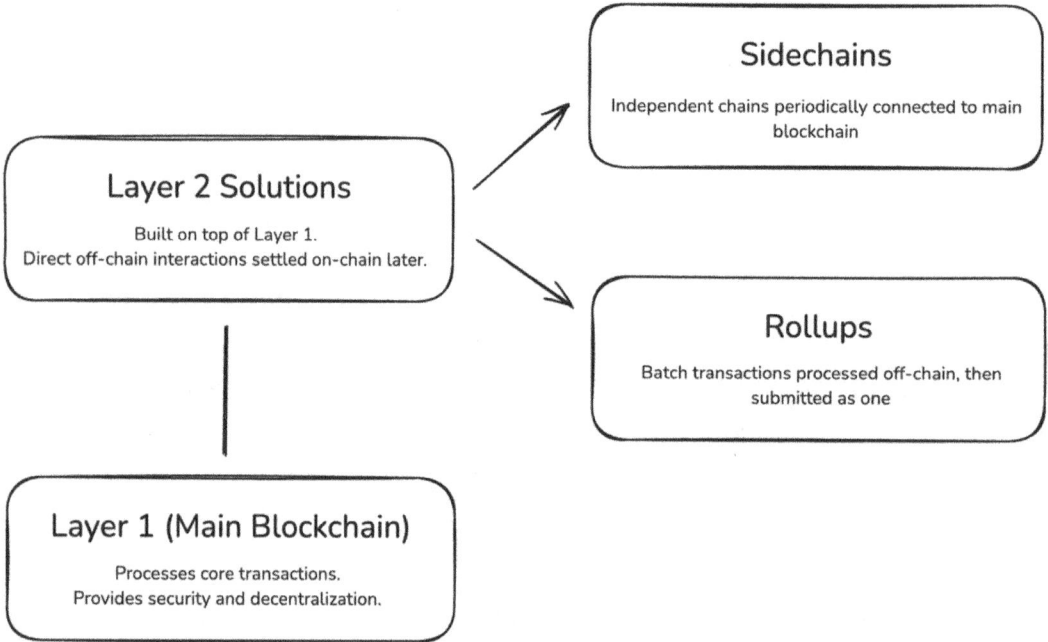

Figure 1-33. Examples of Layer 2 Solutions

Smart Contracts

Smart contracts are self-executing contracts where the terms of the agreement are written directly into code. They are one of the most powerful innovations driving Web3, enabling decentralized applications (DApps) to operate autonomously and securely.

CHAPTER 1　WEB3

1. **How Smart Contracts Work:**

   Smart contracts run on blockchain networks, such as Ethereum, and are executed automatically when predefined conditions are met. See Figure 1-34 for smart contract workflow. For example, a simple smart contract might transfer cryptocurrency from one party to another once a specific condition, like a payment, is fulfilled.

   Because smart contracts are stored on a blockchain, they inherit the properties of transparency, immutability, and security. Once deployed, a smart contract cannot be altered, ensuring that the established terms are enforced without the possibility of manipulation or fraud.

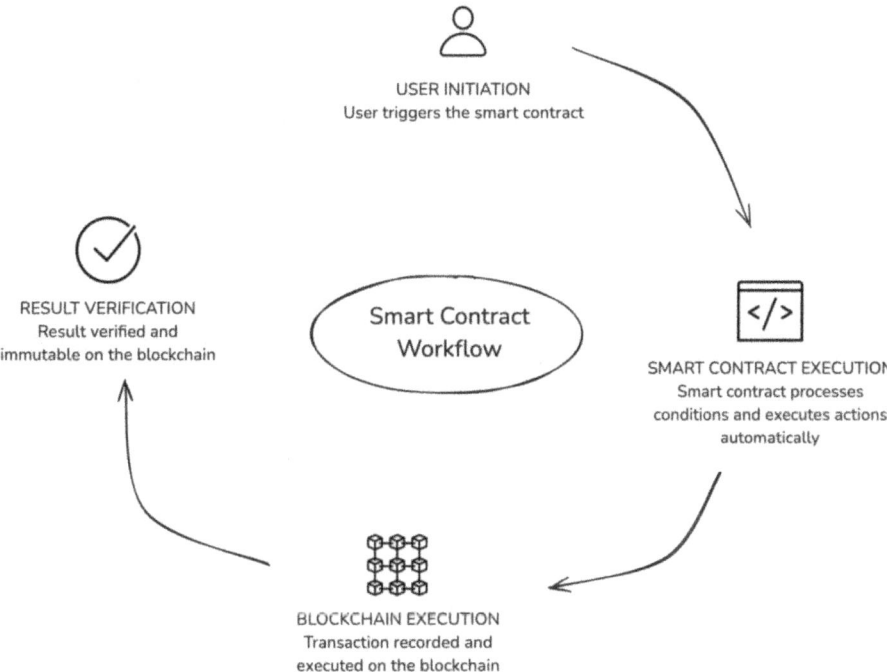

Figure 1-34. Smart Contract Execution Flow

2. **Applications of Smart Contracts:**

   Smart contracts are crucial to many Web3 applications, allowing for a variety of decentralized services. Some of the key applications include:

47

- **Decentralized Finance (DeFi):** DeFi platforms use smart contracts to create financial services, such as lending, borrowing, trading, and investing, without the need for traditional banks or intermediaries. For example, a DeFi platform might use smart contracts to automatically match borrowers with lenders, set interest rates, and distribute loans.

- **NFT Marketplaces:** Smart contracts are used to mint, buy, sell, and transfer non-fungible tokens (NFTs) on blockchain marketplaces. These contracts ensure that ownership of digital assets is transferred securely and that creators can receive royalties on future sales.

- **Decentralized Exchanges (DEXs):** DEXs use smart contracts to facilitate the trading of cryptocurrencies directly between users, without the need for a centralized exchange. These contracts automate the process of matching buy and sell orders, ensuring that trades are executed transparently and securely.

- **Supply Chain Management:** Smart contracts can be used to automate and verify various stages of a supply chain, from manufacturing to delivery. Consider the case of a smart contract: it might automatically release payment to a supplier once a shipment has been confirmed as delivered.

Smart contracts are revolutionizing how agreements are made and enforced in the digital world, providing a secure, efficient, and trustless way to interact in a decentralized environment. Real-world uses are shown in Figure 1-35.

CHAPTER 1 WEB3

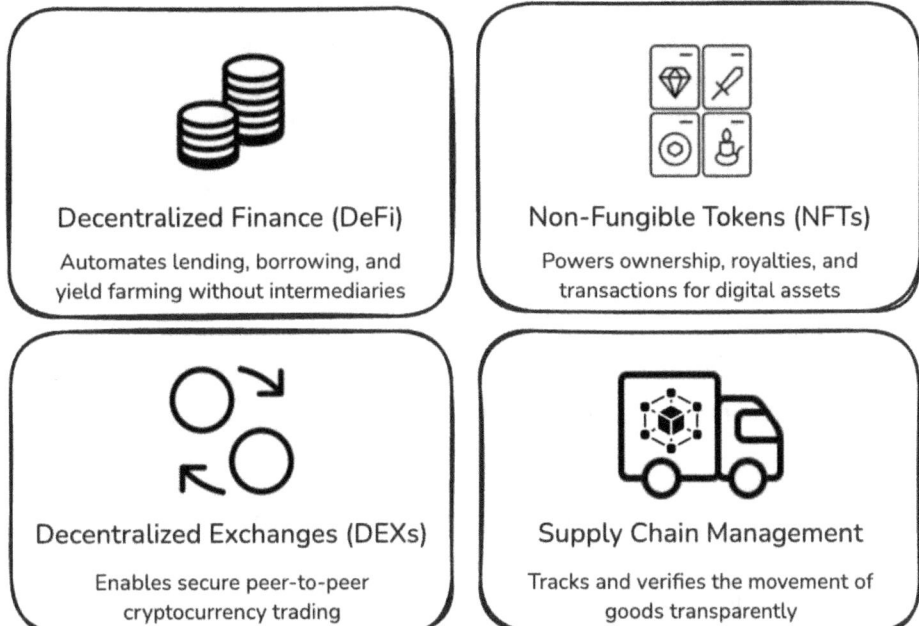

Figure 1-35. Real-World Use Cases of Smart Contracts

Decentralized Storage and Computing

Decentralized storage and computing are critical components of the Web3 ecosystem, enabling the distribution of data and processing power across a network of nodes rather than relying on centralized servers. This decentralization enhances security, privacy and resilience while reducing the risks associated with central points of failure.

1. **Decentralized Storage:**

    In traditional web architectures, data is typically stored on centralized servers owned and operated by companies like Google, Amazon, or Microsoft. This centralization creates vulnerabilities, such as data breaches, censorship, and loss of access if a server goes down or is compromised. Storage differences are visualized in Figure 1-36.

Decentralized storage networks, such as IPFS (InterPlanetary File System) and Arweave, offer an alternative by distributing data across a network of nodes. In these systems, data is broken into small pieces, encrypted, and distributed across multiple nodes. This ensures that no single entity controls the data and that it remains accessible even if some nodes go offline.

2. **Benefits of Decentralized Storage:**

    - **Security and Privacy:** Because data is encrypted and distributed, it is much harder for hackers to access or compromise the entire dataset. Additionally, users retain control over their data, reducing the risk of unauthorized access or abuse by centralized service providers.

    - **Censorship Resistance:** Decentralized storage makes it difficult for any single entity or government to censor or block access to information. Since data is spread across many nodes, it remains available even if some nodes are taken offline.

    - **Data Integrity:** Decentralized storage systems often use content addressing, where each piece of data is identified by a unique cryptographic hash. This ensures that the data cannot be modified, as any variation would change the hash and make the data unrecognizable.

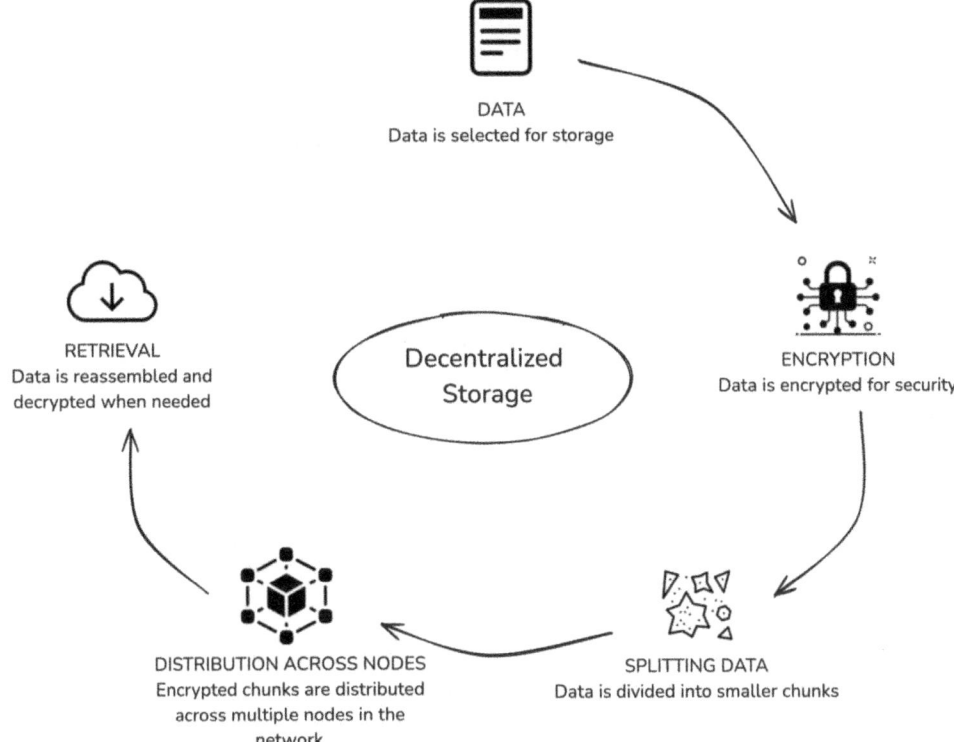

Figure 1-36. *Decentralized Storage Architecture*

3. **Decentralized Computing:**

    Decentralized computing refers to the distribution of computational tasks across a network of nodes rather than relying on a central server or data center. This approach is particularly important for running decentralized applications (DApps) and smart contracts at scale.

    Platforms like Ethereum allow developers to deploy and execute smart contracts across a decentralized network of nodes. However, decentralized computing can also extend to more general-purpose tasks, such as distributed machine learning, rendering, and data analysis.

Projects like Golem and Filecoin are exploring decentralized computing networks where users can rent out their unused processing power or storage in exchange for cryptocurrency. This creates a global, decentralized cloud computing market where resources are allocated based on demand and users can participate without needing access to large-scale infrastructure.

4. **Challenges and Future Developments:**

While decentralized storage and computing offer many benefits, they also present challenges, such as latency, cost, and scalability. Decentralized networks often have higher latency compared to centralized services, and the cost of storing or processing data can be higher due to the redundancy and complexity of the systems.

However, ongoing developments in protocols, consensus mechanisms, and incentive structures are addressing these challenges, making decentralized storage and computing more affordable for a wide range of applications. As these technologies mature, they will play an increasingly important role in the Web3 ecosystem, enabling more resilient, secure, and user-controlled digital infrastructure. Table 1-2 outlines the main challenges of decentralized computing and their solutions.

Table 1-2. Challenges and Solutions in Decentralized Computing

Challenges	Solutions
Latency	Develop optimized protocols and consensus mechanisms to reduce delays in processing.
Cost	Introduce incentive structures and efficient resource allocation to lower costs.
Scalability	Implement Layer 2 solutions like rollups, sidechains, and state channels to enhance scalability.
Interoperability	Develop standards and bridges to ensure compatibility between different blockchain networks.
Data Redundancy	Use advanced data distribution methods to balance redundancy with storage efficiency.
Energy Consumption	Shift from energy-intensive consensus mechanisms (e.g., PoW) to energy-efficient ones (e.g., PoS).
Adoption Barriers	Provide user-friendly interfaces and developer tools to lower the learning curve for new users and developers.
Regulatory Challenges	Collaborate with governments to create fair and adaptable legal frameworks for decentralized computing.

Application Types

Web3 has brought about a new age of internet applications that emphasizes decentralization, transparency, and user empowerment. Unlike traditional web applications, Web3 applications operate on decentralized networks, removing the need for central authorities and giving users control over their data and interactions. In this section, we will explore the different types of applications in Web3, focusing on decentralized applications (DApps) and decentralized finance (DeFi) platforms.

CHAPTER 1   WEB3

Decentralized Applications (DApps)

Decentralized applications, or DApps, are a core component of the Web3 ecosystem. These applications run on blockchain networks and leverage smart contracts to operate without a central authority. DApps can cover a wide range of use cases, from finance and gaming to social media and governance.

1. **What Are DApps?**

    DApps are applications that run on a decentralized network (Figure 1-37 shows DApp architecture), typically a blockchain like Ethereum, rather than relying on a centralized server. The backend code for DApps is stored on the blockchain, and their operation is governed by smart contracts, self-executing contracts with the terms of the agreement directly written into code.

    The decentralized nature of DApps ensures that no single entity controls the application, making it resistant to censorship, downtime, and manipulation. Users interact with DApps through a decentralized interface, often using a cryptocurrency wallet to manage assets, identities, or access rights within the application.

CHAPTER 1   WEB3

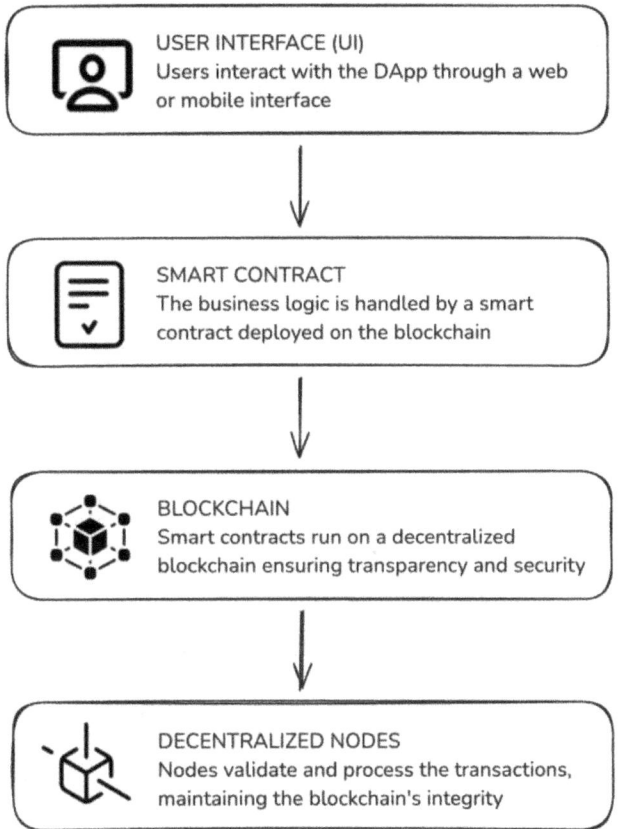

Figure 1-37. *Architecture of a DApp*

2. **Characteristics of DApps:**

   DApps have several key characteristics that differentiate them from traditional web applications (core features are listed in Figure 1-38):

   - **Decentralization:** The backend of a DApp is distributed across a network of nodes, removing the need for a central server. This enhances security and resilience, as there is no single point of failure.

   - **Open Source:** Many DApps are open-source, allowing anyone to inspect, modify, and contribute to the codebase. This transparency fosters trust and collaboration within the community.

CHAPTER 1   WEB3

- **Incentivization:** DApps often incorporate tokens or cryptocurrencies to incentivize participation. Users may earn tokens for contributing to the network, providing services, or engaging in certain activities within the DApp.

- **Smart Contracts:** The logic of a DApp is governed by smart contracts, which automatically execute actions based on predefined conditions. This ensures that the application operates in a trustless and transparent manner.

Key Characteristics of DApps

DECENTRALIZATION
Operates on a decentralized blockchain, ensuring no single point of control

OPEN-SOURCE
Code is publicly available, enabling transparency and community contributions

INCENTIVIZATION
Users and validators are incentivized with tokens for participating in the ecosystem

SMART CONTRACT
Automates processes through programmable, self-executing agreements

Figure 1-38. Key Features of DApps

3. **Examples of DApps:**

    DApps can be found across various sectors, each leveraging the unique capabilities of blockchain technology to provide innovative solutions (examples are summarized in Figure 1-39):

- **Finance:** DApps like Uniswap and Aave are popular in the decentralized finance (DeFi) space. Uniswap is a decentralized exchange (DEX) that allows users to trade cryptocurrencies directly from their wallets, while Aave is a lending platform that enables users to borrow and lend assets without intermediaries.

- **Gaming:** DApps such as Axie Infinity and Decentraland have gained popularity in the gaming industry. Axie Infinity is a blockchain-based game where players can collect, breed, and battle virtual creatures called Axies, while Decentraland is a virtual world where users can buy, sell, and develop virtual real estate using cryptocurrency.

- **Social Media:** DApps like Steemit and Mastodon offer decentralized alternatives to traditional social media platforms. Steemit is a content-sharing platform that rewards users with cryptocurrency for creating and curating content, while Mastodon is a decentralized social network that allows users to host their own servers and control their data.

- **Governance:** DApps like Aragon and Snapshot enable decentralized governance for organizations and communities. Aragon allows users to create and manage decentralized autonomous organizations (DAOs), while Snapshot provides a simple voting interface for DAOs to make decisions based on token-holder votes.

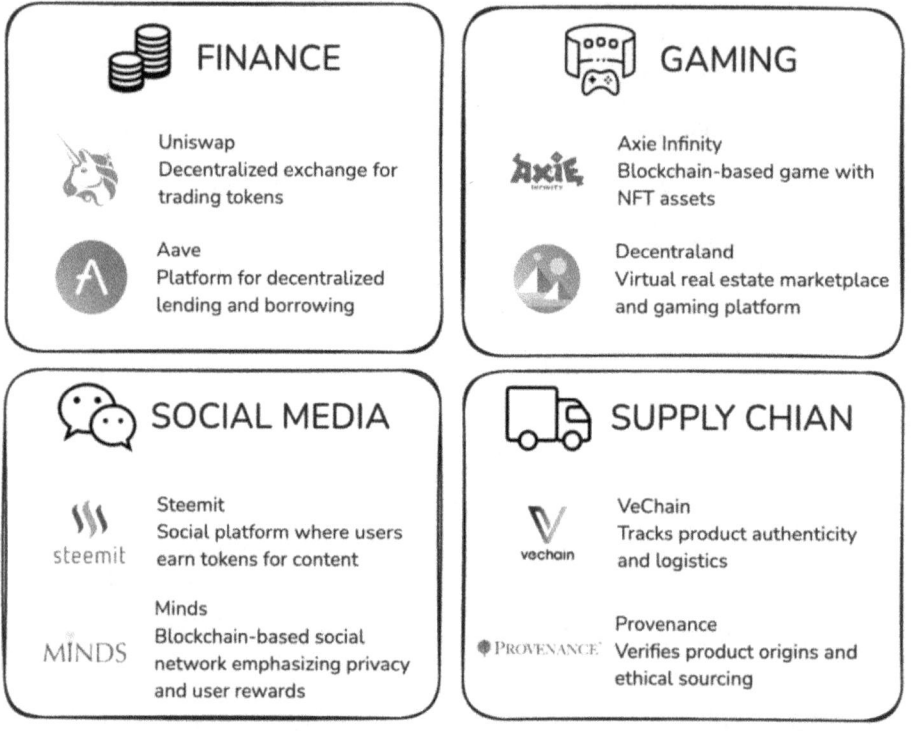

Figure 1-39. Examples of DApps by Sector

Decentralized Finance (DeFi) Platforms

Decentralized finance, or DeFi, represents one of the most transformative applications of Web3. DeFi platforms offer a range of financial services, such as lending, borrowing, trading, and investing, without the need for traditional banks or financial intermediaries. These platforms operate on blockchain networks, providing users with greater control over their assets and enabling financial inclusion on a global scale.

CHAPTER 1 WEB3

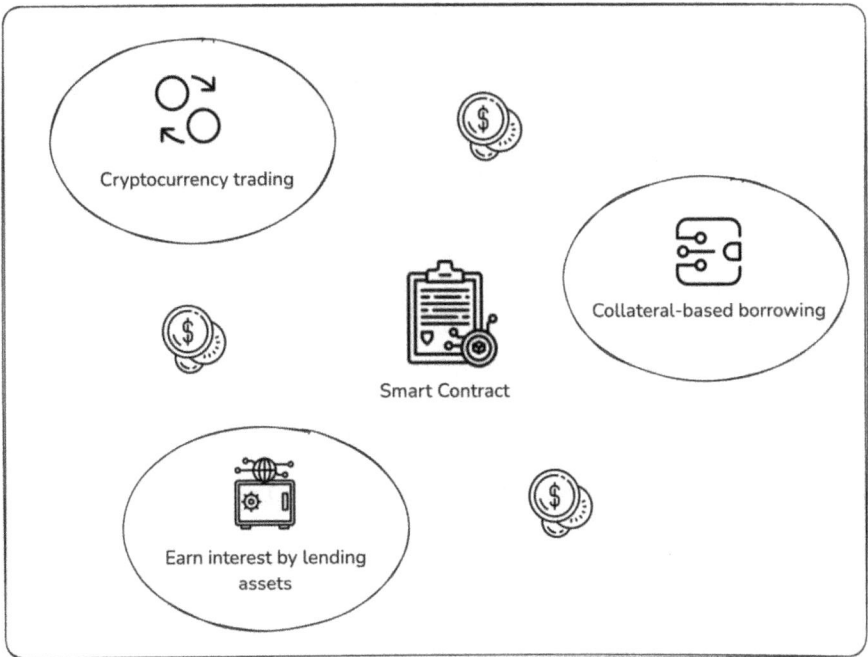

Decentralized Finance (DeFi) Ecosystem

Figure 1-40. *Overview of DeFi Ecosystem*

1. **What Is DeFi?**

   DeFi refers to a broad category of financial applications that are built on decentralized networks. These applications aim to recreate traditional financial services, such as lending, borrowing, trading, and insurance, using blockchain technology and smart contracts. By eliminating intermediaries, DeFi platforms provide more transparent, accessible, and efficient financial services.

2. **Key Components of DeFi:**

   DeFi platforms are composed of several key components, each playing a critical role in the ecosystem:

   - **Decentralized Exchanges (DEXs):** DEXs, such as Uniswap and Sushiswap, enable users to trade cryptocurrencies directly from their wallets without relying on a centralized exchange. Trades are facilitated by automated market makers (AMMs) that use smart contracts to match buy and sell orders.

59

- **Lending and Borrowing Platforms:** Platforms like Aave, Compound, and MakerDAO allow users to lend their cryptocurrencies to others and earn interest or borrow assets by providing collateral. These platforms use smart contracts to manage loans and ensure that all participants comply with the agreed terms.

- **Stablecoins:** Stablecoins are cryptocurrencies that are linked to the value of a fiat currency, such as the US dollar. They provide a stable medium of exchange within the DeFi ecosystem, reducing the volatility associated with other cryptocurrencies. Examples of stablecoins include USDT (Tether), USDC (USD Coin), and DAI (a decentralized stablecoin managed by MakerDAO).

- **Yield Farming and Liquidity Mining:** Yield farming and liquidity mining are strategies used by DeFi users to earn rewards by providing liquidity to platforms or staking tokens. For example, users can provide liquidity to a DEX and earn a portion of the trading fees or receive governance tokens as rewards.

- **Derivatives and Synthetic Assets:** DeFi platforms also offer derivatives and synthetic assets that track the value of real-world assets, such as stocks, commodities, or indices. Synthetix is an example of a platform that enables users to create and trade synthetic assets that mirror the price movements of traditional financial instruments.

3. **Benefits of DeFi:**

DeFi offers several advantages over traditional financial systems:

- **Accessibility:** DeFi platforms are open to anyone with an internet connection and a cryptocurrency wallet, making financial services available to individuals who are unbanked or underbanked.

- **Transparency:** All transactions on DeFi platforms are recorded on the blockchain, providing a transparent and auditable record of activity. This transparency reduces the risk of fraud and allows users to verify the integrity of the system.

- **Control:** DeFi users retain full control over their assets, as they interact directly with the platform via smart contracts. There are no intermediaries that can freeze accounts or block transactions.

- **Efficiency:** DeFi platforms operate 24/7 and can process transactions much faster than traditional banks. The use of smart contracts also automates many processes, reducing the need for manual intervention and lowering costs.

4. **Risks and Challenges:**

   Despite the benefits, DeFi is still an emerging field and comes with its own set of risks and challenges:

   - **Smart Contract Vulnerabilities:** Smart contracts are exposed to bugs and vulnerabilities that can be used by malicious actors. While code audits and security measures are improving, the risk of hacks remains a concern.

   - **Regulatory Uncertainty:** DeFi operates in a largely unregulated environment, which can lead to legal and regulatory challenges. Governments and regulators are still determining how to approach DeFi, and future regulations could impact the growth and operation of these platforms.

   - **Market Volatility:** The cryptocurrency market is highly unpredictable, and the value of assets on DeFi platforms can shift significantly. Users must be aware of the risks associated with price swings and potential liquidations of their collateral.

   - **User Responsibility:** DeFi requires users to manage their own private keys and interact directly with smart contracts. This level of responsibility can be a challenge for beginners and increases the risk of user error.

Table 1-3 compares the advantages of DeFi with the associated risks across key aspects.

Table 1-3. Benefits and Risks of DeFi Platforms

Aspect	Benefits	Risks
Accessibility	Open to anyone with an internet connection and a cryptocurrency wallet.	Users may face technical barriers or lack knowledge to use DeFi platforms effectively.
Transparency	All transactions are recorded on a public blockchain, ensuring a transparent system.	Transparency can expose sensitive transaction data, leading to potential privacy concerns.
Control	Users retain full control over their funds and interact directly with smart contracts.	User errors, such as losing private keys, can result in the permanent loss of funds.
Efficiency	DeFi platforms operate 24/7, with automated processes reducing operational costs.	High network congestion can lead to slower transactions and higher fees.
Yield Potential	Users can earn interest, rewards, or governance tokens through yield farming or staking.	High market volatility can lead to significant losses, especially for inexperienced users.
Innovation	DeFi drives innovation in financial services, introducing new products and services.	Lack of regulation may expose users to scams, rug pulls, and other malicious activities.
Smart Contracts	Smart contracts automate transactions, removing intermediaries and enhancing trust.	Vulnerabilities in smart contracts can be exploited, leading to hacks or financial losses.

5. **Examples of DeFi Platforms:**

    Several DeFi platforms have gained significant traction and are pioneering the development of decentralized financial services (these platforms are shown in Figure 1-41):

    - **Uniswap:** A decentralized exchange (DEX) that allows users to trade Ethereum-based tokens directly from their wallets. Uniswap uses an automated market maker (AMM) model, where users provide liquidity to pools and earn fees from trades.

CHAPTER 1   WEB3

- **Aave:** A decentralized lending and borrowing platform that allows users to lend their assets and earn interest or borrow assets by providing collateral. Aave is known for its innovative features, such as flash loans and credit delegation.

- **MakerDAO:** The platform behind DAI, a decentralized stablecoin linked to the US dollar. MakerDAO allows users to create DAI by locking up collateral (such as Ethereum) in smart contracts. The stability of DAI is maintained through a system of collateralization and governance by MKR token holders.

- **Curve Finance:** A decentralized exchange optimized for stablecoin trading. Curve Finance provides low-slippage trading and high liquidity for stablecoins and other assets with similar price stability.

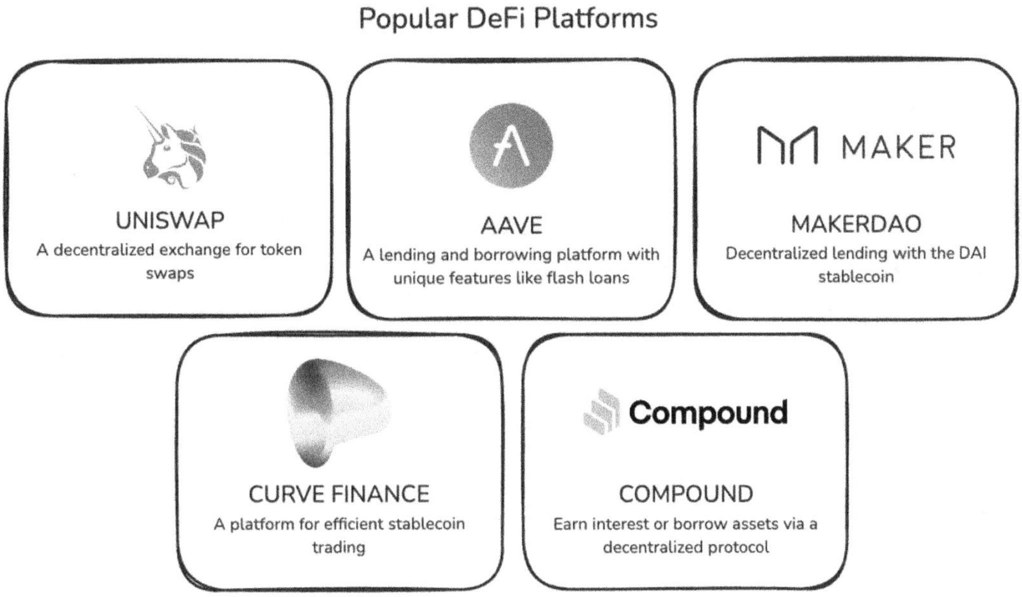

Figure 1-41. Popular DeFi Platforms

CHAPTER 1   WEB3

Conclusion

Web3 represents a transformative shift in how we build and experience the internet. At its core, it challenges the centralized norms of Web2 by introducing decentralization, transparency, and user ownership as fundamental principles. In this chapter, we explored the key characteristics that define Web3, from digital identity and native payments to smart contracts, decentralized applications, and peer-to-peer networks.

We've seen how blockchain enables new forms of trust without intermediaries, how NFTs and tokens empower digital ownership, and how decentralized finance reimagines traditional economic systems. We also examined the risks, trade-offs, and challenges that must be addressed as the ecosystem matures.

What makes Web3 compelling isn't just the technology but the values it brings to the table: openness, inclusivity, and empowerment. As the tools, protocols, and standards continue to evolve, Web3 offers the foundation for a more equitable and participatory digital landscape.

Chapter Summary

Topic	Key takeaways
Web evolution	Web1 (static), Web2 (interactive & centralized), Web3 (decentralized & user-owned)
Key characteristics	Decentralization, trustlessness, digital identity, interoperability, privacy
Security foundations	Public/private keys, zero-knowledge proofs, decentralized governance
Digital ownership	Enabled by blockchain and NFTs: users control content, assets and identity
Native payments	Cryptocurrency enables peer-to-peer, trustless, borderless financial exchange
Transparency	Open-source code, public ledgers, visible governance, immutable transactions
Driving technologies	Blockchain, smart contracts, Layer 2, decentralized storage/computing
Application types	DApps and DeFi platforms spanning finance, gaming, social media, and more

CHAPTER 2

Blockchain

Introduction

This chapter provides a comprehensive foundation for understanding blockchain technology, the core innovation enabling decentralized applications in Web3. We begin by exploring the structure and function of blockchains, from basic concepts to historical milestones. You'll learn how blockchain networks store data securely through distributed ledgers, how consensus mechanisms such as Proof of Work and Proof of Stake ensure trust without intermediaries, and how smart contracts add programmability to these networks.

We'll also cover emerging technologies and protocols that solve current limitations and introduce you to key platforms shaping the space. Through this chapter, you'll develop the technical understanding necessary to engage confidently with blockchain-based applications.

By the end of this chapter, you will be able to

- Describe the core architecture of blockchain systems.
- Distinguish between various consensus mechanisms and their trade-offs.
- Identify key blockchain projects and their use cases.
- Explain transaction lifecycles and network incentives.
- Understand the value and challenges of decentralization.
- Recognize blockchain's security fundamentals and vulnerabilities.

CHAPTER 2   BLOCKCHAIN

Introduction to Blockchain

Definitions and Basic Concepts

Blockchain is a distributed ledger technology that enables secure, transparent, and immutable transactions across a decentralized network. It eliminates the need for intermediaries, allowing direct peer-to-peer transactions, whether for transferring digital assets like cryptocurrencies or recording any type of digital data, such as contracts, votes, or identities.

At its core, a blockchain is a chain of blocks, each containing a collection of transactions. These blocks are linked together using cryptographic hashes, ensuring that the data within them is immutable. Once a transaction is recorded on the blockchain, it cannot be altered or deleted, which provides a high level of security and trust. Figure 2-1 illustrates the basic structure of a blockchain.

HASH: 4X8G
PREV. HASH: 0010

HASH: 3LFH
PREV. HASH: 4X8G

HASH: 3FX5
PREV. HASH: 3LFH

Figure 2-1. *Basic Structure of a Blockchain*

The key concept behind blockchain is decentralization. Unlike traditional centralized systems, where a single entity or authority maintains the ledger, blockchain operates across a distributed network of nodes. Each node has a copy of the entire blockchain, and all nodes work together to validate new transactions. This decentralized nature ensures that no single point of failure exists, and it becomes difficult for bad actors to tamper with the system.

Key Features of Blockchain:

1. **Decentralization:** Instead of relying on a central authority, blockchain relies on a network of nodes, all of which participate in verifying and validating transactions.

CHAPTER 2 BLOCKCHAIN

2. **Immutability:** Once data is added to the blockchain, it becomes practically impossible to change, ensuring that records are permanent and immutable.

3. **Transparency:** All participants in the network can access the same version of the blockchain, creating transparency and trust among users.

4. **Security:** Blockchain uses cryptographic techniques to secure transactions and data, making it highly resistant to attacks or fraud.

Figure 2-2 shows the core features that make blockchain secure and decentralized.

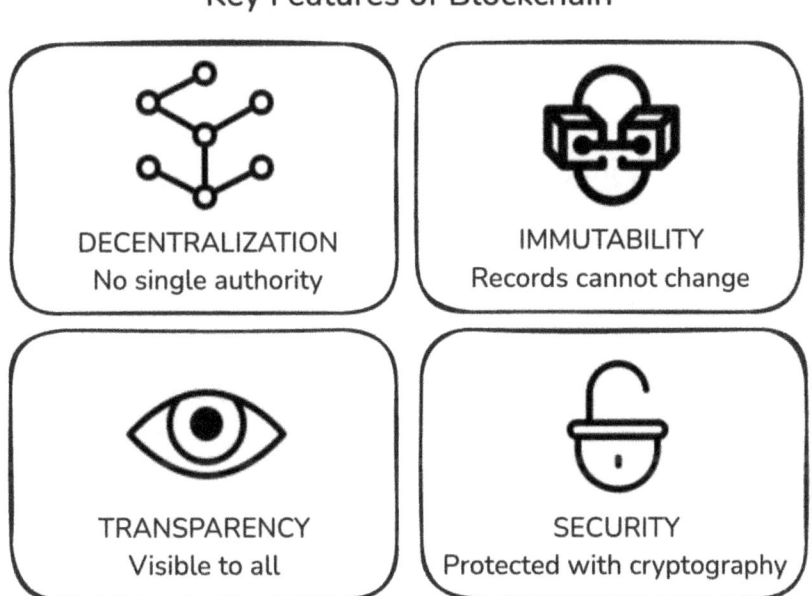

Figure 2-2. Key Features of Blockchain

Historical Background and Evolution

Blockchain technology was first conceptualized in 2008 by an anonymous person or group known as Satoshi Nakamoto. The original purpose of blockchain was to serve as the foundational technology for Bitcoin, a decentralized digital currency that eliminates the need for financial institutions to mediate transactions.

Bitcoin's blockchain was revolutionary because it addressed the double-spending problem, preventing digital assets from being copied and spent multiple times. By using a proof-of-work consensus mechanism, Bitcoin's blockchain ensures that each transaction is unique and verified by the network. This innovation marked the beginning of decentralized finance and peer-to-peer digital currency.

Blockchain 1.0: Bitcoin and Cryptocurrencies

The first generation of blockchain technology, often referred to as Blockchain 1.0, was focused primarily on enabling decentralized digital currencies like Bitcoin. Blockchain 1.0 was limited to handling simple transactions, primarily the transfer of cryptocurrency, but it demonstrated the potential of decentralized systems.

Blockchain 2.0: Smart Contracts and Ethereum

The second phase of blockchain development, known as Blockchain 2.0, emerged with the launch of Ethereum in 2015. Ethereum introduced the concept of smart contracts, self-executing contracts with the terms of the agreement written into code. These smart contracts expanded blockchain's use cases beyond simple transactions to more complex applications, such as decentralized applications (DApps), decentralized finance (DeFi), and tokenization of assets.

Ethereum's blockchain allowed developers to build decentralized applications (DApps) on top of the network, creating an ecosystem where blockchain technology could be used for a wide range of applications, including lending, insurance, and voting systems.

Blockchain 3.0: Scalability and Interoperability

As blockchain adoption grew, scalability became a significant challenge. Bitcoin and Ethereum, the two largest blockchain networks, struggled with network congestion and high transaction fees as their user base expanded. Blockchain 3.0 refers to the current phase of development, which focuses on addressing these challenges by creating more scalable, efficient, and interoperable blockchains. The phases of blockchain evolution are shown in Figure 2-3.

CHAPTER 2 BLOCKCHAIN

Technologies like Proof of Stake (PoS), Layer 2 solutions (such as Lightning Network and Optimistic Rollups), and sharding aim to improve blockchain's scalability. Meanwhile, interoperability protocols are being developed to allow different blockchains to communicate with each other seamlessly, enabling greater collaboration and cross-chain transfers of assets.

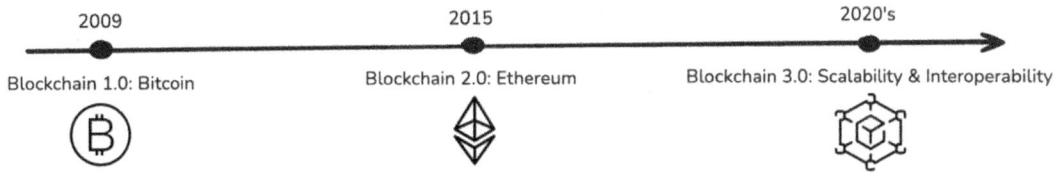

Figure 2-3. Timeline of Blockchain Evolution

Key Players and Projects

Blockchain has seen the emergence of several key players and projects, each contributing to the evolution of technology in different ways.

1. **Bitcoin (BTC):** The first and most well-known blockchain, Bitcoin is often referred to as "digital gold" due to its store-of-value properties. Its primary function is to enable peer-to-peer transactions without intermediaries. Bitcoin's blockchain is secured using Proof of Work (PoW), and while it is slow and resource-intensive, it remains one of the most secure networks in the world.

2. **Ethereum (ETH):** As the second-largest blockchain, Ethereum introduced smart contracts and decentralized applications (DApps). It is the leading platform for decentralized finance (DeFi) and non-fungible tokens (NFTs). Ethereum has recently transitioned from Proof of Work to Proof of Stake with the Ethereum 2.0 upgrade, which is expected to enhance scalability and reduce energy consumption.

3. **Ripple (XRP):** Ripple focuses on providing blockchain-based solutions for cross-border payments and remittances. Unlike Bitcoin and Ethereum, Ripple uses a unique consensus mechanism known as the Ripple Protocol Consensus Algorithm (RPCA), which allows for faster transaction processing and lower fees. Ripple has established partnerships with several banks and financial institutions.

4. **Polkadot (DOT):** Polkadot is a blockchain platform designed to enable interoperability between different blockchains. It allows various blockchains to connect and share information, creating an ecosystem of interconnected chains. Polkadot's unique architecture, known as parachains, allows it to handle many transactions simultaneously, improving scalability.

5. **Cardano (ADA):** Cardano is a blockchain platform that aims to provide a more secure and scalable infrastructure for smart contracts and decentralized applications. Developed with a research-first approach, Cardano focuses on formal verification and peer-reviewed academic research to ensure the security and robustness of its platform.

6. **Solana (SOL):** Solana is a high-performance blockchain known for its speed and low transaction costs. It uses a unique consensus mechanism called Proof of History (PoH), which enables fast processing of transactions. Solana has gained significant adoption in the DeFi and NFT spaces due to its scalability and efficiency.

7. **Chainlink (LINK):** Chainlink is a decentralized oracle network that connects smart contracts with real-world data. Smart contracts typically operate within the blockchain ecosystem, but they often require external data (such as price feeds, weather conditions, or election results) to function. Chainlink solves this problem by securely connecting off-chain data sources to blockchain networks.

As summarized in Table 2-1, platform purposes and features are compiled from primary sources and official documentation for each network.

Table 2-1. *Key Blockchain Platforms*

Platform	Purpose	Key Features
Bitcoin	Digital currency and store of value.	Peer-to-peer transactions, Proof of Work consensus, high security, limited scalability.
Ethereum	Smart contracts and decentralized applications (DApps).	Smart contracts, ERC-20 tokens, transitioning to Proof of Stake for scalability.
Ripple	Blockchain for cross-border payments and remittances.	Fast transactions, low fees, Ripple Protocol Consensus Algorithm (RPCA).
Polkadot	Interoperability between blockchains and scalability.	Parachains architecture, cross-chain communication, Proof of Stake.
Cardano	Secure and scalable platform for DApps and smart contracts.	Formal verification, research-first approach, low energy consumption.
Solana	High-speed, low-cost blockchain for DeFi and NFTs.	Proof of History (PoH) consensus, high throughput, low transaction costs.
Chainlink	Decentralized oracle network to connect smart contracts with off-chain data.	Real-world data feeds, secure off-chain connectivity, scalable oracle solutions.

These projects and others continue to push the boundaries of what blockchain technology can achieve, driving innovation across multiple industries.

Technology Overview

Blockchain technology is a sophisticated system composed of multiple layers and components that work together to enable decentralized, secure, and immutable transactions. This section will provide a detailed overview of the underlying technology behind blockchain, covering its architecture, consensus mechanisms, and network structure.

CHAPTER 2   BLOCKCHAIN

Blockchain Architecture

Blockchain architecture is the fundamental design of how the system works. At its core, a blockchain consists of a series of blocks, each containing a collection of transactions. These blocks are linked together in chronological order to form a chain, which explains the term "blockchain." Each block contains three key components (Figure 2-4):

1. **Data:** The actual transactions or records being stored on the blockchain. For a cryptocurrency like Bitcoin, this data could represent the transfer of digital currency between users. In other blockchain systems, it could store information like contracts, identities, or asset ownership.

2. **Hash of the Previous Block:** This is a cryptographic hash that links the current block to the previous block in the chain. The hash is a unique fingerprint of the block's contents. By linking each block to the previous one, blockchain ensures the immutability of the ledger. Changing the data in any one block would invalidate the hashes of all subsequent blocks.

3. **Nonce (Proof of Work Blockchains):** A nonce is a random number used in proof-of-work blockchains, like Bitcoin, to solve cryptographic puzzles required to validate and add a block to the chain. This process is key to ensuring the integrity of the blockchain in proof-of-work systems.

CHAPTER 2 BLOCKCHAIN

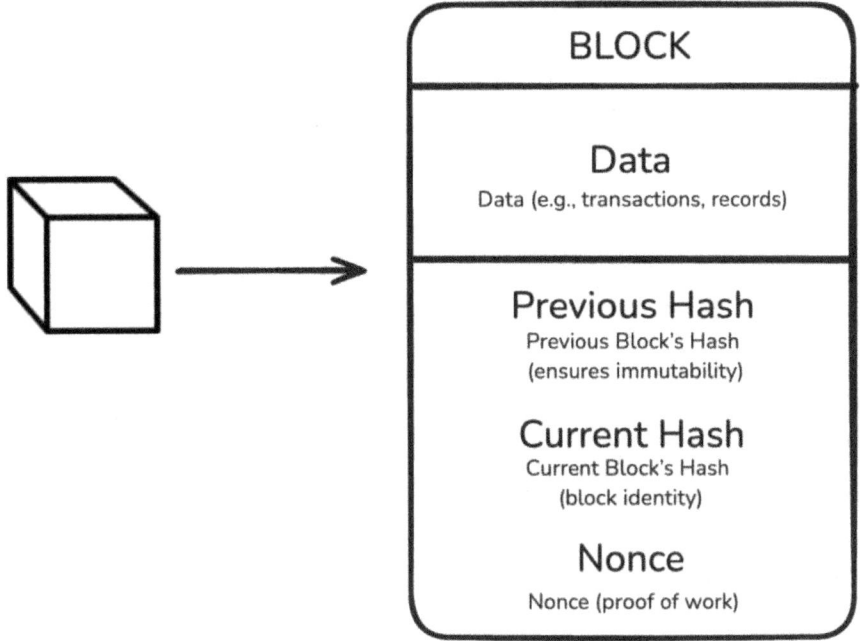

Figure 2-4. *Anatomy of a Blockchain Block*

Blockchain's Structure:

- **Genesis Block:** The first block of any blockchain, which serves as the foundation of the entire chain. Every blockchain has a unique genesis block, which initializes the blockchain's operation.

- **Merkle Tree:** In many blockchains, transactions within a block are arranged in a structure called a Merkle Tree, a binary tree where each leaf node is a transaction hash, and parent nodes are hashes of their child nodes. The root of this tree, known as the Merkle Root, summarizes all transactions in the block, allowing for efficient and secure verification of transaction integrity. Figure 2-5 demonstrates the Merkle Tree used for transaction verification.

73

CHAPTER 2   BLOCKCHAIN

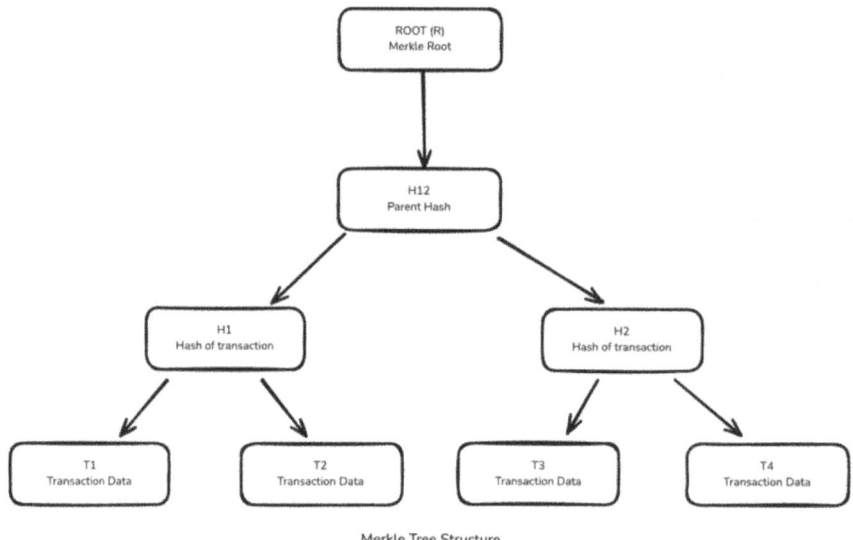

Figure 2-5. *Merkle Tree Structure*

- **Distributed Ledger:** Blockchain operates as a distributed ledger, meaning that the entire database is maintained across multiple nodes, or participants, in the network. Each node holds a copy of the ledger, and consensus mechanisms ensure that all nodes agree on the state of the blockchain.

Blockchain's decentralized architecture ensures that no single point of control exists, making it more secure, transparent, and resistant to manipulation compared to traditional, centralized databases.

Consensus Mechanisms

A key feature of blockchain is the ability to achieve consensus across a distributed network of participants. Consensus mechanisms are the protocols by which all participants in the network agree on the validity of transactions and ensure that the entire system maintains a consistent state. Different blockchains employ various consensus mechanisms, with the most common being Proof of Work (PoW) and Proof of Stake (PoS).

1. **Proof of Work (PoW):**

   Proof of Work (PoW) is the original consensus mechanism used by Bitcoin and other early blockchains. In a PoW system, miners compete to solve complex mathematical puzzles, and the first one to solve the puzzle gets to add a new block to the blockchain. The miner is then rewarded with cryptocurrency for their efforts. The puzzle is difficult to solve, but the solution is easy for other participants to verify.

   PoW is highly secure and decentralized, but it requires significant computational power and energy, which has raised concerns about its environmental impact. The energy-intensive nature of PoW has also limited the scalability of early blockchain networks like Bitcoin, as processing large numbers of transactions is slow and costly.

2. **Proof of Stake (PoS):**

   Proof of Stake (PoS) is an alternative consensus mechanism designed to address some of the limitations of PoW, particularly its energy consumption. In a PoS system, validators are selected to propose new blocks based on the number of tokens they hold and are willing to "stake" as collateral. Validators are incentivized to act honestly because if they behave maliciously, they risk losing their staked tokens.

   PoS is more energy-efficient than PoW because it does not rely on solving computational puzzles. It also tends to allow for faster transaction processing. Ethereum, which started as a PoW blockchain, recently transitioned to PoS as part of its Ethereum 2.0 upgrade.

3. **Delegated Proof of Stake (DPoS):**

   Delegated Proof of Stake (DPoS) is a variation of PoS in which token holders vote to elect a small group of trusted validators, known as delegates or witnesses, to create and validate new blocks. DPoS increases efficiency by reducing the number of nodes involved in the consensus process while maintaining decentralization. Blockchains like EOS and TRON use DPoS.

4. **Proof of Authority (PoA):**

   Proof of Authority (PoA) is a consensus mechanism where a small group of pre-approved validators are authorized to produce blocks. PoA is often used in private or permissioned blockchains, where trust among participants is higher. It offers high transaction processing capacity and efficiency but sacrifices some decentralization. PoA is suitable for enterprise blockchains where permissioned participants are known entities.

5. **Other Consensus Mechanisms:**

   - **Byzantine Fault Tolerance (BFT):** Used in systems like Hyperledger, BFT allows consensus to be reached even if some nodes are acting maliciously or are unreliable.

   - **Proof of History (PoH):** Used by Solana, PoH provides a historical record that proves that an event occurred at a specific moment in time, enabling greater scalability and fast processing.

Each consensus mechanism has its trade-offs, and blockchain projects choose different mechanisms based on their use cases and scalability requirements.

Table 2-2 compares mainstream consensus mechanisms, synthesized from foundational papers and protocol documentation, with examples drawn from the cited networks.

Table 2-2. *Comparison of Consensus Mechanisms*

Consensus Mechanism	Key Features	Advantages	Disadvantages	Examples
Proof of Work (PoW)	Miners solve cryptographic puzzles to validate transactions.	High security, decentralized, resistant to attacks.	Energy-intensive, slow transaction processing, scalability issues.	Bitcoin, Litecoin
Proof of Stake (PoS)	Validators are chosen based on the number of tokens staked.	Energy-efficient, faster transaction processing, scalable.	Can lead to centralization (wealthier users control more of the network).	Ethereum 2.0, Cardano

(continued)

Table 2-2. (*continued*)

Consensus Mechanism	Key Features	Advantages	Disadvantages	Examples
Delegated Proof of Stake (DPoS)	Token holders vote for delegates to validate transactions.	More efficient and faster than PoS, democratic governance.	Less decentralized due to reliance on a small number of delegates.	EOS, TRON
Proof of Authority (PoA)	A set of pre-approved validators create blocks.	High throughput, energy-efficient, ideal for private blockchains.	Limited decentralization relies on trust in validators.	VeChain, Binance Smart Chain
Byzantine Fault Tolerance (BFT)	Achieves consensus even with malicious or faulty nodes.	High fault tolerance, suitable for permissioned blockchains.	Less efficient in large-scale public networks.	Hyperledger Fabric, Stellar
Proof of History (PoH)	Provides a historical record to prove an event's occurrence.	Increases scalability and speeds up processing in conjunction with PoS.	Relatively new and less tested compared to other mechanisms.	Solana

Nodes and Network Structure

In a blockchain network, nodes are the individual participants that maintain a copy of the blockchain and help validate new transactions. The structure and function of nodes can vary, but they are crucial to the decentralized nature of blockchain. Figure 2-6 categorizes different types of nodes in a blockchain network.

1. **Types of Nodes:**

    - **Full Nodes:** Full nodes maintain a complete copy of the blockchain and validate transactions according to the blockchain's consensus rules. In most public blockchains like Bitcoin and Ethereum, full nodes help maintain the network's integrity by ensuring that all transactions and blocks follow the protocol.

- **Light Nodes (SPV Nodes):** Light nodes, or Simplified Payment Verification (SPV) nodes, do not store the entire blockchain. Instead, they store only a portion of the blockchain's data, typically the block headers. Light nodes rely on full nodes to validate transactions but can still participate in the network without the need for extensive storage.

- **Mining/Validator Nodes:** In PoW blockchains, mining nodes are responsible for solving cryptographic puzzles and proposing new blocks. In PoS and DPoS systems, validator nodes are responsible for validating and proposing new blocks based on the consensus mechanism.

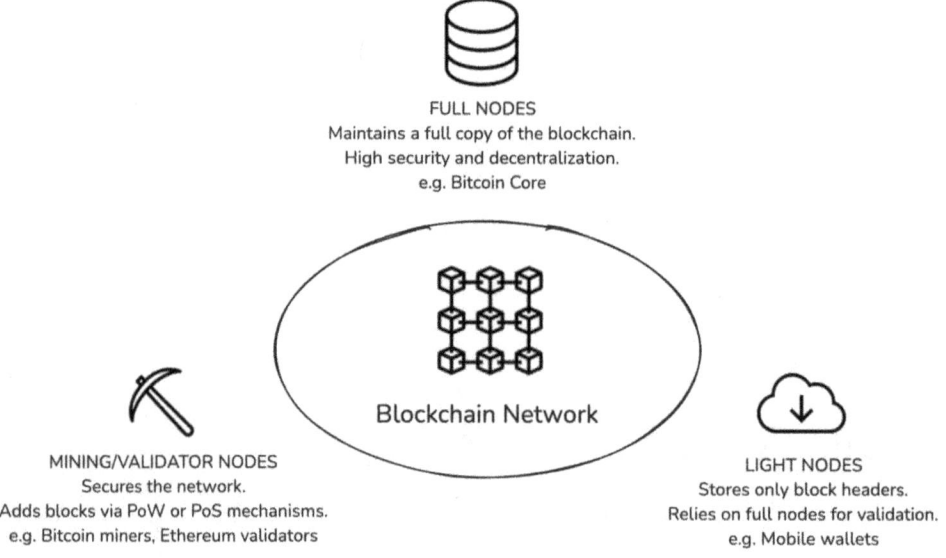

Figure 2-6. Types of Blockchain Nodes

2. **Peer-to-Peer (P2P) Network:**

    Blockchain operates on a peer-to-peer (P2P) network where all nodes communicate directly with each other without a central server. Each node in the network holds a copy of the blockchain and participates in the consensus process.

CHAPTER 2   BLOCKCHAIN

- **Decentralization:** The P2P structure of blockchain ensures decentralization. There is no central point of control, and no single entity can take down the network. Even if some nodes go offline, the blockchain continues to operate as long as most of the nodes are functional.

- **Broadcasting:** When a transaction is initiated, it is broadcast to the entire network. Nodes verify the transaction and add it to the mempool (a pool of unconfirmed transactions). Figure 2-7 shows how nodes interact in a P2P network. Once a miner or validator includes the transaction in a block, it is added to the blockchain.

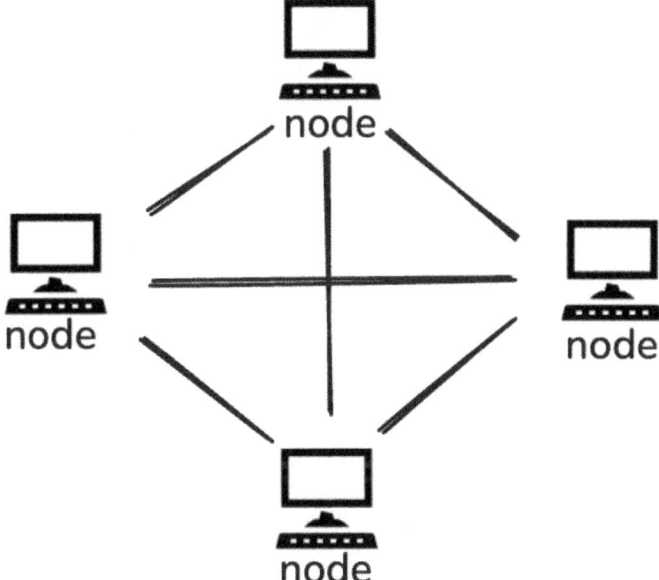

Figure 2-7. *Peer-to-Peer Blockchain Network*

3. **Forks and Upgrades:**

    A blockchain fork occurs when the rules governing the blockchain are changed, resulting in a divergence of the blockchain into two or more paths. Forks can be either **soft forks** (backward-compatible upgrades) or **hard forks** (non-backward-compatible upgrades).

CHAPTER 2 BLOCKCHAIN

- **Soft Fork:** A soft fork occurs when changes are made to the protocol that are backward compatible. This means that nodes running the old version of the software can still participate in the network, but they are encouraged to upgrade to the new version. An example of a soft fork is Bitcoin's SegWit upgrade.

- **Hard Fork:** A hard fork results in a permanent split of the blockchain. Nodes running the old version of the software are no longer compatible with the new version. This creates two separate chains with distinct rules. Figure 2-8 compares hard forks and soft forks in blockchain. Ethereum's hard fork following the DAO hack in 2016 resulted in two blockchains: Ethereum (ETH) and Ethereum Classic (ETC).

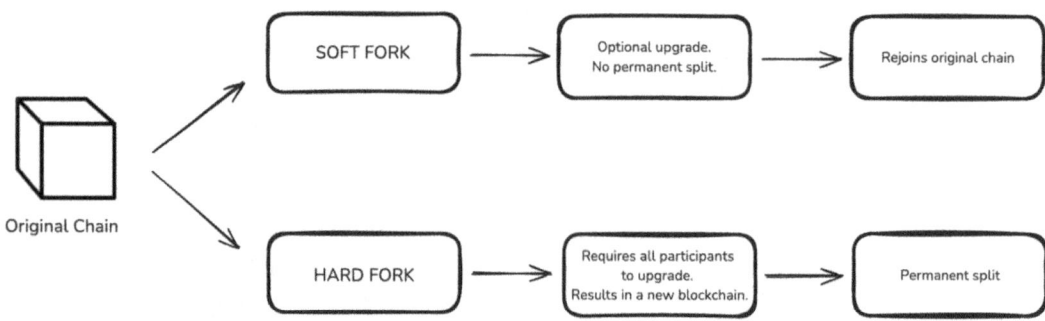

Figure 2-8. *Hard Fork vs. Soft Fork*

Understanding Blockchain Transactions

Blockchain transactions are the fundamental units of activity within a blockchain network, enabling the transfer of assets, recording of data, and execution of smart contracts. In this section, we will break down the lifecycle of a blockchain transaction, explain how transactions are validated and verified, and discuss transaction fees and incentives that drive participation in the network.

Transaction Lifecycle

The lifecycle of a blockchain transaction involves several stages, from its creation to its confirmation and inclusion in a block. Each step is critical to ensuring the transaction's security, immutability, and validity. Figure 2-9 visualizes a transaction's path from creation to finality.

1. **Transaction Creation:**
    - A blockchain transaction is created when a user initiates an action, such as sending cryptocurrency, invoking a smart contract, or recording data on the blockchain. In cryptocurrency networks like Bitcoin or Ethereum, the transaction typically involves transferring coins or tokens from one address (sender) to another address (receiver).
    - The transaction contains several components, including
        - **Input:** The source of funds or digital assets, such as the sender's wallet address or previous unspent transaction output (UTXO)
        - **Output:** The recipient's wallet address or account, specifying where the assets will be sent
        - **Amount:** The quantity of digital assets being transferred
        - **Signature:** A digital signature created using the sender's private key, which proves that the sender is authorized to initiate the transaction

2. **Broadcasting to the Network:**
    - Once the transaction is created and signed, it is broadcast to the blockchain network. In a peer-to-peer (P2P) network, the transaction is propagated to all nodes that receive the broadcast. These nodes verify the transaction for its accuracy (such as ensuring the sender has sufficient funds and the digital signature is valid).

- At this point, the transaction is considered **unconfirmed**, and it waits in a memory pool (or mempool) until it can be included in the next block.

3. **Validation and Verification:**

    - The transaction must be validated by the network. Different blockchain networks employ different methods of validation, depending on the consensus mechanism used (e.g., Proof of Work or Proof of Stake).

    - Validators (in Proof-of-Stake systems) or miners (in Proof-of-Work systems) will check the following:

        - **Funds Availability:** Ensure that the sender has sufficient assets to complete the transaction.

        - **Signature Validity:** Confirm that the transaction has been signed by the rightful owner of the private key associated with the sending address.

        - **Double-Spending Protection:** Ensure that the transaction is not attempting to spend the same funds more than once. Double-spending is a critical issue in digital currencies, and blockchain's distributed consensus helps prevent this problem.

4. **Inclusion in a Block:**

    - Once validated, the transaction is included in a block by a miner (PoW) or validator (PoS). The block contains multiple transactions and is added to the blockchain in chronological order. Each block references the previous one by including its hash, ensuring the immutability of the chain.

    - When the block containing the transaction is added to the blockchain, the transaction is considered **confirmed**. Most blockchain networks require a certain number of confirmations (blocks added on top of the block containing the transaction) before a transaction is considered fully final and irreversible. For example, on the Bitcoin network, six confirmations are typically required to ensure the transaction is secure.

5. **Finality:**

    - Once confirmed, the transaction becomes part of the permanent blockchain record. It cannot be reversed or altered, ensuring immutability. Both the sender and receiver can now see the confirmed transaction in the blockchain ledger, and the assets have been transferred.

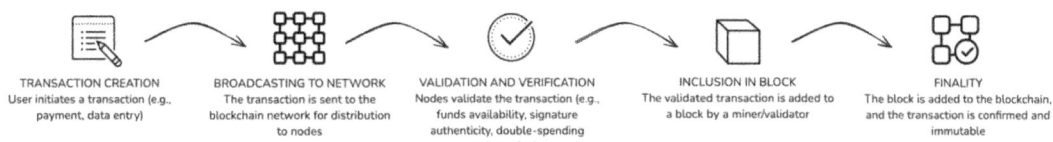

Figure 2-9. Lifecycle of a Blockchain Transaction

Transaction Fees and Incentives

Blockchain transactions are typically subject to fees, which are paid by the sender to incentivize miners or validators to include the transaction in the next block. Transaction fees play a crucial role in ensuring the security and efficiency of the network while also providing economic incentives for participants.

1. **Transaction Fees:**

    - **Bitcoin Fees:** On the Bitcoin network, transaction fees are calculated based on the size of the transaction in bytes. Since Bitcoin blocks have a limited size (currently 1 MB), miners prioritize transactions with higher fees. Users can choose how much they want to pay in transaction fees, with higher fees resulting in faster confirmation times. If the network is congested, users may need to pay higher fees to have their transactions confirmed quickly.

    - **Ethereum Fees:** On Ethereum, transaction fees are based on **gas**, which represents the computational effort required to process a transaction. Gas fees fluctuate based on network demand, and complex transactions (such as executing smart contracts) require more gas. Similar to Bitcoin, users can choose how much gas they are willing to pay, and transactions with higher gas fees are prioritized by validators.

Table 2-3 presents illustrative fee ranges and fee-setting rules, based on protocol fee models and widely used trackers/documentation; values vary over time with network demand.

Table 2-3. *Transaction Fees Across Blockchains*

Blockchain/Layer	Average Transaction Fee	Fee Determination	Impact on Users
Bitcoin (BTC)	$1–$30	Fee based on transaction size (in bytes).	High during congestion; incentivizes larger payments.
Ethereum (ETH)	$0.50–$50+	Determined by gas price and complexity.	Can spike during high demand; affects smart contract executions.
Ethereum Layer 2 (e.g., Optimistic Rollups)	$0.01–$0.10	Aggregated transactions processed off-chain.	Affordable for microtransactions; scalable.
Solana (SOL)	<$0.01	Flat fee for transactions.	Highly affordable; suitable for high-frequency trades.
Binance Smart Chain (BSC)	~$0.10	Flat fee structure.	Low fees; widely adopted for DeFi and NFTs.

2. **Incentives for Miners and Validators:**

    Miners (in PoW) and validators (in PoS) are incentivized to secure the network and validate transactions through the reward system. These rewards come in two forms:

    - **Block Rewards:** When a miner successfully mines a new block (PoW) or a validator proposes a new block (PoS), they receive a reward in the form of newly minted cryptocurrency. For example, in Bitcoin, miners currently receive a reward for each block they mine, though this reward is halved roughly every four years (a process known as the "halving").

    - **Transaction Fees:** Miners and validators also receive the transaction fees included in each block. As block rewards decrease over time (especially in Bitcoin's case), transaction fees become a more important source of income for miners. Figure 2-10 illustrates how miners and validators are incentivized.

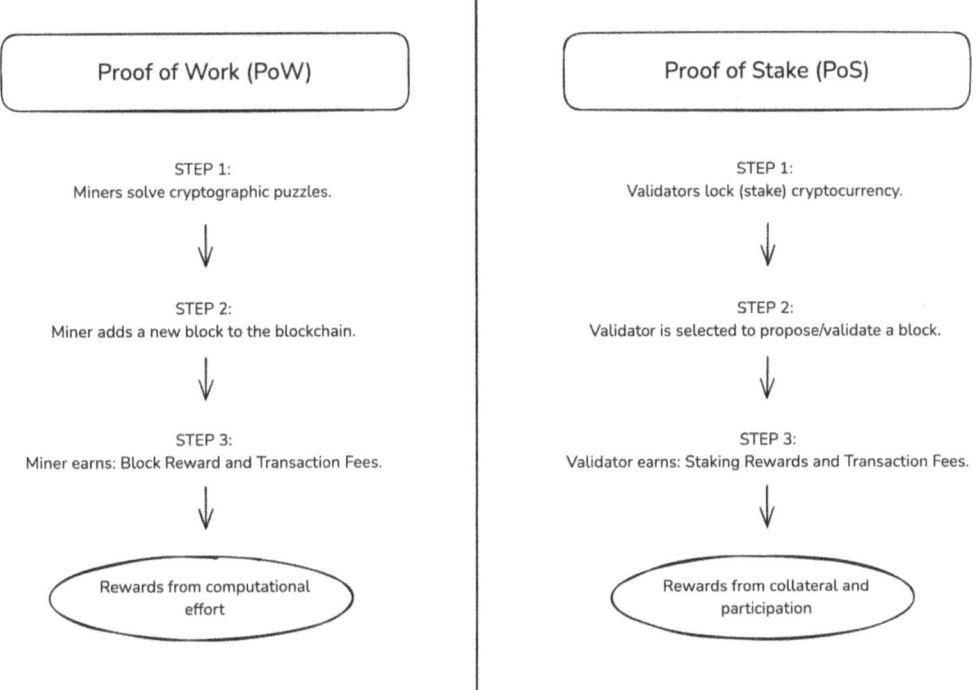

Figure 2-10. *Block Rewards and Transaction Fees*

3. **Fee Market Dynamics:**

    - Transaction fees can fluctuate based on the supply and demand for block space. When the network is congested (e.g., during periods of high demand for transactions or smart contract executions), fees can rise significantly as users compete to have their transactions included in the next block.

    - Blockchains are also exploring solutions to lower fees and increase scalability, such as layer 2 technologies like Bitcoin's Lightning Network or Ethereum's rollups, which bundle multiple transactions together before recording them on the main chain. Figure 2-11 presents techniques to improve blockchain scalability.

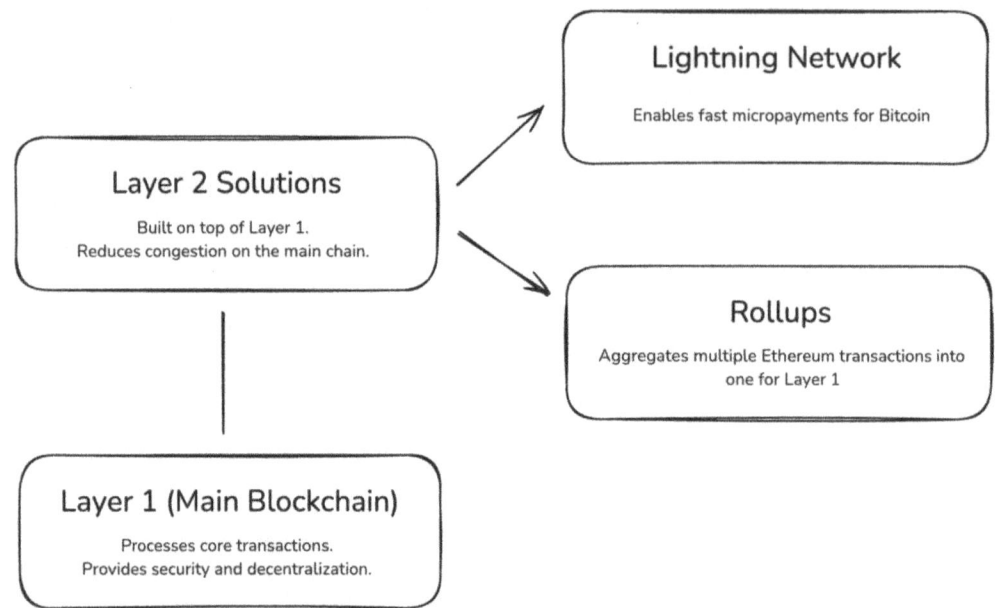

Figure 2-11. Layer 2 Scaling Solutions

The Principle of Decentralization

Decentralization is one of the foundational principles of blockchain technology and Web3, making it unique compared to traditional centralized systems. By removing the need for a central authority, decentralization increases security, transparency, and user control. In this section, we will define decentralization, explore its benefits over centralized systems, and discuss the challenges and trade-offs involved in adopting decentralized architectures.

Definition and Importance

Decentralization refers to the distribution of authority, control, and decision-making across a network of participants, rather than concentrating it within a single entity or central authority. In the context of blockchain, decentralization means that no single party has complete control over the network or its data. Instead, control is distributed across nodes that maintain the network, verify transactions, and reach consensus on the state of the blockchain.

In a decentralized system, power is distributed more equitably, reducing the risk of corruption, fraud, and censorship. Unlike centralized networks, where a single organization or individual can make unilateral decisions, decentralized networks operate on a consensus basis. This means that decisions, such as verifying transactions or updating the protocol, require agreement from a majority of participants.

As illustrated in Figure 2-12, adapted from Baran's seminal work on distributed communications networks (Baran, 1964), the contrast between centralized, decentralized, and distributed architectures highlights how control and decision-making authority can shift across network structures.

 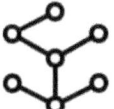 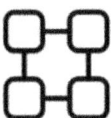

CENTRALIZED
All data flows through one central authority.
Single point of failure.
e.g. Traditional banking systems.

DECENTRALIZED
Control is distributed among multiple key nodes.
Reduces single points of failure.
e.g. Blockchain networks.

DISTRIBUTED
Fully interconnected system.
High redundancy and resilience.
e.g. Peer-to-peer networks.

Figure 2-12. Centralized vs. Decentralized vs. Distributed Networks

Key Features of Decentralization:

1. **Distributed Ledger:** The blockchain itself is a decentralized ledger, meaning it is maintained across multiple nodes, each holding a copy of the data. This redundancy ensures that the system is resilient to failures or attacks.

2. **No Central Authority:** In a decentralized network, there is no single entity that controls or governs the system. This lack of central authority helps protect against censorship, corruption, and abuse by any single party.

3. **Consensus Mechanisms:** Decentralized systems use consensus mechanisms to validate transactions and reach agreement on the current state of the blockchain. These mechanisms ensure that all participants have a voice in maintaining the network.

4. **Security and Transparency:** Decentralization enhances both security and transparency by distributing control among a large number of participants. This makes it difficult for any single actor to manipulate the system or alter records.

Decentralization is critical to the trustless nature of blockchain systems. Participants can engage in transactions, share data, or use decentralized applications (DApps) without needing to trust a central authority to act as an intermediary. This trustless environment reduces reliance on third parties and gives users greater autonomy.

The benefits summarized in Table 2-4 reflect the canonical literature on decentralization and network topology, together with contemporary analyses of blockchain governance.

Table 2-4. Benefits of Decentralization

Feature	Description	Significance
Distributed Ledger	Blockchain is maintained across multiple nodes, each holding a copy of the data. This redundancy ensures resilience against failures or attacks.	Ensures system reliability and data availability even if some nodes go offline.
No Central Authority	There is no single entity controlling or governing the system. This prevents censorship, corruption, or abuse by any single party.	Protects against centralized abuse of power and ensures user autonomy.
Consensus Mechanisms	Used to validate transactions and reach agreement on the current state of the blockchain. These mechanisms give all participants a voice.	Ensures fairness, trust, and consistency in the network's operation.
Security and Transparency	Decentralization enhances security by distributing control among many participants, making it difficult for a single actor to alter records.	Builds trust and ensures tamper-proof, verifiable transactions.

Benefits over Centralized Systems

Decentralization offers several advantages over traditional centralized systems, particularly in terms of security, control, and resilience. These benefits make decentralized technologies attractive for a wide range of applications, from finance and supply chain management to social media and governance. Figure 2-13 illustrates key advantages of decentralization.

1. **Increased Security and Resilience:**
   - In a centralized system, a single point of failure can lead to catastrophic consequences, such as data breaches, system failures, or censorship. If the central authority is compromised or corrupted, the entire network may be vulnerable.

- In contrast, decentralized systems are inherently more secure because there is no central point of failure. Even if some nodes in the network are attacked or go offline, the blockchain continues to operate as long as a majority of nodes remain functional. This resilience makes decentralized networks highly resistant to hacking, fraud, and other malicious activities.

2. **Censorship Resistance:**

    - Centralized systems are vulnerable to censorship because a single authority can control what information is shared, who can participate, or how users can interact with the system. Governments or corporations may suppress certain voices, block access to services, or manipulate content.

    - Decentralized systems are much harder to censor. Since control is distributed among many participants, no single entity can prevent users from accessing the network or censor specific transactions or information. This feature makes decentralized networks perfect for use cases that prioritize freedom of speech, access to information, and privacy.

3. **Enhanced User Control and Ownership:**

    - In centralized systems, users often have limited control over their data and assets. Centralized platforms may collect, store, and even sell user data without explicit consent. Moreover, users rely on intermediaries to manage assets, transactions, and services.

    - Decentralized systems give users full control over their data, identities, and assets. With blockchain-based platforms, users own their private keys, which give them direct access to their assets (cryptocurrency, NFTs, etc.) without needing a third party. This level of control enhances privacy and reduces the risks associated with centralized data storage.

4. **Transparency and Trust:**

    - Centralized systems often operate without transparency, with decisions and processes hidden from public view. This lack of transparency can lead to distrust among users, especially in cases where central authorities have abused their power.

    - Decentralized systems, particularly public blockchains, are fully transparent. All transactions are recorded on a public ledger, which is visible to anyone. This transparency builds trust among users, as they can independently verify the integrity of the system and the transactions that occur within it.

5. **Elimination of Intermediaries:**

    - In centralized systems, intermediaries like banks, payment processors, or service providers are necessary to facilitate transactions, manage services, or verify identities. These intermediaries introduce inefficiencies, add costs, and can become single points of failure.

    - Decentralized systems eliminate the need for intermediaries by relying on peer-to-peer networks and automated smart contracts. For example, decentralized finance (DeFi) platforms allow users to lend, borrow, or trade assets directly with one another without relying on banks or brokers.

CHAPTER 2 BLOCKCHAIN

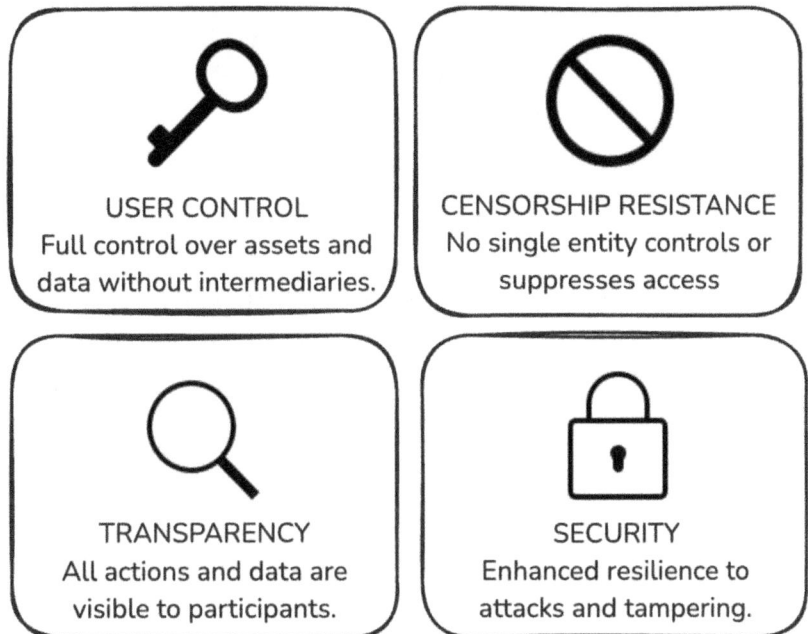

Figure 2-13. Benefits of Decentralization

Challenges and Trade-Offs

While decentralization offers significant advantages, it also presents several challenges and trade-offs. These issues must be carefully considered when designing or adopting decentralized systems. Figure 2-14 outlines the main trade-offs in decentralized systems.

1. **Scalability:**
   - One of the biggest challenges facing decentralized systems is scalability. Public blockchains like Bitcoin and Ethereum have struggled with scaling as their user base grows. Since every node in the network must process and store every transaction, decentralized networks can become slow and congested, leading to higher transaction fees and longer confirmation times.

CHAPTER 2   BLOCKCHAIN

- Solutions such as layer 2 scaling technologies (e.g., Lightning Network, rollups) and sharding are being developed to improve scalability, but achieving global scalability while maintaining decentralization remains a key challenge.

2. **Energy Consumption:**

    - Proof of Work (PoW) consensus mechanisms, like those used in Bitcoin, are energy intensive. Miners compete to solve complex puzzles, which require significant computational power and electricity. This has raised concerns about the environmental impact of blockchain technology.

    - Proof of Stake (PoS) and other consensus mechanisms, such as Proof of Authority (PoA) or Delegated Proof of Stake (DPoS), offer more energy-efficient alternatives, but the environmental impact of large-scale decentralized systems is still a topic of debate.

3. **Governance:**

    - Decentralized systems rely on distributed governance models, such as Decentralized Autonomous Organizations (DAOs), to make decisions about protocol updates, security, and resource allocation. While these models promote inclusivity and transparency, they can also lead to decision-making delays, particularly when there are disagreements among participants.

    - Achieving a balance between decentralized governance and efficient decision-making is a continuous challenge for many blockchain projects.

4. **User Experience:**

    - For most users, interacting with decentralized systems can be more complex than using centralized platforms. Managing private keys, understanding gas fees, and navigating decentralized interfaces can be challenging for those unfamiliar with blockchain technology.

- Improving the user experience (UX) in decentralized applications (DApps) and wallets is critical to increasing adoption and making decentralized systems more accessible to the public.

5. **Regulation and Compliance:**

   - Decentralized systems often operate outside of traditional regulatory frameworks, which can create uncertainty for both users and developers. Governments are still determining how to regulate blockchain technologies, particularly in areas like decentralized finance (DeFi), privacy, and data security.

   - Finding a balance between decentralization and regulatory compliance is a challenging issue that will influence the future of blockchain adoption.

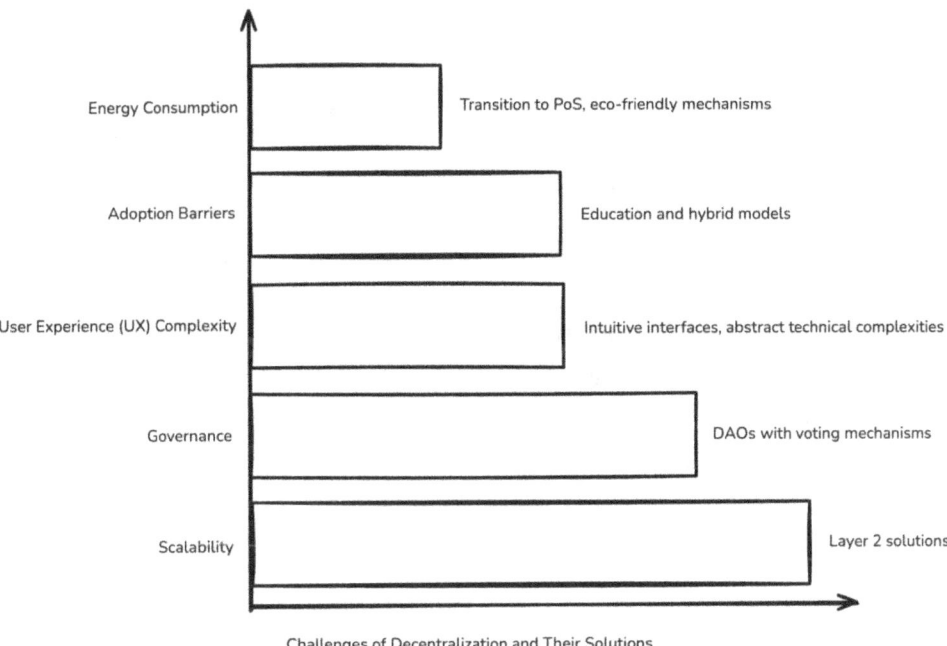

Figure 2-14. Challenges of Decentralization

CHAPTER 2   BLOCKCHAIN

Blockchain Security

Blockchain security is a critical aspect of technology, as it ensures that the decentralized system remains robust, reliable, and resistant to attacks. Security is achieved through a combination of cryptographic techniques, consensus mechanisms, and decentralized network architecture. This section examines different aspects of blockchain security, such as cryptographic methods, network security mechanisms, and case studies of security vulnerabilities and their solutions.

Cryptographic Security

Cryptography is the foundation of blockchain security. It ensures the integrity of transactions, protects user privacy, and secures the network from malicious attacks. The key cryptographic techniques used in blockchain include hashing, digital signatures, and public-key cryptography.

1. **Hash Functions:**

    A hash function takes an input (such as a transaction) and generates a fixed-size string of characters, typically a unique alphanumeric identifier called a hash. Even a small change in the input will result in a completely different hash. In blockchain, hash functions are used for:

    - **Block Hashing:** Each block in the blockchain contains a hash of the previous block, creating a chain of blocks. This ensures the immutability of the blockchain. Changing a single block's data would require changing the hashes of all subsequent blocks, making unauthorized changes nearly impossible. Figure 2-15 shows how hash functions secure blockchain data.

    - **Transaction Verification:** Hash functions are used to create Merkle Trees, where individual transactions are hashed and combined to form a Merkle Root. This allows for efficient verification of transactions within a block without needing to check the entire block.

    Popular cryptographic hash functions used in blockchain include SHA-256 (used by Bitcoin) and Keccak-256 (used by Ethereum).

CHAPTER 2 BLOCKCHAIN

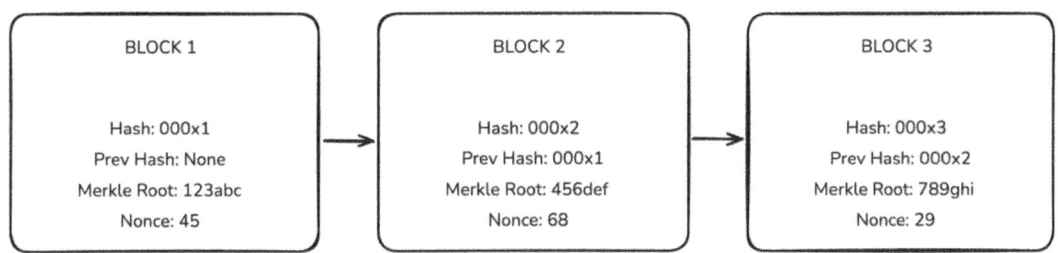

Figure 2-15. *Cryptographic Hash Function*

2. **Digital Signatures:**

   Digital signatures provide a way to verify the authenticity of transactions without revealing the sender's private key. In blockchain, digital signatures are generated using public-key cryptography, where each user has a pair of cryptographic keys:

   - **Public Key:** This key is shared with the network and is used to verify the digital signature of a transaction.

   - **Private Key:** This key is kept secret and is used to sign transactions. The private key generates a unique digital signature for each transaction, proving that the transaction was initiated by the legitimate owner without revealing the private key itself.

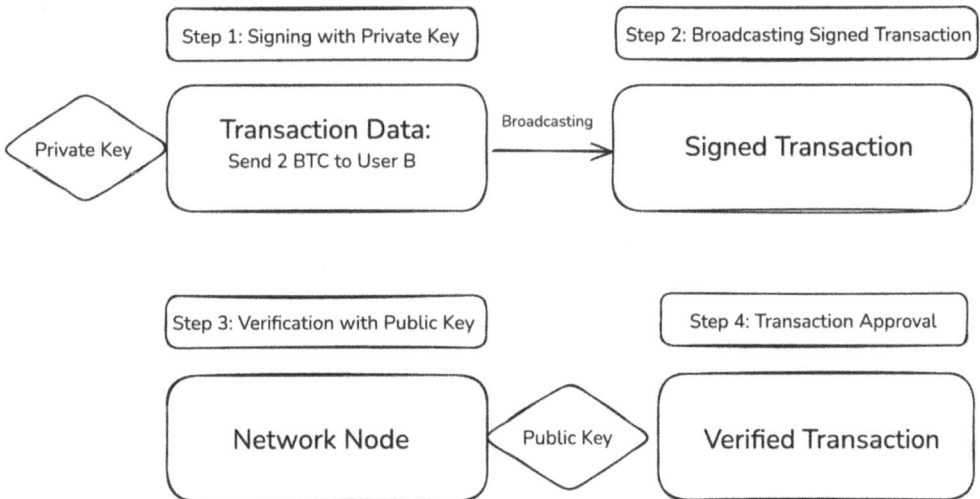

Figure 2-16. *Digital Signature Process*

95

Digital signatures ensure that transactions are both secure and verifiable, meaning that the sender cannot deny initiating the transaction. If the signature matches the public key associated with the sender's wallet, the network confirms that the transaction is valid. Figure 2-16 explains the role of digital signatures.

3. **Public-Key Cryptography:**

   Public-key cryptography (also known as asymmetric cryptography) is used to secure transactions and maintain user privacy in blockchain networks. Each participant in the blockchain has a public-private key pair. Public keys are used to receive funds, while private keys are used to sign transactions and access the funds.

   - **Security of Private Keys:** The security of a blockchain relies on the protection of private keys. If a user's private key is compromised, the attacker can take control of the user's assets. This makes key management critical, as users must securely store their private keys (often using hardware wallets, encrypted storage, or seed phrases).

4. **Elliptic Curve Cryptography (ECC):**

   Many blockchain networks use Elliptic Curve Cryptography (ECC), which is a form of public-key cryptography. ECC provides the same level of security as other cryptographic methods but with smaller key sizes, making it more efficient in terms of computation and storage. Bitcoin and Ethereum both use ECC to secure transactions.

Network Security Mechanisms

In addition to cryptographic techniques, blockchain networks employ several security mechanisms to protect the network from attacks, maintain consensus, and ensure the integrity of the ledger. These mechanisms include consensus algorithms, decentralized node architecture, and defense against common attack methods.

1. **Consensus Mechanisms and Security:**

   Consensus mechanisms play a vital role in maintaining the security and trustworthiness of the blockchain. They ensure that all participants agree on the state of the ledger and that only valid transactions are added to the blockchain.

   - **Proof of Work (PoW):** PoW secures the network by requiring miners to solve complex computational puzzles to validate transactions. This process makes it difficult for an attacker to alter the blockchain, as it would require controlling over 50% of the network's hashing power (a "51% attack"). The immense computational resources needed to carry out such an attack make PoW-based blockchains, like Bitcoin, highly secure.

   - **Proof of Stake (PoS):** PoS secures the network by requiring validators to stake a certain amount of cryptocurrency to participate in block validation. Validators are incentivized to act honestly because malicious behavior can result in the loss of their staked assets. This reduces the risk of attacks compared to PoW, as validators have a financial interest in maintaining the security and integrity of the blockchain.

   - **Byzantine Fault Tolerance (BFT):** BFT consensus mechanisms, such as those used in Hyperledger and Tendermint, secure the network even when some nodes act maliciously or fail. BFT ensures that honest nodes can reach consensus and continue operating, even in the presence of faulty or compromised nodes.

2. **Decentralized Network Architecture:**

   Blockchain's decentralized architecture contributes significantly to its security. By distributing the ledger across many nodes, blockchain reduces the risk of a single point of failure and makes it difficult for an attacker to compromise the entire system.

   - **Distributed Trust:** In centralized systems, trust is placed in a single entity, such as a bank or a service provider. In decentralized blockchain networks, trust is distributed among many participants, making it harder for any single actor to manipulate the system or compromise security.

CHAPTER 2   BLOCKCHAIN

- **Fault Tolerance:** A decentralized network is naturally more resilient because the system can continue operating even if some nodes fail or are attacked. This resilience ensures the network stays operational, which is crucial for applications like financial transactions or supply chains where continuous availability is essential.

3. **Common Attack Vectors:**

   While blockchain networks are generally secure, they are still vulnerable to specific types of attacks. Some common attack vectors include:

   - **51% Attack:** In a 51% attack, a malicious actor gains control of more than 50% of the network's computational power (in PoW) or staked assets (in PoS). With this majority control, the attacker can manipulate the blockchain, such as by reversing transactions (double spending) or censoring new transactions. While technically possible, such attacks are difficult to execute on large, well-established blockchains like Bitcoin and Ethereum due to the prohibitive costs involved.

   - **Sybil Attack:** A Sybil attack occurs when an attacker creates multiple fake identities (or nodes) to gain disproportionate influence over the network. Many blockchain networks use reputation systems or proof mechanisms to mitigate Sybil attacks.

   - **Distributed Denial of Service (DDoS):** A DDoS attack involves overwhelming a network or node with an excessive amount of traffic, causing it to slow down or become unavailable. Blockchain's decentralized architecture helps mitigate the impact of DDoS attacks, as multiple nodes can handle the load and ensure the network remains operational.

   - **Smart Contract Vulnerabilities:** While blockchain itself is secure, smart contracts running on the blockchain can contain vulnerabilities if not properly coded. Attackers can exploit these vulnerabilities to drain funds, manipulate contract behavior, or perform other malicious actions. Smart contracts should receive detailed audits to ensure their security.

Table 2-5 consolidates common attack vectors and mitigations from academic surveys and incident reports, including historical cases such as the Bitcoin Gold 51% attack and the DAO exploit.

Table 2-5. *Blockchain Attack Vectors and Mitigations*

Attack Vector	Description	Example	Prevention Measures
51% Attack	A malicious actor gains control of over 50% of the network's mining power or stake, allowing them to double-spend or censor transactions.	Bitcoin Gold suffered a 51% attack in 2018, leading to the theft of over $18 million.	Use robust consensus mechanisms like Proof of Stake or implement checkpointing.
Sybil Attack	An attacker creates multiple fake identities or nodes to gain influence or disrupt the network.	Peer-to-peer networks without proper identity validation are vulnerable to this type of attack.	Use reputation systems, proof mechanisms, or node authentication to mitigate risks.
DDoS Attack	Overwhelming a network or node with excessive traffic, causing delays or unavailability.	Ethereum and Bitcoin have experienced DDoS attacks targeting mining pools.	Decentralized architecture and rate-limiting mechanisms can help mitigate DDoS attacks.
Smart Contract Exploits	Exploiting vulnerabilities in smart contract code to drain funds, manipulate functionality, or disrupt operations.	The DAO hack on Ethereum in 2016 led to the theft of $50 million in ETH.	Conduct rigorous smart contract audits, use formal verification, and implement upgradeable smart contract frameworks.
Private Key Theft	Stealing private keys to gain unauthorized access to users' assets or wallets.	Individual users or exchanges targeted by phishing attacks or malware.	Encourage the use of hardware wallets, multi-signature wallets, and secure storage practices.

(*continued*)

CHAPTER 2   BLOCKCHAIN

Table 2-5. (*continued*)

Attack Vector	Description	Example	Prevention Measures
Routing Attacks	Intercepting blockchain data during transmission between nodes, potentially leading to double-spending or delayed consensus.	ISPs redirecting or monitoring blockchain traffic to tamper with communication.	Use encryption protocols, virtual private networks (VPNs), and redundant network pathways.
Eclipse Attack	Isolating a node by controlling all its connections to the network, enabling manipulation of the node's view of the blockchain.	Rare but theoretically possible in smaller networks.	Encourage diverse and redundant peer connections for nodes and randomize peer selection.
Social Engineering	Tricking users into revealing private keys, passwords, or sensitive information through phishing or deceptive practices.	Numerous phishing attacks on cryptocurrency exchanges or wallet providers.	Educate users, implement two-factor authentication (2FA), and use anti-phishing tools.

Case Studies of Security Breaches and Solutions

While blockchain is generally considered secure, there have been notable cases of security breaches, often due to vulnerabilities in smart contracts, exchange platforms, or poor key management. Understanding these breaches helps in improving blockchain security moving forward.

1. **The DAO Hack (Ethereum, 2016):**

   In one of the most infamous security breaches, a vulnerability in a decentralized autonomous organization (DAO) built on Ethereum was taken advantage of, resulting in the theft of 3.6 million ETH (worth approximately $50 million at the time). The attacker leveraged a vulnerability in the DAO's smart contract, which enabled them to withdraw funds from the DAO multiple times before the system could update its balance.

- **Solution:** The Ethereum community decided to implement a hard fork to reverse the effects of the hack and return the stolen funds to the rightful owners. This hard fork led to the creation of two separate blockchains: Ethereum (ETH) and Ethereum Classic (ETC), with the second choosing to maintain the original, immutable chain.

2. **The Bitcoin Gold 51% Attack (2018):**

In May 2018, Bitcoin Gold, a fork of Bitcoin, suffered a 51% attack. The attacker gained control of more than 50% of the network's hashing power and used it to reverse transactions, allowing them to double-spend coins. The attacker managed to steal over $18 million worth of Bitcoin Gold by exploiting this vulnerability.

- **Solution:** The Bitcoin Gold team worked to address the vulnerability by upgrading its mining algorithm and enhancing its defenses against 51% attacks. However, the incident highlighted the risks that smaller blockchains face compared to more established networks like Bitcoin and Ethereum.

3. **The Parity Wallet Exploit (Ethereum, 2017):**

In November 2017, a vulnerability in the Parity multi-signature wallet contract was utilized, leading to the freezing of approximately 513,000 ETH (worth around $150 million at the time). A user accidentally triggered a defect in the wallet contract, leaving all funds stored in affected wallets inaccessible.

- **Solution:** The Ethereum community debated how to resolve the issue, but ultimately no hard fork or solution was implemented to recover the funds. The incident highlighted the importance of auditing smart contracts and ensuring that they are rigorously tested for security.

CHAPTER 2   BLOCKCHAIN

Conclusion

Blockchain is the foundation upon which most Web3 technologies are built. In this chapter, we explored its inner workings, from blocks and hash functions to nodes, networks, and consensus protocols. We examined how mechanisms like Proof of Work and Proof of Stake secure decentralized systems and how smart contracts unlock programmable functionality that goes far beyond simple value transfers.

While blockchain offers transparency, immutability, and security, it also faces important limitations: scalability issues, energy consumption, and regulatory uncertainty, among others. These are being addressed through innovations like Layer 2 protocols, modular architectures, and evolving governance models. As the ecosystem matures, developers and architects must understand these trade-offs in order to design reliable and efficient Web3 applications.

Chapter Summary

Topic	Key takeaways
Blockchain fundamentals	Blocks are chained with cryptographic hashes to ensure tamper-proof records.
Distributed ledger	Each node stores the entire ledger, ensuring transparency and resilience.
Consensus mechanisms	PoW and PoS secure the network and validate transactions without central control.
Smart contracts	Programmable contracts that self-execute when conditions are met.
Scalability solutions	Layer 2 solutions and sharding improve performance and reduce fees.
Major platforms	Projects like Bitcoin, Ethereum, and Polkadot offer different use-case focuses.
Decentralization	Promotes security, censorship resistance, and user ownership.
Security considerations	Blockchain security is enforced by cryptography and consensus; vulnerabilities still exist.

CHAPTER 3

Use Cases

Introduction

Blockchain technology has evolved from being the foundation of cryptocurrencies like Bitcoin to becoming a versatile solution for multiple industries. The unique characteristics of it, such as decentralization, transparency, immutability, and security, have opened up new possibilities in multiple domains, from finance to healthcare, supply chains, and governance.

Blockchain has many potential applications due to its revolutionary approach to recording, verifying, and sharing data. Trust is established through cryptography and consensus mechanisms in blockchain, unlike traditional systems that rely on centralized authorities. Innovative use cases have been enabled in various industries due to this paradigm shift, which has addressed long-standing challenges, including inefficiencies, lack of transparency, fraud, and high operational costs.

This chapter explores the practical use cases of blockchain technology and categorizes them into key application areas. Our goal is to demonstrate the power of blockchain to drive innovation and solve complex problems by examining real-world examples and implementations.

Blockchain Applications

The ability to create systems that are more secure, efficient, and equitable is what blockchain applications have in common across a wide range of industries. Blockchain can transform the way information and value are exchanged, from enabling decentralized finance (DeFi) platforms to revolutionizing supply chain management.

CHAPTER 3   USE CASES

Key areas of blockchain applications (Figure 3-1):

1. **Finance**: Blockchain is revolutionizing the financial industry through its use in decentralized finance, cross-border payments, and peer-to-peer lending.

2. **Currency**: Cryptocurrencies, stablecoins, and central bank digital currencies (CBDCs) are redefining how money is created, stored, and transferred.

3. **Property Records**: Blockchain provides an immutable and transparent way to manage property ownership and land registries, reducing fraud and inefficiency.

4. **Smart Contracts**: The automation of complex agreements by these self-executing contracts enables use cases in industries such as insurance, real estate, and logistics.

5. **Supply Chains**: Blockchain enhances the transparency and traceability of supply chains, which ensures ethical sourcing and quality control and reduces fraud.

6. **Voting**: Blockchain-based voting systems offer secure, transparent, and impenetrable solutions for democratic processes.

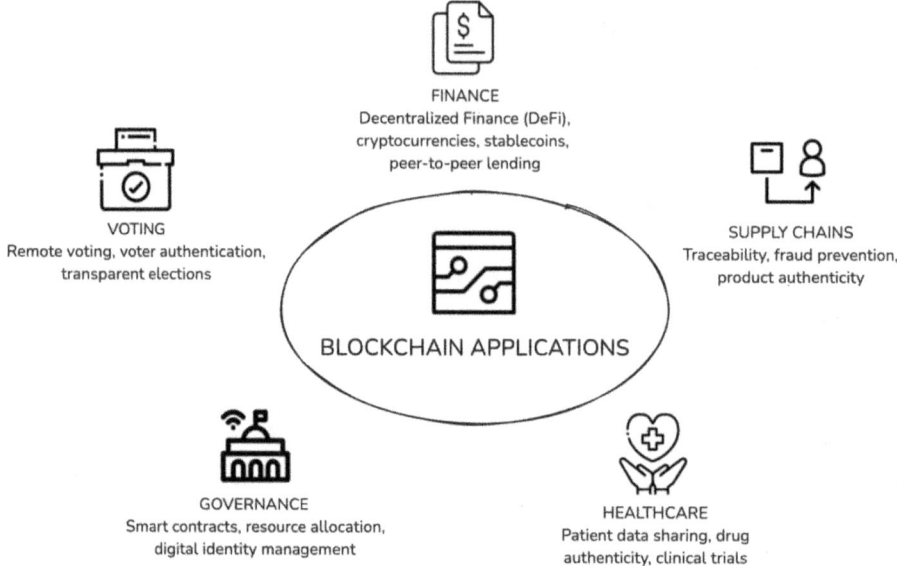

Figure 3-1. *Key Industries Using Blockchain*

CHAPTER 3   USE CASES

While these applications demonstrate the versatility of blockchain, their adoption is not without challenges. To fully realize the potential of blockchain technology, it is necessary to address critical issues such as scalability, regulatory challenges, and user adoption.

Finance

The financial sector has been the first and most prominent adopter of blockchain technology. Blockchain's ability to streamline transactions, eliminate intermediaries, and give global access has led to a wave of innovation in finance. In the following section, we will explore the transformative impact of blockchain on the financial sector, with particular emphasis on decentralized finance (DeFi), cross-border payments, and peer-to-peer lending. The use cases show how blockchain is enabling access to financial services and addressing inefficiencies in traditional systems.

1. **Decentralized Finance (DeFi)**

    Decentralized Finance, or DeFi, represents a new approach in the financial industry. Blockchain technology allows DeFi to eliminate the need for traditional intermediaries such as banks, allowing users to access financial services directly through decentralized platforms.

    Key Features of DeFi:

    - **Permissionless Access:** Anyone with an internet connection and a compatible wallet can access DeFi services without the need for identity verification or credit checks.

    - **Transparency:** Transactions and smart contracts are recorded on a public blockchain, ensuring transparency and auditability.

    - **Interoperability:** DeFi platforms often integrate with each other, creating a seamless ecosystem of financial services.

    Common DeFi Applications (Figure 3-2):

    1. **Decentralized Exchanges (DEXs):** Platforms like Uniswap and PancakeSwap enable users to trade cryptocurrencies directly from their wallets without intermediaries.

2. **Lending and Borrowing:** Platforms like Aave and Compound allow users to lend their assets and earn interest or borrow against their holdings. Smart contracts automate the process, ensuring trustless interactions.

3. **Stablecoins:** DeFi platforms often utilize stablecoins like DAI or USDC for price stability, enabling users to avoid cryptocurrency volatility while interacting with decentralized systems.

Advantages of DeFi:

- **Lower Costs:** By removing intermediaries, DeFi reduces transaction fees and overhead costs.

- **Global Accessibility:** DeFi services are accessible to anyone, including the unbanked and underbanked populations, promoting financial inclusion.

- **Innovation:** DeFi drives rapid innovation, introducing new financial instruments like yield farming, liquidity pools, and flash loans.

Challenges in DeFi:

- **Regulatory Uncertainty:** DeFi platforms frequently operate in a regulatory gray area, resulting in risks for both developers and users.

- **Smart Contract Vulnerabilities:** Bugs in smart contracts can lead to significant losses.

- **Scalability Issues:** High network congestion and gas fees on blockchains like Ethereum can limit accessibility.

CHAPTER 3   USE CASES

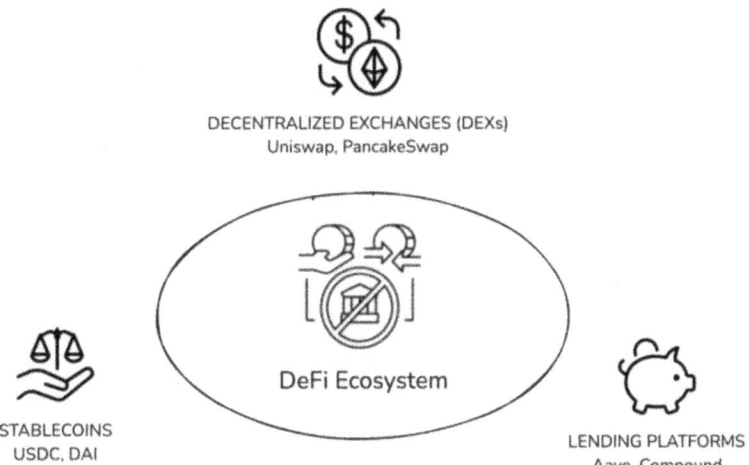

Figure 3-2. *The Decentralized Finance Ecosystem*

2. **Cross-Border Payments**

   Traditional cross-border payments are often slow and costly and rely on intermediaries such as banks or payment processors. Blockchain technology enables faster, more affordable, and more transparent solutions to these processes.

   How Blockchain Transforms Cross-Border Payments:

   - **Reduced Transaction Times:** Blockchain-based systems settle payments within minutes, compared to traditional systems that can take days.

   - **Lower Costs:** By removing intermediaries, blockchain significantly reduces transaction fees, especially for small payments.

   - **Transparency and Security:** All transactions are recorded on an inviolable ledger, which reduces fraud and improves trust among the parties.

   Examples of Blockchain in Cross-Border Payments:

   1. **Ripple (XRP):** Ripple's blockchain and XRP are used by it to facilitate fast and cost-effective cross-border transactions. It has collaborated with banks and financial institutions worldwide.

   2. **Stellar (XLM):** Stellar is designed for cross-border payments and transfers, providing a platform for issuing and transferring digital assets.

CHAPTER 3   USE CASES

3. **Bitcoin and Ethereum:** Both cryptocurrencies are commonly used for international transfers, allowing users to bypass traditional banking systems.

Real-World Impact:

- **Transfers:** Blockchain has made transfer services better, making it possible for migrant workers to send money to their families with lower fees and faster delivery.

- **International Trade:** Businesses use blockchain for cross-border trade payments, enabling quicker transactions and minimizing risks associated with intermediaries.

Challenges in Adoption (Figure 3-3):

- **Regulatory Barriers:** The implementation of blockchain-based payment systems can be complicated by the differences in regulations across countries.

- **Volatility:** Price fluctuations in cryptocurrencies used for cross-border payments can affect transaction value, though stablecoins help with this problem.

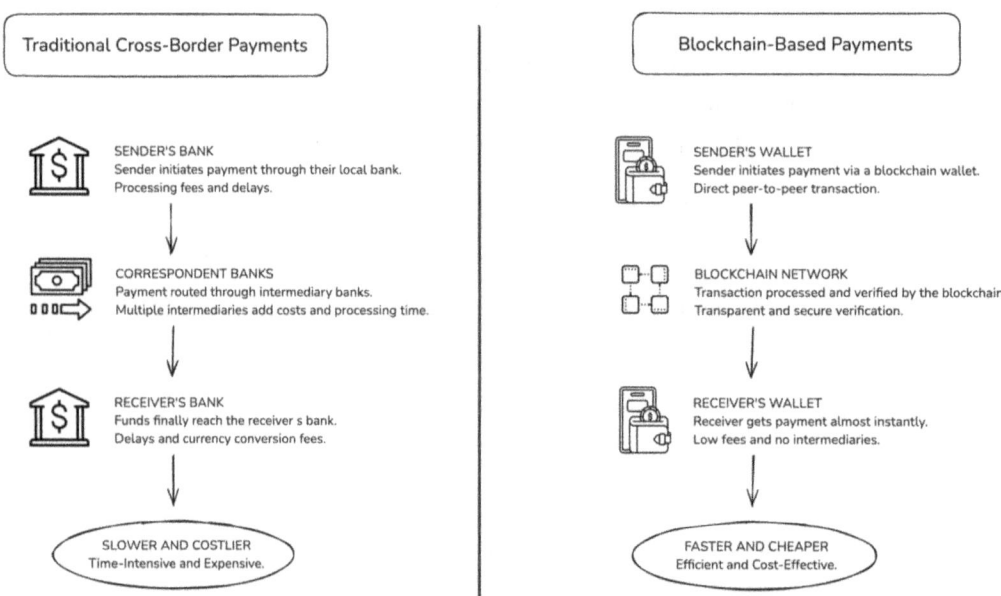

Figure 3-3. *Traditional vs. Blockchain-Based Cross-Border Payments*

3. **Peer-to-Peer Lending**

   Peer-to-peer (P2P) lending platforms that use blockchain technology connect borrowers directly with lenders, making it unnecessary for traditional financial institutions. Smart contracts guarantee trust and efficiency by automating the lending process. Figure 3-4 shows how blockchain facilitates trustless lending and borrowing.

   How Blockchain Enables P2P Lending:

   - **Smart Contracts:** These self-executing contracts enforce the terms of the credit, such as repayment schedules and asset management.

   - **Tokenization of Assets:** Blockchain allows users to tokenize assets, enabling them to borrow against these tokens as security.

   - **Global Access:** P2P lending platforms on blockchain provide global accessibility, allowing users to participate regardless of their location.

   Notable Blockchain P2P Lending Platforms:

   1. **Aave:** A decentralized lending platform that allows users to borrow and lend a wide range of cryptocurrencies.

   2. **MakerDAO:** MakerDAO enables users to borrow its stablecoin, DAI, by locking up Ethereum as a guarantee.

   3. **Celsius Network:** Celsius offers P2P-like lending services with competitive interest rates, but it is more centralized than typical DeFi platforms.

   Advantages of Blockchain-Based P2P Lending:

   - **Lower Interest Rates:** Without banks or intermediaries, lenders and borrowers can negotiate better terms.

   - **Transparency:** All parties are able to see loan terms, repayments, and interest rates on the blockchain.

   - **Automated Collateral Management:** Smart contracts can reduce risks for lenders by liquidating guarantees automatically if repayment conditions are not met.

CHAPTER 3 USE CASES

Challenges:

- **Market Volatility:** The guarantee used in P2P lending is often in cryptocurrencies, which can be highly volatile, increasing risks for borrowers and lenders.

- **Regulation:** Similar to DeFi, P2P lending platforms face regulatory uncertainty, particularly concerning consumer protection and anti-money laundering (AML) compliance.

- **Awareness and Trust:** Mainstream users may be unfamiliar with blockchain-based lending platforms, preventing extensive adoption.

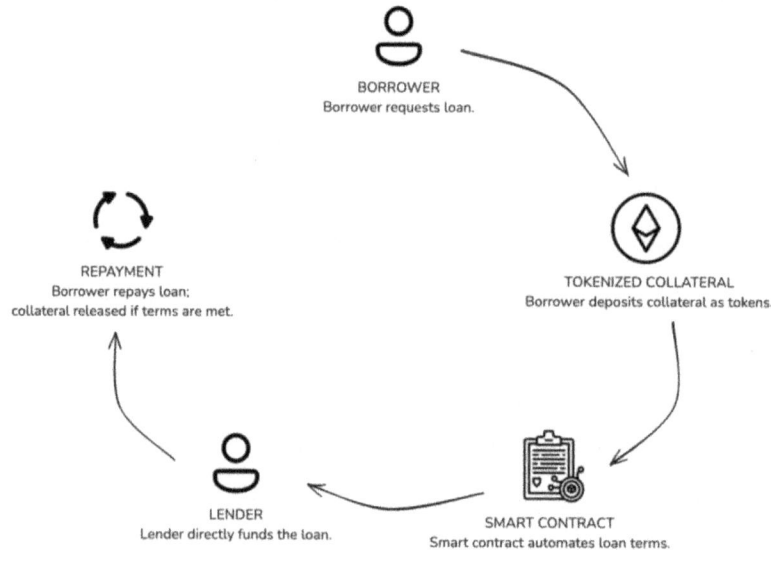

Figure 3-4. Peer-to-Peer Lending with Blockchain

Currency

Blockchain technology has redefined the concept of currency, transforming it from a physical and centralized asset to a digital and decentralized one. From the creation of cryptocurrencies to the development of stablecoins and central bank digital currencies

(CBDCs), blockchain is revolutionizing how value is created, stored, and transferred. In this section, we explore the key use cases of blockchain in currency, including their unique advantages, adoption trends, and potential challenges.

1. **Cryptocurrencies and Stablecoins**

   Cryptocurrencies: Cryptocurrencies are the first and most well-known application of blockchain technology. These are decentralized digital currencies that use cryptographic techniques to secure transactions, control the creation of new units, and verify asset transfers. Bitcoin, created in 2009, was the first cryptocurrency and remains the most well-known example.

   Features of Cryptocurrencies:

   - **Decentralization:** Cryptocurrencies operate without a central authority, relying on a distributed network of nodes to validate transactions.

   - **Transparency:** Transactions are recorded on a public ledger, making them transparent and secure against alterations.

   - **Borderless Transactions:** Cryptocurrencies enable fast, low-cost transactions across borders without intermediaries.

   Notable Cryptocurrencies:

   - **Bitcoin (BTC):** The first cryptocurrency, designed as a decentralized alternative to traditional money.

   - **Ethereum (ETH):** Known for its smart contract functionality, Ethereum has become the foundation for decentralized applications.

   - **Litecoin (LTC):** A peer-to-peer cryptocurrency designed for faster and cheaper transactions than Bitcoin.

   Stablecoins: Stablecoins are a class of cryptocurrencies designed to minimize price volatility by linking their value to a stable asset, such as fiat currency, raw materials, or a collection of assets. They combine the benefits of blockchain technology with the reliability of traditional financial tools. Table 3-1 compares key features of cryptocurrencies and stablecoins.

CHAPTER 3   USE CASES

Table 3-1. Comparison of Cryptocurrencies vs. Stablecoins

Feature	Cryptocurrencies	Stablecoins
Definition	Decentralized digital currencies that operate independently of central authorities.	Cryptocurrencies designed to maintain a stable value by being pegged to an asset like fiat currency or commodities.
Purpose	Designed for peer-to-peer transactions, store of value, and decentralized finance (DeFi) use cases.	Primarily used for price stability in transactions and remittances and as a medium of exchange.
Examples	Bitcoin (BTC), Ethereum (ETH), Litecoin (LTC)	Tether (USDT), USD Coin (USDC), Paxos Gold (PAXG)
Volatility	High; prices fluctuate based on market demand and supply.	Low; value remains stable due to pegging to assets like USD or gold.
Backing	Not backed by any tangible asset.	Backed by fiat currency, commodities, or algorithms.
Key Technology	Blockchain, public-private key cryptography, and decentralized networks.	Blockchain, pegging mechanisms (fiat-backed, commodity-backed, or algorithmic).
Transparency	Transactions are recorded on a public blockchain, ensuring transparency.	Pegging and reserve management vary; some are transparent, others less so.
Adoption Use Cases	Decentralized finance (DeFi), digital payments, cross-border remittances, and investment.	Cross-border payments, stable transactions, and a bridge between crypto and fiat economies.
Challenges	Volatility, scalability, and regulatory uncertainty.	Regulatory challenges, transparency concerns in reserve backing, and algorithmic stability issues.

Types of Stablecoins (Figure 3-5):

1. **Fiat-Backed Stablecoins:** Linked to a fiat currency like USD or EUR. Examples include Tether (USDT) and USD Coin (USDC).

2. **Commodity-Backed Stablecoins:** Secured by tangible assets like gold or oil. Examples include Paxos Gold (PAXG).

CHAPTER 3   USE CASES

3. **Algorithmic Stablecoins:** Maintain their value through algorithmic adjustments of supply and demand. Examples include Terra (LUNA) before its collapse, leading to discussions on algorithmic stability risks.

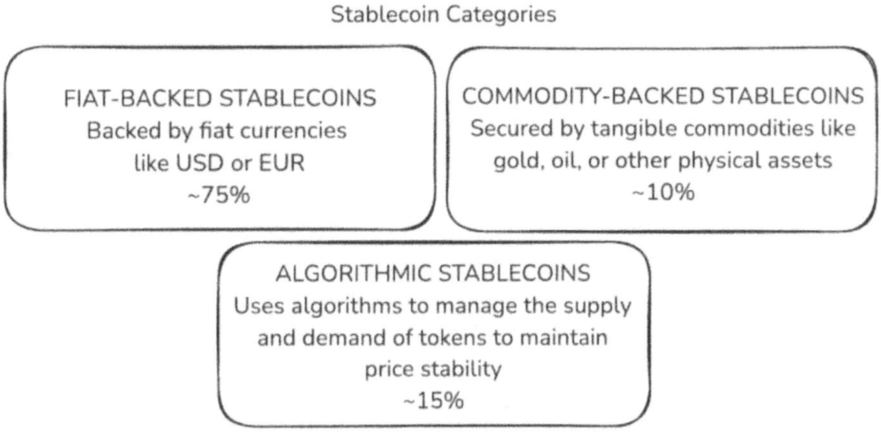

Stablecoin Categories

```
FIAT-BACKED STABLECOINS
Backed by fiat currencies
like USD or EUR
~75%
```

```
COMMODITY-BACKED STABLECOINS
Secured by tangible commodities like
gold, oil, or other physical assets
~10%
```

```
ALGORITHMIC STABLECOINS
Uses algorithms to manage the supply
and demand of tokens to maintain
price stability
~15%
```

Figure 3-5. Types of Stablecoins

Use Cases of Cryptocurrencies and Stablecoins:

- **Remittances:** Provide an affordable way to send money internationally, bypassing traditional banking systems.

- **Decentralized Finance (DeFi):** Used extensively in DeFi platforms for lending, borrowing, and providing liquidity.

- **E-Commerce:** Enable merchants to accept payments in digital currencies, expanding payment options for customers.

Challenges:

- **Regulatory Uncertainty:** Governments and financial institutions remain divided on how to regulate cryptocurrencies.

- **Volatility:** Cryptocurrencies like Bitcoin are highly volatile, making them less suitable for everyday transactions compared to stablecoins.

- **Adoption Barriers:** While adoption is growing, mainstream acceptance of cryptocurrencies is still limited by technological and educational gaps.

2. **Central Bank Digital Currencies (CBDCs)**

   Central Bank Digital Currencies (CBDCs) represent a government-supported digital currency that operates on blockchain or similar distributed ledger technology. Unlike cryptocurrencies, CBDCs are centralized and issued by a nation's central bank, combining the benefits of digital currency with the stability and control of traditional monetary systems.

   Key Features of CBDCs:

   - **Centralized Control:** Managed and regulated by a central authority (e.g., the central bank).

   - **Digital Representation of Fiat:** Functions as a digital equivalent of a country's fiat currency.

   - **Programmable Money:** Can be programmed with specific rules, such as expiration dates or spending limits, enabling greater control over monetary policies.

   Benefits of CBDCs:

   1. **Financial Inclusion:** Provide access to digital financial services for unbanked populations, especially in developing countries.

   2. **Efficiency:** Simplify and speed up domestic and international transactions by eliminating intermediaries.

   3. **Transparency and Security:** Reduce fraud and corruption through immutable transaction records.

   4. **Monetary Policy Control:** Allow central banks to take immediate actions, like providing financial aid or adjusting interest rates, to manage the economy.

   Examples of CBDCs (Figure 3-6):

   - **Digital Yuan (China):** One of the most advanced CBDC projects, aimed at modernizing China's payment system and increasing its global financial influence.

   - **Sand Dollar (Bahamas):** Launched as the first nationwide CBDC, enabling secure and inclusive digital transactions.

CHAPTER 3   USE CASES

- **Digital Euro (EU) and Digital Dollar (USA):** Projects under exploration to enhance cross-border payments and maintain competitiveness in the global digital economy.

Challenges of CBDCs:

- **Privacy Concerns:** CBDCs could give central authorities greater control over citizens' financial data, raising privacy concerns.

- **Implementation Costs:** Developing and integrating CBDC systems with existing financial infrastructure requires significant investment.

- **Competition with Cryptocurrencies:** CBDCs compete with decentralized cryptocurrencies and may struggle to attract users familiar with traditional crypto.

Figure 3-6. CBDC Implementation Initiatives

3. **Use Cases and Adoption**

    The adoption of blockchain-based currencies varies across regions and use cases, driven by specific economic needs and technological advancements.

115

CHAPTER 3   USE CASES

Key Use Cases of Blockchain Currencies:

- **Digital Payments:** Cryptocurrencies and stablecoins are increasingly used for online purchases, tipping, and peer-to-peer payments.

- **Tokenized Economies:** Blockchain currencies are often used to power tokenized ecosystems, such as in-game economies or loyalty programs.

- **Cross-Border Trade:** Businesses use stablecoins and cryptocurrencies for international trade settlements, bypassing delays and costs associated with traditional banking systems.

Adoption Trends:

1. **Developing Economies:** Cryptocurrencies like Bitcoin and stablecoins are gaining traction in regions with unstable fiat currencies or limited banking infrastructure, such as Venezuela and Nigeria.

2. **Institutional Interest:** Financial institutions and corporations, such as PayPal and Tesla, are increasingly integrating cryptocurrencies into their services and balance sheets.

3. **Government Initiatives:** CBDCs are being explored or piloted by over 100 central banks worldwide, with China's Digital Yuan leading the way.

Challenges to Universal Adoption (Table 3-2):

- **Regulatory Uncertainty:** The lack of a global consensus on cryptocurrency and CBDC regulation creates barriers for international adoption.

- **Scalability:** Blockchains like Bitcoin and Ethereum face scalability challenges, limiting their capacity to handle large transaction volumes efficiently.

- **Technological Accessibility:** Ensuring that blockchain currencies are user-friendly and accessible to non-technical users remains a significant challenge.

Table 3-2. *Timeline of Blockchain Currency Adoption and Milestones*

Year	Milestone	Description	Numbers/Stats
2009	Bitcoin Creation	Bitcoin, the first cryptocurrency, was created by Satoshi Nakamoto as a decentralized digital currency.	Initial supply: 50 BTC per block mined.
2015	Ethereum Launch	Ethereum introduced smart contracts, enabling decentralized applications (DApps) and blockchain innovation.	The Initial Coin Offering (ICO) raised over $18 million; ~72 million ETH were initially created.
2018	Stablecoin Adoption	Tether (USDT) and USD Coin (USDC) gained popularity as stable alternatives to volatile cryptocurrencies.	Tether's market cap surpassed $2 billion.
2020	PayPal's Cryptocurrency Integration	PayPal enabled users to buy, hold, and sell cryptocurrencies, including Bitcoin, Ethereum, Litecoin, and Bitcoin Cash.	Over 360 million PayPal users gained access to cryptocurrencies.
2021	Tesla's Acceptance of Bitcoin	Tesla announced it would accept Bitcoin for payments, significantly boosting cryptocurrency visibility.	Tesla purchased $1.5 billion worth of Bitcoin; the Bitcoin price surged over $60,000.
2021	China's Digital Yuan Pilots	China expanded trials of its CBDC, the Digital Yuan, marking a major step in government-backed digital currencies.	Over 261 million digital yuan wallets were created by 2021.
2022	Institutional Investment Surge	Major firms like MicroStrategy, Square, and others added cryptocurrencies to their balance sheets.	MicroStrategy alone held over 120,000 BTC (~$6 billion at the time).
2023	Central Bank Digital Currency (CBDC) Growth	Over 100 central banks began exploring or piloting CBDCs, with projects like the Sand Dollar (Bahamas) and Digital Euro.	114 countries engaged in CBDC research; 11 launched CBDCs by 2023.

(continued)

Table 3-2. (*continued*)

Year	Milestone	Description	Numbers/Stats
2024	Increased Adoption in Developing Economies	Cryptocurrencies like Bitcoin and stablecoins gained traction in countries with unstable fiat currencies or limited banking infrastructure (e.g., Nigeria, Venezuela).	Nigeria's adoption rate reached 45%; remittance costs were reduced by 50% in many regions using stablecoins.

Property Records

Blockchain technology has the potential to revolutionize property record management by providing a secure, transparent, and unchangeable method for documenting ownership and transactions. By eliminating inefficiencies, reducing fraud, and enhancing accessibility, blockchain transforms how property records are managed, verified, and transferred. In this section, we explore the use cases of blockchain in property records, including digital land registries, property ownership verification, and real-world implementations.

1. **Digital Land Registries**

    Traditional land registries often face challenges such as inefficiency, corruption, and a lack of transparency. Blockchain-based digital land registries solve these issues by offering a permanent and decentralized record of property ownership and transactions. Figure 3-7 outlines how land registry processes are automated on blockchain.

    Key Features of Blockchain-Based Land Registries:

    - **Immutability:** Once property records are added to the blockchain, they cannot be altered or deleted, ensuring the integrity of ownership data.

    - **Transparency:** All transactions and changes to property records are visible on the blockchain, creating trust among stakeholders.

    - **Accessibility:** Blockchain simplifies access to property records, reducing administrative delays and improving efficiency.

How It Works:

1. Property details, including ownership history, boundaries, and transaction records, are tokenized and stored on the blockchain.

2. Smart contracts automate processes like title transfers, ensuring compliance with legal and regulatory requirements.

3. Participants, including government agencies, buyers, sellers, and financial institutions, access and update records on the blockchain.

Benefits:

- **Reduced Fraud:** Blockchain eliminates the risk of fraudulent transactions by providing a single, verifiable source of truth for property ownership.

- **Efficiency:** Converting property records to digital formats eliminates paperwork and speeds up processes such as title searches and transfers.

- **Cost Savings:** By eliminating intermediaries and reducing administrative overhead, blockchain significantly lowers costs for buyers, sellers, and governments.

Challenges:

- **Integration with Legacy Systems:** Many land registries rely on outdated systems that are difficult to integrate with blockchain.

- **Regulatory Uncertainty:** Implementing blockchain-based land registries requires alignment with existing legal and regulatory frameworks.

- **Access to Technology:** Ensuring that rural and underserved populations can access blockchain-based systems is a critical hurdle.

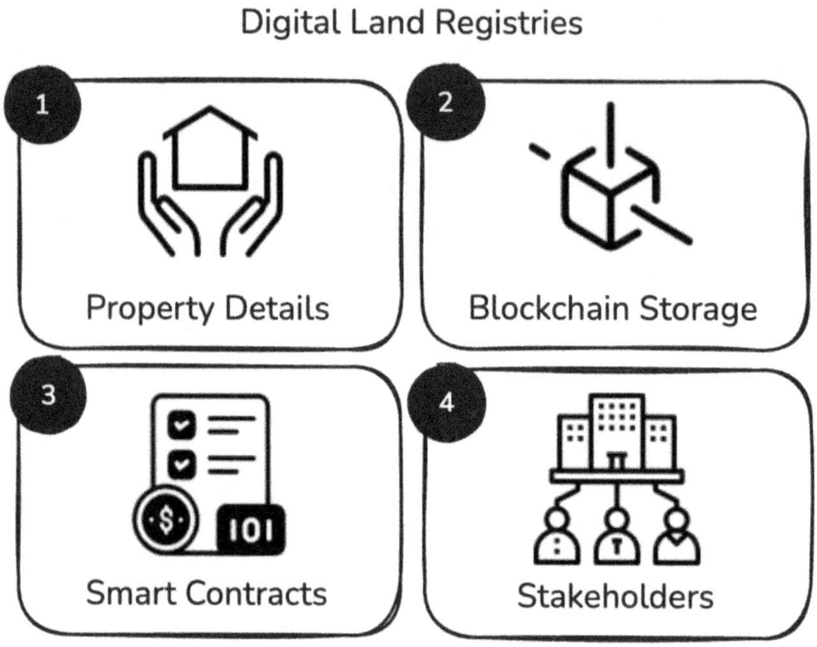

CHAPTER 3   USE CASES

Digital Land Registries

1. Property Details
2. Blockchain Storage
3. Smart Contracts
4. Stakeholders

Figure 3-7. Blockchain-Based Land Registry Architecture

2. **Property Ownership Verification**

    Verifying property ownership is often a complex and time-consuming process, especially in regions with poor record-keeping practices. Blockchain simplifies and secures ownership verification by creating a decentralized and tamper-proof record of ownership. Figure 3-8 depicts the digitization of property titles via blockchain.

    How Blockchain Allows Ownership Verification:

    - **Tokenization:** Property titles are digitized and represented as tokens on the blockchain. These tokens contain metadata about the property, including ownership history, location, and legal documentation.

    - **Smart Contracts:** Smart contracts automate verification processes, ensuring that all required documents and approvals are in place before ownership can be transferred.

CHAPTER 3 USE CASES

- **Immutable Records:** Blockchain ensures that ownership history is accurate and unalterable, reducing disputes and fraud.

Applications:

- **Title Insurance:** Blockchain reduces the need for extensive title searches and insurance by providing a clear and verified record of ownership.

- **Mortgages and Loans:** Lenders can quickly verify ownership and property details, speeding up the approval process for mortgages and loans.

- **Disaster Recovery:** In the event of natural disasters or conflict, blockchain ensures that property ownership records remain secure and accessible.

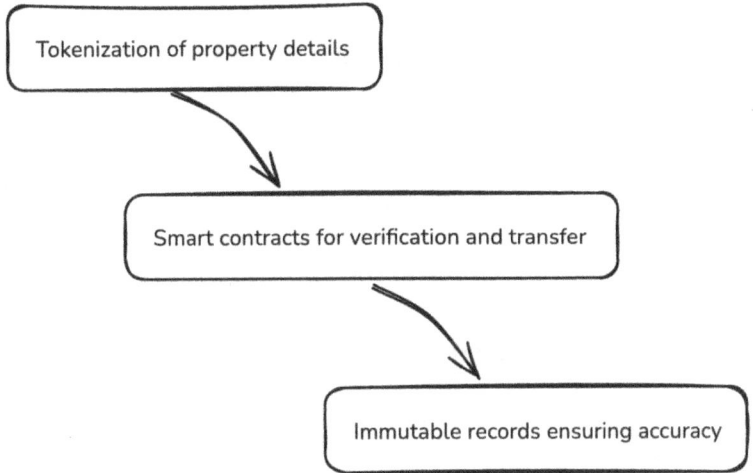

Figure 3-8. Property Ownership Verification with Blockchain

3. **Case Studies and Implementations**

    Several governments and organizations around the world have begun adopting blockchain technology to manage property records and streamline land transactions. These real-world implementations showcase the transformative potential of blockchain in the property sector.

CHAPTER 3   USE CASES

1. **Georgia's National Agency of Public Registry (NAPR):**

    - Georgia has implemented a blockchain-based land registry system in partnership with Bitfury, a blockchain technology company.

    - The system records property transactions on the blockchain, providing an immutable and transparent ledger of ownership.

    - Since its launch, the platform has processed thousands of transactions, reducing fraud and improving trust in the property market.

2. **India's Land Registry Projects:**

    - Several states in India, including Andhra Pradesh and Telangana, have partnered with blockchain firms to digitize and secure land records.

    - These initiatives aim to address issues like corruption, land disputes, and lack of transparency in the country's traditional land registry systems.

    - By using blockchain, the states aim to create a single source of truth for property ownership, accessible to both citizens and government agencies.

3. **Dubai Land Department (DLD):**

    - Dubai has integrated blockchain technology into its land registry system as part of its broader Smart Dubai initiative.

    - The DLD's blockchain platform allows users to conduct property transactions online, including title transfers, payment processing, and contract management.

    - The platform enhances transparency, reduces paperwork, and supports Dubai's goal of becoming a global leader in blockchain adoption.

4. **Honduras Land Title Pilot Project:**

    - Honduras has partnered with Factom, a blockchain technology firm, to create a blockchain-based land registry.

CHAPTER 3   USE CASES

- The project aims to address corruption and land disputes by providing a secure and transparent record of land ownership.
- Although the project faced challenges, it highlights the potential for blockchain to improve land governance in developing countries.

5. **Sweden's Lantmäteriet:**

- Sweden's land registry authority, Lantmäteriet, has been testing a blockchain-based platform for property transactions.
- The system allows buyers, sellers, banks, and government agencies to access and update property records in real time, reducing transaction times from months to weeks.

Figure 3-9 illustrates several real-world implementations of blockchain-based property registries across different countries, highlighting how governments are leveraging distributed ledger technology to enhance transparency, reduce fraud, and improve the efficiency of land management systems (Bitfury, 2017; Factom, 2016; Smart Dubai, 2019; Lantmäteriet, 2018).

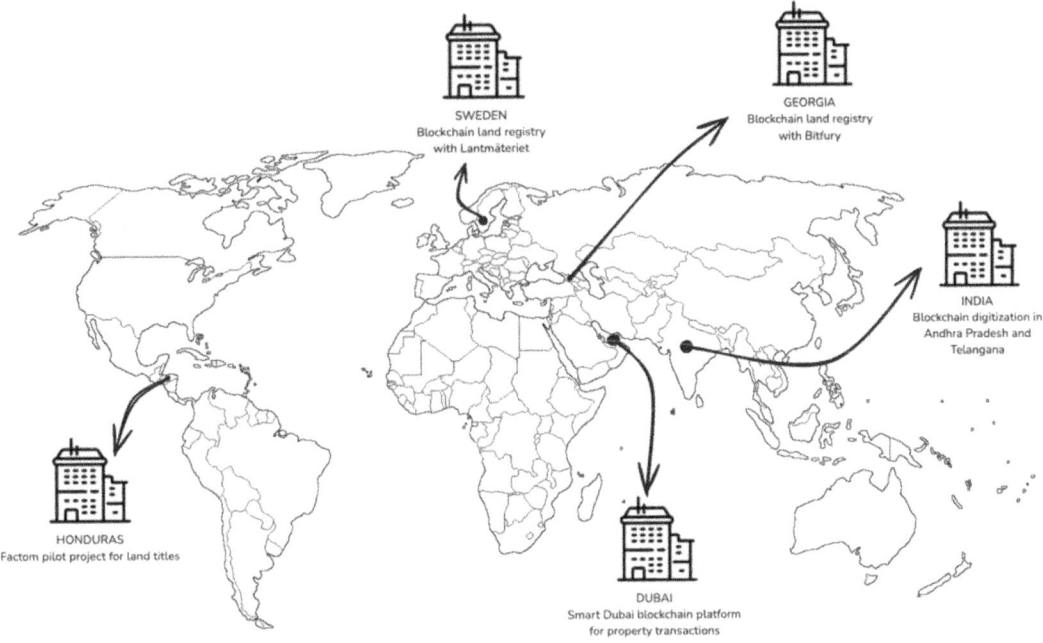

Figure 3-9. Blockchain Property Use Cases Worldwide

123

CHAPTER 3   USE CASES

Smart Contracts

Smart contracts are one of the most transformative applications of blockchain technology, enabling automated, secure, and decentralized agreements between parties. By embedding the terms of an agreement into self-executing code, smart contracts eliminate the need for intermediaries, reduce costs, and increase trust. This section covers the definition and workings of smart contracts, their applications in different industries, and the legal and regulatory aspects associated with them.

1. **Definition and Functionality**

   A smart contract is a self-executing program that runs on a blockchain. The contract's terms and conditions are written directly into its code, ensuring that they are automatically enforced without the need for manual intervention.

   Key Features of Smart Contracts:

   - **Automation:** Smart contracts automatically execute actions when predefined conditions are met.

   - **Decentralization:** They operate on a blockchain, removing the need for a central authority or intermediary.

   - **Immutability:** Once deployed on the blockchain, smart contracts cannot be altered, ensuring trust and security.

   - **Transparency:** The code and execution of smart contracts are visible to all participants in the blockchain network.

   How They Work (Figure 3-10):

   1. **Programming:** Smart contracts are typically written in blockchain-specific programming languages, such as Solidity for Ethereum.

   2. **Deployment:** The contract is deployed on a blockchain, where it becomes an immutable and accessible record.

   3. **Execution:** When triggered by predefined conditions (e.g., receiving payment, meeting a deadline), the contract automatically performs the specified actions, such as transferring assets or sending notifications.

CHAPTER 3 USE CASES

4. **Verification:** The blockchain network validates the contract's execution, ensuring that it operates as intended.

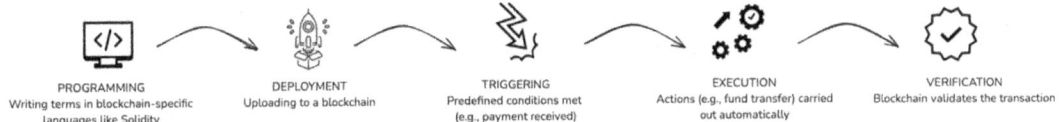

Figure 3-10. Lifecycle of a Smart Contract

2. **Use Cases in Various Industries**

    Smart contracts have a wide range of applications across industries, where they automate processes, reduce costs, and enhance security. Figure 3-11 shows how different industries benefit from smart contracts.

    1. **Finance:**

        - **Decentralized Finance (DeFi):** Smart contracts power DeFi platforms, enabling services like lending, borrowing, and yield farming without intermediaries.

        - **Tokenized Assets:** Smart contracts facilitate the creation and management of tokenized assets, such as stocks, bonds, and real estate, on blockchain platforms.

        - **Escrow Services:** By holding funds in escrow until conditions are met, smart contracts guarantee trust between parties in transactions.

    2. **Real Estate:**

        - **Property Transactions:** Smart contracts automate processes like title transfers and payments, reducing delays and costs.

        - **Leasing and Rentals:** Contracts can automate rental agreements, ensuring on-time payments and enforcing terms without manual intervention.

CHAPTER 3   USE CASES

3. **Supply Chain Management:**
    - **Traceability:** Smart contracts record and verify the movement of goods at every stage of the supply chain, ensuring transparency and authenticity.
    - **Payments:** Payments can be triggered automatically upon the delivery of goods, reducing delays and disputes.

4. **Insurance:**
    - **Claims Processing:** Smart contracts streamline claims processing by automatically verifying conditions and releasing payments to policyholders.
    - **Parametric Insurance:** Contracts automatically execute payouts based on predefined triggers, such as weather data or flight delays.

5. **Healthcare:**
    - **Data Sharing:** Smart contracts facilitate secure sharing of patient data among healthcare providers while ensuring compliance with privacy regulations.
    - **Clinical Trials:** Contracts automate the management of clinical trial data, ensuring transparency and accuracy.

6. **Gaming and NFTs:**
    - **In-Game Economies:** Smart contracts manage in-game assets and currencies, enabling secure and transparent transactions.
    - **NFT Marketplaces:** They power the minting, buying, and selling of non-fungible tokens (NFTs), automating royalty payments and ownership transfers.

CHAPTER 3   USE CASES

Figure 3-11. *Applications of Smart Contracts by Sector*

3. **Legal and Regulatory Considerations**

   While smart contracts offer significant advantages, they also raise legal and regulatory challenges that must be addressed for universal adoption. Figure 3-12 highlights the legal complexities surrounding smart contract use.

   1. **Validity:**

      - Legal systems must determine whether smart contracts are legally binding agreements, particularly when disputes arise.

      - Jurisdictional issues can complicate enforcement, especially in cross-border transactions.

   2. **Compliance:**

      - Smart contracts must comply with existing laws and regulations, such as anti-money laundering (AML) and data protection laws.

      - Developers and users must ensure that the contract's terms align with applicable legal frameworks.

127

3. **Coding Errors:**

    - Smart contracts are immutable once deployed, meaning that errors in the code cannot be corrected. This has led to significant financial losses in cases where vulnerabilities were taken advantage of.

    - Rigorous auditing and testing are essential to reduce the risk of errors.

4. **Liability:**

    - Determining liability in the event of a malfunction or exploit is a complex issue. Questions arise regarding whether the developer, user, or platform is responsible for damages.

5. **Ethical Concerns:**

    - The automation of decisions in smart contracts raises ethical concerns, particularly in scenarios where unexpected circumstances could negatively impact one party.

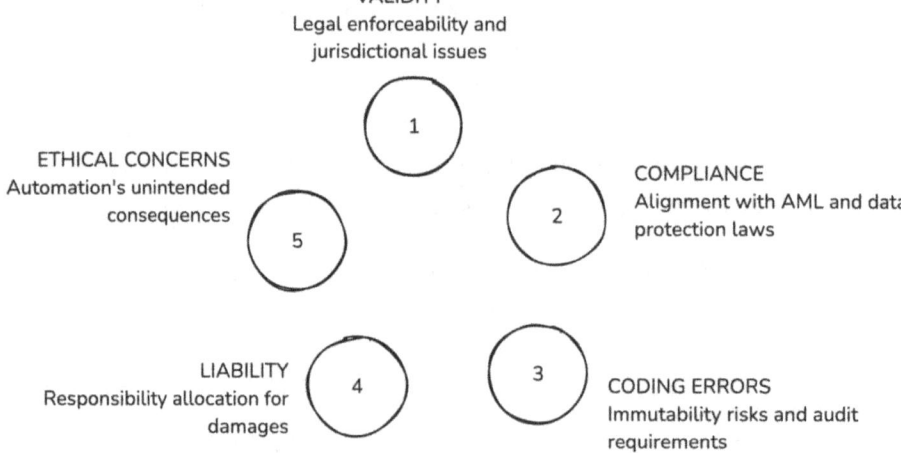

Figure 3-12. Legal and Regulatory Challenges for Smart Contracts

CHAPTER 3 USE CASES

4. **Case Studies and Real-World Examples (Figure 3-13)**

   1. **Ethereum:**

      - Ethereum is the leading blockchain for smart contracts, powering thousands of decentralized applications (DApps) and projects.

      - Examples include Uniswap (a decentralized exchange), MakerDAO (a lending platform), and OpenSea (an NFT marketplace).

   2. **Insurance Platform: Nexus Mutual:**

      - Nexus Mutual uses smart contracts to offer decentralized insurance for blockchain-based projects. Policyholders can claim payouts automatically when predefined conditions are met.

   3. **Real Estate: Propy:**

      - Propy is a blockchain-based platform that enables real estate transactions using smart contracts. Buyers and sellers can complete transactions entirely online, with smart contracts automating title transfers and payments.

   4. **Gaming: Axie Infinity:**

      - Axie Infinity, a blockchain-based game, uses smart contracts to manage in-game assets and rewards. Players can own and trade NFTs representing game characters and items.

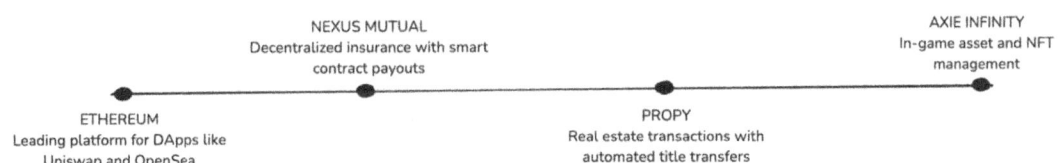

Figure 3-13. *Smart Contract Use Cases and Platforms*

CHAPTER 3   USE CASES

Supply Chains

Supply chain management is a complex and often non-transparent process involving multiple parties, from manufacturers and suppliers to retailers and consumers. Blockchain technology has emerged as a transformative solution, enhancing transparency, traceability, and efficiency across the supply chain. By providing a decentralized and immutable ledger, blockchain ensures that every transaction and movement of goods is recorded and verifiable in real-time. In this section, we explore how blockchain improves supply chain management, highlighting key applications, real-world examples, and challenges.

1. **Transparency and Traceability**

   One of the most significant contributions of blockchain to supply chains is its ability to provide end-to-end transparency and traceability. Traditional supply chains often lack visibility, making it difficult to track the origin, movement, and authenticity of goods. Blockchain addresses these challenges by offering a secure and shared record of all transactions and activities. Figure 3-14 outlines the role of blockchain in supply chain monitoring.

   Key Features:

   - **Immutable Records:** Every transaction, from raw material procurement to product delivery, is recorded on the blockchain and cannot be altered or deleted.

   - **Real-Time Tracking:** Blockchain enables real-time tracking of goods, allowing stakeholders to monitor their status and location at every stage of the supply chain.

   - **Provenance Verification:** Blockchain verifies the origin and journey of products, ensuring authenticity and compliance with regulations.

   Use Cases:

   1. **Food Safety:** Blockchain helps track the origin of food items, ensuring that they meet quality and safety standards. In the event of contamination or product withdrawals, blockchain allows rapid identification and isolation of affected products.

2. **Pharmaceuticals:** Counterfeit drugs are a major issue in the pharmaceutical industry. Blockchain tracks the journey of medicines from manufacturer to retailer to ensure their authenticity.

3. **Luxury Goods:** High-value items like diamonds and designer products can be authenticated using blockchain, preventing counterfeit goods from entering the market.

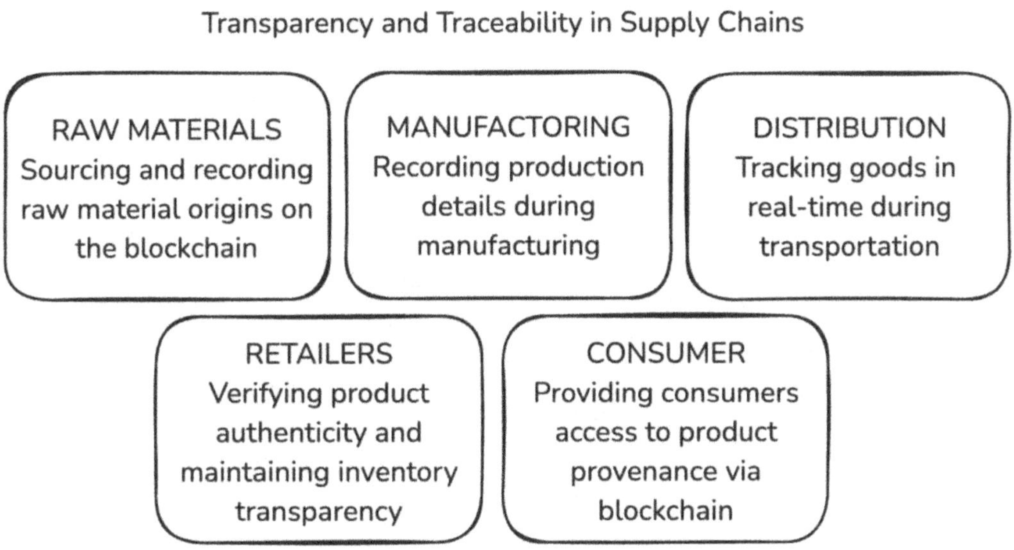

Transparency and Traceability in Supply Chains

- **RAW MATERIALS**: Sourcing and recording raw material origins on the blockchain
- **MANUFACTORING**: Recording production details during manufacturing
- **DISTRIBUTION**: Tracking goods in real-time during transportation
- **RETAILERS**: Verifying product authenticity and maintaining inventory transparency
- **CONSUMER**: Providing consumers access to product provenance via blockchain

Figure 3-14. Supply Chain Transparency via Blockchain

2. **Real-World Examples**

   Several companies and organizations are leveraging blockchain technology to transform their supply chains. These examples demonstrate the practical benefits of blockchain across various industries. Figure 3-15 shows blockchain platforms adopted by logistics and retail companies.

   1. **IBM Food Trust:**

      - IBM Food Trust is a blockchain-based platform that enhances transparency and efficiency in the food supply chain.
      - Partnering with major companies like Walmart and Nestlé, the platform tracks food items from farm to table, ensuring safety and reducing waste.

- Example: Walmart uses IBM Food Trust to trace the origin of mangoes, reducing the time required to track a shipment from days to seconds.

2. **Maersk and TradeLens:**

   - Maersk, a global shipping giant, partnered with IBM to develop TradeLens, a blockchain-based supply chain platform for the shipping industry.

   - TradeLens provides real-time tracking of shipping containers, reduces paperwork, and improves communication between stakeholders.

   - The platform has onboarded over 150 organizations, including ports, shipping lines, and customs authorities.

3. **Everledger:**

   - Everledger uses blockchain to track the provenance of diamonds, ensuring ethical sourcing and reducing the risk of fraud.

   - Each diamond is assigned a unique digital identity recorded on the blockchain, which includes details about its origin, quality, and ownership history.

4. **VeChain:**

   - VeChain is a blockchain platform designed for supply chain management and business processes.

   - It provides tools for tracking and verifying products in industries such as fashion, automotive, and food.

   - Example: VeChain has partnered with wine producers to ensure the authenticity and quality of premium wines.

CHAPTER 3   USE CASES

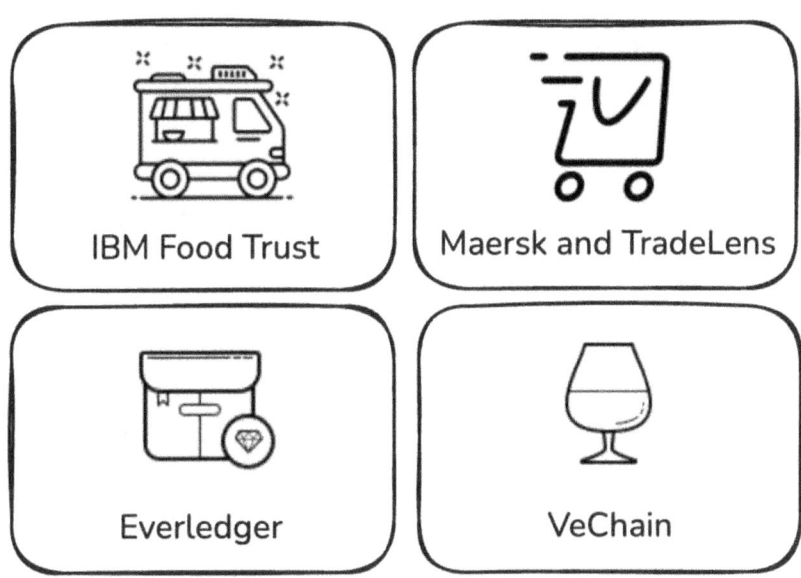

Figure 3-15. *Real-World Blockchain Supply Chain Examples*

3. **Benefits of Blockchain in Supply Chains**

    1. **Enhanced Trust:** Blockchain fosters trust among supply chain participants by providing a single source of truth that all parties can access and verify.

    2. **Improved Efficiency:** By automating processes such as documentation, payments, and compliance checks, blockchain reduces delays and operational costs.

    3. **Fraud Prevention:** Immutable records and traceability make it difficult for counterfeit goods or fraudulent transactions to enter the supply chain.

    4. **Sustainability:** Blockchain enables companies to track and verify sustainable practices, such as ethical sourcing and reduced carbon footprints, appealing to environmentally conscious consumers.

    5. **Customer Confidence:** Consumers can access blockchain-based information about a product's origin, quality, and journey, building trust and loyalty.

    As shown in Figure 3-16, blockchain improves trust and efficiency.

CHAPTER 3 USE CASES

Benefits of Blockchain in Supply Chains

Figure 3-16. Benefits of Blockchain for Supply Chain Management

4. **Challenges and Considerations**

    While blockchain offers significant advantages for supply chains, its implementation is not without challenges. Figure 3-17 summarizes common obstacles to blockchain adoption in logistics.

    1. **Scalability:** Supply chains involve millions of transactions, and many blockchains struggle to handle high volumes of data efficiently.

    2. **Integration with Legacy Systems:** Many organizations rely on legacy systems that are not compatible with blockchain, making integration complex and costly.

    3. **Data Privacy:** While transparency is a strength, some supply chain participants may hesitate to share sensitive business information on a public or semi-public blockchain.

CHAPTER 3 USE CASES

4. **Adoption Barriers:** Blockchain adoption requires buy-in from all stakeholders, which can be challenging in fragmented supply chains with diverse participants.

5. **Initial Costs:** Implementing blockchain systems requires significant investment in technology, infrastructure, and training.

Figure 3-17. Supply Chain Implementation Challenges

5. **Future Outlook**

   As blockchain technology matures, its adoption in supply chains is expected to grow. Innovations such as Layer 2 scaling solutions, hybrid blockchain models, and interoperability protocols will address many of the current challenges. Additionally, the integration of blockchain with emerging technologies like the Internet of Things (IoT) and artificial intelligence (AI) will further enhance supply chain management. Figure 3-18 presents future directions for blockchain in global supply management.

   Predictions:

   1. **IoT Integration:** IoT devices embedded in products and containers will provide real-time data, which can be recorded on the blockchain for enhanced tracking and monitoring.

   2. **Smart Contracts:** Automated contracts will handle payments, compliance, and penalties, streamlining operations and reducing disputes.

   3. **Global Standards:** Industry-wide adoption of blockchain standards will improve interoperability and drive universal adoption.

135

CHAPTER 3   USE CASES

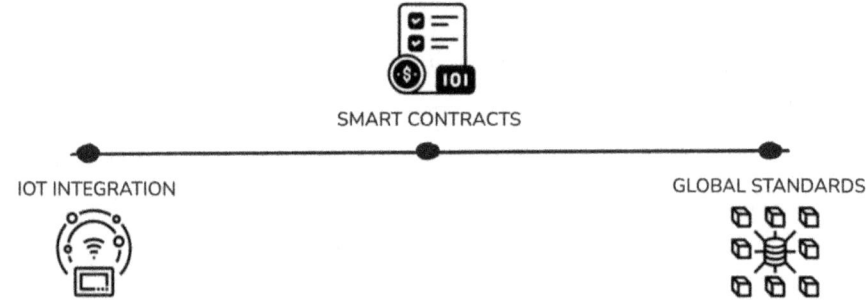

Figure 3-18. Future Trends in Blockchain-Enabled Supply Chains

Voting

Voting is a fundamental part of democratic societies, but traditional voting systems often face challenges such as fraud, lack of transparency, accessibility issues, and inefficiencies. Blockchain technology has emerged as a promising solution to these problems, offering secure, transparent, and immutable voting systems. Using blockchain, elections can become more inclusive, efficient, and trustworthy. In this section, we explore how blockchain enhances voting systems, the benefits it provides, challenges to its adoption and real-world examples.

1. **Blockchain-Based Voting Systems**

    Blockchain-based voting systems use the technology's decentralized and secure features to ensure the integrity of elections. Each vote is recorded as a transaction on the blockchain, creating an immutable and transparent ledger of the election process. Figure 3-19 explains the core flow of a blockchain-enabled election.

    How It Works:

    1. **Voter Authentication:** Voters authenticate their identity using secure methods, such as digital IDs or biometrics.

    2. **Vote Casting:** Votes are cast through an online interface or a blockchain-based application. Each vote is encrypted and recorded on the blockchain as a transaction.

CHAPTER 3   USE CASES

3. **Immutable Record:** Once recorded, votes cannot be altered or deleted, ensuring the integrity of the election.

4. **Real-Time Auditing:** Election results can be audited in real time by authorized participants, increasing transparency and reducing delays.

5. **Decentralized Storage:** The blockchain's distributed nature ensures that no single entity can manipulate the election results.

Key Features:

- **Transparency:** All participants can view the voting process, ensuring trust in the system.

- **Security:** Blockchain's cryptographic methods safeguard votes against alteration and unauthorized access.

- **Accessibility:** Blockchain permits remote voting, making elections more inclusive for individuals unable to vote in person.

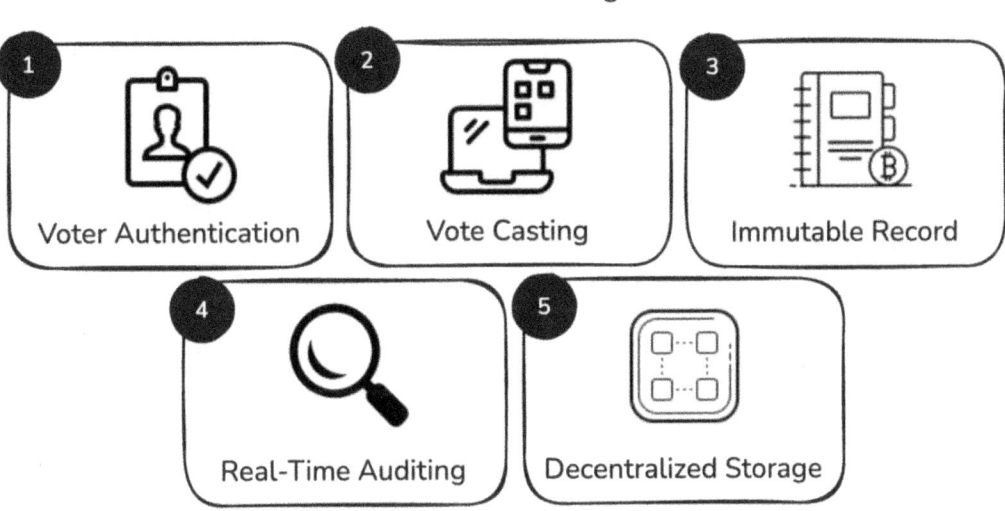

Figure 3-19. *How Blockchain Voting Systems Work*

2. **Benefits of Blockchain-Based Voting (Figure 3-20)**

   1. **Enhanced Security:**

      - Votes are encrypted and stored on an immutable ledger, preventing tampering or unauthorized changes.

- Blockchain eliminates the risk of single points of failure, making elections resistant to cyberattacks.

2. **Transparency and Trust:**
   - The voting process is fully transparent, allowing voters and observers to verify that their votes were counted accurately.
   - Results can be audited in real-time, reducing suspicion of fraud or manipulation.

3. **Accessibility:**
   - Blockchain enables remote and online voting, making elections more inclusive for individuals with disabilities, those living abroad, or those in remote areas.
   - By removing geographical barriers, blockchain increases voter turnout.

4. **Efficiency:**
   - Blockchain automates vote counting and verification, significantly reducing the time required to finalize results.
   - Eliminating intermediaries, such as election officials or manual vote counters, reduces operational costs.

CHAPTER 3   USE CASES

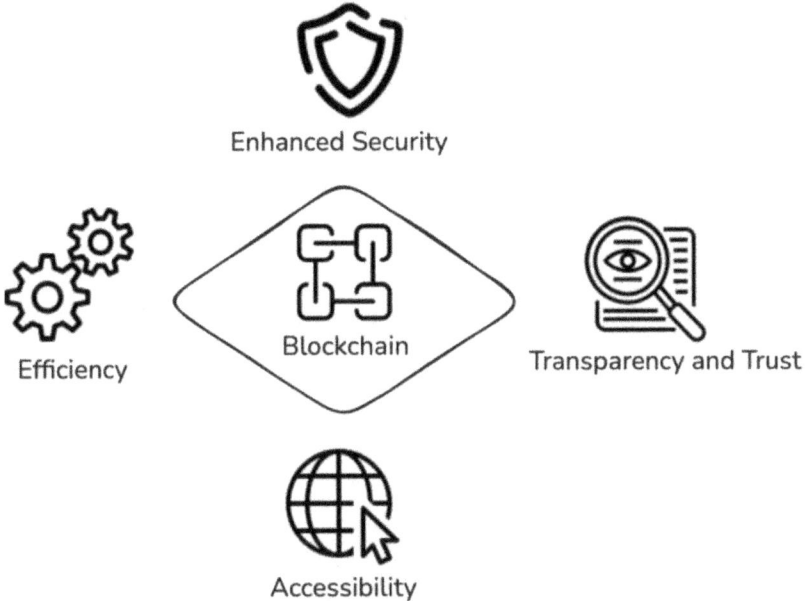

Figure 3-20. *Benefits of Blockchain Voting*

3. **Challenges of Blockchain-Based Voting**

   Despite its advantages, blockchain-based voting faces several challenges that must be addressed before widespread adoption. Figure 3-21 outlines limitations such as scalability and voter authentication.

   1. **Scalability:**

      - Handling millions of votes during national elections requires high-performance blockchains capable of processing large transaction volumes efficiently.

      - Current blockchain networks, such as Bitcoin and Ethereum, face limitations in scalability and transaction speed.

   2. **Voter Authentication:**

      - Ensuring secure and accessible voter authentication methods is critical to preventing fraud and unauthorized voting.

- Integrating digital ID systems with blockchain voting platforms can address this challenge but requires significant infrastructure development.

3. **Privacy Concerns:**
   - While blockchain offers transparency, ensuring voter anonymity is crucial to maintaining privacy in elections.
   - Implementing privacy-preserving technologies, such as zero-knowledge proofs, can balance transparency with confidentiality.

4. **Regulatory and Legal Barriers:**
   - Many countries lack clear regulations or legal frameworks for blockchain-based voting.
   - Aligning blockchain voting systems with existing election laws and standards is essential for adoption.

5. **Public Perception and Trust:**
   - Blockchain technology is still relatively new, and building public confidence in its reliability and security remains a challenge.
   - Educating voters and stakeholders about blockchain's benefits and functionality is critical to building confidence.

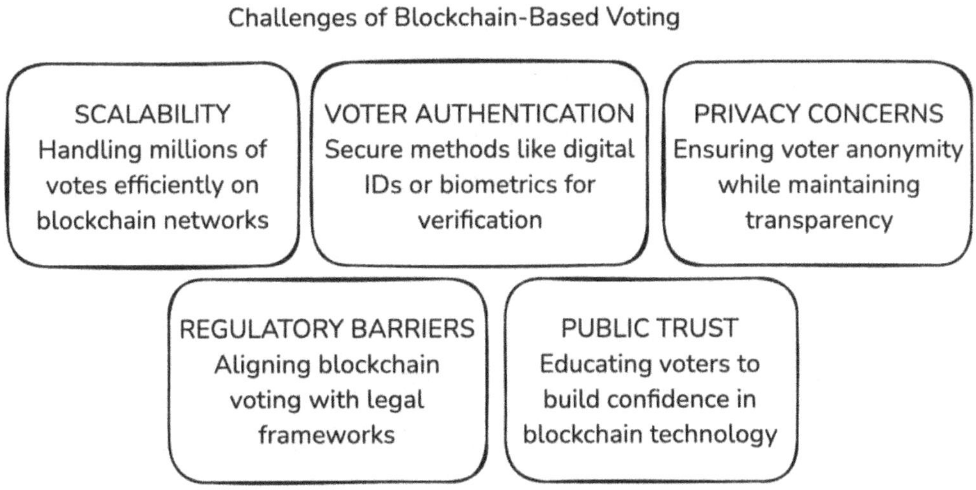

CHAPTER 3　USE CASES

Challenges of Blockchain-Based Voting

- **SCALABILITY** — Handling millions of votes efficiently on blockchain networks
- **VOTER AUTHENTICATION** — Secure methods like digital IDs or biometrics for verification
- **PRIVACY CONCERNS** — Ensuring voter anonymity while maintaining transparency
- **REGULATORY BARRIERS** — Aligning blockchain voting with legal frameworks
- **PUBLIC TRUST** — Educating voters to build confidence in blockchain technology

Figure 3-21. Challenges in Blockchain-Based Voting

4. **Real-World Examples**

   Several organizations and governments have experimented with blockchain-based voting systems, demonstrating the technology's potential to improve election processes. Figure 3-22 presents pilot programs using blockchain in voting worldwide.

   1. **Estonia:**

      - Estonia, a pioneer in digital governance, has explored blockchain for its e-voting system.
      - The country uses digital IDs for secure voter authentication and blockchain to ensure the integrity of election data.

   2. **West Virginia (USA):**

      - During the 2018 midterm elections, West Virginia piloted a blockchain-based voting system for military personnel stationed overseas.
      - The system allowed secure remote voting through a mobile application, enhancing accessibility for eligible voters.

CHAPTER 3   USE CASES

3. **Switzerland:**

    - Switzerland has conducted multiple trials of blockchain-based voting systems at the municipal level.

    - These trials focused on improving transparency and reducing the costs associated with traditional voting systems.

4. **Sierra Leone:**

    - In 2018, Sierra Leone used a blockchain platform to verify election results, becoming one of the first countries to do so.

    - Blockchain helped ensure transparency and trust in the electoral process.

5. **Voatz:**

    - Voatz is a blockchain-based mobile voting platform used in several pilot programs in the USA, including in Utah and Colorado.

    - The platform combines blockchain with biometric authentication to provide a secure and user-friendly voting experience.

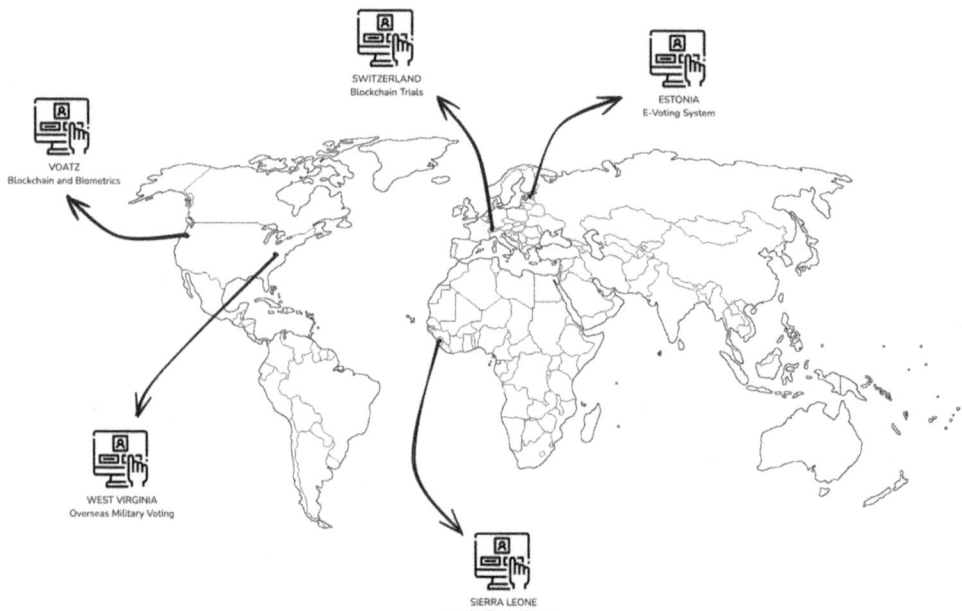

Figure 3-22. *Global Blockchain Voting Initiatives*

CHAPTER 3   USE CASES

5. **The Future of Blockchain Voting**

    The integration of blockchain with emerging technologies, such as artificial intelligence (AI) and biometrics, holds promise for addressing current challenges in blockchain-based voting. Future developments could include (Figure 3-23):

    1. **Layer 2 Solutions:** Using Layer 2 protocols to enhance blockchain scalability and reduce transaction costs for large-scale elections.

    2. **Zero-Knowledge Proofs:** Employing privacy-preserving technologies to ensure voter anonymity while maintaining transparency.

    3. **Global Standards:** Creating international guidelines and regulations for blockchain voting to guarantee compatibility and legal adherence.

As blockchain technology matures, its adoption in voting systems could transform how elections are conducted, making them more secure, transparent, and inclusive.

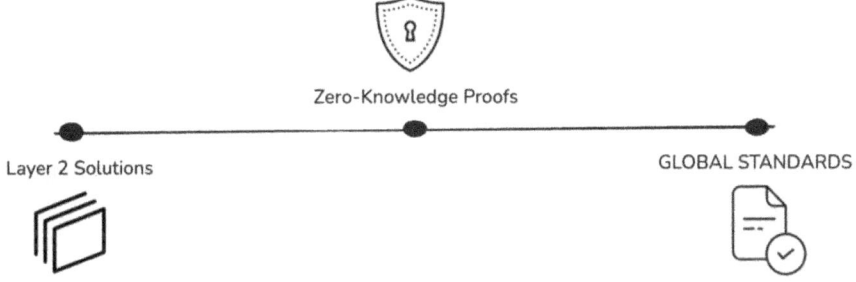

Figure 3-23. The Future of Voting with Blockchain

Conclusion

The use cases explored in this chapter illustrate how blockchain technology is no longer just a theoretical innovation; it is being actively applied across sectors to solve real-world problems. From enabling financial inclusion through DeFi to securing the integrity of elections and property records, blockchain's decentralized model provides tangible benefits like transparency, efficiency, and trust. At the same time, each use case also reveals the current limitations of the technology, including scalability, regulation, and technical barriers.

CHAPTER 3   USE CASES

As adoption grows and technical solutions evolve, such as Layer 2 scaling, interoperability protocols, and regulatory frameworks, blockchain is poised to become a critical infrastructure for digital transformation across industries.

Chapter Summary

Topic	Key takeaways
Finance	Blockchain enables decentralized financial services (DeFi), faster cross-border payments, and P2P lending without intermediaries.
Currency	Cryptocurrencies, stablecoins, and CBDCs redefine how money is created, transferred, and stabilized across global systems.
Property Records	Blockchain secures land ownership and property records, improving efficiency, reducing fraud, and enabling transparency.
Smart Contracts	Self-executing code automates agreements in sectors like insurance, real estate, and logistics, minimizing manual intervention.
Supply Chains	Blockchain increases traceability, ensures product authenticity, and enhances transparency from manufacturing to delivery.
Voting	Blockchain-based voting offers secure, transparent, and remote participation in elections while addressing trust and auditability.
Adoption Challenges	Regulatory uncertainty, scalability issues, and lack of user-friendly access continue to slow mainstream adoption.

CHAPTER 4

Pros and Cons of Blockchain

Introduction

This chapter explores the dual nature of blockchain technology, diving into both its strengths and its current limitations. As adoption grows, it's essential to evaluate the practical implications of decentralization, enhanced security, and transaction efficiency, as well as the operational challenges, such as scalability, energy consumption, and regulatory hurdles.

We will examine how blockchain performs in key areas like cost, speed, and transparency, supported by real-world use cases. The chapter also outlines the evolving regulatory landscape and how governments are responding to the disruptive nature of decentralized technologies.

By the end of this chapter, you will be able to:

- Understand the technical and organizational benefits of decentralization.
- Evaluate how blockchain improves transaction speed, cost-efficiency, and transparency.
- Identify the current technical and legal limitations of blockchain technology.
- Analyze case studies from various sectors applying blockchain in innovative ways.
- Explore the future directions in scalability, regulation, and sustainable blockchain development.

The Benefit of Decentralization

Blockchain technology's most defining feature is its decentralized nature. Unlike traditional centralized systems, where a single entity has control, blockchain operates on a distributed network.

This decentralization offers numerous advantages, addressing many limitations of centralized systems and fostering trust, security, and resilience. Figure 4-1 illustrates the contrast between different systems.

Figure 4-1. Decentralized vs. Centralized vs. Distributed Architecture

Reduced Single Points of Failure

Centralized systems have a critical vulnerability: a single point of failure. This vulnerability can be made use of by malicious actors, resulting in catastrophic failures due to system errors or leading to data loss in the event of a hardware or software malfunction. Distributing data and control across multiple nodes in a blockchain network prevents these risks.

For instance:

- **Data Integrity:** In centralized databases, if the central server is compromised, the entire system is at risk. With blockchain, data is replicated across all participating nodes, ensuring redundancy. Even if one node is compromised, the integrity of the overall system remains intact.

- **Resilience to Attacks:** A distributed network is inherently more resilient to Distributed Denial-of-Service (DDoS) attacks, as attackers must overwhelm a majority of nodes rather than a single server.

This decentralized architecture is both robust and secure for users who rely on the system for critical applications, such as financial transactions or healthcare data storage.

Enhanced Security and Resilience

Decentralization also enhances the security posture of blockchain networks. Security is built into the system via cryptographic mechanisms and consensus protocols, which are essential for guaranteeing the accuracy and reliability of data.

1. **Alteration Resistance:** Each block in a blockchain is cryptographically linked to the previous one. This ensures that altering any part of the data requires re-mining or re-validating all subsequent blocks, which is computationally impractical in most cases. If there is no consensus among the majority of participants, manipulation becomes impossible.

2. **Byzantine Fault Tolerance:** Blockchain networks are designed to operate effectively even in the presence of malicious actors or faulty nodes. Through consensus mechanisms such as Proof of Work (PoW) or Proof of Stake (PoS), the network can reach agreements on transactions, ensuring reliability and trustworthiness.

3. **Resilience Against Failures:** In centralized systems, operations can be severely impacted by a breakdown. For example, when a banking server experiences downtime, customers are unable to access funds or make transactions. Blockchain's decentralized nature distributes the load across multiple nodes, ensuring continuous operation even if some nodes fail. This resilience is highly valuable in industries where operating time and reliability are crucial.

4. **Censorship Resistance:** Decentralized systems are less sensitive to censorship. Since no single entity controls the blockchain, it becomes difficult for governments, organizations, or individuals to block or manipulate specific transactions. This attribute is especially significant in regions where financial or political systems impose stringent restrictions.

CHAPTER 4   PROS AND CONS OF BLOCKCHAIN

Real-World Examples of Decentralization Benefits

The benefits of decentralization are already evident in various sectors (Table 4-1):

- **Finance:** Cryptocurrencies like Bitcoin and Ethereum demonstrate how decentralization enables borderless transactions without reliance on banks or intermediaries. This fosters financial inclusion, particularly in regions with limited access to traditional banking services.

- **Supply Chain:** Blockchain-powered supply chains, such as IBM's Food Trust, use decentralization to track goods transparently and ensure authenticity. By distributing data across participants, they eliminate the risk of data manipulation by any single entity.

- **Healthcare:** Decentralized health data platforms empower patients by giving them control over their medical records. For example, MediBloc enables secure sharing of health information among patients, providers, and researchers without central control.

Table 4-1. *Sector-Specific Benefits of Blockchain Decentralization*

Sector	Use Case	Examples
Finance	Cross-border payments, DeFi	Ripple, Aave, Uniswap
Healthcare	Medical data sharing	MediBloc, Medicalchain
Supply Chain	Provenance, anti-fraud	IBM Food Trust, Provenance
Government	Voting, digital ID	Estonia e-Gov, uPort
Energy	Peer-to-peer energy trading	Energy Web Foundation

Challenges of Decentralization

While decentralization offers immense benefits, it is not without challenges. Understanding these limitations helps in designing more robust blockchain systems. Table 4-2 summarizes the main advantages and trade-offs of blockchain technology.

1. **Coordination and Governance:** In decentralized networks, decision-making can be slow and controversial. Unlike centralized systems where decisions are made unilaterally, blockchain networks require consensus, which can delay critical updates or changes.

2. **Resource Intensity:** Decentralization often requires significant computational and energy resources. For example, Proof of Work (PoW) consensus mechanisms consume vast amounts of electricity, raising concerns about sustainability.

3. **Scalability Issues:** Fully decentralized systems can face scalability challenges. As more nodes join the network, the time required for consensus and data synchronization increases, potentially slowing down transaction processing.

4. **User Responsibility:** Decentralization shifts responsibility from centralized authorities to users. While this empowers individuals, it also means they must manage their private keys securely. Loss of keys often results in irreversible loss of funds or access to data.

Table 4-2. Summary of Blockchain Pros and Cons

Pros	Cons
No single point of failure	Slower decision-making
Enhanced security	High energy/resource consumption
Resilience to attacks	Users must manage private keys securely
Censorship resistance	Scalability remains a technical challenge

Efficient Transactions

Blockchain's ability to enable efficient transactions is one of its most transformative aspects. Figure 4-2 visualizes how blockchain simplifies transactions by removing intermediaries.

CHAPTER 4   PROS AND CONS OF BLOCKCHAIN

By eliminating intermediaries, streamlining processes and leveraging distributed ledger technology, blockchain has revolutionized the way transactions are conducted across various industries. This efficiency is realized through improvements in speed, cost, reliability and accessibility.

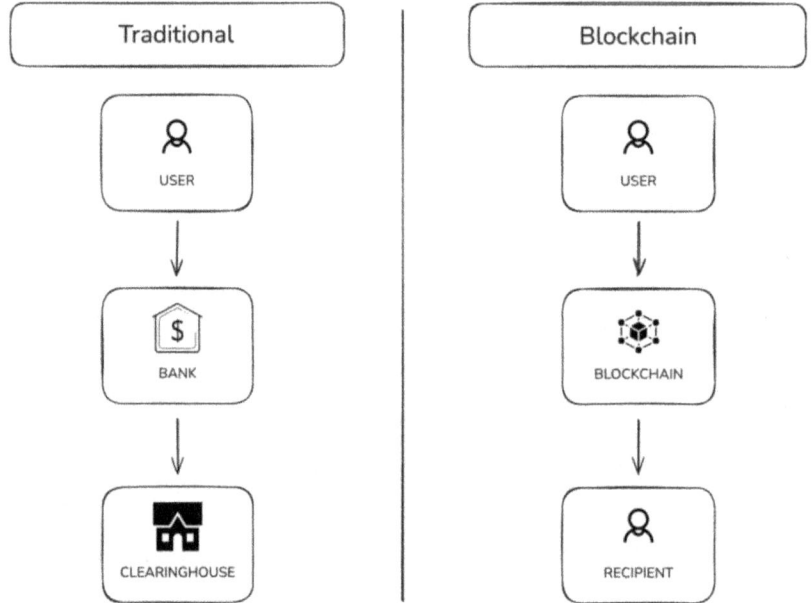

Figure 4-2. *Blockchain-Enabled Transaction Efficiency*

Speed and Cost Benefits

Traditional transaction systems, such as bank transfers or cross-border payments, often involve multiple intermediaries like clearinghouses and banks. These intermediaries not only increase the time required to complete transactions but also add significant costs. Blockchain simplifies this by enabling direct peer-to-peer transactions that are both faster and cheaper.

1. **Instant Settlements:** Blockchain transactions can be settled in near real-time. For example:
    - Bitcoin transactions typically take about 10 minutes to confirm, making it faster than traditional wire transfers, which can take several days.

- Newer blockchain protocols like Solana and Avalanche have reduced settlement times to seconds, providing an experience comparable to real-time payment systems like Visa.

2. **Lower Fees:** Blockchain can decrease transaction costs by eliminating the need for intermediaries. For instance:

    - Cross-border payments via platforms like Ripple cost a fraction of traditional remittance services such as Western Union or SWIFT.

    - Platforms supporting microtransactions, such as those for digital content, benefit from low-cost blockchain transfers, enabling pay-per-use models that were previously expensive due to high fees.

3. **Batch Processing and Automation:** Smart contracts enable automated batch processing of transactions. For example, an escrow service using smart contracts can process multiple transactions simultaneously without manual intervention, reducing costs and increasing speed.

Comparisons with Traditional Systems

Blockchain's efficiency shines when compared to conventional financial systems. Several key comparisons include:

- **Cross-Border Payments:** Traditional systems like SWIFT involve multiple intermediaries, leading to delays and high fees. Blockchain platforms such as RippleNet or Stellar enable instant, low-cost cross-border payments, making international transfers accessible to a broader audience.

- **Settlement Processes:** In traditional markets, clearing and settlement can take up to two business days. Blockchain eliminates the need for clearinghouses, providing same-day or instant settlement for securities and other financial instruments.

- **Microtransactions:** In conventional systems, high fees make small transactions impractical. Blockchain facilitates low-cost microtransactions, enabling innovative business models such as subscription-free digital services or pay-per-view content.

Reliability and Accessibility

Unlike traditional systems that operate during fixed hours and are subject to downtimes, blockchain networks run 24/7. This constant availability ensures that users can initiate and complete transactions at any time, without being constrained by business hours or geographic locations.

1. **Global Reach:** Blockchain is borderless by nature, allowing users in underbanked regions to access financial services without needing a traditional bank account. Projects like Celo and Stellar are targeting these markets with user-friendly blockchain solutions.

2. **Resilience to Failures:** Traditional centralized systems are vulnerable to single points of failure, such as server outages or cyberattacks. Blockchain's decentralized nature ensures that even if some nodes go offline, the network remains operational.

3. **Unbanked Populations:** Over 1.7 billion people worldwide lack access to traditional banking systems, according to the World Bank's Global Findex database. Blockchain projects such as Binance's Blockchain Charity Foundation (BCF) aim to bridge this gap by providing decentralized financial tools and transparent donation mechanisms to underserved communities, enabling access to basic services like savings, remittances, and microloans.

Examples of Efficient Transactions in Practice

- **Remittances:** Blockchain platforms like Ripple and Stellar have revolutionized remittances, enabling instant, low-cost transfers for migrant workers sending money to their families. This efficiency reduces dependence on traditional remittance services with high fees.

- **Supply Chain Payments:** Blockchain automates payments in supply chains using preset conditions.

- **Decentralized Finance (DeFi):** DeFi platforms use blockchain to offer financial services like lending, borrowing, and trading without intermediaries. Protocols like Aave and Uniswap process millions of transactions daily with minimal fees and near-instant settlements.

- **Gaming and Digital Goods:** Blockchain is transforming the gaming industry by enabling fast, cost-effective transactions for in-game assets and NFTs. Platforms like Enjin and Immutable X allow gamers to trade assets seamlessly without centralized platforms taking significant cuts.

Innovative Use Cases for Transaction Efficiency

1. **Micropayments in IoT:** IoT devices can use blockchain for automated micropayments. For instance, electric vehicles can pay for charging at stations based on real-time energy usage, with payments processed instantly on the blockchain.

2. **Healthcare Billing:** Blockchain streamlines healthcare billing by automating insurance claims and reducing administrative overhead. Smart contracts ensure that providers are paid instantly once services are verified.

3. **E-Government Services:** Governments are exploring blockchain for efficient service delivery. For example, Estonia uses blockchain for e-residency programs, enabling fast and secure processing of permits and licenses.

Challenges to Achieving Efficiency

Despite its promise, blockchain faces challenges in delivering consistent Traditional transaction systems:

1. **Scalability Constraints:** High transaction volumes can lead to congestion on popular blockchains like Ethereum, increasing fees and delays. Solutions like Layer 2 protocols (e.g., Polygon) and sharding are being developed to address these issues.

2. **Energy Consumption:** Proof-of-Work (PoW) systems, such as Bitcoin, consume vast amounts of energy. Transitioning to more sustainable consensus mechanisms like Proof-of-Stake (PoS) is critical for long-term efficiency.

3. **Complexity for Users:** The technical complexity of blockchain often prevents it from achieving its efficiency benefits. Simplifying user interfaces and educating the public are essential to increase adoption.

4. **Regulatory Barrier:** Legal uncertainty in many jurisdictions can slow blockchain adoption, particularly in industries like finance and healthcare that are heavily regulated.

Future Trends in Blockchain Efficiency

1. **Advancements in Consensus Protocols:** Emerging protocols like Proof of History (PoH) and DAG-based blockchains promise to enhance speed and scalability while reducing costs.

2. **Integration with AI:** Combining blockchain with artificial intelligence can optimize transaction routing and resource allocation, further improving efficiency.

3. **Cross-Chain Solutions:** Technologies like Polkadot and Cosmos are enabling interoperability between blockchains, ensuring efficient transactions across networks.

Transparency in Blockchain

Transparency is one of the core principles of blockchain technology. By design, blockchain's open and immutable ledger promotes trust among participants, ensures accountability, and lowers the risk of fraud. This transparency has applications across industries and is a key driver for blockchain's adoption. However, its implications extend far beyond operational benefits, transforming how systems operate and interact.

Public Ledger Benefits

1. **Immutable Recordkeeping:** Every transaction on a blockchain is permanently recorded and cannot be altered retroactively. This immutability ensures that the transaction history is accurate and provable, providing a reliable source of truth for all stakeholders involved.

2. **Auditability:** Blockchain's transparency allows stakeholders to audit transactions easily. Businesses can ensure compliance with regulatory standards, while individuals can verify their own transactions without relying on intermediaries. Audits that traditionally required weeks can now be performed in real time with blockchain.

3. **Trust Among Participants:** In traditional systems, trust is often placed in centralized authorities. Blockchain eliminates this dependency by providing a transparent platform where all participants can independently verify data. This feature reduces the risk of fraud and enhances collaboration between parties.

4. **Consensus Validation:** Transactions on a blockchain are validated through consensus mechanisms, ensuring that all entries on the ledger are verified by multiple participants. This adds an additional layer of transparency and accountability, reinforcing trust across the network.

5. **Enhanced Collaboration:** Transparency enables seamless collaboration across organizations. For example, in a multi-party supply chain, all participants can access the same set of verified data, reducing disputes and improving operational efficiency.

CHAPTER 4   PROS AND CONS OF BLOCKCHAIN

Applications in Various Sectors

Blockchain's transparency has transformative potential across multiple industries:

- **Supply Chain:** Blockchain enables end-to-end visibility of supply chains. Consumers can verify the authenticity of products, ensuring they meet ethical and quality standards. For example, Walmart uses blockchain to track food products, enhancing safety and reducing waste. Similarly, companies like Provenance allow users to trace the journey of goods from origin to consumer.

- **Healthcare:** Transparent medical records on blockchain ensure accurate diagnoses and reduce medical errors. Patients can share their records securely with providers, fostering collaboration and improving outcomes.

- **Government and Public Records:** Blockchain-based systems for public records, such as land registries or voting, increase trust in governmental processes. Citizens can access inviolable records, enhancing transparency and accountability. Estonia, for instance, has implemented blockchain to secure and streamline its e-governance services, including tax filings and voting systems.

- **Corporate Governance:** Companies are leveraging blockchain to enhance transparency in corporate governance. For example, shareholder voting and decision-making processes can be recorded on a blockchain to prevent tampering and improve stakeholder trust. Publicly available data can also help investors make informed decisions.

- **Education:** Academic institutions may employ blockchain technology to issue and authenticate credentials, including degrees and certifications. By enhancing transparency, this approach mitigates the risk of fraud and streamlines the hiring process, enabling employers to promptly access verified qualifications.

Innovative Use Cases

1. **Charitable Donations:** Blockchain ensures transparency in donations by allowing contributors to track how their funds are used. Platforms like Binance Charity provide real-time updates on fund allocation, increasing donor trust and minimizing administrative overhead.

2. **Sustainable Practices:** Transparency in blockchain helps organizations track and report their environmental impact. For instance, blockchain can verify carbon offsets, ensuring companies meet sustainability goals without greenwashing. Projects like Energy Web Token focus on creating transparent energy markets.

3. **Intellectual Property Rights:** Blockchain-based platforms enable artists and creators to record proof of ownership and track royalties. This ensures fair compensation, reduces disputes, and simplifies licensing processes. Examples include platforms like Ujo Music and Audius that focus on musicians and content creators.

4. **Transparency in Food Safety:** Blockchain platforms such as IBM Food Trust facilitate detailed traceability of food products, allowing stakeholders to identify sources of contamination throughout the supply chain.

Challenges of Blockchain Transparency

While transparency is a major advantage, it also presents certain challenges:

1. **Privacy Concerns:** While transparency benefits organizations, it may conflict with individual privacy needs. Public blockchains expose transaction details, potentially revealing sensitive user information. Privacy-preserving technologies like zero-knowledge proofs (ZKPs) and private blockchains aim to address this issue by allowing data validation without exposing the data itself.

2. **Complex Implementation:** Integrating blockchain's transparency with existing systems can be technically challenging. Organizations must align blockchain data with legacy systems while complying with regulatory requirements. This often requires significant investment in technology and expertise.

3. **Data Overload:** As blockchain networks grow, the increasing volume of transaction data can lead to storage and scalability challenges. Efficient data compression and off-chain solutions are essential for maintaining transparency without overwhelming the network.

4. **Misinterpretation of Data:** Transparent records alone are not sufficient; stakeholders must have the tools and expertise to interpret blockchain data correctly. Without this, transparency may lead to confusion or misuse, especially in complex systems.

5. **Balancing Transparency with Security:** Exposing too much data can make systems vulnerable to attacks. Finding the right balance between transparency and security is critical for effective blockchain implementation.

Future Trends in Blockchain Transparency

As blockchain technology continues to evolve, new innovations are emerging that further enhance transparency while addressing privacy and scalability concerns. The following trends highlight how blockchain transparency is expected to develop in the coming years:

1. **Decentralized Identifiers (DIDs):** Combining transparency with privacy, DIDs allow users to control their identity while participating in transparent blockchain ecosystems. This innovation is particularly relevant in sectors like healthcare and finance, where identity verification is critical.

2. **Integration with AI:** Artificial intelligence can analyze blockchain data, identifying patterns and anomalies and providing insights for decision-making. AI tools can assist organizations in obtaining actionable intelligence from transparent blockchain records.

3. **Regulatory Support:** Governments are increasingly recognizing the potential of blockchain transparency. Developing global standards for blockchain implementation will ensure uniformity and trust across jurisdictions. Initiatives like the European Union's Markets in Crypto-Assets (MiCA) framework are steps in this direction.

4. **Hybrid Models:** Combining public and private blockchains allows organizations to balance transparency and privacy, optimizing use cases for specific industries. Hybrid models are particularly valuable for applications like supply chain management, where certain data must remain confidential.

5. **Tokenization for Transparency:** Tokenizing assets like real estate or commodities on a blockchain enables transparent ownership tracking and simplifies transactions. This approach is being explored by industries like real estate and art.

6. **Interoperable Systems:** Cross-chain interoperability solutions, such as Polkadot and Cosmos, are enabling seamless data sharing across multiple blockchains. This enhances transparency in multi-network environments, such as global supply chains.

Cost Considerations

Cost is a significant factor in evaluating the adoption and implementation of blockchain technology. While blockchain offers many advantages, understanding its cost structure is essential for determining its feasibility and scalability in specific applications. Beyond the technical expenses, organizations must consider long-term operational costs, environmental impact, and the potential for cost savings through efficiency gains.

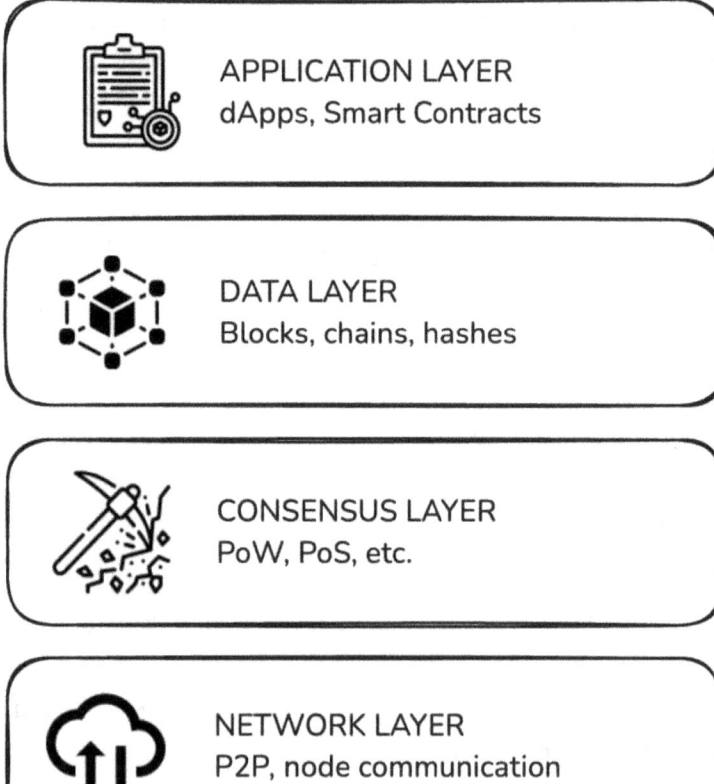

Figure 4-3. *Blockchain-Layered Architecture*

Initial Setup and Operational Costs

1. **Infrastructure Costs:** Setting up a blockchain network requires substantial investment in hardware and software infrastructure. Nodes must be equipped with high-performance servers, robust storage solutions, and reliable internet connectivity to manage the blockchain's increasing demands. For instance:

- Public blockchains rely on decentralized nodes spread globally, which necessitate infrastructure investments from individual participants or mining pools.

- Private blockchains used in enterprises often require centralized infrastructure with severe security measures, which can significantly increase costs.

2. **Development Costs:** Building blockchain-based solutions requires specialized expertise. Developers proficient in blockchain programming languages like Solidity (Ethereum), Rust (Solana), or Go (Hyperledger Fabric) are in high demand and command premium salaries. Additionally, smart contract audits, required to ensure security and functionality, add to development expenses.

3. **Integration Costs:** Integrating blockchain systems with legacy infrastructure is a complex process. Organizations must invest in middleware solutions, API development, and customizations to ensure seamless interoperability. For example:

   - Financial institutions may need to align blockchain solutions with their existing payment processing systems.

   - Supply chain companies often require integrations with IoT devices for real-time tracking and data synchronization.

4. **Energy Consumption:** Blockchain systems that rely on Proof of Work (PoW) consensus mechanisms consume vast amounts of energy. Bitcoin mining, for instance, uses electricity on par with some small countries. Transitioning to energy-efficient alternatives like Proof of Stake (PoS) or Delegated Proof of Stake (DPoS) can mitigate these costs, but such changes require time and investment.

Cost Savings Through Efficiency

Despite the high initial investments, blockchain technology offers significant cost-saving opportunities over time. These efficiencies are particularly impactful in industries plagued by inefficiencies, intermediaries, and fraud.

1. **Reduced Intermediary Fees:** Blockchain eliminates the need for intermediaries, reducing transaction costs across various sectors:

   - **Finance:** Cross-border payments using Ripple or Stellar bypass traditional banks and payment processors, resulting in lower fees.

   - **Supply Chain:** Automated payments through smart contracts eliminate the need for third-party escrow services.

2. **Fraud Mitigation:** Blockchain's tamper-proof ledger reduces the risk of fraud, particularly in sectors like insurance and finance. Fraud prevention not only saves money but also enhances trust and reduces litigation costs.

3. **Automation with Smart Contracts:** Smart contracts streamline operations by automating repetitive tasks. For example:

   - Insurance claims can be processed automatically when predefined conditions are met, reducing the need for manual verification.

   - Payroll systems using smart contracts ensure timely and accurate payments without human intervention.

4. **Operational Efficiency:** Blockchain's transparency reduces time spent on audits and reconciliations. Organizations can verify transactions in real time, speeding up processes and cutting down labor costs.

Balancing Costs and Benefits

Organizations must weigh the costs of implementing blockchain against its potential benefits. This evaluation requires a detailed understanding of both immediate and long-term implications:

- **Scalability Challenges:** Large-scale blockchain implementations can be resource-intensive. Layer 2 solutions, like Polygon for Ethereum, and innovations like sharding help address scalability while reducing costs.

- **Energy Transition:** Moving away from energy-intensive PoW systems to PoS or hybrid models can significantly cut operational expenses.

- **Industry-Specific Suitability:** Blockchain is not a one-size-fits-all solution. Industries with high transparency and decentralization needs, such as finance and healthcare, benefit the most. In contrast, sectors that have centralized operations may find traditional databases to be more cost-effective.

Environmental Costs

The environmental impact of blockchain, particularly PoW systems, is a growing concern. The high energy consumption associated with mining contributes to carbon emissions, which offsets the cost benefits of blockchain. Efforts to address these challenges include:

1. **Carbon-Neutral Mining:** Mining operations powered by renewable energy sources can reduce the environmental footprint. Companies like CleanSpark are exploring sustainable solutions for Bitcoin mining.

2. **Energy-Efficient Consensus Mechanisms:** Proof of Stake (PoS), used by Ethereum 2.0, significantly reduces energy requirements compared to PoW. Other alternatives, like Proof of Authority (PoA), offer similar benefits.

3. **Token Incentives for Sustainability:** Some blockchains incentivize environmentally friendly practices by rewarding participants with tokens for using renewable energy or reducing emissions.

Case Studies of Cost-Saving Implementations

Several organizations across diverse sectors have successfully implemented blockchain solutions to cut costs, improve efficiency, and eliminate intermediaries.

In finance, **RippleNet** has emerged as a leader in reducing the cost of cross-border payments. By enabling instant settlements and bypassing intermediary banks, RippleNet streamlines global transactions and lowers fees. Similarly, **JP Morgan's Onyx** leverages blockchain to enhance wholesale payment systems. Its implementation has led to significant annual savings by reducing friction and improving settlement speeds.

The healthcare sector also benefits from blockchain's potential to lower administrative overhead. For example, **MediBloc** facilitates secure, immutable sharing of medical records between patients and providers, minimizing paperwork and accelerating care coordination. **Chronicled**, on the other hand, uses blockchain to track pharmaceutical supply chains. This not only improves traceability but also reduces financial losses due to counterfeiting and errors.

In the supply chain domain, **Walmart** employs blockchain to trace the origin of food products. This system helps reduce food waste, enhances product safety, and significantly cuts down on manual auditing expenses. Meanwhile, **Maersk**, in collaboration with IBM, launched the **TradeLens** platform to digitize and automate global shipping documentation. This innovation simplifies the movement of goods across borders and leads to substantial operational savings.

Lastly, in the energy sector, the **Energy Web Foundation** enables peer-to-peer energy trading using blockchain. By decentralizing energy markets and automating transactions, utility companies lower their overhead costs while facilitating more efficient renewable energy distribution.

Future Trends in Cost Management

1. **Open-Source Frameworks:** Projects like Hyperledger Fabric allow organizations to build custom blockchain solutions without incurring high licensing fees.

2. **Tokenized Economies:** Blockchain ecosystems increasingly use token incentives to offset operational costs. For example, participants earn tokens for contributing to network security or processing transactions.

3. **Interoperable Blockchains:** Technologies like Polkadot and Cosmos enable cross-chain data sharing, reducing duplication and infrastructure costs.

4. **AI Integration:** Combining blockchain with artificial intelligence optimizes resource allocation and reduces operational inefficiencies, particularly in complex systems like supply chains and financial markets.

Transaction Speed

Transaction speed is a critical metric for evaluating the performance of blockchain systems. Table 4-3 compares transaction speed and settlement time across various systems.

While blockchain offers numerous advantages, its transaction processing speed varies significantly based on the underlying architecture, consensus mechanisms, and network design. Improving transaction speed is essential for achieving scalability and meeting the demands of real-world applications.

This section explores the factors affecting speed, comparisons with traditional systems, innovative blockchain solutions, and the challenges and opportunities ahead.

Table 4-3. Blockchain and Traditional System Speed Comparison

Blockchain/System	Consensus Mechanism	Avg TPS	Settlement Time
Bitcoin	Proof of Work (PoW)	7	~10 minutes
Ethereum (L1)	Proof of Stake (PoS)	15–30	1–5 minutes
Solana	Proof of History	65,000+	~1 second
Visa	Centralized	24,000	Real-time

Factors Affecting Speed

1. **Consensus Mechanism:** The choice of consensus protocol plays a major role in determining transaction speed. For example:

CHAPTER 4   PROS AND CONS OF BLOCKCHAIN

- **Proof of Work (PoW):** Used by Bitcoin, PoW requires complex computations for block validation, resulting in slower transaction speeds (approximately 7 transactions per second, or TPS).

- **Proof of Stake (PoS):** PoS systems, like Ethereum 2.0, achieve higher transaction speeds by selecting validators based on their stake in the network, bypassing the energy-intensive computations of PoW.

- **Delegated Proof of Stake (DPoS):** Platforms like EOS use DPoS to achieve consensus more efficiently, supporting thousands of TPS by delegating validation to selected nodes.

2. **Network Scalability:** The ability of a blockchain to handle increasing numbers of transactions depends on its scalability. Solutions like sharding, sidechains, and Layer 2 protocols (e.g., Lightning Network) enhance scalability and improve transaction throughput, allowing blockchains to manage larger volumes of data efficiently.

3. **Block Size and Time:** Larger block sizes allow more transactions per block, while shorter block times reduce the interval between validations. However, increasing block size can affect decentralization, as it requires more storage and bandwidth from network participants. Ethereum, for instance, balances these factors by dynamically adjusting gas limits based on network activity.

4. **Network Congestion:** High transaction volumes during peak periods can overwhelm blockchain networks, slowing down processing times. This is particularly evident on platforms like Ethereum during token launches or NFT drops. Congestion results in higher fees and delayed confirmations, prompting the need for scalability solutions.

Comparisons with Traditional Systems

1. **Banking Systems:** Traditional financial systems like Visa handle up to 24,000 TPS, far surpassing the speeds of early blockchain systems. However, newer blockchains are closing the gap, with platforms like Solana achieving speeds of 65,000 TPS, making them viable alternatives for financial applications.

2. **Settlement Times:** Blockchain provides faster settlement times compared to traditional banking systems. While bank transfers can take days to clear, blockchain transactions settle in minutes or even seconds, depending on the network. This advantage is particularly valuable for cross-border payments.

3. **Real-Time Processing:** Blockchain's real-time transaction processing, enabled by platforms like Avalanche and Algorand, rivals and often exceeds the efficiency of traditional systems in specific use cases, such as decentralized finance (DeFi).

Examples of High-Speed Blockchains

1. **Solana:** Solana achieves speeds of up to 65,000 TPS using its innovative Proof of History (PoH) mechanism, which timestamps transactions before they are processed. This makes it ideal for applications requiring rapid processing, such as gaming and DeFi.

2. **Avalanche:** Avalanche utilizes a novel consensus protocol to achieve sub-second finality and high throughput. Its architecture supports parallel transaction processing, enhancing speed and scalability.

3. **Polygon:** As a Layer 2 solution for Ethereum, Polygon processes transactions off-chain and then finalizes them on the Ethereum mainnet, significantly improving speed and reducing costs.

4. **Ripple (XRP):** Ripple's consensus mechanism enables fast processing of cross-border payments, making it a leader in financial transactions with settlement times of just a few seconds.

Challenges in Achieving High Speed

1. **Trade-Offs with Decentralization:** Increasing transaction speed often requires reducing the number of nodes participating in consensus, which can compromise decentralization and security. Striking a balance between speed and decentralization is crucial for blockchain adoption.

2. **Energy Consumption:** High-speed blockchains must address energy efficiency concerns, particularly those using resource-intensive consensus mechanisms like PoW. Transitioning to greener alternatives is vital for long-term sustainability.

3. **Technical Complexity:** Implementing advanced scalability solutions, such as sharding and rollups, introduces complexity and increases the risk of software bugs or vulnerabilities. These solutions require careful testing and monitoring.

4. **Interoperability Barriers:** Ensuring seamless communication between high-speed blockchains and other networks is essential to maximize their potential while maintaining transaction efficiency. Technologies like Polkadot and Cosmos are addressing these challenges by enabling cross-chain compatibility.

Innovations in Driving Transaction Speed

1. **Layer 2 Solutions:** Technologies like Optimistic Rollups and zk-Rollups on Ethereum aim to increase transaction speeds by processing transactions off-chain and finalizing them on-chain. These solutions drastically reduce congestion and lower fees.

2. **Dynamic Sharding:** Sharding techniques that dynamically adjust based on network activity can optimize transaction processing and improve scalability. Ethereum's roadmap includes advanced sharding to handle large-scale dApp ecosystems.

3. **Cross-Chain Communication:** Interoperability frameworks like Polkadot and Cosmos enable high-speed blockchains to communicate seamlessly, reducing bottlenecks and enhancing efficiency across ecosystems.

4. **Hardware Acceleration:** Utilizing specialized hardware, such as blockchain accelerators and GPUs, can improve transaction speeds and reduce latency in high-demand applications.

Future Trends in Transaction Speed

1. **Blockchain-as-a-Service (BaaS):** Cloud-based blockchain services are optimizing transaction processing by leveraging scalable infrastructure and distributed computing resources. Providers like IBM and Microsoft are leading this trend.

2. **AI Integration:** Artificial intelligence can optimize transaction routing and resource allocation, further improving efficiency in blockchain networks. AI-driven analytics also enhance congestion management.

3. **Multi-layered Architectures:** Combining multiple layers, such as Layer 2 solutions and sidechains, creates a multi-tiered system for handling transactions at different speeds and costs based on priority.

4. **Decentralized Autonomous Organizations (DAOs):** DAOs are exploring efficient governance models to make decisions about blockchain upgrades and consensus changes that enhance speed without sacrificing security.

Regulatory Challenges

The decentralized and borderless nature of blockchain technology presents unique challenges in the regulatory landscape. Governments and regulatory bodies worldwide are grappling with how to integrate blockchain into existing legal frameworks while addressing its novel characteristics.

CHAPTER 4   PROS AND CONS OF BLOCKCHAIN

These challenges range from legal ambiguity to technical limitations, influencing the adoption and scalability of blockchain systems across industries. Table 4-4 outlines different regulatory approaches to blockchain across countries.

Table 4-4. Global Regulatory Perspectives on Blockchain

Country	Stance	Key Action/Framework
USA	Mixed (State/Federal mismatch)	The SEC treats many tokens as securities
EU	Proactive regulation	MiCA framework
China	Crypto ban, blockchain promotion	BSN (Blockchain Service Network)
El Salvador	Pro-crypto	Bitcoin adopted as legal tender
India	Unclear, evolving	Proposed taxation on digital assets
South Korea	Strict but supportive	Virtual Asset User Protection Act, centralized exchange regulations

Legal and Compliance Issues

1. **Lack of Standardized Regulations:** Blockchain operates across jurisdictions, each with its own regulatory requirements. The absence of international standards leads to uncertainty for businesses and developers, preventing the adoption of blockchain. For example:

    - In the United States, cryptocurrency exchanges face differing state and federal regulations.

    - In contrast, the European Union has introduced more centralized frameworks, such as the Markets in Crypto-Assets (MiCA) regulation.

2. **Classification of Digital Assets:** Governments struggle to categorize cryptocurrencies and tokens:

- **Currencies:** Used for payments (e.g., Bitcoin and Litecoin).
- **Commodities:** Seen as store-of-value assets (e.g., Bitcoin).
- **Securities:** Investment vehicles requiring strict regulation (e.g., tokenized assets like ICOs). This lack of clarity complicates tax reporting, investment regulations, and compliance across borders.

3. **AML and KYC Requirements:** Blockchain's pseudonymous nature raises concerns about its potential misuse for illicit activities, such as money laundering or terrorism financing. Regulatory bodies demand compliance with AML and KYC laws, requiring exchanges and platforms to verify user identities.

4. **Smart Contract Legality:** Smart contracts, which autonomously enforce agreements, present unique legal challenges:
   - How to assign liability for errors or disputes.
   - The enforceability of self-executing contracts in traditional legal systems.

Case Studies of Regulatory Responses

1. **United States:**
   - The SEC considers many tokens securities, applying strict regulations to their issuance and trading.
   - Wyoming has emerged as a blockchain-friendly state, offering legislation for digital asset banking and token issuance.

2. **European Union:**
   - The MiCA framework provides clarity on asset classification, focusing on consumer protection and transparency.
   - GDPR compliance remains a challenge, as blockchain's immutability conflicts with the "right to be forgotten."

3. **China:**
   - China has banned cryptocurrency trading but actively promotes blockchain innovation in supply chain management, digital identity, and state-backed digital currencies.

4. **El Salvador:**
   - El Salvador's adoption of Bitcoin as legal tender exemplifies proactive blockchain integration, leveraging Bitcoin for financial inclusion and tourism.

5. **India:**
   - India's regulatory approach has fluctuated, from bans on cryptocurrency trading to proposals for taxation and regulatory frameworks for digital assets.

6. **South Korea:**
   - South Korea has introduced strict cryptocurrency regulations, focusing on user protection, requiring all exchanges to comply with KYC and AML laws.

Challenges in Regulatory Implementation

1. **Balancing Innovation and Control:** Overregulation can inhibit innovation, while underregulation allows for wrong use. Finding the balance is particularly challenging in fast-evolving industries like DeFi.

2. **Cross-Border Collaboration:** Blockchain's borderless nature necessitates international cooperation. Inconsistent regulations between countries create uncertainty for global businesses, slowing blockchain's adoption.

3. **Technical Complexity:** Many policymakers lack the technical expertise needed to understand blockchain's intricacies, resulting in ineffective or overly restrictive regulations.

4. **Consumer Protection:** Fraudulent ICOs and scams have demonstrated the need for more effective consumer protection strategies. However, implementing these without compromising blockchain's decentralization necessitates innovative approaches.

Opportunities for Regulatory Advancement

1. **Regulatory Sandboxes:** Countries like Singapore and the UK are experimenting with regulatory sandboxes that allow blockchain startups to test applications under relaxed regulations, fostering innovation.

2. **Self-regulation:** Blockchain communities and consortia are establishing their own standards and best practices, reducing the need for external enforcement. For example, the Enterprise Ethereum Alliance (EEA) promotes enterprise-grade blockchain adoption through standardized guidelines.

3. **Tokenized Compliance:** Smart contracts enable automated compliance processes, ensuring transactions adhere to regulatory requirements in real-time. Tokens can prevent transactions to unauthorized wallets or jurisdictions.

4. **Decentralized Identity Systems:** Decentralized identifiers (DIDs) provide a way to comply with KYC and AML requirements while preserving user privacy, balancing regulatory and user needs.

Future Trends in Regulation

1. **Global Frameworks:** Organizations like the Financial Action Task Force (FATF) are working toward global standards for blockchain and cryptocurrency regulation, aiming to promote consistency and reduce jurisdictional conflicts.

2. **Focus on Decentralized Finance (DeFi):** Regulators are increasingly scrutinizing DeFi platforms, balancing the need for innovation with investor protection. Frameworks for auditing smart contracts and ensuring platform security are expected to emerge.

3. **AI and Blockchain Integration:** Artificial intelligence tools are assisting regulators by analyzing blockchain transactions for suspicious activities, helping enforce regulations efficiently.

4. **Environmental Considerations:** Governments may introduce regulations encouraging energy-efficient protocols, penalizing energy-intensive models like PoW while incentivizing greener alternatives.

Expanded Regulatory Applications

1. **Taxation:** Governments are developing blockchain-specific tax regulations, requiring exchanges and users to report capital gains, staking rewards, and mining income.

2. **Digital Identity:** Blockchain-based digital identity systems are increasingly recognized for compliance purposes, allowing individuals to verify identities securely without sharing unnecessary information.

3. **Intellectual Property:** Blockchain simplifies IP management, with regulatory efforts focused on verifying digital ownership and managing royalties.

4. **Voting and Governance:** Regulatory bodies are exploring how blockchain can secure voting processes, ensuring transparency and minimizing fraud.

Conclusion

Blockchain technology is reshaping how we store data, process transactions, and build trust online. Its decentralized nature enhances security, reduces single points of failure, and empowers users, offering real benefits across sectors like finance, healthcare, and supply chain.

Beyond decentralization, blockchain enables faster, cheaper, and more reliable transactions while promoting transparency through immutable ledgers. However, challenges such as high energy consumption, regulatory uncertainty, and scalability must be addressed for broader adoption.

Ultimately, blockchain is not a one-size-fits-all solution but a powerful tool when applied thoughtfully. As technology evolves, its potential to drive efficiency, trust, and innovation continues to grow.

Chapter Summary

Topic	Key takeaways
Decentralization	Eliminates single points of failure, enhances security, and promotes censorship resistance.
Security and Resilience	Cryptographic structures and consensus mechanisms improve data integrity and fault tolerance.
Transaction Efficiency	Reduces costs and speeds up processing by removing intermediaries and enabling automation.
Transparency	Immutable public ledgers increase trust, support audits, and ensure accountability across sectors.
Cost Considerations	Upfront infrastructure and energy costs are high but offset by automation and fraud reduction.
Transaction Speed	Performance varies across blockchains; Layer 2 and new consensus protocols enhance scalability.
Regulatory Landscape	Diverse global approaches; legal clarity and technical understanding are key for adoption.

CHAPTER 5

Blockchain Applications

Introduction

Blockchain technology was once exclusively associated with cryptocurrencies, but now it has become a powerful force that can reshape industries outside of finance. The concept of decentralized networks is transforming how we manage identity, value, ownership, and even governance. As seen previously, blockchain applications extend into sectors like healthcare, supply chains, social media, finance, and even national infrastructure projects.

In this chapter, we will explore the breadth of blockchain's applications, with a focus on the critical architectural changes it brings, the new user experiences it enables, and the decision-making frameworks needed to choose the right blockchain for a project. We begin by understanding the key differences between the traditional Web2 internet and the emergent world of Web3, a shift that is foundational to every blockchain innovation.

Differences Between Web2 and Web3

Architectural Differences

The evolution of the internet from its early days to its current decentralized visions has been marked by profound shifts not only in technology but also in philosophy. To understand blockchain applications, one must first grasp the fundamental architectural differences between Web2 and Web3. These differences go beyond technical details and represent competing worldviews about trust, ownership, and control.

Web2, often called the Social Web," is built on client-server models where users interact with centralized services that handle authentication, data storage, and content delivery. Every time a user logs into a platform like Facebook or Google, they interact with servers that not only process their requests but also store and manage their data. The centralized model ensures rapid response times, highly curated experiences, and seamless integration of various services. However, at the core, it creates a significant imbalance: users do not own the infrastructure nor the data they generate; they merely access services under the terms dictated by corporations.

In contrast, Web3 introduces a peer-to-peer, decentralized architecture enabled by blockchain networks. Here, the logic of the application, its backend, is no longer a proprietary black box owned by a company but transparent, verifiable, and immutable code living on a blockchain. Instead of relying on a corporation's promise, users can independently verify the behavior of smart contracts, check the integrity of transactions, and directly own their digital interactions.

This decentralization is not just a technical rearrangement; it reconfigures power dynamics. Control shifts away from institutions to individuals. It reduces the risks associated with data breaches, censorship, and monopolistic behavior. However, decentralization also introduces its own challenges: performance bottlenecks, user complexity, and governance dilemmas.

The essence of architectural difference can be summarized clearly (Table 5-1):

Table 5-1. Key Differences Between Web2 and Web3

Aspect	Web2	Web3
Ownership	Platform owns content/data	Users own their assets/data
Infrastructure	Centralized servers	Decentralized nodes
Identity	Email, password, KYC	Wallet address, decentralized ID
Trust Model	Trust in platforms	Trust in protocols and code
Data Storage	Corporate-controlled databases	Distributed ledgers, IPFS

Each of these aspects represents not just a technological switch but a different way of relating to the internet itself. In Web2, users rent space. In Web3, users claim ownership. In Web2, corporations arbitrate disputes. In Web3, the code becomes the arbiter.

This architectural transformation lays the foundation for everything else: the way users experience the web, the strategies behind business models, and the legal frameworks that regulate it.

User Experience Changes

The impact of architecture on users is profound, often in ways that are not immediately apparent. As the backend changes, so does the frontend: the experience of interacting with the internet shifts fundamentally in Web3. Figure 5-1 compares login flows between Web2 and Web3 ecosystems.

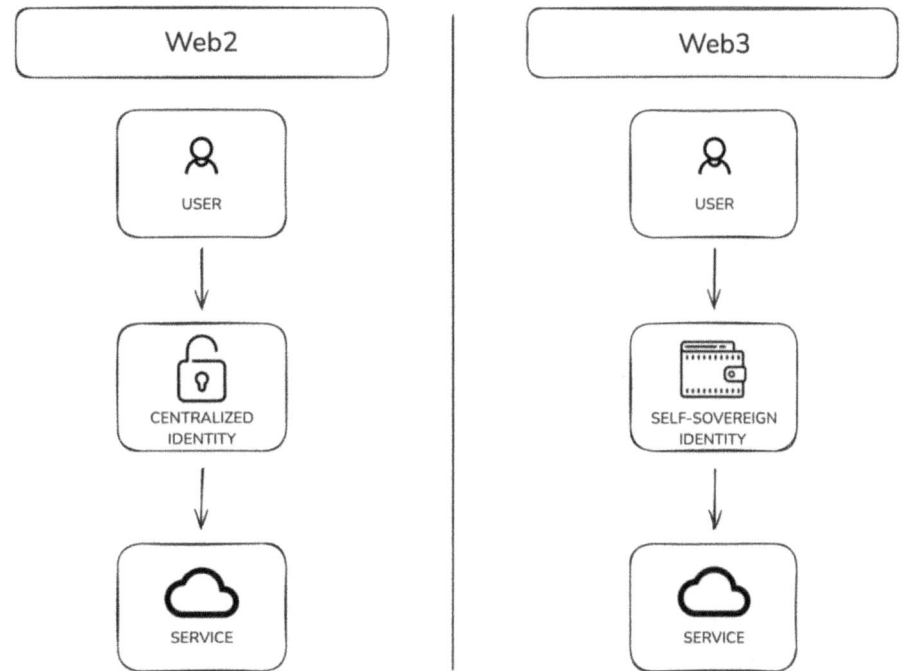

Figure 5-1. *Web2 vs. Web3 Login Flow*

Identity and Access

Perhaps the most immediate difference a user encounters when stepping into Web3 is the concept of self-sovereign identity. In Web2, identities are federated and managed by companies. Single sign-on (SSO) features enable users to log into a multitude of websites using a Google or Facebook account. Recovery mechanisms are handled by these entities. If a user forgets their password, recovery is a simple email away.

In Web3, identity is cryptographic and non-custodial. Users create a public-private key pair, typically managed through a crypto wallet. If a user loses their private key, no corporation can help them recover access. While this reality introduces responsibility and risk, it also grants freedom: no single entity can revoke a user's identity, censor their account, or monetize their personal information without consent.

This shift towards cryptographic identities brings philosophical and practical consequences. It returns ownership of identity to individuals but demands that users become much more technically literate and cautious. Wallet management, seed phrase backups, and understanding transaction approvals become everyday concerns.

Financial Interactions

Financial behavior on the internet also changes dramatically in Web3. Where Web2 transactions require trust in intermediaries, such as banks, card processors, and escrow services, Web3 enables peer-to-peer programmable money through cryptocurrencies.

Consider the act of sending money overseas. Web2 frequently demands bank wires, currency conversions, anti-fraud verifications, and waiting periods. In Web3, the same task can happen in minutes, using assets like Ethereum or stablecoins, with global accessibility and minimal fees.

This is not merely about speed. Web3 takes down financial gatekeeping: anyone with an internet connection and a crypto wallet can access global financial systems without asking permission. Of course, this openness also introduces exposure to volatility, scams, and poorly secured platforms.

Content Ownership

The content users create, such as tweets, videos, and blogs, is largely platform property in Web2. Users publish under terms-of-service agreements that allow companies to monetize and even remove user content at their discretion.

In Web3, content is tokenized. A blog post could be an NFT. A music album could be streamed directly via decentralized protocols with built-in royalty payments. Ownership is cryptographically secured and verifiable on public blockchains. Monetization can happen without platform intermediaries taking massive cuts. As shown in Figure 5-2, Web3 redefines how content is owned and monetized.

CHAPTER 5 BLOCKCHAIN APPLICATIONS

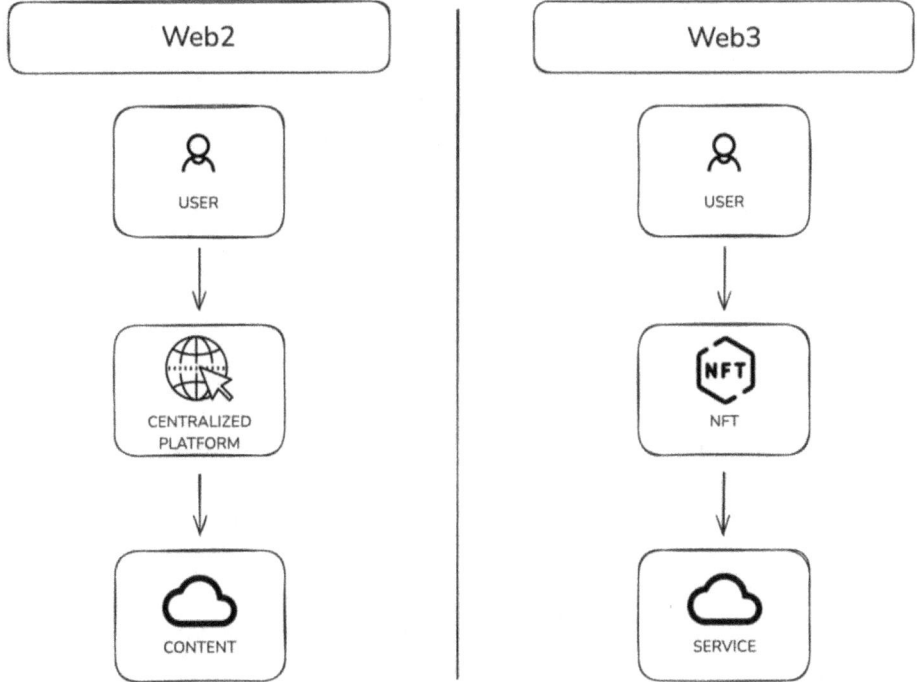

Figure 5-2. Content Ownership in Web2 vs. Web3

In short, Web3 alters the social contract between users and the internet itself. Users of the internet are now more than just consumers: they are also owners and participants, which comes with greater personal responsibility and learning curves.

Case Studies of Transition

In order to gain a better understanding of how these differences are manifested in practice, we can examine real-world examples of industries moving from Web 2 models to Web 3 paradigms.

1. **Social Media:** From Twitter to Lens Protocol
   In Web2 social media like Twitter, users create content, but their reach, visibility, and monetization are determined by platform algorithms. Accounts can be suspended without warning. Content can be demonetized. Data can be sold to advertisers without explicit user consent.

Lens Protocol, built on the Polygon blockchain, gives an idea of a Web3 alternative. On Lens, profiles are NFTs. Posts are NFTs. Users can port their social graph across applications. Monetization flows directly between creators and fans. Ownership is real, not metaphorical.

This shift empowers creators to truly own their presence but introduces new challenges: onboarding complexity, gas fees, and issues around content moderation without centralized authorities.

2. **Finance:** from traditional banks to Decentralized Finance (DeFi)

Traditional banks serve as custodians, intermediaries, and gatekeepers. DeFi platforms like Aave and Compound, by contrast, offer lending, borrowing, and trading services through smart contracts. No bank tellers, no account managers, no paperwork.

Users offer liquidity to earn yield, borrow assets against collateral, and trade derivatives, with all these activities being managed by open-source code. Access is global, permissionless, and 24/7. However, DeFi also carries risks: smart contract bugs, volatile assets, and immature insurance systems. The absence of traditional consumer protections means users must rely on community audits, personal research (DYOR), and careful risk management.

3. **Cloud Storage:** From Dropbox to Filecoin/IPFS (Figure 5-3)

Dropbox epitomizes Web2 cloud storage: convenience at the cost of trust. Users upload files to Dropbox's servers, trusting that the company will keep them safe, private, and accessible.

In Web3, decentralized storage solutions like Filecoin and IPFS distribute encrypted fragments of files across hundreds or thousands of independent nodes. New user responsibilities are introduced when managing decentralized storage, including retrieval, encryption keys, and storage contracts, as data becomes harder to censor or lose.

Decentralized storage promotes resilience and user sovereignty but can complicate access, recovery, and user interfaces.

CHAPTER 5 BLOCKCHAIN APPLICATIONS

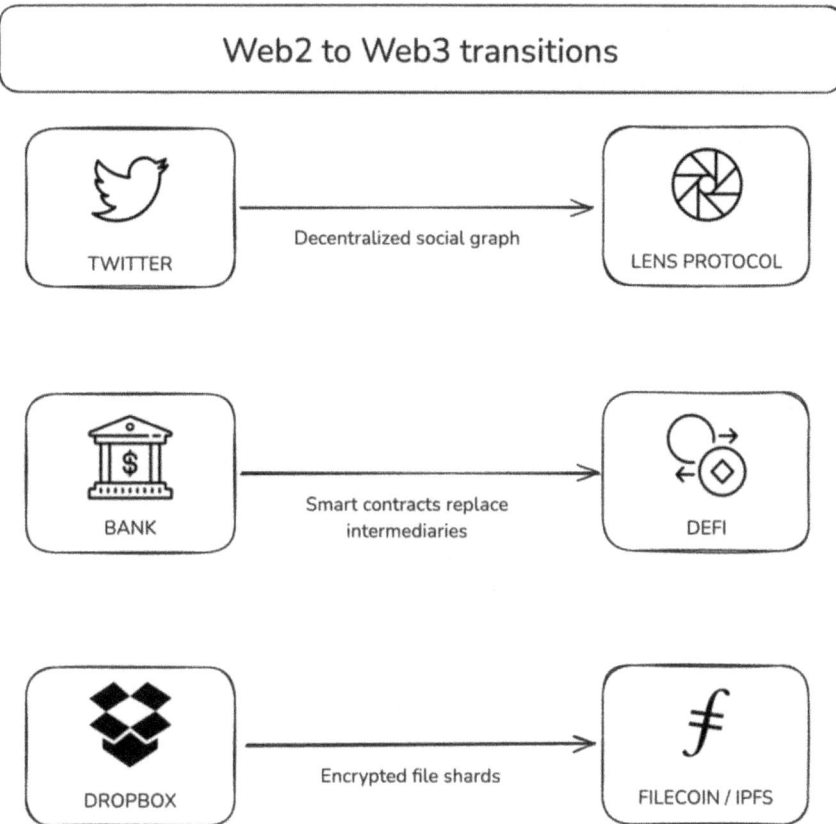

Figure 5-3. *Industry Transitions from Web2 to Web3*

Choosing the Right Blockchain

In the ever-evolving world of blockchain applications, selecting the right blockchain platform is one of the most critical decisions any developer, entrepreneur, or organization must make. The selection of a blockchain has an impact on everything, from scalability and security to user adoption and regulatory compliance. The success or failure of a project can be determined by a strategic, long-term commitment, not just a technical decision.

Before diving into specific blockchain options, it is important to establish a comprehensive understanding of the factors that should guide this choice. Figure 5-4 outlines key decision criteria for selecting a blockchain platform.

CHAPTER 5   BLOCKCHAIN APPLICATIONS

Factors to Consider

When evaluating blockchain platforms, several key factors come into play. These considerations are interconnected: prioritizing one often involves trade-offs with another.

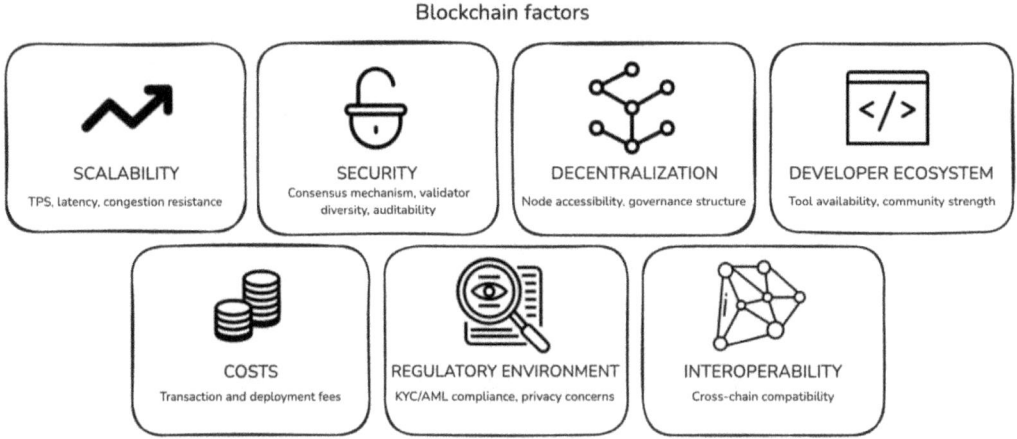

Figure 5-4. *Blockchain Platform Considerations*

Scalability

Scalability refers to the blockchain's ability to handle an increasing number of transactions efficiently as the network grows. This is crucial for applications expecting high user adoption or frequent transactions, such as gaming platforms, DeFi protocols, or supply chain tracking systems.

Scalability metrics include:

- **Transactions per Second (TPS):** How many transactions the blockchain can process in a second.

- **Latency:** The time it takes for a transaction to be confirmed.

- **Network Congestion Resistance:** How well the blockchain handles high transaction volumes without massive fee spikes or delays.

Example:

Ethereum's early scalability issues, leading to extremely high gas fees during periods of congestion, highlighted the need for Layer 2 solutions like optimistic rollups and sidechains. Figure 5-5 compares scalability metrics across major blockchains.

CHAPTER 5   BLOCKCHAIN APPLICATIONS

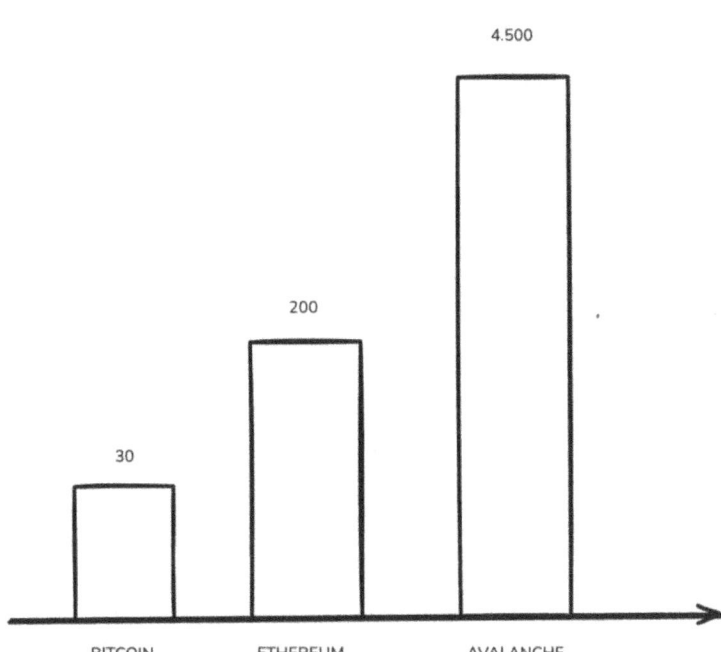

Figure 5-5. *Blockchain Scalability Comparison*

Security

Security remains the backbone of blockchain integrity. Without robust security, blockchains risk being attacked, manipulated, or rendered unreliable.

Security factors include:

- **Consensus Mechanism Robustness:** How resistant is the blockchain to attacks such as a 51% attack?

- **Validator Diversity:** How decentralized is the network's node/validator structure?

- **Auditability:** Are smart contracts and platform updates subject to rigorous external audits?

Example:

Bitcoin's Proof of Work system, while energy-intensive, remains arguably the most battle-tested and secure public network to date.

> **Important Note** Security often comes at the cost of scalability and performance, a trade-off famously known as the Blockchain Trilemma:
>
> *"You can optimize for two out of three: decentralization, scalability, and security, but never all at once."*

Decentralization

Decentralization is a philosophical and practical principle: it refers to how much control or influence is distributed across the network's participants.

Questions to ask:

- How easy is it to run a node or validator?
- How geographically and institutionally diverse are the validators/miners?
- Does any single entity or consortium hold disproportionate influence?

Example:
Solana, despite its high TPS, has faced criticism for its validator set being relatively small compared to Bitcoin or Ethereum, raising questions about decentralization robustness.

Developer Ecosystem

A blockchain's future depends heavily on its developer community.

Signs of a healthy developer ecosystem:

- Abundant tools, SDKs, and APIs.
- Vibrant open-source communities and hackathons.
- Educational resources and developer incentives.

Example:
Ethereum boasts the largest developer ecosystem in blockchain, fueling innovations in DeFi, NFTs, and DAOs.

A strong ecosystem not only accelerates development but also ensures future support, upgrades, and security patches.

Costs

Transaction fees, deployment fees, and maintenance costs vary dramatically across blockchains.

Projects need to factor in not just today's fees but future projections as adoption grows. Table 5-2 compares average transaction fees across leading blockchain platforms.

Table 5-2. *Blockchain Fees Comparison*

Blockchain	Average Transaction Fee (approx.)	Notes
Bitcoin	$1–$20	Depends heavily on congestion.
Ethereum (Layer 1)	$2–$100	High fees during congestion; rollups help reduce costs.
Polygon	<$0.01	Extremely cheap transactions on Layer 2.
Solana	<$0.001	Very low fees, but it depends on network reliability.

Regulatory Environment

Some blockchains may be more sensitive to regulatory pressures based on their architecture, anonymity features, or centralization levels.

Key considerations:

- Does the blockchain comply with KYC/AML requirements?
- Are privacy features (e.g., ZCash and Monero) likely to trigger regulatory scrutiny?
- How adaptable is the blockchain if regulations evolve?

Example:

Projects like Circle's USDC stablecoin chose to launch on Ethereum, Polygon, and Solana, chains considered more "regulator-friendly" compared to fully privacy-focused chains like Monero.

Interoperability

In an increasingly multi-chain world, the ability for a blockchain to interact with others (interoperability) is vital.

Key questions:

- Can the blockchain bridge assets easily to other chains?
- Are standards like ERC-20, ERC-721, or Cosmos IBC supported?
- Is cross-chain communication a priority in its roadmap?

Example:

Polkadot was designed explicitly to support interoperable "parachains," while Cosmos offers the IBC (Inter-Blockchain Communication) protocol to facilitate chain-to-chain messaging.

Comparisons of Popular Blockchains

Let's now compare some of the most influential blockchains based on the factors outlined above. Table 5-3 compares leading blockchain platforms based on their strengths and weaknesses.

Table 5-3. *Comparison of Popular Blockchains*

Blockchain	Strengths	Weaknesses
Bitcoin	Ultimate security and decentralization; proven stability.	Limited programmability; slow transactions.
Ethereum	Massive developer community; smart contract leader; highly decentralized.	High fees; scalability still improving.
Solana	High TPS; low transaction costs.	Network outages; decentralization concerns.
Avalanche	Subnets for custom chains; fast finality.	Still growing developer ecosystem.
Polygon	Low-cost Ethereum scaling; easy onboarding.	Depends heavily on Ethereum security.
Polkadot	True interoperability focus; scalable.	Complex architecture; longer learning curve.
Algorand	High throughput, near-instant finality.	Smaller community compared to Ethereum.

Decision-Making Framework

Given the complexity of options, how should individuals or organizations systematically choose the right blockchain for their needs?

Here's a simple, adaptable framework (Figure 5-6):

1. **Define Your Priorities**

    Start by ranking what matters most to your project (Table 5-4):

    Table 5-4. Defining Project Priorities When Choosing a Blockchain

Priority	Examples
Scalability	High TPS needed for a DeFi platform.
Security	Enterprise data management project.
Low fees	Micropayments system or gaming economy.
Decentralization	Privacy-focused social media app.

    Clarify your "must-haves" versus "nice-to-haves."

2. **Match Platform Strengths to Needs**

    Using the comparison table earlier, shortlist 2–3 blockchains that align best with your priorities.

    Example:

    If you need extreme scalability and cheap fees: Solana or Polygon.
    If decentralization and composability are critical: Ethereum.

3. **Pilot and Test**

    Before full commitment, develop a Minimum Viable Product (MVP) or pilot application on the shortlisted platforms. Measure performance: transaction times, costs, developer ease, and ecosystem support.

    Pilot data can save you months of regret later.

CHAPTER 5   BLOCKCHAIN APPLICATIONS

4. **Consider Long-Term Evolution**

   Blockchains evolve. Upgrades like Ethereum's shift to Proof of Stake (Merge), the rise of Layer 2s, and new consensus innovations like Danksharding will change the landscape.

   Choose a platform not only for today's needs but also for its roadmap alignment with your future vision.

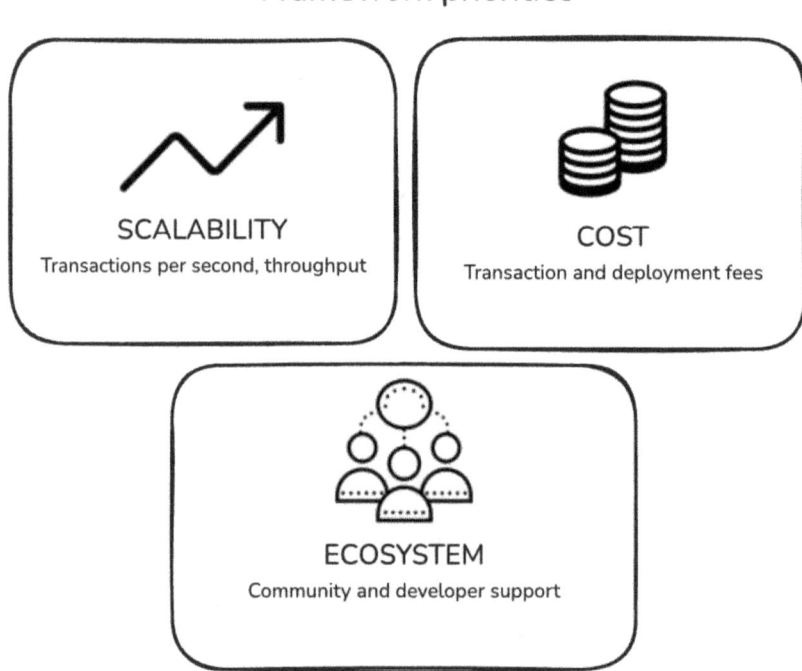

Figure 5-6. *Blockchain Framework Priorities*

Introduction to Ethereum

Ethereum is a milestone in the evolution of blockchain technology. While Bitcoin demonstrated that it was possible to create a decentralized digital currency, Ethereum went further: it offered the first decentralized computing platform, allowing anyone to create and deploy complex applications on top of a blockchain.

Overview of the Ethereum Platform

Ethereum was born out of necessity. In 2013, Vitalik Buterin, a programmer deeply involved with Bitcoin development, noticed a limitation: Bitcoin's scripting system was too rigid. It could only support simple transaction logic such as sending and receiving currency, but not complex interactions such as financial contracts, decentralized organizations, or identity management.

Buterin, frustrated, suggested a blockchain that could run smart contracts—self-executing code not needing third parties. This led to the Ethereum whitepaper published later that year.

In 2014, Ethereum raised over $18 million in a public crowdsale, one of the first examples of a blockchain-based funding model. A year later, in July 2015, Ethereum's first live version, known as Frontier, launched. It was basic but functional, setting the stage for the explosion of decentralized applications (DApps) we see today. Figure 5-7 highlights the milestones in Ethereum's development.

Ethereum was a new type of platform that extended blockchain technology to every type of human interaction, not just another cryptocurrency.

CHAPTER 5   BLOCKCHAIN APPLICATIONS

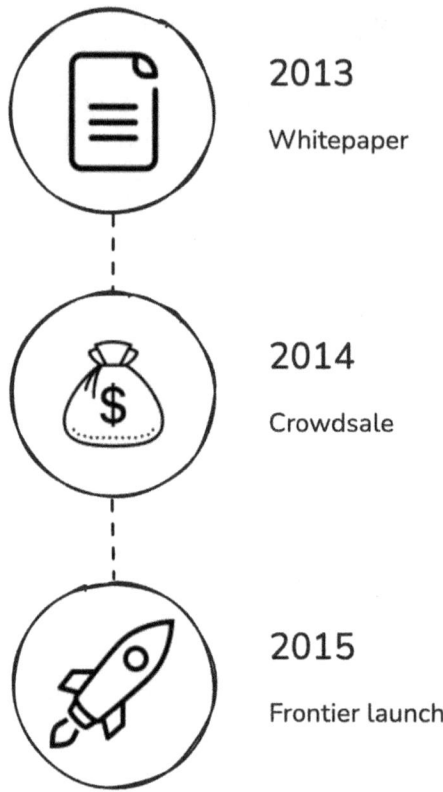

Ethereum creation

Figure 5-7. The Creation of Ethereum

Ethereum's Vision

The vision behind Ethereum can be summarized simply: to be the world's decentralized computer. Instead of relying on centralized companies to host websites or apps, Ethereum allows these applications to be hosted and operated by thousands of nodes globally.

This approach has profound implications:

- **Resilience:** Applications are harder to shut down because there is no single point of failure.

- **Censorship Resistance:** No company or government can arbitrarily block users or activities.

- **Innovation:** Developers are free to create applications that challenge traditional industries, from finance to art to governance.

CHAPTER 5   BLOCKCHAIN APPLICATIONS

The structure of how we interact online is being redefined by this transformation, which is not just technological. Trusted intermediaries such as tech giants, payment providers, and social networks are relied upon by users in a Web2 world to facilitate communication, transactions, and content sharing.

In a Web3 reality powered by Ethereum, the reliance on these gatekeepers is dismantled. Ownership, governance, and control revert back to the users themselves. Data becomes portable and open. Financial services become accessible without permission. Creative expression flourishes without centralized curation.

Ethereum provides not just new tools but also a new digital society. Figure 5-8 illustrates Ethereum's role in reshaping the digital economy.

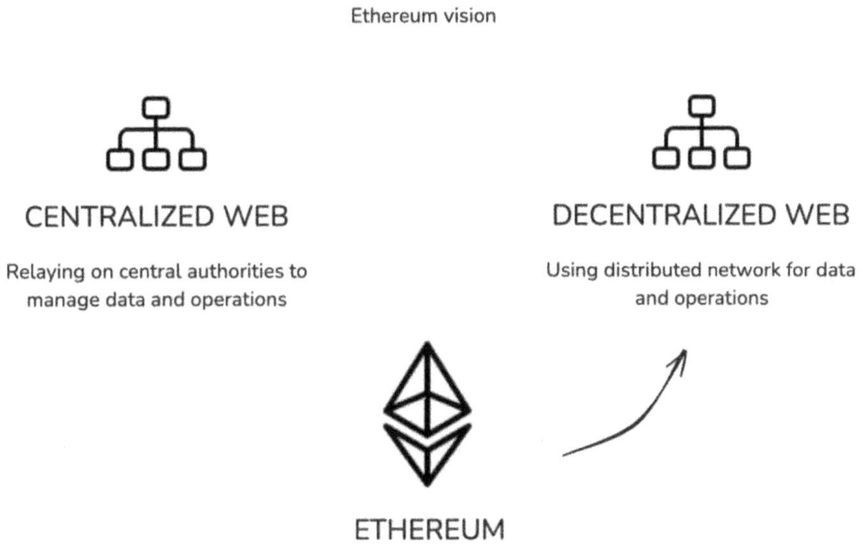

Figure 5-8. Ethereum's Role in Web3

Key Features and Functionalities

Ethereum's design is a fusion of multiple innovations, each carefully crafted to extend the possibilities of what a blockchain can achieve. Ethereum aimed to be a programmable platform that could be used to build entire decentralized ecosystems, not just payments like Bitcoin. This ambition required not just a native currency but a way to process arbitrary computation, secure complex digital contracts, and empower global collaboration. Every core component of Ethereum, from its virtual machine to its token standards, contributes to this broader mission of building an open and decentralized future.

CHAPTER 5   BLOCKCHAIN APPLICATIONS

Let's explore them in detail (Figure 5-9):

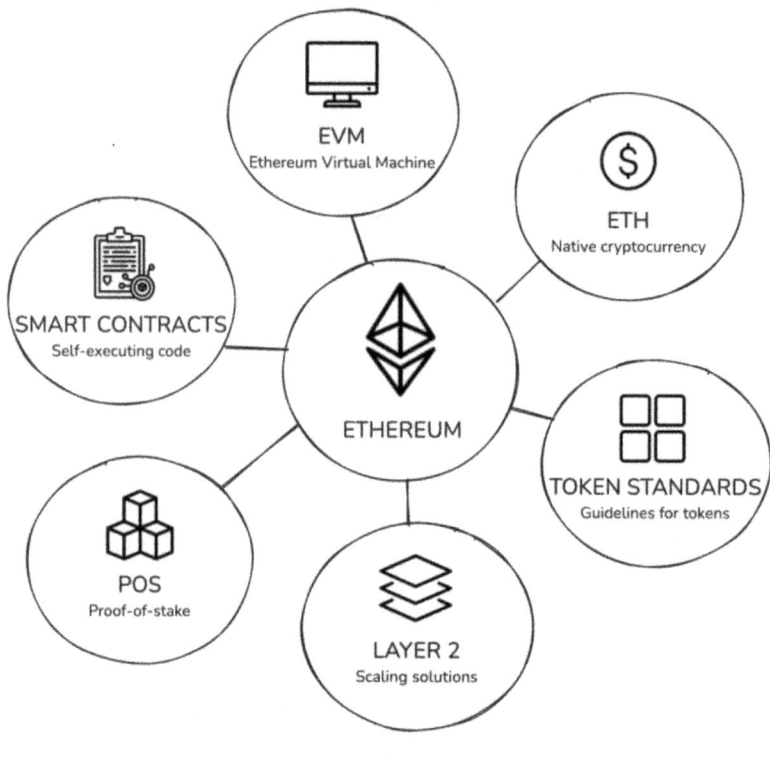

Figure 5-9. Core Components of Ethereum

Smart Contracts

Smart contracts are the cornerstone of Ethereum. These are self-executing programs stored on the blockchain, running exactly as programmed without any possibility of downtime, censorship, or fraud.

When we say "smart contract," think of:

- An automated escrow service, releasing payment only when a delivery is confirmed.

- A decentralized voting system that automatically counts and validates votes.

- A digital rights management system that distributes royalties transparently.

CHAPTER 5   BLOCKCHAIN APPLICATIONS

Each smart contract operates under deterministic rules. Once a smart contract is deployed, it is irreversible and cannot be altered. This immutability builds trust because users know that the code, not the developer, controls the contract's behavior. Figure 5-10 illustrates how smart contracts are deployed and executed.

Moreover, every smart contract is transparent: anyone can inspect the code and audit its behavior before interacting with it.

Example:

A decentralized lottery DApp uses a smart contract to collect bets, select a random winner, and distribute prizes, without any human management.

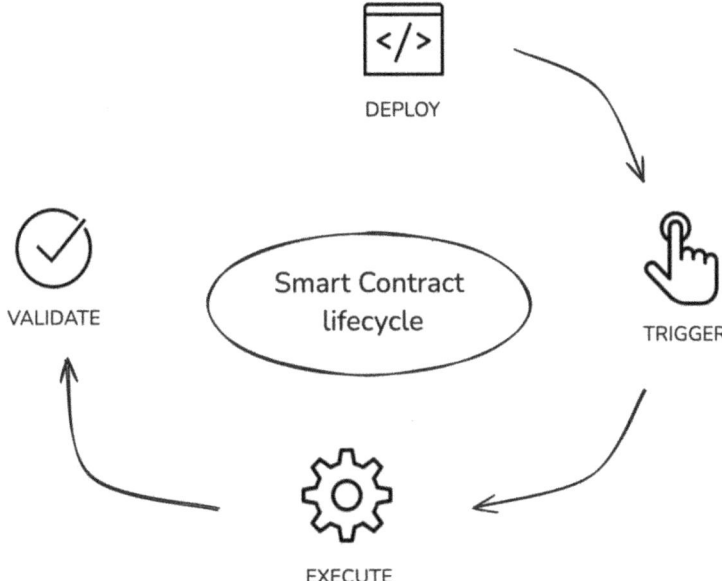

Figure 5-10. How Ethereum Smart Contracts Work

Ethereum Virtual Machine (EVM)

At the heart of Ethereum lies the Ethereum Virtual Machine (EVM), a decentralized computation engine.

195

The EVM plays a critical role:

- It standardizes the execution of smart contracts across different machines.
- It isolates contracts from each other to prevent one faulty contract from crashing the network.
- It ensures deterministic execution: every node should arrive at the same result after running the same contract.

The EVM is often called the global computer because, no matter where you are on the planet, every Ethereum node runs the same EVM code, ensuring global consensus (Figure 5-11).

To prevent abuse, Ethereum charges a fee for computation (measured in gas). This means that complex operations are more expensive, discouraging inefficient code and resource waste.

CHAPTER 5   BLOCKCHAIN APPLICATIONS

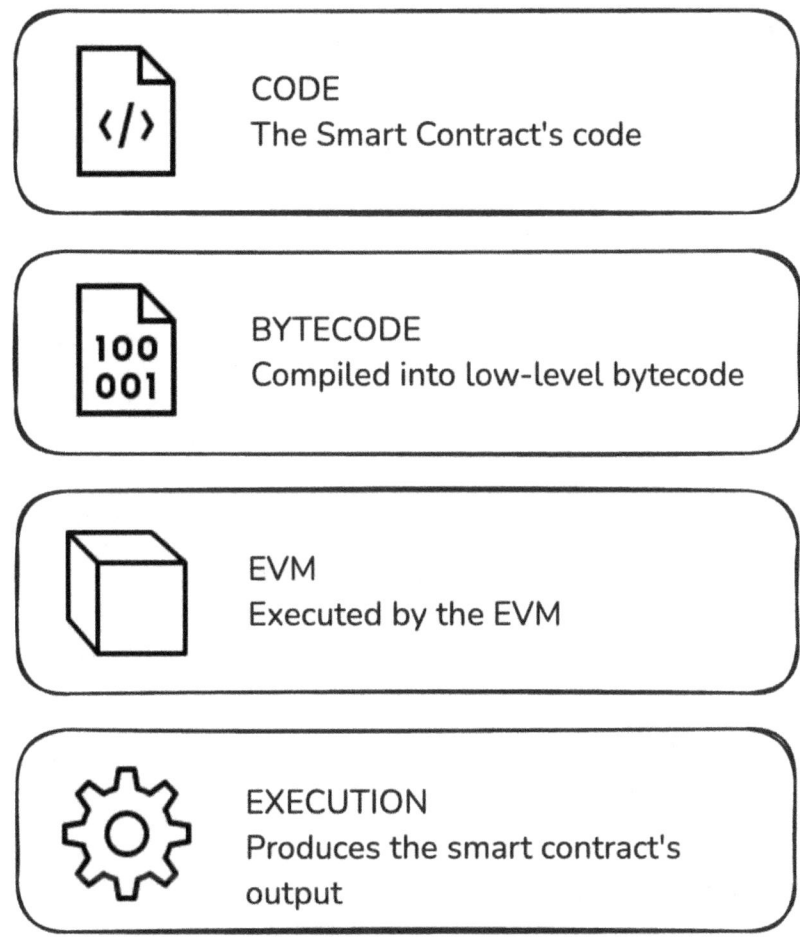

Figure 5-11. *The Ethereum Virtual Machine (EVM) in a Smart Contract Process*

Ether (ETH)

Ether (ETH) is the native currency of Ethereum, and it serves multiple essential purposes:

- **Transaction Fees:** Users pay ETH to submit transactions or deploy smart contracts.
- **Staking:** Validators stake ETH to secure the network in Ethereum 2.0 (Proof of Stake).

- **Value Transfer:** ETH functions like Bitcoin, as a store of value and medium of exchange.

Since the EIP-1559 upgrade in August 2021, part of every transaction fee is burned (destroyed), reducing the overall supply of ETH and potentially making it deflationary over time.

Gas System in Ethereum (Figure 5-12):

- **Base Fee:** Mandatory minimum fee burned by the network.
- **Tip:** Optional bonus for faster processing, paid to validators.

This two-tiered fee system stabilizes gas fees and incentivizes honest behavior among validators.

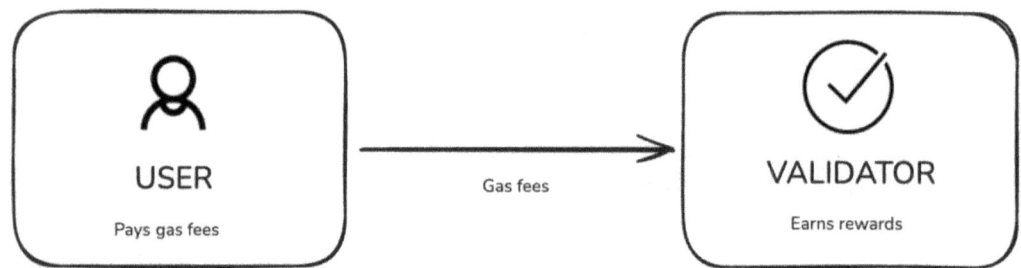

Figure 5-12. *Ether and the Gas System*

Proof of Stake (PoS)

Ethereum's transition to Proof of Stake (PoS) with The Merge in September 2022 marked one of the most important technological upgrades in blockchain history.

Under PoS:

- Validators are selected randomly to propose new blocks.
- Other validators attest (verify) that a proposed block is valid.
- Validators must stake ETH as a security deposit; bad behavior (like creating fraudulent blocks) results in losing part or all of the staked ETH (called slashing).

CHAPTER 5 BLOCKCHAIN APPLICATIONS

Impact of PoS:

- Reduced energy consumption by 99.95%.

- Increased accessibility: anyone can become a validator by staking ETH.

- Improved network security by introducing economic penalties for bad actors.

PoS rewards honest validators and penalizes dishonest ones. Figure 5-13 explains Ethereum's PoS consensus process.

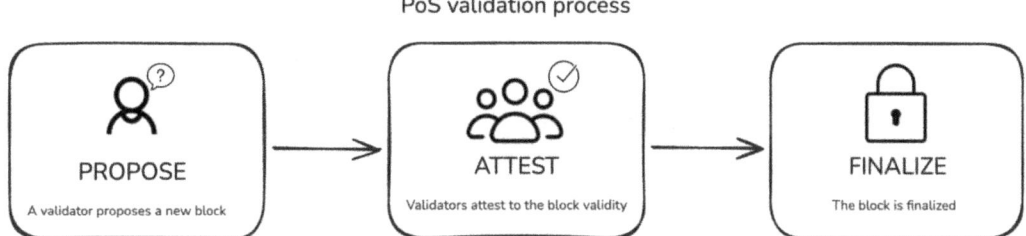

Figure 5-13. Ethereum Proof of Stake Process

Layer 2 Scaling Solutions

Ethereum's popularity has caused scalability bottlenecks, particularly high gas fees during periods of heavy use.

Layer 2 solutions offer a remedy. They process transactions off-chain (or semi-off-chain) before posting final results back to Ethereum's main chain.

Main Layer 2 Technologies:

- **Optimistic Rollups:** Assume transactions are valid and correct them if fraud is detected later.

    (Example: Optimism, Arbitrum)

- **ZK-Rollups:** Use zero-knowledge proofs to prove correctness without revealing transaction details.

    (Example: zkSync, StarkNet)

CHAPTER 5 BLOCKCHAIN APPLICATIONS

Layer 2 solutions:

- Increase transaction throughput (thousands of transactions per second).
- Drastically reduce fees.
- Maintain Ethereum's underlying security guarantees.

In short, Layer 2 scaling makes Ethereum affordable and scalable for global use.

Token Standards

Ethereum introduced standardized methods for creating digital tokens, enabling massive ecosystems of decentralized assets.

Main token standards (Table 5-5):

Table 5-5. *Token Standards and Their Use Cases*

Standard	Description	Use Cases
ERC-20	Fungible tokens (identical units)	Stablecoins (USDC), utility tokens (LINK)
ERC-721	Non-fungible tokens (unique units)	Art NFTs (CryptoPunks, BAYC)
ERC-1155	Hybrid tokens (both fungible and non-fungible)	Gaming assets, virtual real estate

These standards act like "universal languages" for creating digital assets. Developers can now avoid inventing new protocols for every token by following existing templates like ERC-20 or ERC-721, which ensures compatibility across wallets, exchanges, and DApps. This standardized approach not only accelerates innovation but also promotes interoperability, one of the pillars of Web3. Without these standards, building a tokenized economy would be chaotic and fragmented. Ethereum's presence led to an increase in creativity and commerce on the blockchain.

Real-world impact:

- ERC-20 enabled the ICO boom in 2017.
- ERC-721 fueled the NFT explosion from 2020 onward.
- ERC-1155 allowed flexible asset creation for games and marketplaces.

This transformation cannot be overstated. By offering standardized, programmable money and assets, Ethereum unlocked new digital markets that simply could not exist before. From global fundraising through ICOs to the explosion of digital art, gaming economies, and virtual real estate, Ethereum proved that decentralized ownership could thrive at scale. The repercussions of this go beyond cryptocurrency. It has impacted the way value is created, exchanged, and experienced online.

Ethereum Ecosystem and Community

Ethereum is a technology company that thrives on decentralization, not only in code but also in culture, unlike traditional tech companies with centralized leadership. Conferences like Devcon, hackathons like ETHGlobal, and online communities like Ethereum Magicians create an atmosphere where relentless innovation is encouraged. Figure 5-14 maps out the global Ethereum developer network.

Vitalik Buterin may be Ethereum's most famous voice, but the project's strength lies in its distributed collective: countless independent teams building, improving, and challenging the status quo.

This community-driven approach ensures that Ethereum evolves organically, based on the needs and dreams of its users rather than corporate mandates.

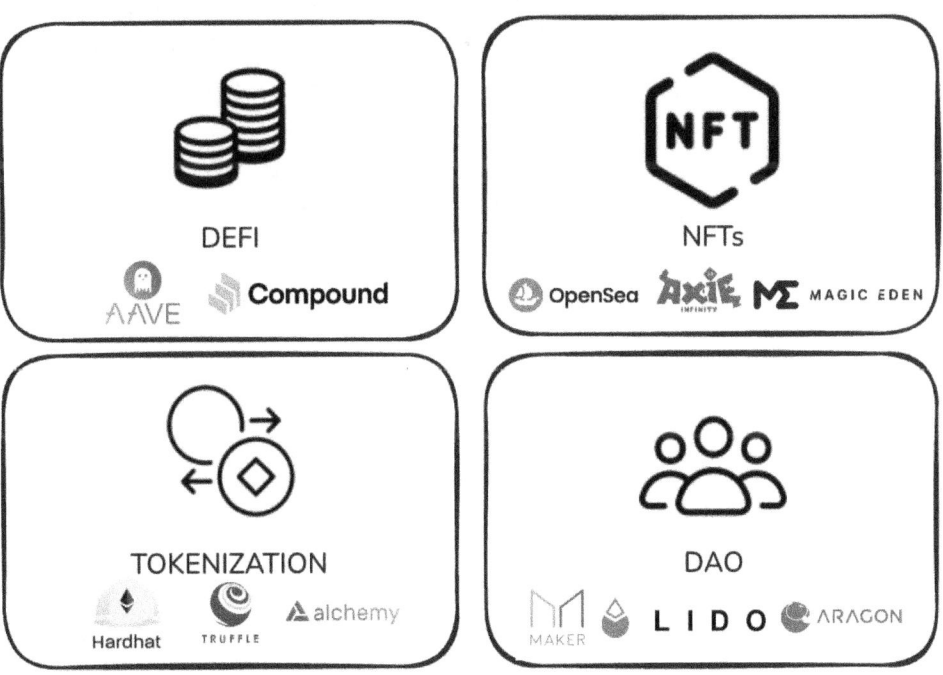

Figure 5-14. Ethereum Developer Tools

CHAPTER 5 BLOCKCHAIN APPLICATIONS

DeFi on Ethereum

Ethereum holds the title as the home of Decentralized Finance (DeFi).

In DeFi, traditional financial services are reimagined as decentralized protocols (Table 5-6):

Table 5-6. *DeFi Services on Ethereum*

Service	DeFi Examples	Description
Lending	Aave, Compound	Users earn interest or borrow against assets.
Trading	Uniswap, SushiSwap	Decentralized exchanges with automated liquidity.
Asset Management	Yearn.Finance	Automated yield optimization across protocols.

DeFi has created a parallel financial universe (Figure 5-15):

- No banks.

- No brokers.

In this new financial paradigm, users are no longer subject to arbitrary fees, account closures, or exclusion based on geography. Financial sovereignty is restored: a smartphone and an internet connection are all that's needed to participate. Smart contracts replace lawyers, escrow agents, and bankers, executing transactions transparently and automatically.

DeFi isn't just an alternative to traditional finance; it's a complete reinvention, offering efficiency, transparency, and accessibility that centralized systems struggle to match.

CHAPTER 5　BLOCKCHAIN APPLICATIONS

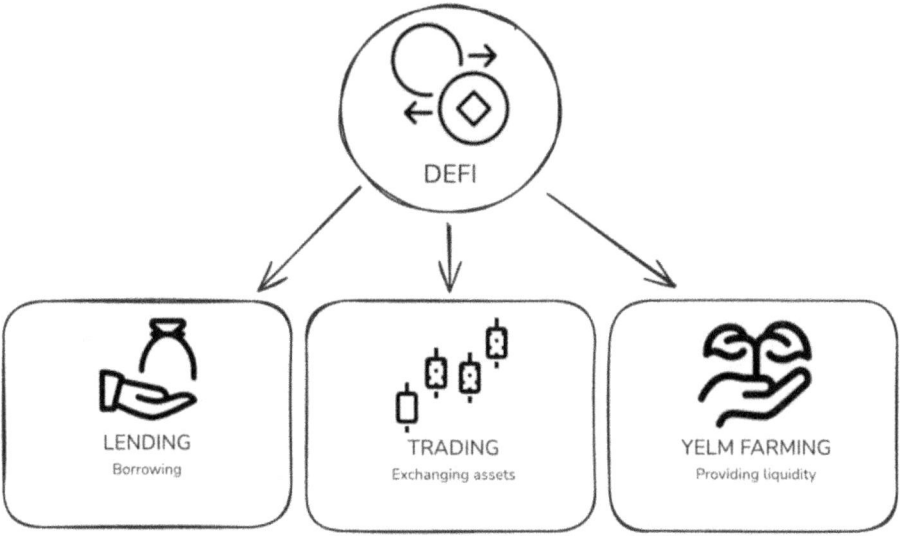

Figure 5-15. *DeFi Ecosystem on Ethereum*

NFTs and the Creator Economy

Ethereum's ERC-721 standard gave rise to the NFT revolution.
NFT Use Cases:

- Digital art (Beeple's $69M sale).

- Virtual real estate (Decentraland, The Sandbox).

- Music royalties and tickets.

- In-game assets with real-world value.

NFTs empowered creators by allowing direct monetization without relying on traditional gatekeepers like galleries, publishers, or labels. Figure 5-16 outlines real-world use cases for NFTs on Ethereum.

203

Chapter 5 Blockchain Applications

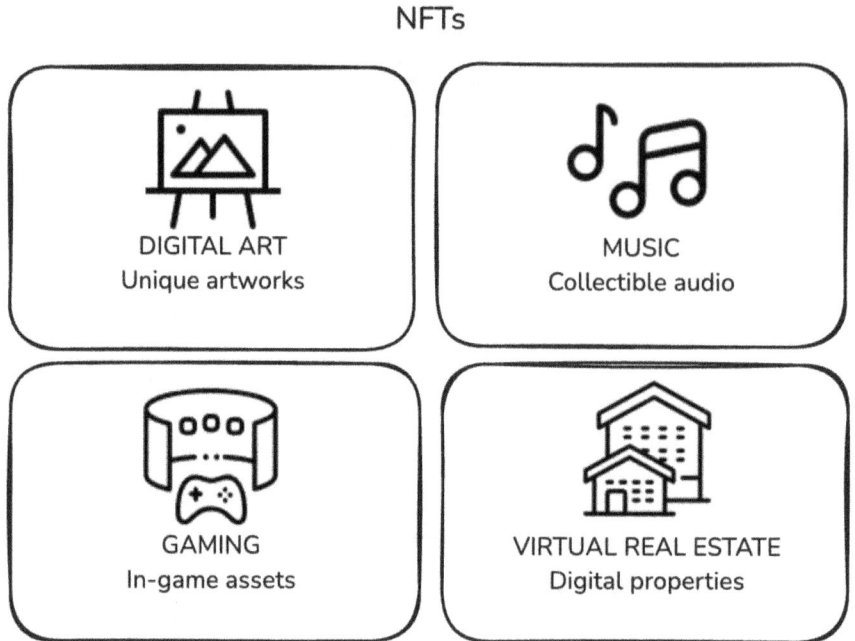

Figure 5-16. NFT Use Cases

DAOs and Decentralized Governance

Decentralized Autonomous Organizations (DAOs) are a new way for communities to govern themselves.

In a DAO:

- Members hold governance tokens.

- They propose and vote on decisions.

- Code enforces outcomes automatically.

DAOs are emerging in every field: investment clubs, nonprofits, protocol governance, and even journalism. Figure 5-17 visualizes how a DAO proposal and voting mechanism work.

Figure 5-17. DAO Governance Process

Developer Ecosystem

Ethereum glories:

- Thousands of active developers globally
- Dozens of annual hackathons (e.g., ETHDenver and ETHCC)
- Hundreds of open-source projects

The Ethereum developer ecosystem is often described as the largest and most active in the blockchain world. This critical mass of talent drives constant innovation, from Layer 2 scaling solutions to radical experiments in decentralized governance.

Open-source culture permeates the space, encouraging collaboration over competition. Every breakthrough, whether it be on zero-knowledge proofs, rollup technology, or user-friendly wallets, enhances the entire network. In many ways, Ethereum is not a project led by a company but an idea being collaboratively built by the world.

Ethereum's Future

Vitalik Buterin outlined Ethereum's ambitious roadmap (Table 5-7):

Table 5-7. Ethereum Roadmap Phases

Phase	Goal
Surge	Massive scaling through rollups and sharding.
Verge	Simplify storage with Verkle trees.
Purge	Clean up protocol complexity and historical data.
Splurge	Miscellaneous upgrades and improvements.

CHAPTER 5   BLOCKCHAIN APPLICATIONS

The goal is not only technical but also philosophical. Ethereum refuses to compromise on its founding values of openness, censorship resistance, and inclusivity, even as it faces the immense pressures of mass adoption. Scaling to millions of users means not just increasing raw throughput but doing so without creating new centralized bottlenecks. It demands elegant cryptographic innovations, global collaboration, and thoughtful governance. As Ethereum moves through each phase of its roadmap, it strives to achieve what no platform has done before: a truly decentralized, scalable, and resilient global infrastructure, capable of supporting finance, culture, governance, and creativity for generations to come.

Conclusion

Blockchain is no longer confined to the world of cryptocurrencies; it's becoming the foundational layer for a new internet: Web3. In this chapter, we explored how the transition from Web2's centralized platforms to Web3's decentralized architectures changes identity, ownership, and participation. From user-controlled wallets to tokenized content, blockchain redefines how individuals interact online.

Choosing the right blockchain is not a purely technical decision; it's a strategic one. It's important to strike a balance between scalability, security, decentralization, and community support. Ethereum stands out as a versatile platform, not only for its pioneering smart contracts but also for the thriving ecosystem it has enabled, from DeFi and NFTs to DAOs and developer innovation.

As we move forward, understanding these building blocks equips us to design applications that are more transparent, resilient, and user-empowered, core principles at the heart of the blockchain revolution.

Chapter Summary

Topic	Key takeaways
Web2 vs. Web3	Web2 is centralized and corporate-controlled; Web3 introduces decentralized infrastructure and user ownership.
User Experience	Web3 changes identity, payments, and content ownership, empowering users but requiring greater responsibility.
Industry Transitions	Case studies in social media, finance, and cloud storage demonstrate Web3's impact on traditional systems.
Blockchain Selection	Key factors include scalability, decentralization, developer ecosystem, and regulatory considerations.
Ethereum Architecture	Ethereum introduced smart contracts, the EVM, PoS consensus, and token standards for programmable assets.
DeFi, NFTs, DAOs	Ethereum powers decentralized financial protocols, creator economies, and community-led governance models.
Ecosystem and Future	Ethereum's large developer base and clear roadmap make it a cornerstone of blockchain innovation.

CHAPTER 6

Wallet

Introduction

As blockchain technology reshapes finance, identity, and ownership, the concept of a cryptocurrency wallet becomes central to interacting with this new decentralized world. In traditional banking, an individual's wealth is secured by trusted institutions. In the blockchain universe, individuals assume direct control and responsibility for their assets. Although this empowerment is revolutionary, it also presents new challenges, particularly the need for impeccable security and technical understanding.

A cryptocurrency wallet is not just a place to store coins. It is your gateway to managing digital assets, interacting with decentralized applications (DApps), signing transactions, participating in decentralized finance (DeFi), voting in governance systems, and safeguarding your digital identity. Proper wallet management is critical for both financial sovereignty and personal security in Web3.

In this chapter, we will deeply explore what cryptocurrency wallets are, how they function, the critical importance of mnemonic phrases, how public and private keys interplay, the various types of wallets available, and best practices for setting up and securing your digital life.

We will also highlight common mistakes, demystify technical terms, and prepare you for safe and effective participation in the blockchain ecosystem.

Understanding Cryptocurrency Wallets

In the world of blockchain and digital assets, the term "cryptocurrency wallet" is fundamental. Yet, for newcomers, the concept can often feel abstract or confusing. Unlike a leather wallet in your pocket, a cryptocurrency wallet does not physically hold coins or tokens. Instead, it acts as a secure portal, allowing you to access, manage, and transact your digital wealth on decentralized networks.

CHAPTER 6   WALLET

Understanding how wallets function is crucial because, in a decentralized world, there is no customer service hotline if you lose access. Ownership, security, and autonomy all converge inside this simple but powerful tool. In this section, we will explore what cryptocurrency wallets are, how they work, why they matter, and how they fit into the larger blockchain ecosystem.

What Is a Cryptocurrency Wallet?
Definition

At its core, a cryptocurrency wallet is a software program, hardware device, or even a paper artifact that stores **private and public keys**. These keys are essential to interact with a blockchain, manage your digital assets, and authorize transactions.

The wallet allows users to:

- **Send cryptocurrencies** to other addresses
- **Receive cryptocurrencies** securely
- **Store keys** safely over long periods
- **Sign and verify ownership** of digital assets

The crucial point: **The assets themselves always live on the blockchain**. The wallet merely manages your access to them.

Purpose

Cryptocurrency wallets fulfill several indispensable roles:

- **Authentication:** They verify that the person initiating a transaction is authorized to do so.
- **Authorization:** Wallets sign transactions to be broadcast onto the blockchain.
- **Security:** They protect your private keys from being exposed to external threats.

- **Identity:** In Web3 applications, your wallet address often doubles as your online identity.

- **Accessibility:** They make digital assets available for daily use, like trading, staking, or interacting with decentralized applications (DApps).

In short, a wallet is your personal "bank branch," "passport," and "keychain" to the blockchain.

How Wallets Work

Understanding the mechanics of wallets requires grasping two fundamental concepts: **asymmetric cryptography** and **blockchain interaction**.

Asymmetric Cryptography

Every wallet relies on a cryptographic system involving two keys (Figure 6-1):

- **Private Key:** A long, randomly generated string of characters that must remain secret. Whoever possesses this key can fully control the assets tied to it.

- **Public Key:** Derived mathematically from the private key. This is safe to share and serves as your receiving address.

CHAPTER 6   WALLET

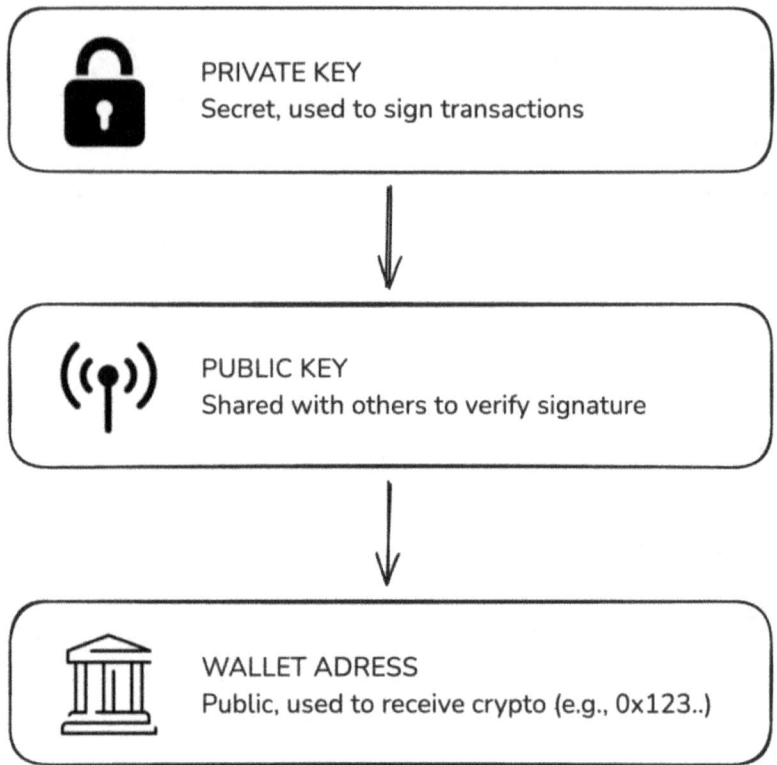

Figure 6-1. Cryptography in Wallets

When you create a wallet, the software generates these two keys. The **private key** must be guarded at all costs because losing it means losing access to your funds forever.

Transaction Process

Here's what happens during a cryptocurrency transaction:

1. You enter the recipient's address and the amount to send.
2. Your wallet software **signs** this information with your private key.
3. The signed transaction is broadcast to the blockchain network.
4. Blockchain nodes validate the signature and record the transaction.

CHAPTER 6   WALLET

Importantly, **your private key is never transmitted** during this process. Only the signature, derived from your private key, is exposed.

Types of Wallets

While the basic principles remain constant, there are several types of wallets, each catering to different needs. Hot and cold wallets are compared in Table 6-1.

1. **Hot Wallets**

    - **Definition:** Wallets connected to the internet.
    - **Examples:** Browser wallets (MetaMask), mobile wallets (Trust Wallet), and desktop wallets (Exodus).
    - **Pros:** Easy access, user-friendly.
    - **Cons:** Vulnerable to online attacks if not secured properly.

    Hot wallets are excellent for daily transactions but should not be used for long-term storage of large sums.

2. **Cold Wallets**

    - **Definition:** Wallets disconnected from the internet.
    - **Examples:** Hardware wallets (Ledger and Trezor), paper wallets.
    - **Pros:** Extremely secure against online threats.
    - **Cons:** Less convenient for frequent transactions.

Cold wallets are considered the gold standard for storing significant amounts of cryptocurrency.

Table 6-1. Comparison of Hot and Cold Wallets

Feature	Hot Wallets	Cold Wallets
Connectivity	Connected to the internet (e.g., web/mobile apps, browser extensions)	Completely offline (e.g., hardware wallets, paper wallets)
Security	More vulnerable to hacks, phishing, and malware	Safer from online attacks, but physical security is critical
Convenience	Easy to access and use for frequent transactions	Less convenient; ideal for long-term storage or large amounts
Cost	Usually free or low-cost	May require purchasing hardware (e.g., Ledger, Trezor)
Use Case	Daily spending, quick trades, DeFi interaction	HODLing, savings, cold storage of large funds
Recovery	Often tied to cloud backups or seed phrases	Seed phrase-based; physical loss could mean loss of access
Examples	MetaMask, Trust Wallet, Coinbase Wallet	Ledger Nano S/X, Trezor, Paper Wallets

Custodial vs. Non-custodial Wallets

Another important distinction:

- **Custodial Wallets:** A third party (like an exchange) holds your private keys.

    - You trust the platform to secure your assets.

    - Example: Coinbase wallet on the exchange platform.

- **Non-custodial Wallets:** Only you have access to the private keys.

    - You are solely responsible for your security.

    - Example: MetaMask, Trust Wallet.

CHAPTER 6 WALLET

"**Not your keys, not your coins.**" — A mantra in the crypto community emphasizing the importance of non-custodial control.

Importance of Wallet Security

It is crucial to manage a cryptocurrency wallet responsibly. Great power comes with great responsibility, which means you can't call customer service for help.
Key security practices:

- **Back up your recovery phrase** (mnemonic phrase) securely.
- **Use hardware wallets for significant funds.**
- **Enable two-factor authentication (2FA) whenever possible.**
- **Stay vigilant against phishing attacks.**
- **Never share your private key or recovery phrase.**

Real-World cautionary tale:
In 2021, over $100 million worth of cryptocurrency was stolen from users who fell victim to phishing scams impersonating popular wallet providers.

Common Misconceptions About Wallets

1. **"If I lose my wallet app, I lose my money."**
   - False. If you have your backup recovery phrase, you can restore your wallet on any compatible device.
2. **"Wallets store coins inside them."**
   - False. Wallets store private keys. Coins remain on the blockchain.
3. **"All wallets are equally safe."**
   - False. Poorly secured hot wallets are vastly riskier than hardware wallets.

215

Real-World Examples

- **Metamask:** A popular non-custodial browser extension wallet for Ethereum and EVM-compatible blockchains.
- **Ledger Nano X:** A cold storage hardware wallet highly regarded for security.
- **Trust Wallet:** A mobile wallet supporting a wide variety of assets.
- **Trezor Model T:** Another top-tier hardware wallet.

These examples show the diversity of choices available depending on whether a user prioritizes convenience or security.

Cryptocurrency wallets are much more than simple storage devices. They embody the very philosophy of decentralization: empowering individuals with direct control over their assets and identity.

Choosing the right wallet, understanding how it works, and practicing good security habits are critical steps for anyone engaging with blockchain technology. In a world without intermediaries, your wallet is your fortress, your passport, and your bank vault, all rolled into one.

Mnemonic Phrases and Their Importance

Security is essential in the world of cryptocurrency. Unlike traditional banking systems, where passwords can be reset and accounts can often be recovered through customer support, the decentralized nature of blockchain technology places full responsibility on the user. One of the most critical elements in securing a cryptocurrency wallet, and by extension, the digital assets it holds, is the mnemonic phrase.

What Is a Mnemonic Phrase?

Creating a new cryptocurrency wallet generates a mnemonic phrase, which is a sequence of typically **12, 18, or 24 words**. These words may seem random, but together, they encode all the cryptographic information necessary to regenerate your wallet's private keys and addresses. This system is based on the **BIP-39 standard**, which ensures that every word belongs to a pre-approved list of easy-to-write, hard-to-confuse English words.

Your mnemonic phrase is essentially your **master key**. It allows you to:

- Restore your wallet on any compatible device.
- Access all your funds and transaction history.
- Maintain full ownership, independent of any company, device, or nation.

Your crypto assets cannot be recovered without your mnemonic phrase, and there is no way to recover them through password reset, customer support ticket, or phone call. This concept can be shocking to those used to centralized systems, where assistance is always just a phone call away. In blockchain, finality is absolute: the ledger does not lie, and no entity has the power to reverse it. The harsh reality isn't a weakness; it's a characteristic, and it's a result of removing intermediaries and providing users with complete control. The upside is liberation from third-party risks; the downside is that the safety net is removed. You are the first and last line of defense. The role of mnemonic phrases is depicted in Figure 6-2.

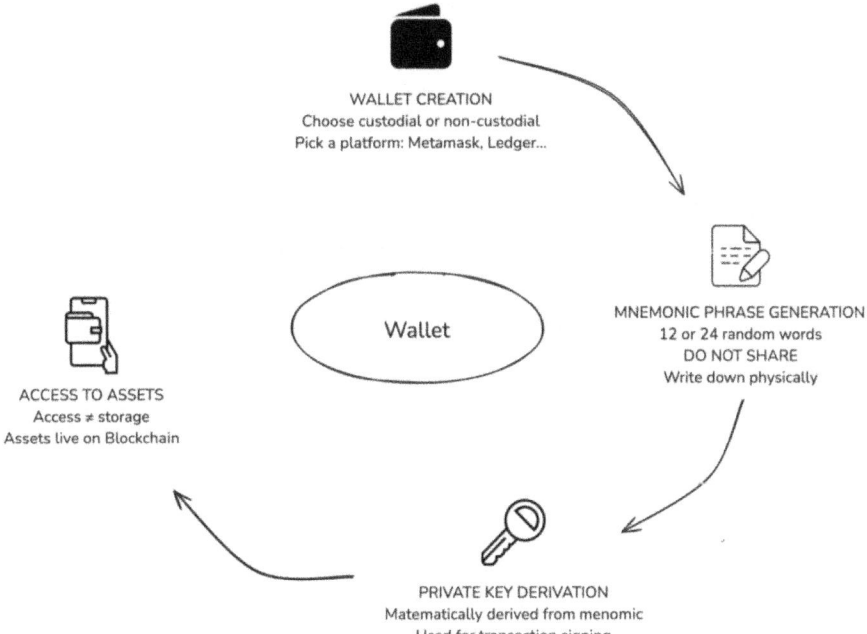

Figure 6-2. Wallet flow

CHAPTER 6   WALLET

Why Is It Important?

The mnemonic phrase is the sole method of recovery, not just a convenient option. Losing it means losing everything. This isn't an exaggeration; it's the fundamental rule of self-custody in Web3. Unlike traditional systems, there's no "forgot password" button and no customer support line to call. Security in this world must be **proactive**, not reactive.

This shift comes with a trade-off: **radical empowerment in exchange for radical responsibility**. You control your assets fully. But that also means you alone are responsible for securing them. A single point of failure, like exposing your mnemonic phrase, can result in total, irreversible loss.

Here's why your mnemonic phrase is so critical:

- **Backup and Recovery**: Devices fail. Phones get lost. Your mnemonic ensures your crypto assets aren't tethered to a single piece of hardware.

- **Portability**: Travel anywhere or switch devices; your assets follow with just 12 or 24 words.

- **Complete Ownership**: No government, company, or third party can access or confiscate your funds, unless you give them access.

This level of sovereignty is powerful, but it requires a new mindset. Think of your mnemonic phrase like **physical gold or bearer bonds**: valuable, irreplaceable, and vulnerable if left unsecured.

Many early users learned this the hard way. In the Web3 world, **personal vigilance is the price of financial freedom**. For those prepared, this autonomy is liberating. For the careless, it can be catastrophic.

Best Practices for Mnemonic Phrase Security

Your mnemonic phrase is more than just a password; it's the **key to a vault** that may hold life-changing sums of money, irreplaceable data, or personal identity proofs. Think of it as **both the map and the combination** to that vault. A failure at either level, losing it, or letting it fall into the wrong hands can result in irreversible loss.

Securing your mnemonic isn't a one-time task. It's an **active, ongoing responsibility** that should become part of your broader digital hygiene, just like renewing your insurance, backing up your files, or testing your smoke detectors.

Figure 6-3 shows recommended practices for securing your mnemonic phrase. This phrase deserves **physical**, **digital,** and **procedural** protection:

- Store it offline in a secure, fireproof location.
- Avoid photographing or typing it into internet-connected devices.
- Share it with no one, ever.

Your mnemonic is the backbone of your **financial sovereignty**. Treat it with the seriousness it demands.

Table 6-2 summarizes best practices.

Table 6-2. Best Practices for Mnemonic Phrase Security

Best Practice	Description
Write it down securely	Create multiple physical copies, avoid digital storage
Store in safe locations	Use safes, separate storage sites
Never share your phrase	Guard it like you would a treasure, assume any request is a scam
Consider sharding your backup	Split into parts stored separately
Regularly verify your backup	Check backups periodically to ensure readability and existence

Now, let's break down each best practice carefully. Table 6-2 summarizes best practices for securing mnemonic phrases.

1. **Write It Down Securely**

    At first, this might seem old-fashioned. In a world dominated by cloud storage, physical notes feel obsolete. However, storing your mnemonic phrase digitally exposes it to a vast array of online risks: malware, hackers, cloud breaches, phishing links, or device theft.

    Instead:

    - Write it legibly, using **archival-quality** pens and paper.

- Make **at least two physical copies**.
- **Double-check** each word; even one mistake can render the entire backup useless.

Some users go even further:

- **Metal Wallets:** Specialized steel sheets designed to survive fire, flood, and physical damage.

A properly written and preserved backup ensures that even in catastrophic scenarios, such as floods, fires, and thefts, your ability to recover your assets remains intact.

2. **Store in Safe Locations**

   One backup isn't enough. Two might not be either. In the world of irreversible crypto loss, **redundancy is non-negotiable**.

   Store **multiple copies** of your mnemonic phrase in **physically separated, secure locations**. A house fire, flood, or break-in should never be able to wipe out your entire recovery plan.

   If any backup is stored in a less secure environment, consider encrypting it. However, make sure the decryption method is well-documented and accessible to you when needed.

   Also consider **geopolitical risk**: in regions facing instability, it may be wise to store at least one copy **in another country**, providing protection from localized threats like political unrest or asset seizure.

   The goal is balance: maximum security without compromising recoverability. It's dangerous to have too little redundancy, but so is complexity without clarity.

3. **Never Share Your Phrase**

   Your mnemonic phrase is **never** meant to be shared. No legitimate service, including a wallet, exchange, or dApp, will ever require it. Not for support. Not for upgrades. Not for verification. **Never.**

   If someone asks for your seed phrase, they're trying to steal your assets. **No exceptions.**

Scammers often seem professional and convincing. Some pretend to be support agents. Others send emails, Discord messages, or popups mimicking trusted services. But they almost always want one thing: **your seed phrase**, the ultimate access key.

Treat it like a sacred secret. And if you help others onboard into crypto, teach them this rule. Most social engineering scams succeed not through technology, but through **ignorance**.

Remember:

- Emails, Discord messages, SMS, "support agents," or popup ads that request it are all scams.

4. **Consider Sharding Your Backup**

    For those seeking a higher level of protection, **sharding** your mnemonic phrase is a powerful strategy. This means **splitting your seed into multiple parts**, each stored in a different secure location.

    Examples:

    - Divide a 24-word phrase into two 12-word halves, each stored in separate cities.

    - Use **Shamir's Secret Sharing** to mathematically split the phrase into multiple shares, requiring a specific threshold (e.g., 2 out of 3) to reconstruct it.

    Benefits of Sharding:

    - A single compromised shard is **useless on its own**.

    - Attackers would need to locate **multiple secured locations** to access your full wallet.

    - Even natural disasters or thefts affecting one site won't compromise your assets.

    Think of it like placing valuables in **two locked safes in different buildings**: breaking into one gives nothing. The more **independent security hurdles** you introduce, the harder it becomes for anyone, including you, to make a costly mistake.

> **Important** If you use sharding, ensure that your reconstruction plan is clear, secure, and accessible, especially in an emergency.

5. **Regularly Verify Tour Backup**

   Creating a secure backup is essential, but **keeping it intact over time** is just as important. Physical degradation happens faster than most people expect. Paper can yellow, ink can fade, metal can corrode, and even bank vaults aren't immune to floods, fire, or humidity.

   Just like reviewing your insurance or updating your will, **check your wallet backups regularly**, ideally once or twice a year.

   What can go wrong:

   - Ink fades
   - Paper becomes brittle
   - Metal plates corrode in coastal or humid climates
   - Safe combinations are lost or forgotten

   What to do:

   - **Inspect** backups for readability and physical condition
   - **Restore** a wallet from your backup (on a secure, offline device) to ensure it still works
   - **Replace or rotate** materials that show signs of wear

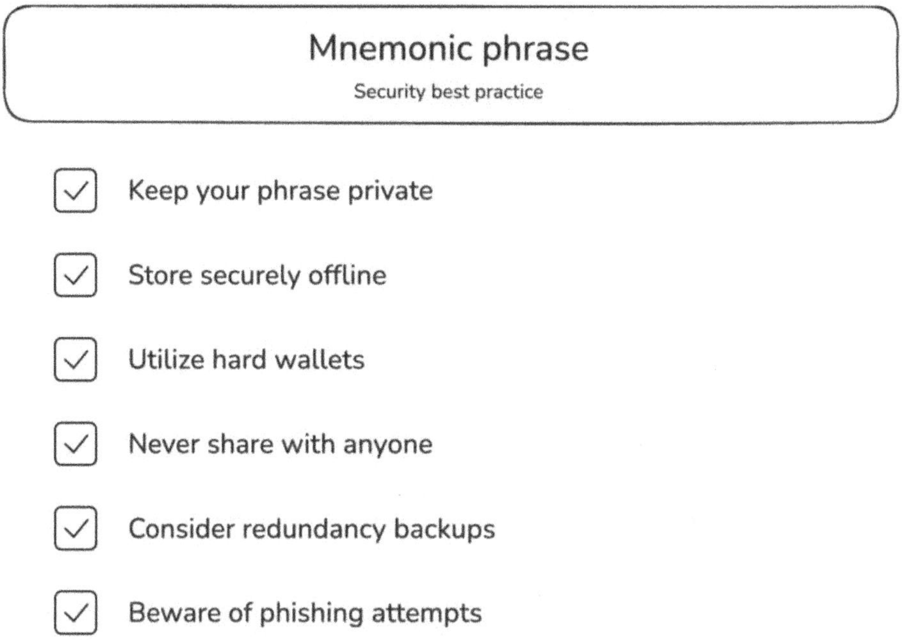

Mnemonic phrase
Security best practice

- [✓] Keep your phrase private
- [✓] Store securely offline
- [✓] Utilize hard wallets
- [✓] Never share with anyone
- [✓] Consider redundancy backups
- [✓] Beware of phishing attempts

Figure 6-3. Mnemonic Phrase Security Best Practices

Real-World Lessons: Horror Stories

The importance of securing a mnemonic phrase is often driven home by cautionary tales from the crypto community:

- **The Lost Drive**: A user accidentally threw away a hard drive containing the only copy of his Bitcoin wallet's mnemonic phrase, an estimated $300 million in lost Bitcoin.

- **The Phishing Scam**: Another user fell for a fake "wallet update" email, entering their mnemonic phrase into a fraudulent website. Within minutes, their wallet was drained.

These stories underline a grim but vital truth:

> **Responsibility in Web3 is binary; you either have complete control or none at all.**

There's no such thing as partial loss in crypto. You either retain full access to your cryptographic keys, or you lose everything.

Blockchain systems **don't recognize human error, forgotten passwords, or customer support tickets**. Their strength lies in this rigidity: decentralized networks operate under strict, incorruptible logic. There are no exceptions. No appeals. No authorities.

This can feel unforgiving, and it is. But it's also what makes Web3 systems **resilient, neutral, and tamper-proof**.

Ownership in crypto is binary:

- **You have your keys** → You have control.
- **You lose them** → You lose everything.

That's why securing your mnemonic phrase isn't a helpful tip; it's a **survival skill** in the decentralized world.

Advanced Security Techniques

As the crypto space matures, so do the tactics used to exploit it. What once passed for "good enough" security is now insufficient, especially for users managing significant funds or digital assets.

For those looking to move beyond the basics, a range of **advanced security strategies** offer deeper protection:

- **Multisignature wallets** for shared or distributed authorization
- **Hardware-based cold storage** to keep keys offline
- **Decoy wallets** (plausible deniability setups)
- **Sharded backups** stored across multiple geographic locations

These techniques represent the **new gold standard** for serious participants in the space.

But they come with a trade-off: **greater complexity can introduce new risks**, especially if procedures aren't clearly documented or regularly maintained. The key is finding the right balance between **security and usability**.

Encrypting Your Mnemonic

- Use passphrases (BIP-39 extensions) to add another layer to your recovery phrase.
- This is like setting an extra password that must be entered alongside the mnemonic to regenerate your wallet.
- Without the correct passphrase, the mnemonic phrase alone is useless.

Multi-signature Wallets

- Instead of a single key controlling the wallet, multiple keys are required to authorize a transaction.
- This is excellent for organizational setups (e.g., treasury management) or added redundancy for individuals.
- For example, you could require 2 out of 3 signatures to move funds, protecting against single-point failure.

Hidden Wallets

- Some users create **hidden wallets** layered within their main wallet, unlocked only with a specific password.
- This method provides a "decoy" wallet (containing small amounts) and a "hidden" wallet with the main holdings.
- In the event of coercion, a user could reveal the decoy wallet while keeping their true holdings safe.
- Wallets like BitBox and Ledger support such advanced setups.

Cold Storage Solutions

- For long-term holdings, storing mnemonic phrases and wallets completely offline (cold storage) is the gold standard.

CHAPTER 6   WALLET

- This could involve air-gapped computers or specialized hardware designed never to connect to the internet.
- Devices like Coldcard, Keystone, and custom-built air-gapped systems are popular choices.

Mnemonic phrases are the foundation of self-custody in the crypto world. They empower users with full ownership and access to their digital assets, but with great power comes great responsibility. Protecting your mnemonic phrase means protecting your financial freedom, your identity, and your place in the new digital economy.

Keys: Public and Private

At the heart of blockchain technology, beneath the layers of smart contracts, tokens, and decentralized applications, lies a critical and elegant system: public and private key cryptography. Without it, blockchain would simply not be possible. Every transaction, every ownership proof, and every digital signature relies on the unbreakable bond between a public key and a private key.

Understanding this pairing is essential for anyone wishing to interact securely and confidently in the blockchain world. Just as mnemonic phrases act as the ultimate recovery tool, public and private keys act as the mechanism of daily operation: they authenticate transactions, prove ownership, and protect your assets.

Definition and Differences

What Is a Private Key?

A **private key** is an ultra-sensitive, randomly generated alphanumeric code. It acts as a **master password**, not to a website or service, but to your actual wealth, identity, and digital existence on the blockchain.

Think of your private key as the equivalent of:

- The only key to a high-security vault.
- The only password to your sovereign digital identity.
- The only signature needed to validate powerful financial transactions.

Properties of a Private Key:

- It must remain secret and protected at all costs.
- It can generate (but not be reverse-engineered from) a corresponding public key.
- It is used to *sign* transactions, proving ownership and authorization.

The strength of a private key lies in mathematics: the probability of guessing a valid private key is so astronomically low (about 1 in 2^{128}) that it's effectively impossible, even with the combined computing power of the universe.

Technical Details:

- **Format:** 256-bit number (typically shown as 64 hexadecimal characters).
- **Example (truncated):** 0x1f5b1a8e9c46c3eabfe12c0b7db5b0e6c8af8283c35c5f7d96f6b0d9c5de7c4a

In simpler terms, your private key is your *power of attorney* over your digital assets. Lose it, and you lose everything. Expose it, and you invite irreversible theft.

What Is a Public Key?

The **public key** is generated directly from the private key through a one-way cryptographic function. While private keys must remain secret, public keys are designed to be shared freely.

Properties of a Public Key:

- It allows others to verify your signatures.
- It enables others to send you cryptocurrency or messages.
- It poses no danger if publicly exposed (as long as the private key remains secret).

The public key is like your **public-facing address**: people can know it, use it to interact with you, and trust it for communication or transactions, but they cannot use it to take anything away from you.

CHAPTER 6 WALLET

Technical Details:

- **Format:** Depending on the blockchain, public keys can be compressed or uncompressed.

- In Ethereum, public keys are often hashed further to generate shorter **wallet addresses** (40 hexadecimal characters prefixed by 0x).

Example Ethereum Address: 0x742d35Cc6634C0532925a3b844Bc454e4438f44e

Key Differences: Private vs. Public

While both private and public keys are fundamental to blockchain security, they serve distinct purposes. Table 6-3 summarizes the main differences between the two, highlighting their visibility, role in transactions, and importance in maintaining asset security. The differences between private and public keys are also outlined.

Table 6-3. Private Key vs. Public Key Differences

Feature	Private Key	Public Key
Visibility	Kept secret	Shared openly
Purpose	Authorizes transactions	Verifies transactions, receives funds
Criticality	Loss means total loss of assets	Loss can be recovered if private key is safe
Mathematical Relation	Basis for generating public key	Derived from private key
Role in Signature	Signs transactions	Verifies signatures

Why Is This System Brilliant?

This asymmetry, where one key can sign and another can verify, underpins the **trustless security model** of blockchains.

In traditional finance:

- Trust is placed in banks, auditors, and governments.

In blockchain:

- Trust is placed in **math and open code**.

- Transactions don't require approval from third parties; they require cryptographic proof.

Public and private keys make it possible to:

- Move money across the world without banks.
- Own property without relying on governments.
- Vote in decentralized organizations without fear of fraud.
- Authenticate identities without passwords or centralized databases.

They are the glue holding decentralized systems together.

Importance of Key Management

In traditional banking, losing access to your account might be an inconvenience, but a few forms and phone calls can recover your funds. In blockchain, **key management is absolute**: if you lose your private key, you lose access permanently. If your private key is stolen, your assets can be drained immediately and irreversibly.

This brutal finality underscores why managing your private key responsibly is one of the most critical skills in Web3.

Key management involves:

- **Secure Generation**: Always create wallets and keys through reputable, audited software. Never accept keys generated by online forms or third parties.
- **Safe Storage**: Private keys should never be stored in plain text, in email inboxes, on cloud services, or unencrypted on devices.
- **Access Control**: Only the wallet owner should have access to the private key. Never share it, not even with support teams or trusted individuals.
- **Backup Strategies**: Keys should be backed up securely, ideally offline, across multiple locations and, if possible, using advanced techniques like sharding or encryption.

- **Lifecycle Management**: If you suspect your key may have been exposed, migrate your funds immediately to a new wallet with freshly generated keys.

Common Key Management Strategies

Managing private keys effectively is essential for maintaining security and avoiding irreversible loss of funds. Different approaches offer varying levels of safety and convenience. Table 6-4 outlines common strategies for key management, their descriptions, and associated risk levels and also highlights common key management strategies with their risk levels.

Table 6-4. Key Management Strategies and Risks

Strategy	Description	Risk level
Memorizing keys	Remembering the private key manually.	Extremely risky (forgetfulness, mental error).
Writing keys on paper	Physical backup written on paper.	Risk of fire, theft, and fading.
Hardware wallet storage	Using devices like Ledger or Trezor.	Low (if the device is secured properly).
Air-gapped cold storage	Keeping keys entirely offline.	Very low, but complex setup.
Multi-signature solutions	Requiring multiple keys to approve a transaction.	Very low if configured properly.

Real-World Key Management Failures

The crypto world is filled with cautionary tales that illustrate the life-or-death importance of key management.

- **Mt. Gox Bankruptcy (2014)**:

    Though primarily a case of theft, many Mt. Gox users lacked personal wallet control, relying on the exchange to hold their private keys, and paid the ultimate price when the exchange collapsed.

- **Hard Drive Losses**:

    Countless users have lost fortunes by losing hardware wallets, misplacing computers, or failing to back up their keys. The famous case of James Howells, who lost 8,000 Bitcoin in a landfill, stands as a stark warning.

- **SIM-Swapping Attacks**:

    Hackers hijack phone numbers to access email and cloud backups, but if private keys are securely offline, such attacks are useless. Otherwise, they can lead to devastating thefts.

These stories reinforce a simple truth: **security practices must be airtight from day one**.

Advanced Key Management Strategies

For users securing significant assets or managing organizational wallets, additional techniques can offer enhanced security:

Multi-signature Wallets

- Require multiple private keys to authorize transactions.
- Example: "2 out of 3" wallets require 2 signatures out of 3 possible key holders.
- Adds redundancy and protection against single points of failure.

Hardware Wallets

- Devices like Ledger, Trezor, and Coldcard store private keys in secure environments isolated from the internet.
- Protects against malware, phishing, and most common attacks.

CHAPTER 6   WALLET

Air-Gapped Devices

- Wallets created and operated entirely offline.
- Private keys never touch internet-connected devices, drastically reducing the attack surface.

Hierarchical Deterministic (HD) Wallets

- HD wallets derive multiple addresses from a single master seed.
- Allow structured backups and easier management of multiple addresses without exposing the underlying private keys individually.

Owning cryptocurrency isn't just about holding digital coins — it's about assuming full custody of powerful cryptographic keys that secure your place in the decentralized world.

In Web3:

- **You are your keys.**
- **You are your wallet.**
- **You are your own bank.**

This is both the great promise and great peril of blockchain: ultimate freedom paired with ultimate responsibility.

Managing your keys properly is not optional — it is the price of admission into the world of true financial sovereignty.

Wallet Setup Process

Setting up a cryptocurrency wallet is the very first act of sovereignty in the blockchain world. The moment you leave centralized custodianship, which is the domain of banks, brokers, and tech giants, and enter personal financial freedom.

Yet, with freedom comes complexity and responsibility. Wallet setup is not a trivial process like signing up for an email account. Done improperly, it can expose you to irreversible loss, theft, or frustration. Done correctly, it builds a strong, private foundation for everything you will do in Web3.

In this section, we walk through the wallet creation process meticulously, highlighting not only *what* to do but also *why* it matters. We'll also explore the common traps that newcomers fall into and how to avoid them, ensuring you move into the world of decentralized ownership fully prepared.

Step-by-Step Guide to Setting Up a Wallet

Whether you are setting up a mobile wallet, a browser extension wallet, or a hardware wallet, the general principles remain the same. Let's break it down:

Step 1: Choose Your Wallet Type

Before setting anything up, you must first decide what kind of wallet suits your needs.

Table 6-5. Comparison of Wallet Types (Hardware, Software, and Paper)

Wallet Type	Description	Ideal for
Software wallet	Apps or browser extensions like MetaMask, Trust Wallet.	Beginners, light everyday use.
Hardware wallet	Physical devices like Ledger, Trezor.	Long-term storage, larger amounts.
Paper wallet	Mnemonic, or private key, is printed/stored offline.	Cold storage with high manual control.
Custodial wallet	Managed by third parties (exchanges).	High convenience but no true ownership.

Important Decision: Choosing between convenience and control. Self-custody (software or hardware wallets) offers full control but requires vigilance. Custodial wallets sacrifice control for ease, at the cost of true sovereignty.

Step 2: Install and Verify the Wallet Software/Device

- **Software Wallets:**
    - Download from the official website or app store.
    - Verify authenticity by checking for official reviews, website HTTPS certificates, and published checksums.

CHAPTER 6   WALLET

- **Hardware Wallets:**
  - Order **directly from the manufacturer** or trusted vendors.
  - Always check packaging for tampering.
  - Perform firmware updates directly from official sources.

Why This Matters: Fake wallets and tampered devices are a favorite tool of hackers. Installing from unofficial sources can silently expose your private keys during setup.

Real-World Example: In 2021, Ledger users reported phishing scams where attackers sent fake replacement devices claiming they needed an urgent update, stealing private keys from unsuspecting users.

Step 3: Create a New Wallet

Upon first opening the wallet software or device, you'll be prompted to:

- **Create a new wallet** or
- **Import an existing wallet** (using mnemonic phrase)

Choose **Create New Wallet** if starting fresh.

At this stage:

- The system generates your **private key** and **public key** internally.
- The **mnemonic phrase** will be shown. Usually **12, 18, or 24 words**.

You are now entering the most critical moment of the process.

Step 4: Back Up Your Mnemonic Phrase

The wallet will **display the mnemonic phrase once**, usually with strong warnings to write it down.

DO NOT:

- Screenshot it.
- Save it in cloud storage.
- Email it to yourself.
- Copy it to the clipboard without care.

INSTEAD:

- **Write it down carefully** on paper.
- **Verify** spelling and word order.
- **Create multiple backups** if possible.

Key Insight: You are now the sole guardian of your assets. This is your bank, your vault, and your passport to Web3.

Step 5: Confirm Your Mnemonic Phrase

Most wallets will **test** you immediately:

- Asking you to re-enter some or all the words in the correct order.
- This ensures you have backed up the phrase accurately.

Take this seriously: This step is not a formality. It catches errors now, when they can be fixed, rather than later, when they could cause irreversible loss.

Step 6: Set a Strong Password (If Available)

Many software wallets add an **additional layer** of password protection for daily access:

- Encrypts access to the local app or device.
- Adds protection against unauthorized access if your device is stolen.

Password Best Practices:

- Use long, random, complex passwords.
- Store passwords separately from the device (password manager or physical storage).
- Avoid using the same password as other services.

Example of a Strong Password: F3!rS4nm8#Aq9zT!Yx7vBqW@p

Note This password protects the interface, **not the blockchain access itself**. If someone has your mnemonic, your password won't matter. But a password buys valuable time and complexity.

Step 7: Customize Wallet Settings

Once inside your new wallet:

- **Set network preferences** (e.g., Ethereum mainnet, testnets, and Binance Smart Chain).
- **Enable security settings** like biometric locks (Face ID and fingerprint).
- **Label accounts** for easier tracking.
- **Create multiple accounts** if planning to use wallets for different purposes (investment, trading, and saving).

Important Tip Separate operational wallets (for frequent use) from cold storage wallets (for long-term holdings).

Step 8: Test with a Small Transaction

Before depositing large sums:

- Send a **small amount** of cryptocurrency (like $5 worth) to your new address.
- Confirm it arrives.
- Try **sending it back** to a known account.

This real-world testing verifies:

- The wallet is functional.
- The mnemonic works.
- You understand how to send and receive securely.

Remember: The best time to discover problems is before real money is at risk.

Common Pitfalls and Solutions

1. **Rushing the Setup**

   Mistake: Clicking "next" blindly during wallet setup, skipping mnemonic backup or security warnings.

   Consequence: Losing access if the device crashes, the app uninstalls, or data is wiped.

   Solution: Slow down. Treat wallet setup like setting up a secure vault, not installing a game.

2. **Saving the Mnemonic Digitally**

   Mistake: Saving the recovery phrase in cloud storage, email drafts, or even text messages.

   Consequence: Hackers target online repositories and phishing links to harvest these keys.

   Solution: Only store backups **offline**: paper, metal plates, and secure offline devices.

3. **Underestimating Physical Risks**

   Mistake: Keeping the only written backup in one house vulnerable to fire, flood, or theft.

   Consequence: Total asset loss if disaster strikes.

   Solution: Distribute backups across different secure physical locations.

4. **Falling for Fake Wallets**

   Mistake: Downloading wallets from unofficial sources or random app stores.

   Consequence: Phishing or malware that steals your private key during setup.

   Solution: Always verify the source. Bookmark official websites. Use wallet apps vetted by the community.

5. **Losing Passwords**

   Mistake: Using weak passwords or forgetting the password that locks your wallet interface.

   Consequence: Exposure to physical theft or frustration in accessing assets.

   Solution: Use strong, unique passwords. Store them securely using trusted methods.

   Setting up a wallet is **an act of self-empowerment**. Just like using any powerful tool, from fire to encryption, it requires respect.

Your entire crypto journey is shaped by the small choices made during setup, such as where you write your mnemonic, how you secure backups, and how you test your transactions.

In blockchain, mistakes are final. But so are victories. Once properly configured, your wallet becomes your passport to a new digital frontier: a realm where you, and only you, control your wealth, identity, and destiny.

In Web3, you don't create an account. You create your own sovereign presence.

Types of Wallets

Cryptocurrency wallets come in many forms, each offering different balances between **security**, **accessibility**, and **user experience**.

Choosing the right wallet type is like choosing the right kind of safe:

- A desktop wallet is like a lockbox in your home, convenient but exposed.

- A hardware wallet is like a fortified vault, highly secure but slightly less accessible.

- The ultimate offline security is achieved by burying a paper wallet, but it is vulnerable to physical degradation.

Understanding the types of wallets available and when and why to use them is fundamental to mastering personal crypto security.

Hardware Wallets

What Is a Hardware Wallet?

A hardware wallet is a **physical device** designed to **securely store your private keys** offline. Rather than exposing keys to potentially infected computers or mobile devices, hardware wallets isolate cryptographic operations within a tamper-proof chip.

Think of it as **a vault in your pocket**: Even if your laptop is hacked, your crypto remains safe because your private key never leaves the hardware device.

Popular Examples:

- Ledger Nano S, Ledger Nano X
- Trezor Model T, Trezor One
- BitBox02
- Keystone Pro

How Hardware Wallets Work

When you initiate a transaction (e.g., sending Ethereum), the steps are:

1. The transaction details are sent **to the hardware wallet**.
2. **Inside the device**, the transaction is signed using your private key.
3. The signed transaction (but **not** your private key) is sent back to your computer or phone and broadcasted to the blockchain.

Important Insight: The private key **never** touches the internet, even for a second.

Advantages of Hardware Wallets

Hardware wallets offer several benefits that make them the preferred choice for securely storing cryptocurrencies, particularly for long-term holdings or large balances. Table 6-6 summarizes their main advantages:

Table 6-6. *Advantages of Hardware Wallets*

Advantage	Description
Maximum Security	Offline storage shields keys from online threats like phishing, malware, and viruses.
Resistance to Tampering	Most devices are physically hardened and encrypted.
Multi-currency Support	Manage Bitcoin, Ethereum, NFTs, and thousands of tokens in one device.
Recovery Flexibility	Restore your wallet using your mnemonic phrase if the device is lost or damaged.

Disadvantages of Hardware Wallets

Despite their strong security, hardware wallets also present some drawbacks that may affect usability or cost. Table 6-7 highlights these disadvantages:

Table 6-7. *Disadvantages of Hardware Wallets*

Disadvantage	Description
Cost	Typically, between $50 and $250.
Setup Complexity	More steps and security measures compared to simple apps.
Accessibility	Requires carrying or accessing the device for every transaction.
Physical Risk	Device loss, theft, or damage still requires proper backup planning.

When to Use a Hardware Wallet

- Holding significant sums (> $1,000) for the medium or long term.
- Active DeFi users managing multiple protocols.
- NFT collectors wanting to protect valuable digital art.
- Builders and developers working in Web3 ecosystems.

Real-World Example

During the massive DeFi boom of 2021, multiple users with browser extension wallets (like MetaMask) fell victim to phishing attacks. However, users who linked their MetaMask to a hardware wallet avoided total loss because **transactions could not be signed** without physical confirmation on the device itself.

Key Takeaway: Even if your hot wallet (online wallet) is compromised, a hardware wallet acts as a final line of defense.

Software Wallets

What Is a Software Wallet?

A software wallet is a **program** or **application** that stores your private keys on your computer or mobile device. They are the most common form of wallet, offering **ease of use** and **instant access** to crypto assets.

Popular Examples:

- MetaMask (browser extension and mobile app)
- Trust Wallet (mobile)
- Exodus (desktop and mobile)
- Rainbow Wallet (Ethereum-focused)

How Software Wallets Work

Unlike hardware wallets, software wallets keep the private keys **within the device memory** or **encrypted local storage**.

When you send a transaction:

1. The wallet software signs the transaction **directly** on your device.
2. The signed transaction is broadcast to the blockchain.

Because your device is connected to the internet, this makes software wallets **convenient but inherently more vulnerable**.

CHAPTER 6   WALLET

Advantages of Software Wallets

Software wallets are popular due to their accessibility and flexibility. They enable users to quickly interact with decentralized applications and manage multiple assets at no cost. Table 6-8 outlines their primary advantages:

Table 6-8. *Advantages of Software Wallets*

Advantage	Description
Convenience	Quick access for frequent trading, NFT minting, and dApp interactions.
Free to use	Most wallets are open-source and cost nothing to install.
Multi-chain capabilities	Manage assets across different blockchains easily.
Integrated dApp browsers	Many wallets allow direct interaction with decentralized apps inside the wallet.

Disadvantages of Software Wallets

While convenient, software wallets introduce certain risks, especially since they operate on internet-connected devices. Table 6-9 summarizes the main disadvantages:

Table 6-9. *Disadvantages of Software Wallets*

Disadvantage	Description
Exposure to malware	Private keys reside on devices connected to the internet.
Social engineering risks	Phishing links, fake wallets, and impersonation attacks.
Device loss or failure	If backups aren't properly made, wallet access can be lost.
Permission complexity	Authorizing smart contract interactions can expose tokens if users approve malicious contracts unknowingly.

When to Use a Software Wallet

- Frequent traders who need fast transaction access
- New users exploring DeFi, NFTs, or staking
- Daily interactions with decentralized apps (dApps)

Pro Tip If using a software wallet, **pair it with a hardware wallet** whenever possible for signing critical transactions.

Real-World Example

Many early adopters of NFTs during the 2021 bull run minted new tokens directly through MetaMask connected to OpenSea. While highly convenient, this led to frequent phishing scams; fake mint sites tricked users into granting approvals to malicious contracts.

Lesson: Software wallets demand constant vigilance in checking what permissions are being granted.

Paper Wallets

What Is a Paper Wallet?

A paper wallet is a **physical printout** of a private key and public address. It is one of the oldest forms of "cold storage," a way to keep crypto assets completely offline.

At its core, a paper wallet is nothing more than a piece of paper containing:

- Your public address (to receive funds)
- Your private key (to access and spend funds)

CHAPTER 6   WALLET

How Paper Wallets Work

After generating a paper wallet (typically offline):

- You can **send** funds **to** the public address.
- To **spend** or **move** the funds, you must **import** the private key into a software wallet and sign transactions from there.

Advantages of Paper Wallets

Paper wallets provide one of the simplest and most secure ways to store cryptocurrency completely offline. Table 6-10 summarizes their main advantages:

Table 6-10. *Advantages of Paper Wallets*

Advantage	Description
Total offline storage	Immune to online hacks, malware, or phishing.
Cost-free	Requires no special device or software beyond generation tools.
Simplicity	No software updates or device maintenance needed.

Disadvantages of Paper Wallets

Despite their offline security, paper wallets come with significant risks and limitations. Table 6-11 highlights these disadvantages:

Table 6-11. *Disadvantages of Paper Wallets*

Disadvantage	Description
Fragility	Paper can tear, burn, fade, or be stolen easily.
Complexity of spending	Must be imported into a hot wallet to spend, reintroducing online exposure.
Risk of theft	If anyone finds the paper, they can access your funds without additional security.
Generation risks	Must be created offline; online generation can expose private keys to malware.

When to Use a Paper Wallet

- Long-term holding of small to moderate crypto balances.
- Gifting cryptocurrency securely.
- Archival storage where digital systems are undesirable.

Important Caution   If you use paper wallets, **generate them completely offline**, preferably using an air-gapped computer running a secure, open-source generator.

Real-World Example

Bitcoin "gift cards" using paper wallet formats were popular in the early days of Bitcoin (2011–2015). However, improperly generated wallets, using online services, led to major thefts once users realized their private keys had been compromised.

Lesson: Paper wallets offer ultimate offline protection **only if** properly generated and stored securely.

Comparing Wallet Types

Choosing the right wallet type requires balancing security, convenience, and intended use. Table 6-12 compares the main characteristics of hardware, software, and paper wallets:

Table 6-12. Comparison of Wallet Types (Hardware, Software, and Paper)

Feature	Hardware Wallet	Software Wallet	Paper Wallet
Security	Highest (offline keys)	Moderate (online keys)	Highest (offline, if generated securely)
Cost	$50–$250	Free	Free (except printing costs)
Accessibility	Medium	High	Low
Risk	Physical loss/theft	Malware, phishing	Physical degradation/theft
Best use	Large, long-term holdings	Daily interactions, frequent trading	Cold storage, gifts

Choosing the right type of wallet is **personal**. It depends on your financial goals, technical comfort level, risk tolerance, and intended use cases.

If you're investing serious capital, a hardware wallet is not optional; it's essential. **If you're learning and experimenting,** start with a software wallet, but secure your mnemonic carefully. **If you're building cold storage for future generations,** consider secure paper wallets or advanced multi-signature setups.

Conclusion

Cryptocurrency wallets are the cornerstone of digital asset ownership in the blockchain era. Unlike traditional banking, where third parties safeguard your funds, wallets place full control and responsibility into your hands. From managing public and private keys to securing mnemonic phrases and choosing the right wallet type, each decision determines the safety and accessibility of your assets.

Mastering wallets is not just about storing coins; it's about understanding sovereignty in Web3. With proper setup, vigilant security practices, and thoughtful use of tools like hardware wallets or multisignature solutions, you can protect your digital identity and confidently navigate decentralized ecosystems.

Chapter Summary

Topic	Key takeaways
Definition of Wallet	Manages public/private keys and gateway to blockchain assets, not physical storage of coins.
Asymmetric Cryptography	Private keys sign transactions, public keys verify them, and assets stay on-chain.
Hot vs. Cold Wallets	Hot wallets are online and convenient but less secure; cold wallets are offline and ideal for long-term storage.
Custodial vs. Non-Custodial	Custodial wallets rely on third parties; non-custodial wallets give full ownership and responsibility to the user.
Mnemonic Phrases	Critical for wallet recovery, losing it means losing access permanently.
Public and Private Keys	Core cryptography ensures secure, trustless transactions.
Wallet Setup Process	Step-by-step procedure including secure backup, password protection, and test transactions.
Types of Wallets	Hardware, software, and paper wallets offer different balances of security and accessibility.
Advanced Security Techniques	Multisignature wallets, hidden wallets, sharding backups, and cold storage enhance protection.
Key Management	Proper handling of keys prevents irreversible loss and ensures true financial sovereignty.

CHAPTER 7

Provider

Introduction

Blockchain technology, at its core, promises decentralization, transparency, and self-sovereignty. Interacting with a blockchain network involves technical procedures that require specific knowledge, hardware, and ongoing maintenance. This is where **providers** come in. Providers form the essential infrastructure layer that connects decentralized networks with the users, applications, and developers that rely on them. They are the unsung heroes of the Web3 movement, quietly handling the complex backend operations that enable seamless blockchain interactions.

Without providers, mass adoption of blockchain technology would be virtually impossible. Every user would be forced to run their own full node, a process that demands significant computational resources and expertise. Instead, providers abstract these complexities, offering standardized, reliable, and often user-friendly interfaces to blockchain ecosystems.

In this chapter, we will dive deep into the world of providers: their roles, types, security considerations, key differences between wallet and RPC providers, and how their design choices shape the future of blockchain technology.

Role of Providers in Blockchain

Providers are the silent engines that power nearly every interaction users have with blockchain networks.

Whether minting an NFT, swapping tokens on a decentralized exchange (DEX), participating in decentralized finance (DeFi), or simply checking a wallet balance, every blockchain operation relies, directly or indirectly, on one or more providers.

CHAPTER 7   PROVIDER

Understanding what providers are, the different types that exist, and why they matter is fundamental to mastering blockchain development and architecture.

What Is a Provider?

At its core, a **provider** is a service or software component that acts as an intermediary between two parties (Figure 7-1):

- A **client** (which could be a user, application, or smart contract platform interface)
- A **blockchain network** (such as Ethereum, Polygon, Arbitrum, or Solana)

Providers abstract away the technical complexities of directly communicating with decentralized networks.

They expose standardized interfaces, typically through protocols like **JSON-RPC**, **GraphQL**, **WebSocket,** or **gRPC**, that allow applications to:

- **Read blockchain state** (e.g., query account balances)
- **Submit transactions** (e.g., transfer tokens and interact with smart contracts)
- **Listen to blockchain events** (e.g., when an NFT is transferred)

Without providers, users and applications would have to operate their own full blockchain nodes, an impractical requirement for most.

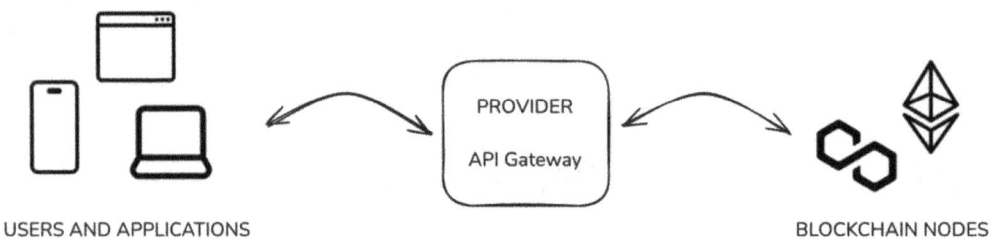

Figure 7-1. Providers as bridges between clients and blockchain networks

Why Providers Are Needed

Blockchain networks are distributed, complex systems:

- Nodes must **validate** transactions independently.
- Data must be **synchronized** across the entire network.
- State queries often require traversing large datasets (especially with smart contracts).

Running a full node:

- Requires significant storage (Ethereum full node ≈ 1–2TB as of 2025)
- Needs stable, high-bandwidth internet
- Demands constant maintenance (software upgrades, security patches)

By using providers, dApps and wallets can

- **Outsource** the heavy lifting of running nodes.
- **Accelerate** development cycles.
- **Improve** application uptime and performance.

Historical Evolution of Providers

In the early days of blockchain (2014–2017), developers interacted with networks like Bitcoin or Ethereum directly by running local nodes:

- **Bitcoin Core** clients for Bitcoin
- **Geth** or **Parity (OpenEthereum)** clients for Ethereum

This model, while decentralized, was

- **Technically difficult** for non-specialists
- **Resource intensive** for applications needing real-time access
- **Error-prone** due to protocol upgrades (e.g., Ethereum hard forks)

CHAPTER 7   PROVIDER

Recognizing the friction, companies like Infura, a well-known blockchain infrastructure provider, emerged.

Infura allowed developers to interact with Ethereum without maintaining local infrastructure, simply by sending HTTPS requests to their cloud-managed Ethereum nodes.

This innovation catalyzed the first **Web3 boom**:

- ICOs of 2017
- Early DeFi protocols (e.g., MakerDAO)
- NFT experiments (e.g., CryptoKitties)

Today, the provider landscape has expanded massively, supporting dozens of Layer 1 and Layer 2 networks, specialized indexing, transaction relaying, enhanced APIs, and privacy-preserving technologies. The historical growth of providers is illustrated in Figure 7-2.

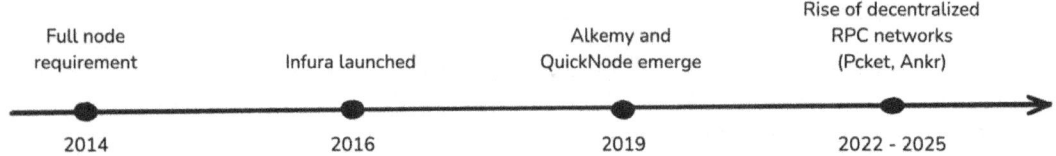

Evolution of Providers

Figure 7-2. *Evolution of Providers in Blockchain*

Types of Providers

Providers specialize based on the needs they serve.

While all providers act as blockchain intermediaries, their specific functions vary widely.

Let's explore each major type in detail.

Full Node Providers

Full Node Providers run blockchain clients (e.g., Geth, Besu, and Erigon) and expose their full functionality without significant abstraction.

These nodes:

- Validate all blocks independently
- Maintain the entire blockchain history
- Enable trust-minimized querying and transaction submission

Figure 7-3 illustrates a typical full node provider setup.

Advantages:

- Maximum decentralization
- Direct protocol compliance (no middle layers)
- Full archive access (essential for certain DeFi protocols)

Challenges:

- High hardware costs (SSDs, memory, bandwidth)
- Operational complexity (e.g., handling Ethereum upgrades like Cancun and Dencun)

Examples:

- Self-hosted Geth node
- Blockdaemon full node services

Figure 7-3. Full Node Provider Setup

RPC Providers (Remote Procedure Call Providers)

Most dApps use **RPC providers** to interact with blockchains via lightweight protocols. RPC providers:

- Abstract away node complexity
- Offer fast read/write access to blockchain data
- Scale horizontally to serve thousands of concurrent users

Standard RPC methods (Ethereum example):

- *eth_blockNumber*: Latest block number
- *eth_getBalance*: Wallet balance
- *eth_call*: Smart contract read without gas cost
- *eth_sendRawTransaction*: Broadcast signed transactions

Table 7-1 lists common Ethereum RPC methods.

Each transaction executed through these RPC calls consumes **gas**, the unit of computational cost required by the Ethereum Virtual Machine (EVM). Gas ensures fair compensation for node operators and prevents network abuse like infinite loops. *(See Chapter 8 for a more detailed explanation of gas and gas optimization techniques.)*

Examples:

- **Infura** (Ethereum, IPFS)
- **Alchemy** (Ethereum, Polygon, Arbitrum, Optimism)
- **QuickNode** (Multi-chain)

Table 7-1. Common RPC Methods for Ethereum

Method	Description
eth_blockNumber	Returns the number of the most recent block
eth_getBalance	Fetches the balance of an address
eth_getTransactionByHash	Retrieves a transaction by its hash
eth_sendRawTransaction	Submits a signed transaction for broadcast
eth_call	Executes a new call without creating a transaction
net_version	Returns the current network ID

Wallet Providers

Wallet providers specialize in **key management** and **user authentication**.

CHAPTER 7   PROVIDER

Their responsibilities include:

- Securely storing private keys
- Prompting users to sign transactions
- Managing sessions and dApp connections

Types of Wallet Providers:

- **Hot Wallets**: Browser extensions (MetaMask, Rabby)
- **Mobile Wallets**: Trust Wallet, Rainbow
- **Hardware Wallets Integration**: Ledger Live with MetaMask

Example Flow (Figure 7-4):

1. dApp requests signature from MetaMask.
2. MetaMask prompts the user for approval.
3. User signs, and MetaMask either sends or returns the signed transaction.

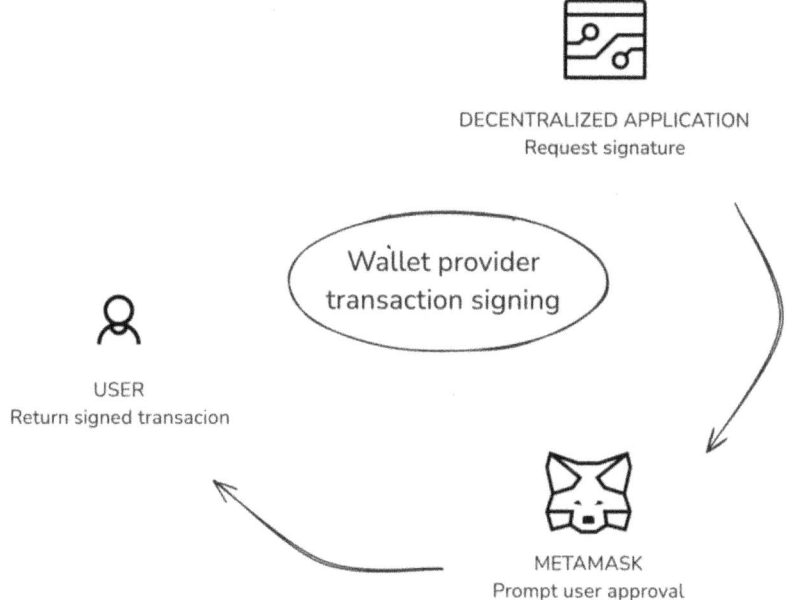

Figure 7-4. *Wallet Provider Transaction Signing Process*

CHAPTER 7   PROVIDER

Gateway Providers

Some providers offer **more than basic RPC** access, bundling:

- Enhanced APIs
- Real-time webhooks
- Developer analytics
- NFT metadata hosting
- Gas price optimization APIs

These **gateway providers** aim to accelerate development and improve dApp reliability.

Examples:

- **Alchemy Enhanced APIs**: Transaction receipts with richer metadata.
- **Moralis**: User authentication + NFT querying + database syncing.

Why Important:

By abstracting blockchain complexities even further, gateways reduce development time dramatically.

Indexing and Querying Providers

Blockchain data is not naturally structured for easy querying:

- Finding all NFTs owned by an address
- Searching for historical DeFi positions
- Listing DAO proposals and votes

Indexing providers solve this by:

- Running custom indexers
- Structuring blockchain data into GraphQL or REST endpoints
- Allowing advanced, application-specific queries

Figure 7-5 shows how indexing providers structure blockchain data.

256

Examples:

- **The Graph**: Open source, subgraph-based indexing.
- **Covalent**: Rich REST APIs for blockchain data.

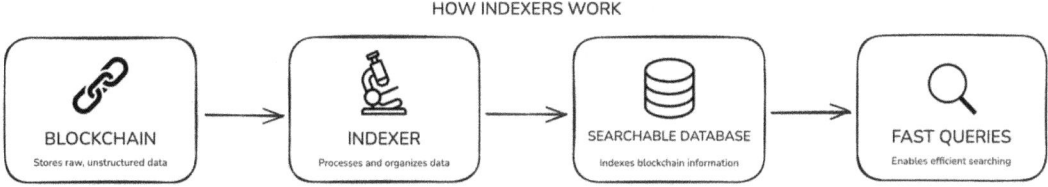

Figure 7-5. Indexing Providers Workflow

Hybrid Providers

Many modern providers combine multiple functionalities:

- RPC + WalletConnect integration
- Indexing + Webhooks
- Multi-chain support (Ethereum + Solana + BNB Chain)

Examples:

- **Alchemy**: RPC + Enhanced APIs + NFT APIs
- **Ankr**: RPC + decentralized node access

Hybridization helps developers avoid stitching multiple providers manually.

Why Providers Are Critical to Blockchain Growth

Without providers:

- Decentralized applications would be much slower and harder to build.
- Users would face technical hurdles setting up full nodes.
- Enterprises would hesitate to integrate blockchain solutions at scale.

Providers enable:

- **Scalability** (handling millions of users)
- **Accessibility** (simple APIs instead of node setup)
- **Resilience** (redundancy, fallbacks)

In Web2, companies rely on cloud providers like AWS, Azure, and Google Cloud.

In Web3, dApps and users rely on providers like Infura, Alchemy, QuickNode, and increasingly decentralized alternatives to power the decentralized world.

Network Considerations for Providers

When selecting a provider for blockchain applications, technical performance alone is not sufficient. One must also evaluate how a provider manages network connections, handles reliability challenges, ensures security against external and internal threats, and respects user privacy.

In decentralized systems, **the provider** becomes a critical trust layer. Any weaknesses at this level can expose users to attacks, cause downtime in critical financial systems, and undermine the very goals of decentralization. A deep understanding of network considerations is therefore mandatory for any serious blockchain architect or developer.

This section dives into the four major areas that define a provider's operational quality: **performance**, **reliability**, **security,** and **privacy**.

Performance Metrics

Performance is one of the first things users notice when interacting with blockchain-based applications. If loading times are slow, transactions fail to broadcast, or data appears outdated, users lose confidence immediately.

When evaluating the performance of providers, the most critical metrics include the following metrics.

Latency

Latency measures the time taken between a user action and the system's response.

CHAPTER 7 PROVIDER

In blockchain terms,

- Latency is the delay between submitting a transaction request and receiving confirmation that it has been accepted by a node.

- It also applies when reading data. For example, fetching an account balance or smart contract state.

Low latency is essential for

- High-frequency trading applications (e.g., decentralized exchanges like Uniswap).

- Gaming applications relying on real-time blockchain events.

- Wallets needing to display near-instant balance updates.

Sources of Latency:

- Geographical distance between user and provider servers.

- Internal processing time at the provider's data centers.

- Blockchain network congestion itself.

Figure 7-6 visualizes latency in provider server communication.

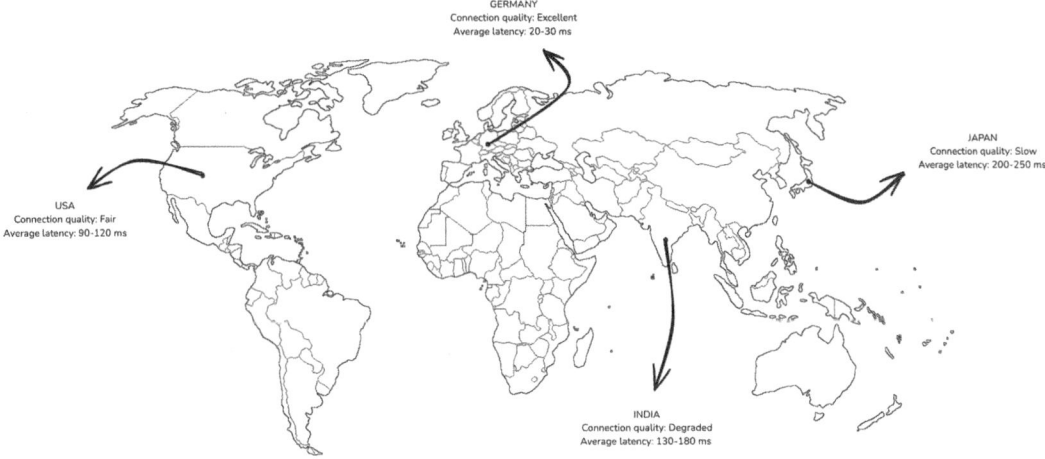

Latency metrics to illustrate how geographic distance affects performance, here the provider server is based in Frankfurt, Germany

Figure 7-6. *Latency in Provider Infrastructure*

Ideal Targets:

For consumer-grade applications, latency under 200 ms is considered excellent. For financial applications, sub-100 ms is ideal.

Throughput

Throughput defines how many requests per second (RPS) a provider can handle reliably without performance degradation.

In blockchain contexts, this could include

- Simultaneous *eth_getBalance* queries for many users
- Bulk reading thousands of NFTs
- Submitting many small transactions for batch minting or airdrops

Higher throughput allows

- Scalability of dApps during high traffic (e.g., NFT launches)
- Preventing rate limiting during critical operations

Factors influencing throughput (Figure 7-7):

- Backend architecture (load balancers and sharded databases)
- Node software optimization (e.g., Geth vs. Erigon performance)
- Horizontal scaling capabilities (adding more servers dynamically)

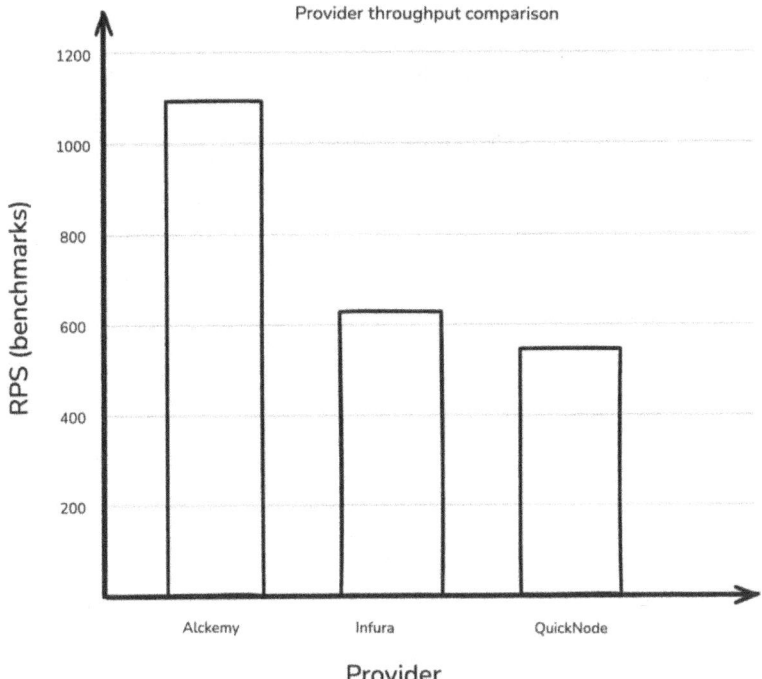

Figure 7-7. *Provider Throughput Comparison*

Example:

During high-profile NFT launches, throughput needs often spike by 10x within minutes. Providers unable to scale suffer outages and API errors, leading to failed mints and lost revenue.

Uptime

Uptime measures the percentage of time the provider's services are available without interruption.

Even brief downtimes can cripple decentralized applications, especially financial systems handling live assets.

Typical uptime tiers (Figure 7-8):

- **99.9% ("Three Nines")**: Acceptable for basic dApps
- **99.99% ("Four Nines")**: Standard for DeFi and financial applications
- **99.999% ("Five Nines")**: Desired for mission-critical blockchain infrastructure (e.g., liquid staking, cross-chain bridges)

CHAPTER 7   PROVIDER

Strategies Providers Use for Uptime:

- Geographic redundancy (multiple regions and availability zones).
- Automated failover between cloud providers (AWS, Azure, GCP).
- Proactive DDoS protection and traffic management.

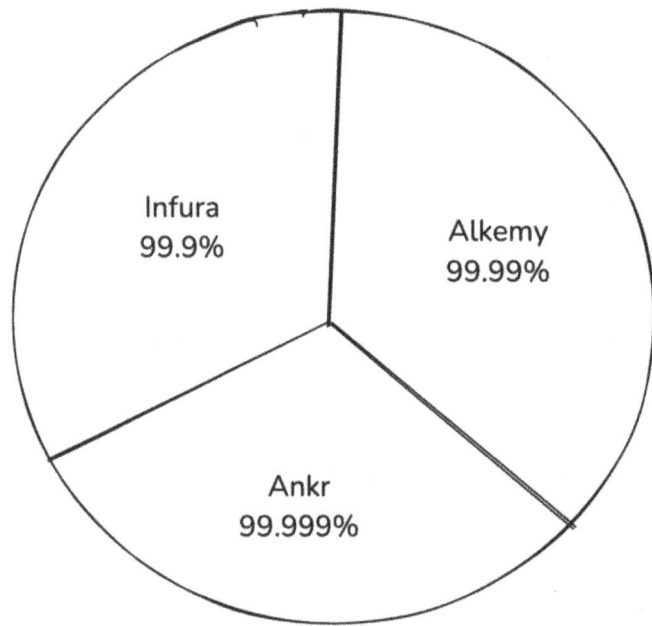

Uptime Guarantees by Leading Providers

Figure 7-8. *Leading Provider Uptime*

Global Geographic Coverage

Since blockchain users are worldwide (Figure 7-9), providers must distribute their infrastructure accordingly:

- North America, Europe, Asia, Africa, and South America
- Emerging markets where Web3 adoption is growing rapidly (e.g., India and Nigeria)

Global server presence reduces

- Connection latency
- Risk of regional outages
- Legal exposure to country-specific bans or service disruptions

Example:

A dApp that's only performant for users in North America would fail to scale globally, especially as Web3 adoption grows fastest in Asia and Africa.

Figure 7-9. Global Provider Server Deployment

Reliability and Failover Strategies

Reliability is not just about uptime in normal conditions; it's about how gracefully a system handles unexpected failures.

Blockchain applications, especially financial ones, must maintain availability during

- Network outages
- Hardware failures
- Regional disasters
- DDoS attacks

CHAPTER 7   PROVIDER

Multi-region Redundancy

Leading providers maintain clusters of nodes and API gateways across multiple physical regions and cloud providers. Figure 7-10 shows a multi-region setup for failover reliability.

If an outage occurs in one region, traffic is automatically routed to another without interruption.

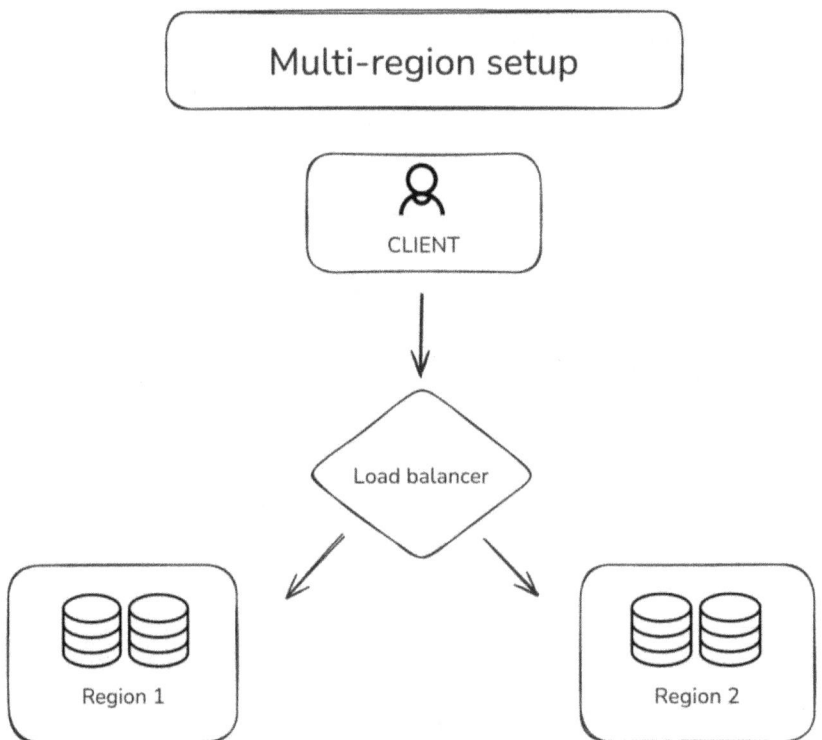

Figure 7-10. *Multi-region Provider Setup*

Automatic Retries and Circuit Breakers

When a request fails (e.g., RPC timeout), applications should:

- Retry automatically with exponential backoff (wait 1s, then 2s, then 4s...).
- Use **circuit breakers** to prevent overwhelming a failing system.

264

Example:

An NFT marketplace may implement retries if the primary RPC fails to respond within 300 ms. After three failed attempts, it switches to a backup provider.

Provider Fallback Mechanisms

Fallback systems mean integrating multiple providers simultaneously and dynamically switching between them when errors are detected. Provider failover logic is depicted in Figure 7-11.

Popular fallback designs include

- **Primary–Secondary:** Use one provider until it fails.
- **Round-Robin:** Alternate providers on every request.
- **Weighted Failover:** Prefer higher-performance providers until they degrade.

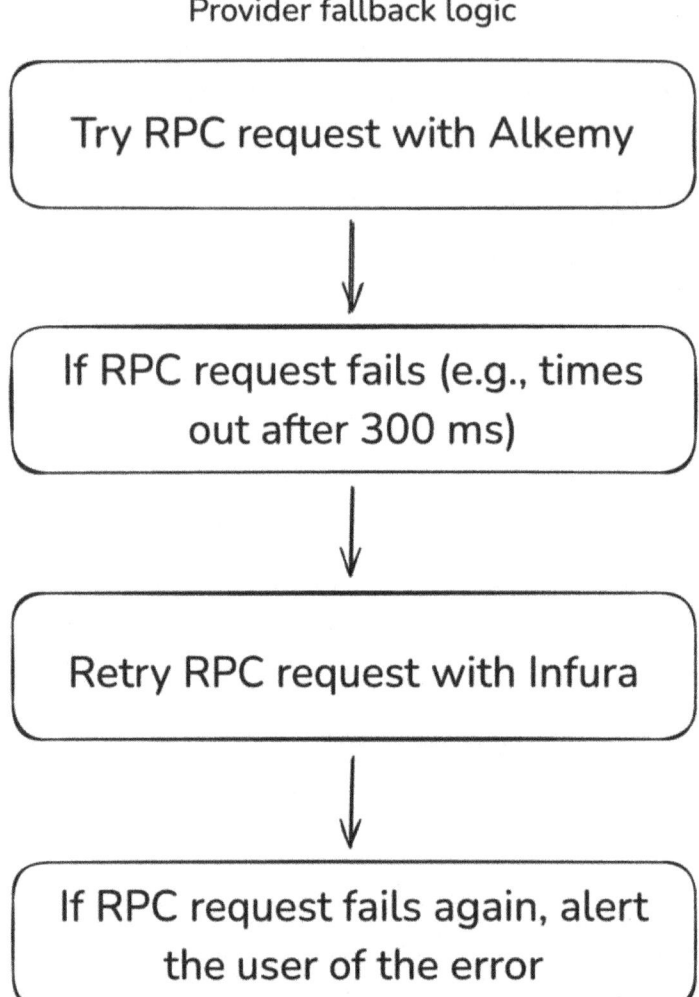

Figure 7-11. Provider Fallback Logic

Security Implications

Providers, by their nature, become trusted intermediaries.

If a provider is compromised, it can:

- Serve malicious blockchain data to applications.
- Steal users' private data if wallet interactions are mishandled.
- Delay or censor transactions selectively.

Understanding security risks is essential when designing robust dApps.

Man-in-the-Middle (MITM) Risks

If connections between applications and providers are not encrypted (using HTTPS/TLS), attackers can intercept and manipulate traffic.

Attack Scenario (Figure 7-12):

- A user submits a transaction.
- A malicious actor intercepts the transaction, modifies it (e.g., changes the recipient address), and then forwards it.

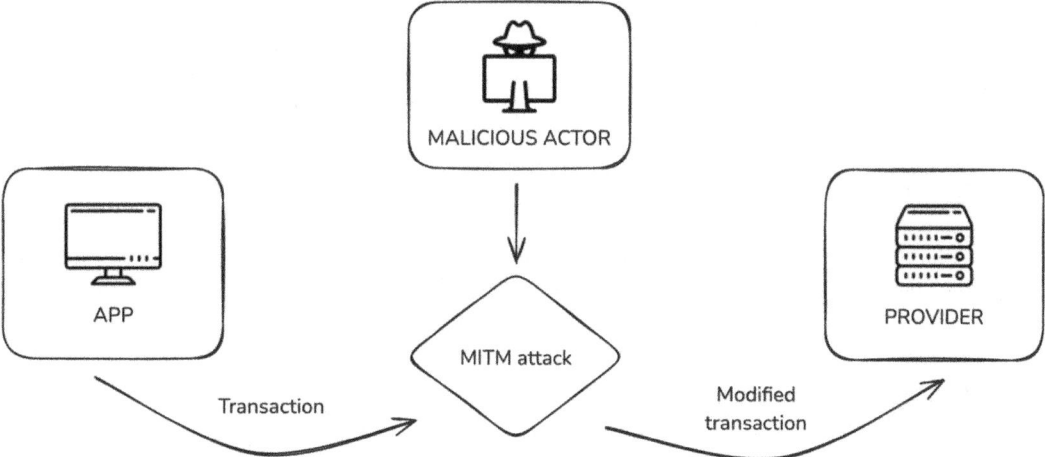

Figure 7-12. *Man-in-the-Middle Attack on Providers*

Mitigation:

Always enforce HTTPS, verify SSL certificates, and optionally use end-to-end encryption techniques where feasible.

Data Injection Attacks

An insecure provider could inject falsified responses to RPC requests, tricking a dApp into:

- Displaying incorrect balances
- Signing fraudulent transactions
- Showing incorrect smart contract states

Mitigation:

Use providers that offer verifiable proof of blockchain state (e.g., zk-proofs or Merkle proofs in the future).

Key Management

Wallet providers must manage user private keys securely:

- Never transmit private keys over the network.
- Use encrypted local storage, hardware security modules (HSMs), or hardware wallets.

Failures in key management are catastrophic, leading to full asset loss.

Privacy Considerations

Decentralization promotes pseudonymity, but providers can unintentionally erode user privacy if not carefully designed.

IP Address Exposure

Whenever a user connects to a provider, their IP address is revealed, creating a link between the user and their blockchain activity.

Example:

Using Infura directly from a web browser without a VPN exposes both the IP and the wallet address to the provider.

Transaction Metadata Leakage

Providers may log

- Smart contract interactions
- Token transfers
- NFTs minted

Over time, this metadata can be used to profile users.

Techniques to Preserve Privacy

Solutions include (Figure 7-13):

- **VPNs** and **Tor** routing to obfuscate IPs
- Using privacy-focused providers
- Homomorphic encryption techniques (experimental)

Figure 7-13. Enhancing Privacy in Providers

Example of Privacy-Preserving Approach:

BlockWallet encrypts transactions locally and routes them through multiple nodes to protect user anonymity.

Comparing Wallet Providers vs. RPC Providers

The blockchain space is powered by an intricate network of providers, but not all providers serve the same purpose.

Understanding the **critical differences** between wallet providers and RPC providers is key to building secure, scalable, and user-friendly decentralized applications.

Although both types act as intermediaries between users/applications and blockchain networks, they operate at **different layers** of the blockchain interaction stack and have **different threat models, infrastructure needs,** and **design implications**.

This section provides a comprehensive analysis of wallet providers and RPC providers, with detailed technical insights, real-world examples, and architectural comparisons.

CHAPTER 7   PROVIDER

Wallet Providers

A **wallet provider** is responsible for managing the **keys, identities, and signatures** necessary for interacting securely with a blockchain.

While blockchains are public ledgers, writing to them requires proving ownership of a private key associated with a blockchain address.

Wallet providers facilitate this ownership without forcing users to manage cryptographic materials manually.

Key Responsibilities of Wallet Providers

Private Key Management

At the heart of blockchain identity lies the **private key**, a piece of cryptographic information that allows a user to authorize transactions and claim ownership over blockchain assets.

Wallet providers ensure:

- **Secure storage** of private keys.
- **Isolation** of keys from dApp environments.
- **Recovery mechanisms** (seed phrases, social recovery, smart contract wallets).

Without proper key management:

- Assets can be stolen.
- Users can lose access permanently.
- dApps can suffer from fraud and legal liabilities.

Technical Approaches:

- **Software-based hot wallets** (encrypted private keys stored locally).
- **Hardware-based wallets** (private keys stored on dedicated hardware chips, never exposed to the computer or network).
- **Smart contract wallets** (abstract accounts managed by smart contracts, enabling features like social recovery).

CHAPTER 7 PROVIDER

Transaction Construction and Signing

Wallet providers are responsible for

- Receiving transaction payloads from dApps
- Prompting users to approve or reject the transaction
- Applying cryptographic signatures using the user's private key
- Optionally broadcasting the signed transaction to the network

Example Flow:

1. dApp constructs a transaction (e.g., swap 1 ETH for DAI).
2. Wallet provider (e.g., MetaMask) shows the transaction details.
3. User approves.
4. Wallet signs the transaction locally.
5. The dApp either broadcasts it directly or lets the wallet broadcast.

Figure 7-14 details the transaction signing process.

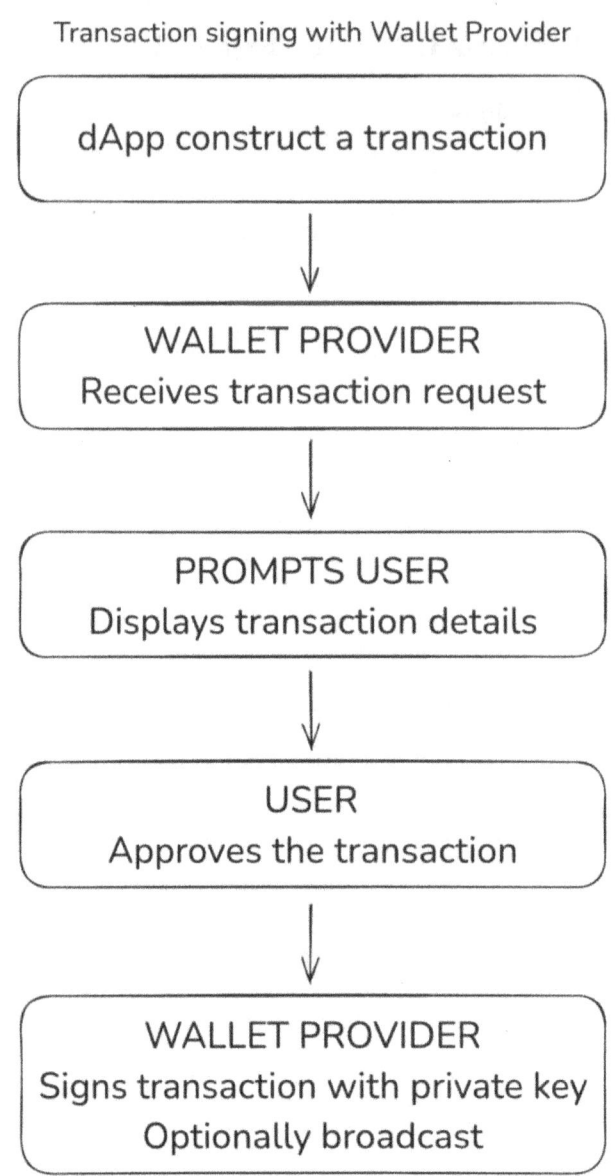

Figure 7-14. Wallet Provider Signing Flow

Session Management and Permissions

Modern wallet providers manage **sessions** between users and dApps:

- Which dApps a wallet is connected to.
- Which accounts are exposed.

- Which permissions (signing, read-only) are granted.

Best practices:

- Session expiration mechanisms.
- User notifications for new connection requests.
- Limiting dApp access only to necessary data.

Categories of Wallet Providers

Wallet providers come in various flavors (Table 7-2):

Table 7-2. *Wallet Provider Categories*

Type	Examples	Characteristics
Browser extension wallets	MetaMask, Rabby, Phantom	Easy to integrate; fast UX; browser dependency
Mobile wallets	Trust Wallet, Rainbow	Mobile-native; deeper hardware access
Smart Contract wallets	Argent, Safe (formerly Gnosis Safe)	Programmable security; social recovery
Hardware wallets	Ledger, Trezor	Cold storage; physical confirmation required

Real-World Case Study: MetaMask

MetaMask, the most popular Ethereum wallet, illustrates how a wallet provider operates at scale:

- **Key Storage**: Locally encrypted inside the browser or mobile device.
- **Connection Model**: User manually connects to each dApp.
- **Signing**: Only transaction payloads are exposed to MetaMask, never full user private keys.
- **Fallback RPC**: MetaMask uses Infura by default to submit transactions after signing, separating the wallet function from the node relay function.

CHAPTER 7   PROVIDER

Important Concept:
Wallet providers and RPC providers are often combined **at the UX level** (e.g., MetaMask users unknowingly using Infura), but **conceptually they are separate roles**.

RPC Providers

While wallet providers manage user identities and signatures, **RPC providers** focus purely on **data access** and **transaction relaying**.

RPC stands for **Remote Procedure Call**, a computer science term referring to calling functions on remote servers as if they were local.

In blockchain contexts, RPC protocols allow applications to:

- Query blockchain state (e.g., account balances, smart contract storage).
- Submit signed transactions for inclusion in the blockchain.
- Subscribe to blockchain events (e.g., new blocks, emitted events).

Key Responsibilities of RPC Providers

API Exposure

RPC providers expose blockchain networks via APIs such as

- **JSON-RPC over HTTP/S**: Most common for Ethereum and EVM-compatible chains.
- **WebSocket APIs**: For real-time event subscriptions.
- **GraphQL APIs**: For structured, flexible querying (used in newer chains like The Graph).

Common Ethereum JSON-RPC methods include (Table 7-3):

- *eth_blockNumber*
- *eth_getTransactionReceipt*
- *eth_estimateGas*
- *eth_sendRawTransaction*

Table 7-3. RPC Provider JSON-RPC Methods

Method	Description	Parameters	Results
eth_blockNumber	Get the latest block number	—	Block number
eth_getTransactionReceipt	Get the receipt of a transaction	Transaction hash	Receipt object
eth_estimateGas	Estimate gas needed for a transaction	Transaction object	Gas amount
eth_sendRawTransaction	Submit a signed transaction	Signed transaction	Transaction hash

Node Management and Scaling

Behind the scenes, RPC providers:

- Operate pools of blockchain nodes.
- Monitor node health and synchronization.
- Implement caching layers for frequent queries.
- Scale horizontally across regions to support global dApp usage.

High-end providers like Alchemy or QuickNode maintain:

- **Dedicated node fleets** (not just shared infrastructure).
- **Archive nodes** (full history of blockchain state).
- **Real-time analytics dashboards**.

Real-World Case Study: Infura

Infura operates one of the largest Ethereum RPC infrastructures:

- Serves billions of API requests per day.
- Provides Ethereum, IPFS, and Layer 2 (Optimism and Arbitrum) endpoints.

- Critical infrastructure for dApps like MetaMask, Uniswap, and OpenSea.

Notably, in November 2020, Infura experienced a brief outage during an Ethereum upgrade, highlighting that **centralized RPC dependencies** can become points of failure, even in decentralized ecosystems.

Key Differences: A Deeper Comparison

While wallet providers and RPC providers can both be integrated into dApps, their internal architectures and risk models are fundamentally distinct. Table 7-4 compares main security concerns for wallet vs. RPC providers.

Table 7-4. Security Comparison: Wallet vs. RPC Providers

Aspect	Wallet Providers	RPC Providers
Focus	User keys, identity, transaction signing	Blockchain data access, transaction broadcasting
Handles private keys	Yes	No
User authentication	Required	Not needed
Security risks	Key theft, phishing, social engineering	Data integrity issues, censorship
Examples	MetaMask, WalletConnect, Ledger Live	Infura, Alchemy, QuickNode
Monetization	Fee on swaps, premium services (e.g., MetaMask Swaps)	API usage tiers, dedicated node hosting
Failure impact	Total asset loss (if compromised)	Data unavailability, transaction delays

Choosing the Right Provider(s)

In practice, most modern blockchain applications require **both types** of providers:

- Wallet providers for user interaction and signing.
- RPC providers for data querying and transaction relaying.

Designing a production-ready dApp involves

- Allowing users to connect with different wallets.
- Supporting multiple RPC endpoints for reliability.
- Separating signing (wallet) from broadcasting (RPC) responsibilities cleanly.

Best Practice Tip:
Architect dApps to treat wallet and RPC providers as **pluggable modules**, allowing easy switching or redundancy for both.

Provider Selection Criteria

Choosing the right provider is one of the most critical architectural decisions when building a blockchain-based application.

The provider becomes a core part of the system's reliability, performance, security, and even legal compliance.

A poor choice can result in:

- Downtime at critical moments
- User loss due to slow performance
- Security breaches
- Legal vulnerabilities due to regulatory non-compliance

The right provider, on the other hand, can help your project scale confidently, deliver excellent user experiences, and position itself at the forefront of blockchain innovation.

This section examines all major factors that must be considered when evaluating and selecting providers, going far beyond simple uptime guarantees.

Speed and Performance

Speed is often the first tangible quality users perceive, even before security or decentralization becomes relevant.

A blockchain application that lags during wallet connection, transaction submission, or balance display creates user frustration immediately.

CHAPTER 7   PROVIDER

Fast providers are critical to building products that feel modern, reliable, and responsive.

Key Performance Indicators (KPIs)

Table 7-5 summarizes the main performance indicators to consider when evaluating blockchain providers. These metrics help assess speed, scalability and suitability for different Web3 applications.

Table 7-5. Key Performance Indicators (KPIs)

Metric	Ideal Value	Why It Matters
API latency	< 200 ms roundtrip globally	Faster UI updates; better trading UX
Throughput capacity	10,000+ RPS (requests per second)	Handles surges during NFT drops and DeFi trading spikes
Block propagation speed	Immediate or near-instant	Critical for miners/validators and real-time apps
Archive access	Available on demand	Supports historical queries (important for DeFi apps)

Importance of Regional Distribution

Global audiences demand regional optimization:

- Users in Europe should not connect to servers in North America unless necessary.

- Emerging markets (Africa and Southeast Asia) should have minimal latency.

Leading providers like Alchemy, Infura, and Ankr maintain distributed server fleets to minimize geographic latency.

Case Study: NFT Minting Stress Test

During a popular NFT mint (e.g., Otherside by Yuga Labs), RPC providers faced sudden surges of **50x normal traffic** within seconds.

CHAPTER 7 PROVIDER

Projects connected to scalable providers succeeded, while others saw:

- API rate limits exceeded
- Transactions stuck pending
- Failed mints and major financial losses

Decentralization and Trust Models

Blockchain aims for decentralization, but many providers today are **centralized** entities.

Choosing a provider also means deciding how much **trust** you are placing in a single infrastructure point.

Levels of Decentralization

When evaluating providers, it's important to understand the varying degrees of decentralization they offer. Table 7-6 outlines three common levels, their characteristics, and examples:

Table 7-6. Levels of Decentralization in Providers

Level	Characteristics	Examples
Fully centralized	Single entity controls all nodes and APIs	Infura, Alchemy (default configurations)
Partially decentralized	Some nodes spread across different operators	Pocket Network, Ankr decentralized RPC
Self-hosted	You run your own node(s)	Complete control, maximum decentralization

Why Trust Models Matter

Centralized RPC Risks:

- Single-point failure: If the provider goes down, your app goes down.
- Censorship potential: Provider could block certain transactions (e.g., OFAC compliance).

- Data manipulation: Provider could lie about blockchain state (though difficult without wide collusion).

Decentralized RPC Benefits:

- Multiple independent operators relay requests.
- Reduced censorship risk.
- Greater resilience to attacks and political pressure.

Case Study: Infura Outage (2020)

In November 2020, Infura suffered a major outage during an Ethereum network upgrade. Because many wallets (e.g., MetaMask) were configured to use Infura exclusively:

- Users could not send transactions.
- Many DeFi apps broke temporarily.
- Confidence in centralized provider reliance was shaken.

Security and Compliance

Security must be **built into** your provider choice, not assumed afterward.

While blockchains themselves are highly secure, the **infrastructure connecting to them** (providers) can be attacked, censored, or surveilled.

Security Factors to Evaluate

When selecting a provider, ensuring strong security measures is crucial to protect applications and users from vulnerabilities. Table 7-7 summarizes key factors to assess and their recommended best practices:

Table 7-7. Security Factors for Provider Evaluation

Factor	Description	Best Practice
HTTPS/TLS	Secure data in transit	Mandatory
Data Validation	Ensure no injected data manipulation	Always validate RPC responses
Key Isolation	No key leakage between wallet and RPC layers	Use separation of concerns
DDoS Protection	Handle high-volume attacks	Confirm provider anti-DDoS infrastructure

Regulatory and Legal Compliance

Providers must sometimes comply with regulations:

- **KYC/AML laws** (e.g., in exchanges/wallet providers)
- **OFAC sanctions compliance** (blocking sanctioned wallets)
- **GDPR** (Europe) and **CCPA** (California) for data privacy

If your app handles sensitive industries (e.g., finance, healthcare, and national security), selecting a provider with clear compliance policies is essential.

Case Study: Tornado Cash Sanctions (2022)

When the US government sanctioned Tornado Cash smart contracts, centralized providers like Infura and Alchemy began **blocking** RPC requests involving sanctioned addresses.

Consequence:

Even though blockchains are decentralized, users interacting through certain providers experienced censorship.

Cost and Pricing Structures

While many providers offer **free tiers**, usage can become expensive quickly as dApps scale.

Common pricing models:

- **Request-based** (per million API calls)
- **Bandwidth-based** (per GB transferred)
- **Dedicated node hosting** (monthly subscription)

Cost Factors to Compare

Pricing can vary significantly across providers depending on usage levels, request volume, and whether dedicated infrastructure is required. Table 7-8 outlines typical costs to consider when selecting an RPC provider:

Table 7-8. Typical RPC Provider Pricing

Feature	Typical Costs
Free tier	1M–3M requests per month
Paid APIs	~$50–$300/month for 20M–100M requests
Dedicated nodes	$500–$2,000+/month depending on chain and service

Optimizing Costs

- Use caching aggressively to minimize RPC hits.
- Optimize frontend apps to batch multiple blockchain queries.
- Negotiate enterprise deals if scaling past free tiers.

Developer Experience (DX)

The **developer experience (DX)** can make or break a project's momentum.
Key DX factors:

- Clear documentation
- Easy onboarding (SDKs, examples, quickstarts)

- Multilingual SDK support (JavaScript, Python, Rust, Go, etc.)
- Community support and forums
- Analytics dashboards for usage monitoring

Multichain and Scalability Support

Web3 is not just about Ethereum anymore.

Leading projects often operate across:

- Ethereum mainnet
- Layer 2s (Optimism, Arbitrum, zkSync, and Starknet)
- Alternative L1s (Solana, Avalanche, and Polygon)

Choosing a provider that **natively supports multichain development** reduces integration complexity dramatically. Table 7-9 compares provider multichain capabilities.

Table 7-9. Multichain Provider Support

Provider	Supported Chains
Alchemy	Ethereum, Polygon, Arbitrum, Optimism
QuickNode	Ethereum, Solana, BSC, Polygon, Fantom
Infura	Ethereum, Optimism, Arbitrum

Future-Readiness: Emerging Technologies

Providers must also be evaluated for readiness in emerging areas:

- **Zero-knowledge proof (ZK) networks** (zkSync and StarkNet)
- **Decentralized storage** (IPFS and Filecoin integrations)
- **Privacy-enhanced blockchains** (Aztec and Secret Network)

Choosing a forward-compatible provider now ensures smoother scaling later.

CHAPTER 7   PROVIDER

Advanced Provider Topics

As the blockchain space matures, the demands placed on providers are growing more complex.

While basic RPC access and wallet connections are essential, advanced applications often require **custom infrastructure solutions,** especially in areas like DeFi, gaming, and Layer 2 scaling.

Self-Hosting RPC Endpoints

One approach to achieving **maximum control** and **decentralization** is **self-hosting your own blockchain nodes** rather than relying on third-party providers.

Self-hosting provides:

- **Full sovereignty** over your connection to the blockchain
- **Freedom from API rate limits or third-party censorship**
- **Direct access** to all node data, including historical state (with archive nodes)

However, it introduces significant operational complexity and costs.

Requirements for Running Full Nodes

Hardware Requirements (Ethereum Example):

- SSD storage (at least 2 TB for mainnet full node; 12 TB+ for full archive node)
- High-throughput, stable internet (at least 100 Mbps recommended)
- Reliable server uptime ($\geq 99.9\%$)
- At least 32 GB RAM (recommended)

Software Choices:

- **Geth** (Ethereum's Go implementation)
- **Nethermind** (optimized for performance, especially on Windows)
- **Besu** (enterprise-oriented, Java implementation)

Figure 7-15 illustrates a self-hosted full node setup.

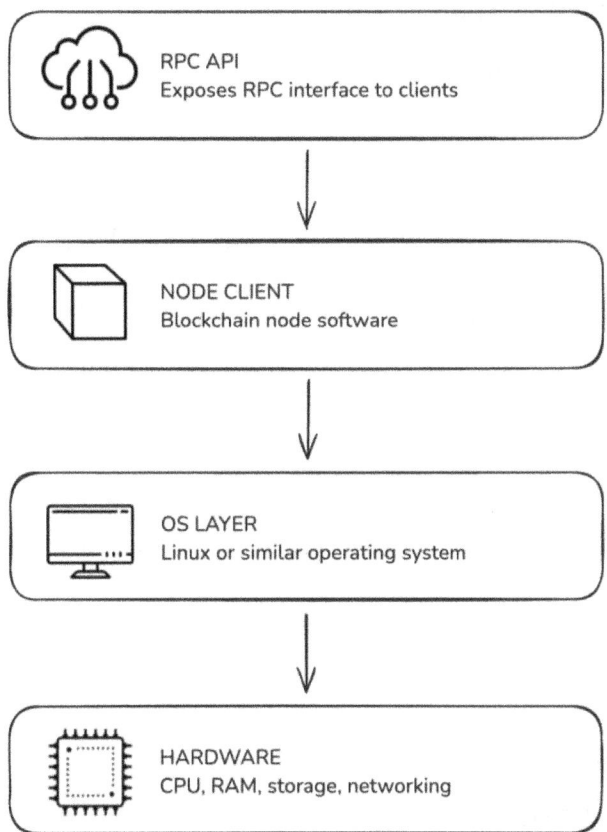

Figure 7-15. *Self-Hosted Full Node Architecture*

Operational Challenges

- **Synchronization Time**: Initial sync for Ethereum full nodes can take **days or weeks**, depending on hardware and network conditions.

- **Maintenance Overhead**:
    - Node upgrades (hard forks and security patches)
    - Monitoring node health (peering status and sync status)
    - Protecting nodes from DDoS attacks

- **Cost Factors:**
  - Cloud servers capable of running archive nodes can cost **$500–$1,000+ per month**.
  - Or you must manage your own on-premises servers.

When Self-Hosting Makes Sense

Table 7-10 highlights common scenarios where self-hosting blockchain nodes is beneficial, along with the primary reasons organizations might choose this approach.

Table 7-10. Scenarios and Benefits of Self-Hosting Blockchain Nodes

Scenario	Why Self-Host?
Financial protocols (DeFi)	Need for absolute transaction censorship resistance
DAOs and Governance tools	Want to avoid reliance on centralized entities
Analytics platforms	Require full historical chain access without provider limits
Blockchain infrastructure companies	Provide service to others based on self-hosted nodes

Hybrid Architectures

Many projects deploy a **hybrid model**:

- **Primary reliance on third-party RPCs** (for speed and scale)
- **Secondary fallback to self-hosted nodes** (for resilience and sovereignty)

This balances cost, performance, and decentralization. Figure 7-16 shows a hybrid setup combining self-hosted and RPC nodes.

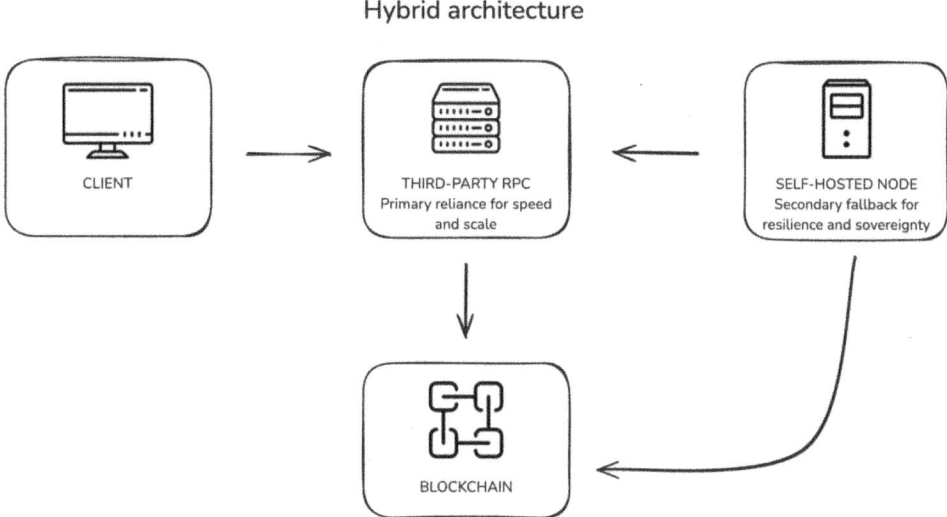

Figure 7-16. Hybrid Architecture for Providers

Decentralized RPC Networks

Centralized providers, while convenient, create single points of failure.

Decentralized RPC networks aim to solve this problem by distributing the responsibility of serving RPC requests across a **network of independent nodes**.

Key Features of Decentralized RPC

- **Multiple node operators** handle traffic, reducing reliance on any single party.

- **Rewards for node operators** incentivize reliable service (typically via blockchain tokens).

- **Dynamic routing** ensures traffic is directed to available, healthy nodes.

- **Censorship resistance**: No central authority can block specific addresses or transactions.

Examples of Decentralized RPC Networks

Table 7-11 lists popular decentralized RPC networks.

Table 7-11. Decentralized RPC Network Examples

Network	Description
Pocket network	RPC layer for dozens of chains, uses POKT token for incentivization
Ankr decentralized RPC	RPC endpoints powered by node pools
Chainstack decentralized infrastructure	Hybrid decentralized node marketplace

Challenges of Decentralized RPC

- **Consistency of Data**: Ensuring all nodes are synced and trustworthy.
- **Latency**: Routing across decentralized networks may introduce slight delays.
- **Economic Sustainability**: Token incentive models must remain viable long-term.

Case Study: Pocket Network Growth

Pocket Network, founded in 2017, has become one of the largest decentralized RPC networks:

- Serves billions of relayed requests monthly.
- Supports Ethereum, Polygon, Solana, and dozens of other chains.
- Uses economic slashing to punish misbehaving nodes.

Provider Aggregators and Fallback Systems

Another advanced technique for achieving resilience and performance is using **multiple providers simultaneously**.

Instead of trusting a single RPC provider, your application can:

- Attempt primary provider first.
- On error, retry with backup providers.

CHAPTER 7 PROVIDER

- Distribute load across multiple providers simultaneously.

This reduces downtime risk dramatically.

Example Strategies

When using multiple providers for improved resilience, developers can choose from different aggregation strategies. Table 7-12 summarizes the most common approaches:

Table 7-12. Provider Strategy Types for Aggregation

Strategy	Description
Simple failover	Use Provider B if Provider A fails
Weighted load balancing	70% traffic to Provider A, 30% to Provider B
Intelligent routing	Dynamically select a provider based on latency, health, or geolocation

Libraries Supporting Provider Aggregation

- **ethers.js FallbackProvider**: Allows configuring multiple providers in order of priority.
- **web3modal**: Frontend library supporting multi-wallet, multi-provider connection options.
- **Custom SDKs**: Some apps write their own provider orchestration logic.

Example in ethers.js:

```
1. import { providers } from 'ethers';
2.
3. const provider = new providers.FallbackProvider([
4.   new providers.InfuraProvider('mainnet', INFURA_KEY),
5.   new providers.JsonRpcProvider('https://rpc.ankr.com/eth'),
6.   new providers.AlchemyProvider('mainnet', ALCHEMY_KEY),
7. ]);
```

This fallback system ensures maximum uptime and minimal disruption.

Multichain Application Design

Modern applications often must support **multiple blockchains simultaneously**, especially in DeFi, NFT marketplaces, and bridges.

A multichain-ready application must:

- Maintain connections to RPC endpoints across chains (Ethereum, Polygon, Arbitrum, Solana, etc.).
- Handle differing transaction formats (e.g., Solana vs. EVM).
- Dynamically switch between providers based on user-selected chain.

Evolving Responsibilities of Providers

Blockchain technology is often described as "trustless," yet the reality is more nuanced. **Trust shifts**: from centralized authorities to decentralized protocols, from traditional institutions to cryptographic proofs. In that landscape, **providers** emerge as critical actors: they are the invisible scaffolding that supports every blockchain application.

Best Practices for Working with Providers

To build production-ready applications, developers should:

Separate Concerns:

- Treat wallet providers and RPC providers as distinct modules.
- Never expose private keys to any RPC provider.

Design for Redundancy:

- Always configure fallback providers.
- Prepare for partial network failures gracefully.

Prioritize User Privacy:

- Minimize metadata leakage.
- Use decentralized RPC networks where possible.

Plan for Multichain Reality:

- Abstract blockchain interactions behind chain-agnostic layers.
- Choose providers that natively support multiple chains.

Stay Flexible:

- Provider ecosystems evolve rapidly.
- Architect your application to switch providers if needed, without major refactoring.

The Future of Providers

The next generation of blockchain applications will demand even more from providers. Key trends shaping the future include:

1. **Decentralized Infrastructure at Scale**

    Decentralized RPC networks like Pocket Network and Ankr are just the beginning. Future decentralized networks will offer:

    - Peer discovery without centralized servers.
    - Verifiable computation proofs.
    - Node reputation systems to ensure quality.

2. **Zero-Knowledge Proofs for Trustless RPCs**

    Imagine querying blockchain data and receiving a **cryptographic proof** that the response is accurate – no need to trust the provider. Early research in **zkRPC** aims to make this vision a reality:

    - RPC providers will return both data and zk-proofs.
    - dApps will verify proofs locally before trusting responses.

3. **Privacy-Preserving Provider Interactions**

    Increased awareness of blockchain metadata privacy will drive adoption of:

    - Tor and VPN routing at the provider layer.
    - Homomorphic encryption for private queries.

CHAPTER 7   PROVIDER

- Private smart contract execution networks (e.g., Secret Network, Aztec).

Future providers must integrate privacy as a default, not an optional add-on.

4. **Multichain Orchestration as a Standard**

   Already today, leading dApps operate across 5–10 blockchains. Tomorrow, **seamless multichain orchestration** (handling wallets, transactions, and queries across dozens of Layer 1s and Layer 2s) will become the norm.

   Providers that offer unified multichain APIs, SDKs, and smart routing will dominate. Figure 7-17 visualizes multichain orchestration for providers.

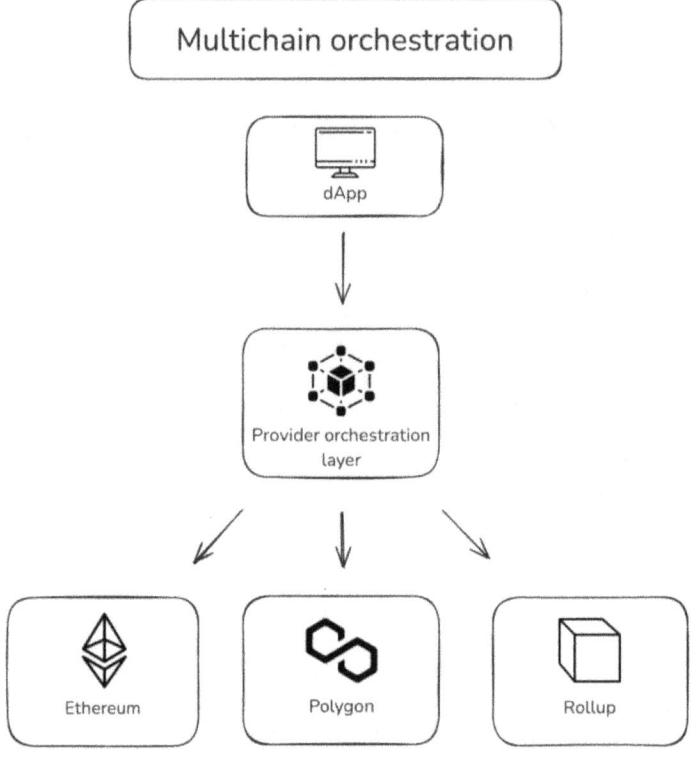

Figure 7-17. Multichain Orchestration Future Vision

Conclusion

Blockchain aims to build systems that **don't rely on trust**, but until fully decentralized, verifiable infrastructure is the norm, **providers remain trusted bridges** in the Web3 ecosystem.

Selecting, integrating, and designing around providers is not just a technical decision; it's a matter of philosophy:

- How much do you want to decentralize?
- How much resilience do you require?
- How much trust are you willing to outsource?

Informed developers and architects treat providers with the **respect they deserve**, designing architectures that leverage their strengths while mitigating their weaknesses.

Providers today are **infrastructure**. Providers tomorrow will be **protocols**. The future belongs to those who build with that vision in mind.

Chapter Summary

Topic	Key Takeaways
Definition of Providers	Providers are intermediaries connecting clients (users, apps) with blockchain networks.
Types of Providers	Full node, RPC, wallet, gateway, indexing, and hybrid providers with different roles and capabilities.
Performance Considerations	Metrics like latency, throughput, uptime, and global server distribution affect user experience.
Reliability and Failover	Multi-region setups, fallback mechanisms, and circuit breakers ensure high availability.
Security and Privacy	TLS encryption, key isolation, protection against MITM attacks, and privacy-preserving techniques.

(*continued*)

CHAPTER 7   PROVIDER

Topic	Key Takeaways
Wallet vs. RPC Providers	Wallet providers manage keys and signing; RPC providers handle data querying and transaction relay.
Provider Selection Criteria	Evaluate speed, decentralization, security, compliance, cost, and multichain support.
Advanced Topics	Self-hosting nodes, decentralized RPC networks, multi-provider aggregation, and hybrid architectures.
Future of Providers	Moving toward decentralized protocols, zkRPC verification, enhanced privacy, and multichain orchestration.

CHAPTER 8

Smart Contracts and Decentralized Applications

Introduction

Smart contracts and decentralized applications (dApps) form the **core building blocks of Web3**. While previous chapters introduced blockchain fundamentals and providers, this chapter shifts focus to **programmable, self-executing agreements** that run directly on decentralized networks.

In this chapter, you will

- Understand what smart contracts are and how they differ from traditional contracts
- Explore their internal architecture, lifecycle, and common design patterns
- Learn how they enable decentralized finance, NFTs, DAOs, gaming, and supply chain solutions
- Discover the tools and frameworks used to write, test, deploy, and integrate smart contracts into real-world dApps

By the end of this chapter, you will have a solid understanding of **how to design and implement smart contracts** and connect them to decentralized applications, preparing you to build fully functional Web3 solutions in the upcoming chapters.

Deep Dive into Smart Contracts

What Are Smart Contracts?

A **smart contract** is a self-executing piece of code stored on a blockchain that runs when predetermined conditions are met. Figure 8-1 visually compares a traditional contract process with a smart contract workflow.

It acts as an autonomous agreement: once deployed, it can **no longer be changed** and **always executes as written**, not as intended.

The term "smart contract" was coined in the 1990s by cryptographer Nick Szabo, long before Ethereum existed. Szabo envisioned computer protocols that could enforce contractual agreements without human intervention, the kind of automation we now associate with blockchain-powered smart contracts.

Core Properties

Smart contracts, especially as implemented on Ethereum and other EVM-compatible chains, are defined by several key properties. Table 8-1 outlines the core properties that make smart contracts deterministic, immutable, and autonomous.

Table 8-1. Core Properties of Smart Contracts

Property	Description
Deterministic	Given the same input, a smart contract will always produce the same output.
Immutable	Once deployed, the contract code cannot be altered. Only new versions can be deployed.
Transparent	Anyone can inspect the code and its state (on public blockchains).
Trustless	Execution does not require a trusted third party.
Autonomous	Once triggered, contracts execute on their own, without intermediaries.

These characteristics make smart contracts ideal for **financial, legal, and governance applications**, where verifiability and predictability are paramount.

How Smart Contracts Differ from Traditional Contracts

The comparison between traditional and smart contracts is summarized in Table 8-2.

Table 8-2. *Traditional Contracts vs. Smart Contracts*

Feature	Traditional Contract	Smart Contract
Medium	Legal document	Computer code
Enforcement	Courts or intermediaries	Blockchain network
Execution	Manual	Automatic
Modification	Negotiated	Immutable
Transparency	Private	Public (on-chain)
Cost of enforcement	High	Low (gas fees only)

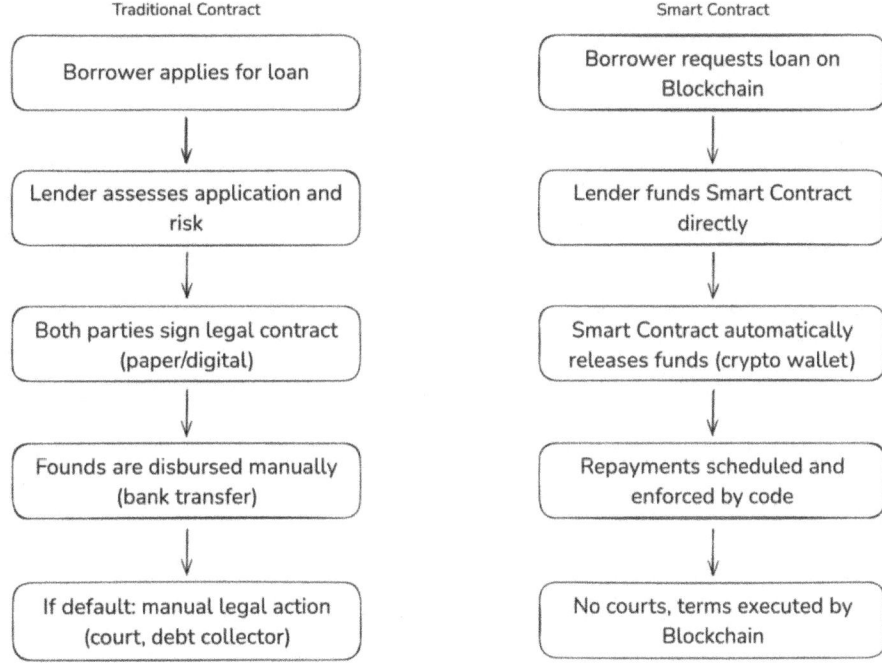

Figure 8-1. *Traditional vs. Smart Contract*

Example:

A traditional escrow contract for real estate requires lawyers, banks, and intermediaries.

A smart contract can serve the same purpose with code: when the buyer transfers funds, the seller's NFT (representing ownership) is automatically released.

How Smart Contracts Work (Under the Hood)

A smart contract is compiled into **bytecode** and deployed to the blockchain at a specific address. Once on-chain, users and other contracts can **call** its public functions and **query** its state.

Most smart contracts

- Are written in **Solidity** (Ethereum)
- Contain **functions** that perform logic
- Can **store data** in on-chain variables
- Can **emit events** to signal important activity

Example code (Solidity):

```solidity
// SPDX-License-Identifier: MIT
pragma solidity ^0.8.0;

contract SimpleStore {
    uint256 public value;

    function set(uint256 _value) public {
        value = _value;
    }

    function get() public view returns (uint256) {
        return value;
    }
}
```

This contract stores a single number. Any user can set it or retrieve it.

CHAPTER 8   SMART CONTRACTS AND DECENTRALIZED APPLICATIONS

That's the fundamental power of a smart contract: **public logic with persistent storage**, secured by cryptography.

The Ethereum Virtual Machine (EVM)

The **Ethereum Virtual Machine (EVM)** is the environment in which smart contracts run. Figure 8-2 depicts the execution stack of smart contracts within the EVM.

Every Ethereum node runs an EVM instance, which executes contract bytecode as part of processing each block.

Key features of the EVM:

- **Isolated** from the outside world (no internet access, clock, or file system)

- Executes smart contract functions securely and deterministically

- Uses **gas** to measure and limit resource usage

Technical Note   Solidity, Vyper, and other smart contract languages compile into **EVM bytecode**, not machine code.

This makes smart contracts portable across EVM-compatible blockchains (e.g., Polygon, Avalanche, Optimism, and BNB Chain).

CHAPTER 8   SMART CONTRACTS AND DECENTRALIZED APPLICATIONS

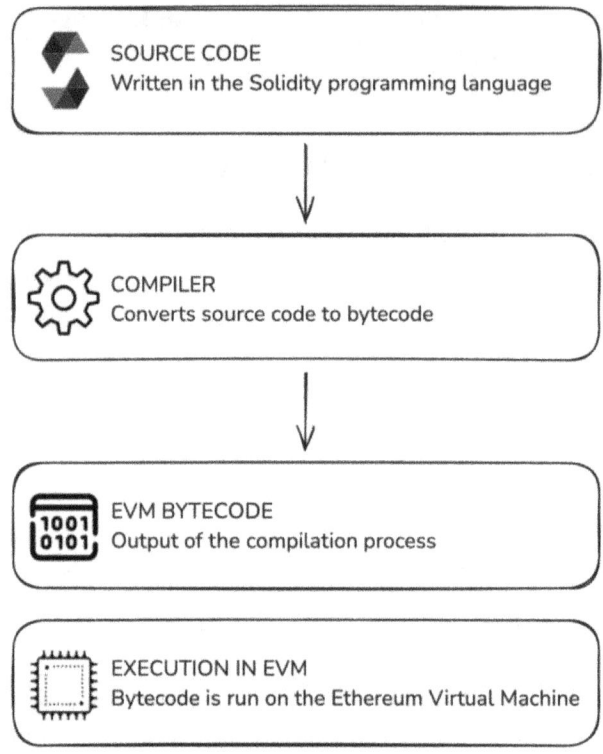

Figure 8-2. *EVM Smart Contract Execution Stack*

Limitations and Design Constraints

Smart contracts offer powerful benefits, but they're not general-purpose programs. Developers must design within several constraints (Table 8-3).

Table 8-3. *Design Constraints and Limitations of Smart Contracts*

Constraint	Description
No external calls	Smart contracts can't call web APIs directly (use oracles instead).
No randomness	Contracts can't generate secure random numbers on their own.
Gas costs	Execution is paid for in gas, so efficiency matters.
Immutability	Bugs can't be fixed after deployment (upgrades are possible but complex).

These constraints encourage **minimalist, security-focused** design.

CHAPTER 8 SMART CONTRACTS AND DECENTRALIZED APPLICATIONS

Real-World Examples of Simple Contracts

- **ERC-20 Token**

    A smart contract that defines a fungible token with balance tracking and transfer logic.

- **NFT Contract (ERC-721)**

    A unique asset tracker that stores metadata and ownership.

- **Escrow Contract**

    Holds funds until both parties meet specific conditions.

- **DAO Voting Contract**

    Allows users to vote on proposals using governance tokens.

Figure 8-3 highlights common real-world use cases for smart contracts.

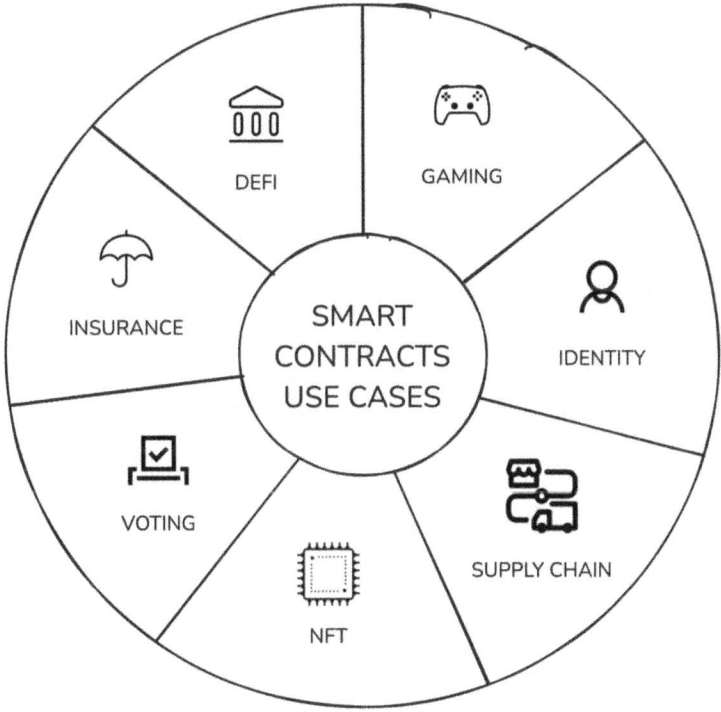

Figure 8-3. Popular Smart Contract Use Cases

301

Why Smart Contracts Matter

Smart contracts are not just "backend logic," they're the foundation of

- Decentralized Finance (DeFi)
- Token economies
- Permissionless governance
- Cross-border asset transfers
- Web3 business models

They enable applications where **trust is enforced by code**, not by institutions.

Smart Contract Architecture

Designing smart contracts goes far beyond simply writing functions in Solidity.

It requires thoughtful architectural choices around **data modeling**, **interaction surfaces**, **modularity,** and **gas efficiency**.

A well-architected contract is:

- Secure
- Maintainable
- Efficient
- Composable

In this section, we explore the internal anatomy of smart contracts and how their architecture affects usability, performance, and upgradability.

On-Chain vs. Off-Chain Logic

One of the most important architectural decisions is determining **which logic should live on-chain** versus what can safely exist off-chain. Table 8-4 illustrates which components are typically implemented on-chain versus off-chain.

Table 8-4. On-Chain vs. Off-Chain Logic

Component	On-Chain	Off-Chain
Token balances, governance logic	✓	✗
UI rendering, analytics, graphs	✗	✓
Access control, ownership tracking	✓	✗
Wallet integrations, frontend logic	✗	✓
Game state (e.g., scores, positions)	Sometimes	Often

The rule of thumb: **only put logic on-chain when decentralization, integrity, or transparency demands it.**

Why?

- **Gas costs** make on-chain operations expensive.
- On-chain logic is immutable (hard to patch bugs).
- Blockchain storage is limited.

Contract Interfaces and ABIs

In Ethereum and EVM-compatible blockchains, smart contracts expose **public functions** and **events** via their **Application Binary Interface (ABI)**.

The ABI is a **compiled schema** that allows tools like ethers.js or web3.js to

- Encode function calls (e.g., transfer(address,uint256))
- Decode return values
- Parse emitted events

This makes contracts **interoperable**, meaning other contracts or applications can interact with them as long as the ABI is known.

Example ABI Fragment (ERC-20 Transfer):

```
1. {
2.   "name": "transfer",
3.   "type": "function",
```

```
 4.   "inputs": [
 5.     { "name": "to", "type": "address" },
 6.     { "name": "amount", "type": "uint256" }
 7.   ],
 8.   "outputs": [{ "name": "", "type": "bool" }],
 9.   "stateMutability": "nonpayable"
10. }
```

Developer Tip When integrating with third-party contracts (e.g., Uniswap, Aave), you only need their ABI, not the source code.

Storage and State Design

Smart contracts persist data **on-chain**, meaning all state variables are stored in the blockchain's state trie.

Common types of state:

- Scalars (uint256, bool, address)
- Mappings (mapping(address => uint256))
- Arrays and structs

Example:

1. `mapping(address => uint256) public balances;`

Gas efficiency is critical when designing storage layouts (Figure 8-4):

- Use smaller types (e.g., uint32 instead of uint256) when possible.
- Pack variables in the same storage slot to save gas.
- Minimize writes; storage writes are more expensive than reads.

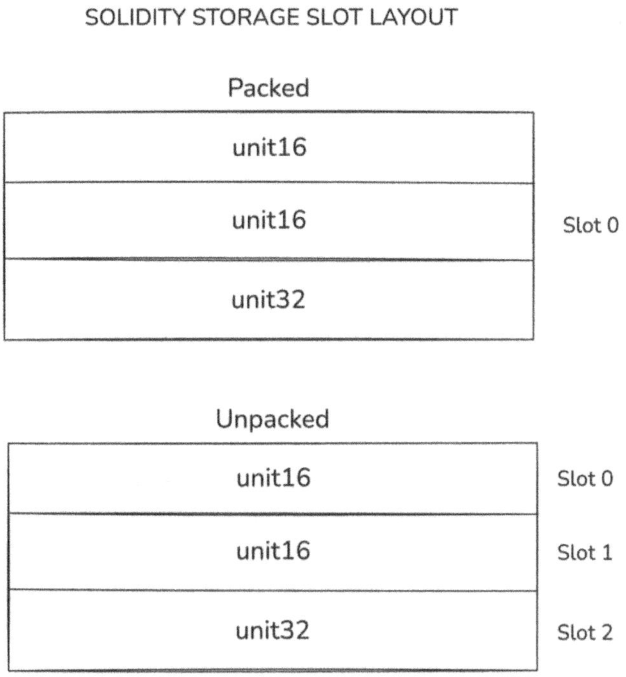

SOLIDITY STORAGE SLOT LAYOUT

```
Packed
┌─────────────────┐
│     unit16      │
├─────────────────┤  Slot 0
│     unit16      │
├─────────────────┤
│     unit32      │
└─────────────────┘

Unpacked
┌─────────────────┐
│     unit16      │  Slot 0
├─────────────────┤
│     unit16      │  Slot 1
├─────────────────┤
│     unit32      │  Slot 2
└─────────────────┘
```

Figure 8-4. *Solidity Storage Layout*

Modularity and Contract Composition

Larger projects split logic across multiple contracts using **inheritance** or **delegation**. This promotes:

- Separation of concerns
- Code reuse
- Easier auditing and testing

Inheritance

Solidity supports multiple inheritance. For example:

```
1. contract Ownable { /* ... */ }
2. contract Pausable { /* ... */ }
3.
```

```
4. contract MyToken is Ownable, Pausable {
5.    // Combines both access control and pause functionality
6. }
```

Delegation (Proxy Pattern)

Delegation uses the *delegatecall* opcode to forward calls to an implementation contract. Figure 8-5 shows the proxy pattern used for upgradeable smart contracts.

Used in:

- Upgradable contracts (OpenZeppelin Proxy)
- Modular systems like Diamond Standard (EIP-2535)

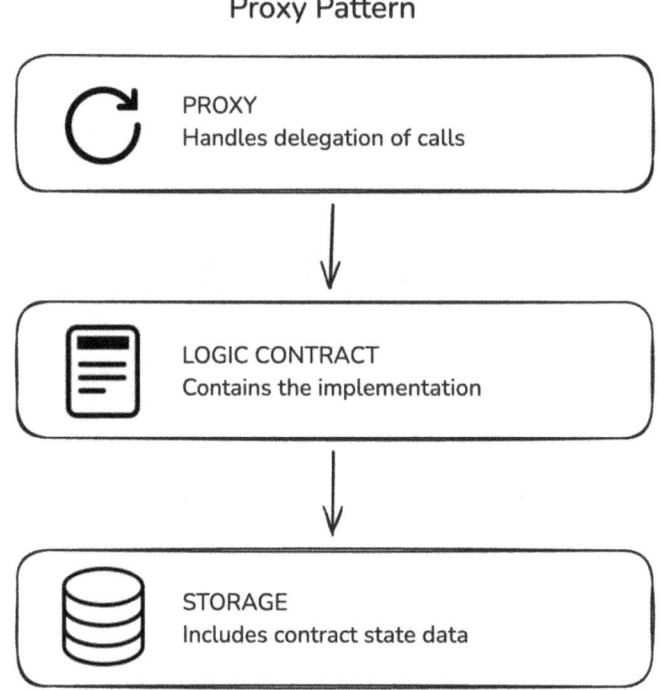

Figure 8-5. *Proxy Pattern for Upgradable Contracts*

Events and Logs

Smart contracts can **emit events**, which are logged in transaction receipts.

While these logs are **not part of the contract state**, they are extremely useful for:

- Frontend UIs (e.g., showing transfers)
- Indexers (The Graph, Covalent)
- Auditing and analytics

Example:

```
1. event Transfer(address indexed from, address indexed to, uint256
   amount);
2.
3. function transfer(address to, uint256 amount) public {
4.     balances[msg.sender] -= amount;
5.     balances[to] += amount;
6.     emit Transfer(msg.sender, to, amount);
7. }
```

Reentrancy and Call Context

Smart contracts can call each other, which introduces risk.

Reentrancy happens when a contract sends funds to another contract, and that contract calls back into the original before it finishes execution.

This can be exploited to drain funds.

Best Practice:

- Use **checks-effects-interactions** pattern:
    1. Check conditions
    2. Update state
    3. Interact with external contracts

Better:

- Use **ReentrancyGuard** from OpenZeppelin

```
1. modifier nonReentrant {
2.     require(!_locked, "Reentrant call");
```

```
3.    _locked = true;
4.    _;
5.    _locked = false;
6. }
```

Composability and Interoperability

Smart contracts can call other contracts seamlessly, a concept called **composability**. This enables

- dApps built on top of other protocols (e.g., Yearn on Curve + Aave)
- Flash loans and atomic operations across DeFi
- Cross-protocol strategies (e.g., arbitrage, staking + lending)

Risks of Composability:

- If a dependency fails (e.g., a lending pool), your dApp can break.
- Chain of reentrancy risks and gas exhaustion.

Popular Use Cases for Smart Contracts

Smart contracts are not just a theoretical tool; they've been widely adopted in **live, high-value protocols** that move billions of dollars daily.

Their programmability, transparency, and automation capabilities make them ideal for powering complex systems where trust must be minimized or eliminated.

In this section, we'll explore the **most impactful use cases** for smart contracts in today's blockchain ecosystems, from decentralized finance to gaming, identity, and governance.

Decentralized Finance (DeFi)

DeFi is arguably the most transformative application of smart contracts so far.

DeFi replaces traditional financial services with **open-source protocols**, enabling

- Lending and borrowing
- Trading

CHAPTER 8   SMART CONTRACTS AND DECENTRALIZED APPLICATIONS

- Yield generation
- Stablecoins and synthetic assets

All of these are powered by smart contracts.

1. **Lending Protocols (e.g., Aave and Compound)**

   Users deposit tokens into a pool; borrowers provide collateral to take loans.

   All interest rates, liquidations, and repayments are enforced automatically via smart contracts.

   How It Works:

   - User deposits 10 ETH into Aave.
   - Aave's smart contract issues interest-bearing aETH tokens.
   - Borrowers deposit USDC as collateral to borrow ETH.

   Smart Contract Concepts Illustrated:

   - Collateral ratios
   - Interest rate models
   - Liquidation thresholds
   - Governance upgrades (changing parameters)

2. **Automated Market Makers (e.g., Uniswap and Curve)**

   AMMs allow users to trade tokens directly through liquidity pools without order books.

   Uniswap's smart contracts maintain a **liquidity invariant** (e.g., $x * y = k$) and rebalance token reserves after each swap.

   Example:

   - User swaps 100 DAI for ETH.
   - The pool adjusts prices automatically.
   - Liquidity providers earn fees, all handled by code.

Smart Contract Concepts Illustrated:

- Constant product formula
- Slippage protection
- Fee collection and distribution

3. **Yield Farming and Aggregators (e.g., Yearn Finance)**

   These contracts automate complex DeFi strategies:

   - Move funds between protocols for best yield.
   - Auto-compound rewards.
   - Rebalance risk.

   Yearn's contracts interact with dozens of other protocols like Curve, Aave, and Compound, all in a **composable way**.

   Smart Contract Concepts Illustrated:

   - Composability
   - Modular vault logic
   - Permissioned vs. permissionless execution

Non-Fungible Tokens (NFTs)

NFTs are **unique, verifiable digital assets** on-chain, most commonly implemented via smart contracts using the **ERC-721** or **ERC-1155** standards.

NFT smart contracts manage:

- Ownership
- Transfers
- Metadata links (image, audio, game asset)
- Royalties and secondary sales

Example:
A simple ERC-721 contract holds metadata for a piece of digital art.
When someone buys it, the smart contract updates ownership and emits a Transfer event.

Marketplace Contracts (e.g., OpenSea and Blur)

Marketplace contracts enable buying, selling, and bidding on NFTs.
These smart contracts often include

- Escrow logic
- Royalty distribution
- Signature verification

Smart Contract Concepts Illustrated:

- *approve()* patterns for sales
- Event logs for frontend updates
- Payment splitting and royalties

Decentralized Autonomous Organizations (DAOs)

DAOs use smart contracts to encode **governance rules**, enabling groups to make decisions **without centralized leadership**.

Examples:

- **MolochDAO**: Uses smart contracts for membership and funding proposals.
- **ENS DAO**: Controls domain name ownership policy on-chain.
- **Gitcoin**: Uses quadratic funding logic implemented in smart contracts.

DAO contracts handle:

- Voting (e.g., token-based and quadratic)
- Treasury disbursement
- Proposal creation and execution

Smart Contract Concepts Illustrated:

- Token-based voting
- Proposal lifecycle logic
- On-chain vs. off-chain governance bridges

Escrow and Conditional Payments

Smart contracts are ideal for **holding funds until conditions are met**.

Example:

- A freelancer completes a job.
- The client submits funds to an escrow smart contract.
- When both parties agree, the contract releases the funds.

These use cases require

- Time locks
- Multi-signature approvals
- Dispute resolution logic (or oracles) – *Oracles are external services that feed real-world data (such as delivery confirmation or legal ruling outcomes) into the blockchain, enabling smart contracts to resolve disputes based on off-chain information.*

Identity and Reputation Systems

Projects like **BrightID**, **Proof of Humanity,** and **Gitcoin Passport** use smart contracts to manage

- Human verification
- Unique identity claims
- Trust scores

Use cases:

- Preventing Sybil attacks
- Whitelisting verified users
- Limiting claimable rewards to one per person

Smart Contract Concepts Illustrated:

- Non-transferable tokens (soulbound tokens)
- Identity attestation
- Reputation-linked actions

Gaming and Virtual Economies

Games like **Axie Infinity**, **Decentraland,** and **Zed Run** rely on smart contracts to:

- Manage in-game assets
- Enable trading
- Record achievements
- Handle payouts

In many cases, **smart contracts are the game's backend**.
Smart Contract concepts illustrated:

- Tokenized game items (ERC-1155)
- Rental and upgrade logic
- Inter-game composability

Supply Chain and Real-World Asset Tracking

Smart contracts can track the provenance and status of physical goods, as long as reliable data is provided (via oracles or IoT devices).

Use cases:

- Tracking organic certifications
- Recording shipping milestones
- Authenticating luxury goods (e.g., NFTs for watches or handbags)

The Smart Contract Lifecycle

Developing a smart contract is not a one-click operation; it's a lifecycle involving writing, compiling, deploying, verifying, interacting, and maintaining code that lives permanently on a public blockchain.

Each phase requires different tools, mindsets, and best practices. Understanding this lifecycle is essential not just for writing Solidity code but for designing systems that are scalable, secure, and maintainable over time. Figure 8-6 visualizes the full lifecycle of a smart contract, from drafting to maintenance.

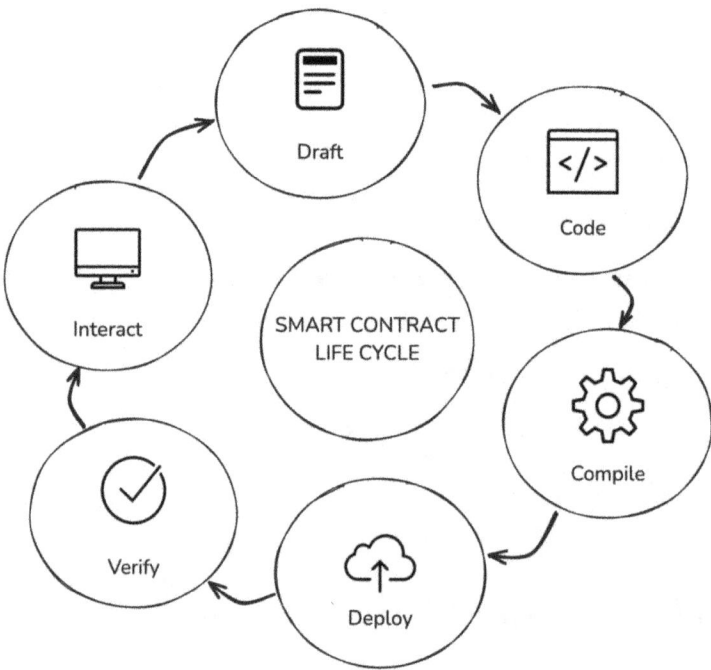

Figure 8-6. Smart Contract Development Lifecycle

Drafting the Contract Logic

Before writing a line of code, a developer should design

- **What the contract should do**
- **Who can call each function**
- **What data needs to be stored**
- **What risks exist**

This can be done in plain English or diagrammed as a flowchart or state machine.

Example (for a basic token):

- Owner can mint new tokens
- Users can transfer tokens
- Balances should be tracked
- Total supply should be capped

Writing the Contract (Solidity)

Most smart contracts today are written in **Solidity**, a statically typed, object-oriented language inspired by JavaScript and C++.

Example, ERC-20 token:

```solidity
// SPDX-License-Identifier: MIT
pragma solidity ^0.8.0;

contract MyToken {
    string public name = "MyToken";
    mapping(address => uint256) public balanceOf;

    function mint(uint256 amount) public {
        balanceOf[msg.sender] += amount;
    }

    function transfer(address to, uint256 amount) public {
        require(balanceOf[msg.sender] >= amount, "Insufficient balance");
        balanceOf[msg.sender] -= amount;
        balanceOf[to] += amount;
    }
}
```

Compiling the Contract

Solidity source code must be compiled into **EVM bytecode** before deployment.

Tools used:

- **Solc** (Solidity compiler)
- **Hardhat** (npx hardhat compile)
- **Foundry** (forge build)
- **Remix IDE** (browser-based with auto-compilation)

The compiler produces:

- bytecode: to be deployed on-chain
- ABI: for interacting with the contract off-chain

Best Practice: Always compile with **optimization enabled** and clearly specify your **Solidity version range** to avoid compatibility issues.

Deploying the Contract

Contracts can be deployed to:

- A local blockchain (for testing)
- A public testnet (Goerli, Sepolia, Mumbai, etc.)
- A mainnet (Ethereum, Polygon, Arbitrum, etc.)

Tools for deployment:

- **Hardhat scripts** (JavaScript/TypeScript)
- **Remix Deploy Plugin**
- **Foundry forge create**
- **Third-party tools like Thirdweb, Alchemy, and Infura Dashboards**

Hardhat deployment script example:

```
1. async function main() {
2.     const [deployer] = await ethers.getSigners();
3.     const Token = await ethers.getContractFactory("MyToken");
```

```
4.    const token = await Token.deploy();
5.    console.log("Contract deployed to:", token.address);
6. }
7. main();
```

Verifying the Contract

After deployment, it's standard practice to **verify your contract** so others can read its source code on block explorers like **Etherscan, Polygonscan,** or **Blockscout.**

Verification links your source code to the on-chain bytecode, enabling:

- Code transparency
- Public audits
- Easier debugging

Methods:

- Hardhat plugin (npx hardhat verify)
- Manually via Etherscan UI
- Foundry's forge verify-contract

Why It Matters: Verified contracts are essential for gaining user trust, especially in DeFi and NFT platforms.

Interacting with the Contract

Once deployed, the contract becomes **live** and callable by:

- Wallets (e.g., MetaMask)
- dApps (via web3.js or ethers.js)
- Other smart contracts

Example (Using ethers.js):

```
1. const contract = new ethers.Contract(address, abi, signer);
2. await contract.mint(100);
```

Frontends usually use providers like Infura, Alchemy, or self-hosted nodes to send these transactions.

Monitoring and Maintaining

Although contracts are immutable, developers still need to:

- Monitor usage (transactions, logs, balances)
- Respond to exploits or bugs (via upgradeable patterns or migration)
- Push new versions (e.g., V2 contracts)
- Coordinate community decisions (especially in DAO contexts)

Monitoring Tools:

- **Tenderly**: transaction debugging, gas profiling
- **Etherscan Watchlist**
- **Blocknative**, **Alchemy Notify**, or custom bots

Maintenance Strategy: Use versioning contracts (e.g., TokenV1 and TokenV2) or **proxy upgradeability** (OpenZeppelin UUPS) with caution; upgrades must be audited and secure.

Gas, Costs, and Efficiency

Smart contracts don't run for free. Every operation executed on the Ethereum Virtual Machine (EVM) requires **gas**, a unit of computational cost paid by the sender of a transaction. This mechanism prevents abuse (like infinite loops) and ensures that nodes are compensated for executing the contract's logic.

Understanding gas is not just important for users; it's essential for developers to write contracts that are efficient, scalable, and affordable.

What Is Gas?

Gas is the **execution cost unit** for smart contract operations in Ethereum and EVM-compatible blockchains.

CHAPTER 8 SMART CONTRACTS AND DECENTRALIZED APPLICATIONS

Each operation (e.g., storing data, adding two numbers, calling another contract) has a **predefined gas cost** in the Ethereum Yellow Paper.

Users pay for gas using the network's native currency (e.g., ETH on Ethereum, MATIC on Polygon).

Equation:

$$\text{Total Fee} = \text{Gas Used} \times \text{Gas Price}$$

- **Gas Used**: Computational effort
- **Gas Price**: Set by the user (in gwei)
- **Max Fee/Tip**: Introduced in EIP-1559 for fee predictability

Figure 8-7 shows the components of Ethereum transaction fees.

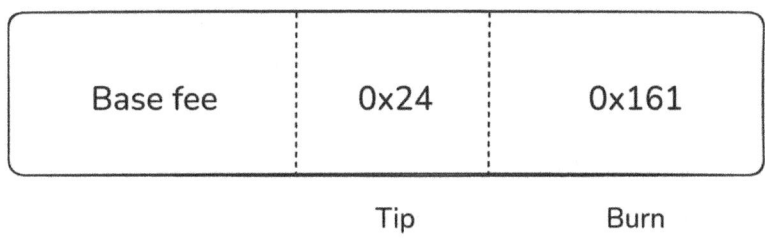

Figure 8-7. Ethereum Transaction Fee Breakdown

Why Gas Efficiency Matters

For Users:

- Lower gas = cheaper transactions
- High gas usage = fewer users can afford to interact

For Developers:

- Gas-efficient contracts are **faster**, **cheaper,** and **more scalable**
- Contracts with excessive gas costs may **fail to execute** if they exceed the block gas limit

- Gas-efficient dApps gain a **competitive advantage** in DeFi and NFT sectors

For Protocol Design:

- Enables **batched transactions**, **flash loans**, and **composable systems**

- Reduces friction in **governance**, **staking**, and **multi-step workflows**

Common Gas Costs for Operations

Table 8-5 shows approximate gas costs for typical EVM operations.

Table 8-5. *Common Gas Costs for EVM Operations*

Operation	Estimated Gas Cost
Add two numbers (+)	3
Store to storage (sstore)	20,000 (first write)
Read from storage (sload)	2,100
Emit event (log)	375 + 8 per byte
Calling another contract	700 + execution
Transfer ETH	21,000

Optimizing Contract Design for Gas Efficiency

1. **Minimize Storage Writes**

   Storage operations are the **most expensive** part of contract execution.

Tips:

- Avoid writing to storage more than once per variable.

- Use memory instead of storage for temporary variables inside functions.

- Use calldata for external function arguments (cheaper than memory).

2. **Use Smaller Data Types When Possible**

   Use uint8, uint16, or uint32 instead of uint256 when high ranges aren't needed.

   Smaller types can **pack into a single storage slot**, saving gas.

   ```
   1. struct Packed {
   2.    uint128 a;
   3.    uint128 b; // Both fit in 1 slot
   4. }
   ```

3. **Pack Structs and Mappings Carefully**

   Poorly aligned variables result in unused storage space and higher gas costs.

Tips:

- Order struct fields from largest to smallest types.
- Don't mix uint256 and bool unless necessary — each type affects alignment.

---

4. **Avoid Redundant Checks or Repeated Computation**

   Move reusable logic to internal functions or store results in temporary variables.

   Example:

   ```
   1. uint256 value = someMapping[msg.sender];
   2. require(value > 10, "Too low");
   3. doSomething(value); // Use cached result
   ```

5. **Use Events Instead of Storage for Logging**

   Events are **cheaper** than writing data to state and are **indexed** for easy access.

Use them for

- Logging transfers
- Audit trails
- Notifications

Testing and Profiling Gas Usage

Use tools to **measure gas before deployment.**

Tools for Gas Profiling

Developers can use the tools in Table 8-6 to profile and optimize gas usage.

Table 8-6. Tools for Gas Profiling

Tool	Description
Hardhat Gas Reporter	Outputs gas usage per function
Foundry's Forge Test	Shows gas usage alongside tests
Tenderly	Visual simulation and gas tracking
Remix Gas Analyzer	Built-in view of gas usage by line

Gas Limits and Out-of-Gas Errors

Each block has a **block gas limit** (currently ~30 million gas on the Ethereum mainnet). If a transaction exceeds this, it will **fail** and **consume the gas anyway.**

Implications:

- Large loops, deeply nested operations, or recursive calls may hit gas limits.
- Batch operations (e.g., minting 100 NFTs) must be optimized or split into multiple txs.

Design Rule: Avoid unbounded loops in smart contracts. Always ensure operations are **bounded by function input or data length.**

Gas Optimization Tradeoffs

While writing efficient smart contracts is crucial for reducing transaction costs, developers should be cautious about over-optimizing. Aggressive optimization techniques can lead to reduced code readability, complex debugging, and even security vulnerabilities. Table 8-7 highlights common optimization techniques and their potential trade-offs, emphasizing the importance of balancing efficiency with safety and maintainability.

Table 8-7. Trade-Offs in Gas Optimization Techniques

Optimization	Potential Tradeoff
Bitwise hacks	Low readability
Storage packing	Complex debugging
Inline assembly	Hard to audit, prone to bugs
Minimal checks	Security risk

Use optimization **only after your contract is working, secure, and well-tested**.

Implementation of Smart Contracts and dApps
Development Tools Overview

Developing smart contracts isn't just about writing Solidity code; it's about having the right tools to **compile, deploy, test, debug, and maintain** code safely and efficiently.

Over the years, the Ethereum developer ecosystem has matured with powerful frameworks that handle:

- Project scaffolding and dependency management
- Compilation and deployment
- Local test blockchain environments
- Automated testing and gas reporting
- Contract verification and debugging

Let's walk through the most commonly used frameworks and tools in the ecosystem.

Hardhat

Hardhat is one of the most popular JavaScript/TypeScript-based Ethereum development frameworks.

It provides a complete toolbox for developing, testing, and deploying smart contracts.

Key features

- Built-in local Ethereum node (Hardhat Network)
- Plugin system (for ethers.js, gas reporter, Etherscan verification, etc.)
- TypeScript and JavaScript support
- Console and scripting environment

Best for

- Web3 developers using JavaScript/TypeScript
- Teams building full-stack dApps
- Projects requiring deployment scripts and plugin integrations

Common commands

```
1. npx hardhat compile          # Compile contracts
2. npx hardhat test             # Run unit tests
3. npx hardhat node             # Run a local Ethereum node
4. npx hardhat run scripts/deploy.js --network localhost
```

Integration Tip Hardhat works seamlessly with **ethers.js**, making it ideal for frontend–backend contract integrations.

Figure 8-8 illustrates the typical workflow when developing contracts with Hardhat.

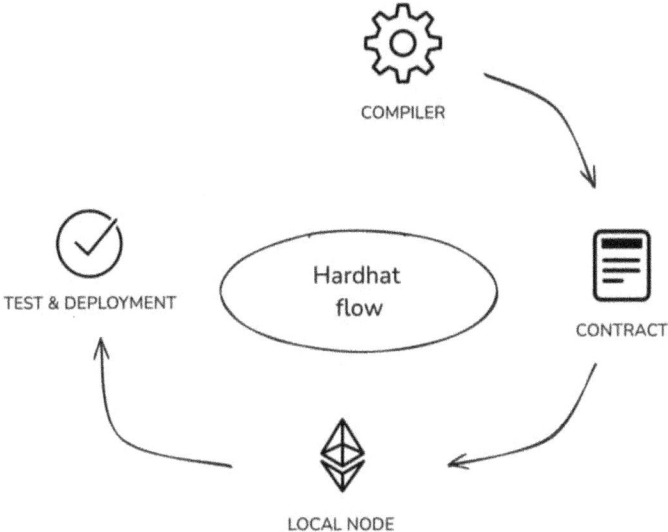

Figure 8-8. Hardhat Development Workflow

Foundry

Foundry is a **blazing-fast** smart contract development toolkit written in Rust.

It has quickly become a favorite among advanced solidity developers and security researchers.

Key features

- Native support for Solidity scripting (no JavaScript)
- Super-fast test runner (forge test)
- Built-in fuzzing and property-based testing
- Deployment with forge create
- Contract interaction with cast (CLI tool)

Best for

- Low-level contract developers
- Auditors, security engineers
- Speed-focused teams

Common commands

```
1. forge init              # Scaffold new project
2. forge build             # Compile contracts
3. forge test              # Run tests + gas reporting
4. forge script ...        # Deploy or simulate actions
5. cast call ...           # Query live blockchain data
```

Security Bonus: Foundry has native support for **fuzz testing**, making it a great choice for pre-audit hardening.

Truffle

Truffle was one of the first major Ethereum dev frameworks, known for its integration with Ganache (a personal Ethereum blockchain).

Though now less dominant, it remains widely used and supported.

Key features

- Simple contract compilation and migration
- Support for both web3.js and ethers.js
- Integration with Ganache for local testing
- Mocha test environment

Best for

- Legacy projects
- Educational and proof-of-concept dApps
- Developers already using Ganache or older web3 tooling

Common commands

```
1. truffle init
2. truffle compile
3. truffle migrate
4. truffle test
```

CHAPTER 8 SMART CONTRACTS AND DECENTRALIZED APPLICATIONS

Remix IDE

Remix is a browser-based Solidity IDE that allows developers to **write, compile, test, and deploy smart contracts without installing anything**.

Key features

- Web-based and zero-install
- Solidity compiler and deployment GUI
- Static analysis and gas estimation
- Support for plugins (e.g., Slither and Etherscan verification)
- Deploy to MetaMask or injected Web3 provider

Best for

- Beginners learning Solidity
- Prototyping or testing one-off contracts
- Teaching environments and workshops

Tool Comparison Table

Table 8-8 compares features of major development tools used for smart contract projects.

Table 8-8. Workflow Recommendation by Project Type

Feature/Tool	Hardhat	Foundry	Truffle	Remix
Language Support	JS/TS	Solidity	JS	Solidity
Speed	Medium	🚀 Fast	Slow	Medium
Test Framework	Mocha	Native	Mocha	Manual
Built-in Blockchain	Yes	Yes	Ganache	No
Fuzzing	Plugin	Native	✗	✗
Best Use Case	Full-stack apps	Audits, R&D	Legacy/edu	Prototyping

Plugin Ecosystem and Extensions

The best tools are extensible.

Hardhat and Foundry both support powerful plugins and custom scripts.

Hardhat Plugins

- @nomiclabs/hardhat-ethers
- hardhat-gas-reporter
- hardhat-etherscan
- hardhat-deploy

Foundry Add-Ons

- Integration with dapptools, slither, and forge coverage
- Easy cross-compatibility with Hardhat ABIs or deployments

Workflow Recommendation by Use Case

Table 8-9 recommendeds tool stacks for different smart contract project types.

Table 8-9. *Workflow Recommendation by Use Case*

Project Type	Recommended Stack
dApp with frontend	Hardhat + ethers.js
Security-focused protocol	Foundry + Slither + Echidna
Beginner prototyping	Remix or Truffle
Teaching Solidity	Remix + GitHub Pages
Gas-sensitive DeFi app	Foundry + Hardhat fallback

Writing Your First Contract (Line by Line)

Let's now apply what we've learned by building a **real smart contract from scratch**.

This contract covers

- Reading and writing on-chain state

- Managing addresses
- Emitting events
- Basic access control (onlyOwner)
- Require statements and gas-saving patterns

Contract Goals

Let's define what the contract should do

- Allow users to vote "Yes" or "No" on a single question.
- Count how many voted "Yes" and "No."
- Prevent double-voting.
- Only the contract owner can close voting.
- Store the result on-chain.

Full Code (Solidity 0.8+)

```
1.  // SPDX-License-Identifier: MIT
2.  pragma solidity ^0.8.18;
3.
4.  contract VoteBox {
5.      address public owner;
6.      bool public isVotingOpen = true;
7.
8.      uint256 public yesVotes;
9.      uint256 public noVotes;
10.
11.     mapping(address => bool) public hasVoted;
12.
13.     event Voted(address voter, bool vote);
14.     event VotingClosed(uint256 totalYes, uint256 totalNo);
15.
16.     modifier onlyOwner() {
```

```
17.        require(msg.sender == owner, "Not owner");
18.        _;
19.    }
20.
21.    modifier votingOpen() {
22.        require(isVotingOpen, "Voting is closed");
23.        _;
24.    }
25.
26.    constructor() {
27.        owner = msg.sender;
28.    }
29.
30.    function voteYes() external votingOpen {
31.        require(!hasVoted[msg.sender], "Already voted");
32.        hasVoted[msg.sender] = true;
33.        yesVotes += 1;
34.        emit Voted(msg.sender, true);
35.    }
36.
37.    function voteNo() external votingOpen {
38.        require(!hasVoted[msg.sender], "Already voted");
39.        hasVoted[msg.sender] = true;
40.        noVotes += 1;
41.        emit Voted(msg.sender, false);
42.    }
43.
44.    function closeVoting() external onlyOwner {
45.        isVotingOpen = false;
46.        emit VotingClosed(yesVotes, noVotes);
47.    }
48. }
```

Walkthrough by Section
Pragma and License

```
1. // SPDX-License-Identifier: MIT
2. pragma solidity ^0.8.18;
```

- SPDX-License: Declares the contract's open-source license.

- pragma: Sets the Solidity compiler version. Always use exact or fixed ranges for security and compatibility.

State Variables

```
1. address public owner;
2. bool public isVotingOpen = true;
3.
4. uint256 public yesVotes;
5. uint256 public noVotes;
6.
7. mapping(address => bool) public hasVoted;
```

- owner: Stores who deployed the contract (for access control).

- isVotingOpen: A toggle to allow/disallow votes.

- yesVotes, noVotes: Count user input.

- hasVoted: Tracks who has voted to prevent double voting.

Storage Reminder: Mappings are not iterable; we use them for lookup, not lists.

Events

```
1. event Voted(address voter, bool vote);
2. event VotingClosed(uint256 totalYes, uint256 totalNo);
```

- Voted: Logs each vote (can be indexed and shown on frontends).

- VotingClosed: Useful for indexing and final state tracking.

Modifiers

```
1. modifier onlyOwner() {
2.     require(msg.sender == owner, "Not owner");
3.     _;
4. }
```

- Custom logic inserted before function logic.
- Common for **access control**, **state checks**, **pausing**, etc.

    ```
    1. modifier votingOpen() {
    2.     require(isVotingOpen, "Voting is closed");
    3.     _;
    4. }
    ```

- Ensures users can't vote once voting is closed.

Gas Tip Modifiers are just syntactic sugar; they don't reduce gas, but they keep code readable.

Constructor

```
1. constructor() {
2.     owner = msg.sender;
3. }
```

- Called once when deployed. Sets the deploying wallet as the owner.

Vote Functions

```
1. function voteYes() external votingOpen {
2.     require(!hasVoted[msg.sender], "Already voted");
3.     hasVoted[msg.sender] = true;
4.     yesVotes += 1;
5.     emit Voted(msg.sender, true);
6. }
```

CHAPTER 8 SMART CONTRACTS AND DECENTRALIZED APPLICATIONS

- Ensures only new voters can vote.
- Updates internal state and logs the event.
- Uses external for gas savings when no internal calls are expected.

Same for *voteNo()*, but sets *noVotes* i+= 1.

Close Voting (Owner Only)

```
1. function closeVoting() external onlyOwner {
2.     isVotingOpen = false;
3.     emit VotingClosed(yesVotes, noVotes);
4. }
```

- Ensures only the owner can disable voting.
- Prevents new votes while preserving transparency via event logs.

Testing Your Contract

You can test this contract in:

- **Remix**: Deploy and click vote buttons manually.
- **Hardhat**:
    ```
    1. it("allows a user to vote once", async () => {
    2.     await contract.voteYes();
    3.     await expect(contract.voteYes()).to.be.revertedWith("Already voted");
    4. });
    ```
- **Foundry:**
    ```
    1. function testVoteYes() public {
    2.     voteBox.voteYes();
    3.     assertEq(voteBox.yesVotes(), 1);
    4. }
    ```

Compiling and Deploying Your Contract

Once you've written and tested your smart contract, the next step is to **compile** it into deployable bytecode and **send it to the blockchain**. This transforms your Solidity code into an **immutable, on-chain application**, visible and usable by anyone in the world.

This section explains how to go from Solidity source to a **live, deployed contract** using three different tools: **Hardhat**, **Foundry**, and **Remix**.

Understanding the Compilation Process

Solidity code must be **compiled into bytecode** for the Ethereum Virtual Machine (EVM). Figure 8-9 depicts the process of compiling Solidity source code into deployable bytecode. During compilation, your tools generate:

- **Bytecode**: Low-level instructions the EVM understands
- **ABI**: Contract interface used by external apps (e.g., dApps, wallets)
- **Metadata**: Used for verification and debugging

Compiler Tip   Use Solidity versions ^0.8.x unless you have specific legacy requirements. Always lock compiler versions for reproducibility.

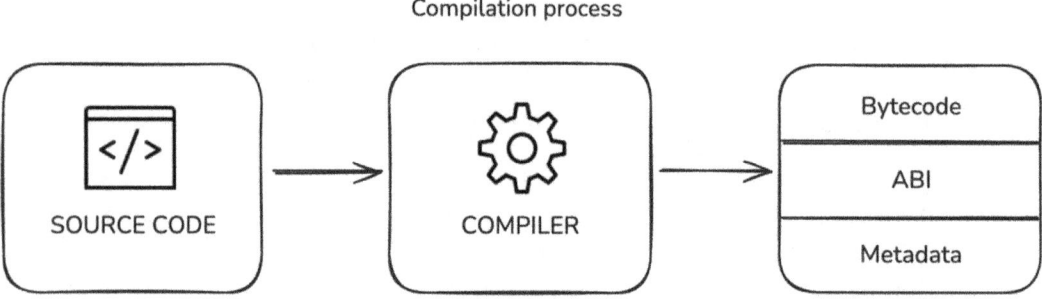

Figure 8-9. *Solidity Compilation Process*

1. **Deploying with Hardhat**

    Hardhat is one of the most widely adopted frameworks for full-stack Ethereum development.

CHAPTER 8 SMART CONTRACTS AND DECENTRALIZED APPLICATIONS

Project setup

1. `npm init -y`
2. `npm install --save-dev hardhat`
3. `npx hardhat`

Choose "Create a basic sample project." It scaffolds a working folder with example contracts and scripts.

Compile the Contract

1. `npx hardhat compile`

Outputs compiled contracts in the artifacts/ directory.

Write a Deployment Script

Create scripts/deploy.js:

```
1.  async function main() {
2.    const [deployer] = await ethers.getSigners();
3.    const VoteBox = await ethers.getContractFactory("VoteBox");
4.    const voteBox = await VoteBox.deploy();
5.    await voteBox.deployed();
6.    console.log("VoteBox deployed to:", voteBox.address);
7.  }
8.  main().catch((error) => {
9.    console.error(error);
10.   process.exitCode = 1;
11. });
```

Deploy Locally

Start a local testnet:

1. `npx hardhat node`

Then run:

1. `npx hardhat run scripts/deploy.js --network localhost`

You'll get an address like:

```
VoteBox deployed to: 0x123...def
```

Deploy to Testnet (e.g., Sepolia)

1. Set up .env file:

   1. `PRIVATE_KEY=your_wallet_private_key`
   2. `INFURA_API_KEY=your_infura_key`

2. Configure hardhat.config.js:

   ```
   1. sepolia: {
   2.   url: `https://sepolia.infura.io/v3/${INFURA_API_KEY}`,
   3.   accounts: [PRIVATE_KEY]
   4. }
   ```

3. Deploy to Sepolia:

   1. `npx hardhat run scripts/deploy.js --network sepolia`

Testnet Tip Use faucets to get test ETH for Sepolia or Goerli.

---

2. **Deploying with Foundry**

   Foundry is CLI-first and super fast. Perfect for scripting deployments in Solidity.

   Install and init project

   ```
   1. curl -L https://foundry.paradigm.xyz | bash
   2. foundryup
   3. forge init vote-box
   4. cd vote-box
   ```

   Place your VoteBox.sol file in the /src directory.

   Compile

   ```
   1. forge build
   ```

   Outputs compiled files into /out and ABI into /out/VoteBox.sol/VoteBox.json.

CHAPTER 8   SMART CONTRACTS AND DECENTRALIZED APPLICATIONS

Deploy

Use the forge create command:

```
1. forge create --rpc-url https://sepolia.infura.io/v3/<API_KEY> \
2.              --private-key <YOUR_PRIVATE_KEY> \
3.              src/VoteBox.sol:VoteBox
```

You'll get:

- Deployed contract address
- Transaction hash

Gas Tip   Use --verify flag to auto-submit the source to Etherscan.

Verify on Etherscan (optional)

```
1. forge verify-contract <address> src/VoteBox.sol:VoteBox <ETHERSCAN_API_KEY>
```

3. **Deploying with Remix**

Remix is the fastest way to deploy for simple contracts or demos.

Open Remix IDE

- Go to remix.ethereum.org
- Paste or upload your contract into the editor

Compile Contract

- Go to the "Solidity Compiler" tab
- Select version (match your pragma)
- Click **Compile VoteBox.sol**

Deploy

- Go to "Deploy & Run Transactions" tab
- Choose environment:
  - **JavaScript VM**: Temporary local chain (no real deployment)
  - **Injected Web3**: Use MetaMask for testnet/mainnet

CHAPTER 8 SMART CONTRACTS AND DECENTRALIZED APPLICATIONS

- Click **Deploy**
- Confirm transaction in MetaMask

You'll get the address, and a full UI to test your contract directly.

Verifying and testing your deployment

After deployment:

- Try calling your functions (e.g., voteYes())
- Use Etherscan or Sepolia Explorer
- Submit your source for verification (for transparency)

Verified contracts:

- Show full code
- Enable UI interaction directly on block explorers
- Build trust with users and other devs

Deployment Best Practices

Table 8-10 summarizes the key practices developers should follow when deploying smart contracts to ensure security, transparency, and reliability.

Table 8-10. Deployment Best Practices

Practice	Why It Matters
Use .env for secrets	Avoid leaking keys in source control
Verify contracts	Makes your contract transparent and callable from explorers
Automate deployments	Use scripts to avoid mistakes and enable reproducibility
Use constructor parameters wisely	Immutable values save gas vs. storage writes
Deploy to testnet first	Always dry-run deployments to test safety and correctness

Testing and Security Best Practices

Writing and deploying a smart contract is just the beginning. Smart contracts are **immutable**, **public,** and often **control real assets,** which means a single vulnerability can lead to **irreversible loss of funds** or **exploitable behavior.**

This section focuses on:

- Proper testing techniques
- How to write good test cases
- Common vulnerabilities
- How to audit and secure your contracts
- Tools for automatic analysis and simulation

It teaches developers how to write **robust and safe contracts** that won't break under pressure or under attack.

The Role of Testing in Smart Contract Development

Smart contract testing has **two goals**:

1. Prove that the code behaves correctly
2. Detect potential bugs, edge cases, or attack vectors

Unlike traditional applications, smart contracts:

- Cannot be patched post-deployment (unless upgradeable, and even that has risks)
- Operate in hostile environments with **economic incentives to attack them**
- Interact with other contracts that may behave unexpectedly

That's why testing is **non-negotiable** in any Web3 project.

Types of Smart Contract Tests

Table 8-11 summarizes the different types of tests and the tools used for each.

Table 8-11. Testing Types and Tools for Smart Contracts

Test Type	What It Covers	Tools
Unit Tests	Single-function correctness and expected behavior	Hardhat, Foundry
Integration	Interactions between functions and other contracts	Hardhat, Ganache, Foundry
Property-Based (Fuzz)	Test invariants under randomized inputs	Foundry, Echidna
Simulation/Fork Testing	Real-world mainnet behavior and edge cases	Tenderly, Anvil
Static Analysis	Detect known bug patterns in code	Slither, MythX

Writing Unit Tests with Hardhat

Hardhat uses Mocha/Chai for writing tests in JavaScript or TypeScript.

Example:

```
1.  describe("VoteBox", function () {
2.    it("should allow voting once", async function () {
3.      const [user] = await ethers.getSigners();
4.      const VoteBox = await ethers.getContractFactory("VoteBox");
5.      const contract = await VoteBox.deploy();
6.
7.      await contract.connect(user).voteYes();
8.      await expect(contract.connect(user).voteYes()).to.be.
         revertedWith("Already voted");
9.    });
10. });
```

Writing Tests in Foundry

Foundry uses **Solidity itself** to write tests.

```solidity
1.  contract VoteBoxTest is Test {
2.      VoteBox voteBox;
3.
4.      function setUp() public {
5.          voteBox = new VoteBox();
6.      }
7.
8.      function testVoteYes() public {
9.          voteBox.voteYes();
10.         assertEq(voteBox.yesVotes(), 1);
11.     }
12.
13.     function testFailDoubleVote() public {
14.         voteBox.voteYes();
15.         voteBox.voteYes(); // Expected to fail
16.     }
17. }
```

Test Prefixes:

- test... → Should pass
- testFail... → Should fail
- fuzz_... → Run with random inputs

Fuzz Testing and Invariant Checks

Fuzzing randomly generates inputs to find edge-case bugs. Figure 8-10 demonstrates the fuzz testing process for identifying edge-case bugs.

Foundry example:

```
1. function testFuzzVote(uint256 choice) public {
2.     vm.assume(choice == 0 || choice == 1);
3.     if (choice == 0) voteBox.voteYes();
4.     else voteBox.voteNo();
5. }
```

Invariant testing ensures a rule is **always true**, no matter what inputs or function call order.

Example:

"Total votes = yesVotes + noVotes"

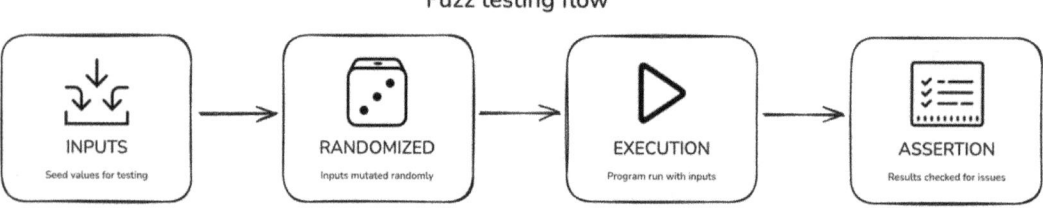

Figure 8-10. Fuzz Testing Flow

Common Smart Contract Vulnerabilities

Table 8-12 highlights common vulnerabilities developers must address before deployment.

Table 8-12. Common Smart Contract Vulnerabilities

Vulnerability	Description
Reentrancy	Attacker calls back into contract before state is updated
Arithmetic Overflows	uint256 variables exceed their max value (less common post-0.8)
Unprotected self-destruct	Allows funds to be destroyed or redirected
Uninitialized Storage Pointers	Can corrupt state
Timestamp Manipulation	Miners can manipulate block.timestamp
Gas Griefing	Operations that force out-of-gas failures
Front-Running/MEV	Timing-sensitive logic like auctions or DeFi positions

Using Static Analysis Tools

Automated tools help detect known patterns and logic errors.

Slither

Static analysis tool by Trail of Bits

- Detects reentrancy, uninitialized storage, dangerous modifiers
- Run with:

    1. slither contracts/VoteBox.sol

MythX

Cloud-based formal verification and vulnerability scanning

- Detects deep logic bugs
- Integrates with Remix or CI pipelines

Foundry Coverage

Analyze which functions and branches were actually tested

- *forge coverage*

Auditing Basics

Even small contracts should undergo **manual review**. Larger protocols should get **formal audits** by professional firms (e.g., OpenZeppelin, Trail of Bits, Sigma Prime).

Checklist Before Deployment:

- All functions tested
- Public/external functions reviewed
- Fallback and receive functions restricted
- Modifiers + access control verified

CHAPTER 8 SMART CONTRACTS AND DECENTRALIZED APPLICATIONS

- Slither reports addressed
- Stable storage layout (especially for upgradeable contracts)

Real-World Testing Strategy

Table 8-13 outlines the recommended testing strategies for each stage of contract development.

Table 8-13. Real-World Testing Strategy by Development Stage

Stage	Tests to Run
Local development	Unit, gas, coverage
Pre-testnet	Integration, fuzz
Testnet	UI-connected testing, long-term monitoring
Pre-mainnet	Static analysis + peer review
Post-deployment	Simulations + alerting systems

Integrating Smart Contracts into Decentralized Applications (dApps)

Smart contracts don't live in isolation; they power **decentralized applications**.

The frontend (React, Vue, Angular, etc.) connects users to the blockchain by:

- Displaying contract data
- Triggering transactions
- Listening for events
- Managing wallet connections
- Handling confirmations, errors, and state changes

This section explains how to **bridge smart contracts and users**, step-by-step, using real code, tools like **ethers.js**, and industry-standard UX patterns.

dApp Architecture Overview

Most decentralized apps follow this general flow:

1. User → Wallet (e.g., MetaMask) → dApp Frontend → RPC Provider → Smart Contract

Each component has its own job (Table 8-14):

Table 8-14. dApp Architecture Layers

Layer	Role
Wallet	Signs transactions, holds keys (e.g., MetaMask and WalletConnect)
Frontend	Calls contract methods via JavaScript libraries
Provider	Relays requests to blockchain (e.g., Infura and Alchemy)
Smart Contract	Executes logic, stores state

Connecting to Wallets

Wallets expose an **Ethereum provider object** to your app (commonly window.ethereum).

To connect:

1. await window.ethereum.request({ method: 'eth_requestAccounts' });

You can also use **ethers.js** to wrap it:

```
1. import { ethers } from 'ethers';
2.
3. const provider = new ethers.providers.Web3Provider(window.ethereum);
4. const signer = provider.getSigner();
```

This signer can now **send transactions**, call contract methods, and query blockchain data.

Best Practice: Handle network switching and account changes via event listeners:

```
1. window.ethereum.on('accountsChanged', handleAccountsChanged);
2. window.ethereum.on('chainChanged', () => window.location.reload());
```

Using ethers.js to Call Contracts

You need two things:

- The **contract address**
- The **ABI** (Application Binary Interface)

1. `const contract = new ethers.Contract(contractAddress, abi, signer);`

Calling View Functions (No Gas)

1. `const yesCount = await contract.yesVotes();`

Sending Transactions (Costs Gas)

1. `const tx = await contract.voteYes();    // Triggers MetaMask popup`
2. `await tx.wait();                        // Wait for confirmation`

Displaying Events and Real-Time Feedback

Contracts emit **events**, which your frontend can subscribe to:

1. `contract.on("Voted", (voter, vote) => {`
2. `  console.log(`${voter} voted ${vote ? 'YES' : 'NO'}`);`
3. `});`

Use Case: Update the UI in real time as new votes arrive, no need to refresh or poll.

Handling Gas, Errors, and Confirmations

You should

- Show estimated gas fees
- Handle failed transactions gracefully
- Display status while waiting for confirmation

Example TX lifecycle handler:

```
1. try {
2.     const tx = await contract.voteYes();
3.     setStatus("Transaction sent. Waiting for confirmation...");
4.     await tx.wait();
5.     setStatus("Vote recorded!");
6. } catch (err) {
7.     setStatus("Transaction failed: " + err.message);
8. }
```

User Experience Tip Always give users a progress status; otherwise, they'll assume something broke.

Network Management and Testnets

Your contract may live on

- Local testnets (Hardhat and Anvil)
- Public testnets (Sepolia and Mumbai)
- Mainnet (Ethereum, Polygon, etc.)

Use window.ethereum.networkVersion or provider.getNetwork() to check current chain.

Prompt for switching:

```
1. await window.ethereum.request({
2.     method: 'wallet_switchEthereumChain',
3.     params: [{ chainId: '0x1' }] // Ethereum Mainnet
4. });
```

Security Tip Always verify the chain before sending real funds.

CHAPTER 8 SMART CONTRACTS AND DECENTRALIZED APPLICATIONS

Using Frontend Libraries and Frameworks

Popular tools:

- **Web3Modal**: wallet connection popups
- **RainbowKit**: UI + wallet integration
- **wagmi**: React hooks for Ethereum
- **useDApp/EtherSWR**: stateful contract queries

These frameworks simplify:

- Wallet state
- Gas fee management
- Contract interaction wrappers

UI/UX Patterns for Web3

Table 8-15 lists essential UX patterns that improve usability and reliability in dApps.

Table 8-15. UI/UX Patterns for Web3 Applications

UX Element	Why It Matters
"Connect Wallet" button	First point of interaction
Pending TX indicator	Reduces uncertainty
Gas cost preview	Builds trust
Error toasts	Show MetaMask or revert messages clearly
Event-driven updates	Real-time UI = better experience

Anti-pattern to avoid: Don't reload the page after a transaction; update the state with events instead.

Conclusion

Smart contracts are not simply code; they are **decentralized, self-enforcing agreements** that serve as the backbone of the modern Web3 ecosystem. From managing multi-billion-dollar DeFi protocols to issuing NFTs, running DAOs, and powering on-chain games, smart contracts have transformed the way applications are written, trusted, and deployed.

But raw contract code isn't enough. Real impact comes when smart contracts are **paired with decentralized applications** that expose intuitive UIs, allow wallet-based interaction, and bridge users to the blockchain in a secure and seamless way.

This chapter has taken you through the full lifecycle, from understanding what smart contracts are to writing them, testing them, deploying them, and integrating them into robust applications. You've also seen the most important tools, patterns, and pitfalls along the way.

Armed with this knowledge, you're no longer just reading about Web3. You're ready to **build it.**

Chapter Summary

Section	Key Takeaways
Smart Contracts Basics	Defined as immutable, deterministic code that enforces agreements without intermediaries.
Architecture and Design	Covers on-chain vs. off-chain logic, storage design, modular contracts, and proxy patterns.
Use Cases	Includes DeFi, NFTs, DAOs, gaming, supply chain, and identity management.
Development Lifecycle	Drafting ➤ Coding ➤ Compiling ➤ Deploying ➤ Verifying ➤ Interacting ➤ Monitoring.
Gas and Efficiency	Gas determines cost; optimization techniques improve scalability and reduce expenses.
Tools and Frameworks	Hardhat, Foundry, Truffle, and Remix enable building, testing, and deploying contracts.
Testing and Security	Includes unit tests, fuzzing, vulnerability checks, audits, and real-world testing strategies.
dApp Integration	Explains how contracts integrate into frontends, wallets, providers, and full applications.

CHAPTER 9

Web Development with Angular

Introduction

Modern web applications demand more than beautiful interfaces. They need robust architecture, predictable state management, excellent developer experience, and the flexibility to grow. Angular provides a complete, opinionated framework for building complex, maintainable web applications that scale gracefully from small sites to large enterprise platforms.

Before diving into blockchain integrations, it's essential to understand how to craft a well-structured web application using the modern Angular ecosystem. This chapter will walk you through the foundational concepts that make Angular a trusted choice for high-performance web development, from components and services to routing, state management, and performance strategies. Along the way, you'll see how recent advancements in Angular's design philosophy, tooling, and reactivity models strengthen your ability to build responsive, maintainable applications.

By mastering these principles now, you'll be ready to extend your skills into the next level: combining modern frontend architecture with decentralized technologies.

Introduction to Angular

Angular is a robust, full-featured framework designed to build dynamic, maintainable, and scalable web applications. Over the years, it has evolved significantly, earning its place as a trusted choice for complex projects in industries ranging from finance to healthcare, e-commerce, and government platforms.

CHAPTER 9   WEB DEVELOPMENT WITH ANGULAR

A Brief History

Angular's journey began with its early predecessor, commonly known today as AngularJS. Initially released in 2010, it introduced concepts that reshaped how developers approached web interfaces: declarative templates, dependency injection, and two-way data binding. However, as web standards advanced and application requirements became more sophisticated, a complete architectural rethink was necessary.

This need for modernization led to the creation of Angular as we know it today: a framework built from the ground up with performance, modularity, and maintainability in mind. Unlike its predecessor, this modern Angular was rewritten with TypeScript at its core, enabling better tooling, strong typing, and a more predictable development experience.

From Rewrite to Reinvention

One of the most significant shifts was the separation of concerns through a component-based architecture. Applications are now organized into cohesive, reusable building blocks: components for UI logic and rendering, services for encapsulating shared behavior, and modules for organizing related features.

This emphasis on modular design allows teams to scale projects with confidence, sharing responsibilities across multiple developers while maintaining clear boundaries between features.

Another cornerstone of Angular's design is its commitment to declarative programming: templates define **what** should appear, while the framework handles the **how** behind updates and rendering. This philosophy reduces the manual synchronization between state and DOM that plagues older JavaScript solutions.

Core Design Principles

At its heart, Angular rests on three guiding principles:

1. **Modularity**. Applications are composed of small, focused units that can be reused, tested, and maintained independently.

2. **Dependency Injection**. A powerful built-in mechanism that manages how classes and services depend on each other, simplifying configuration and promoting testability.

3. **Type Safety and Tooling**. The TypeScript-first approach provides developers with static analysis, auto-completion, and early detection of potential bugs, enhancing long-term project maintainability.

Over time, Angular's ecosystem has introduced various innovations that keep it aligned with the changing demands of web development. Features like a new rendering engine, streamlined build processes, advanced reactivity through signals, standalone components, and zoneless change detection reflect its continued focus on performance, developer productivity, and maintainability.

Who Uses Angular Today?

Angular continues to be widely adopted by large enterprises and teams building mission-critical applications. Its structure and opinionated approach make it especially suitable for projects that benefit from clear conventions, long-term support, and robust tooling.

Beyond the enterprise, a vibrant community contributes to its evolution through open-source libraries, educational resources, and best practices. The framework's rich ecosystem includes UI libraries, state management solutions, and integrations with modern development workflows, ensuring that developers have the tools they need to deliver sophisticated user experiences.

Staying Current

A hallmark of Angular's sustainability is its commitment to a steady release cadence and transparent roadmap. Developers benefit from predictable updates, progressive enhancements, and a thriving community that supports continuous learning and innovation.

As this chapter unfolds, you'll explore the foundational architecture, core patterns, and modern capabilities that make Angular a reliable choice for building sophisticated web applications and why it remains a strong candidate for powering decentralized applications and integrating seamlessly with blockchain technology in the chapters ahead.

Angular Architecture and Core Concepts

To build effective, scalable web applications with Angular, it is essential to understand its core architecture and the fundamental building blocks that define how an application is structured and how data flows through it. This section explores these concepts, explaining how they work together to support clean design, maintainability, and robust user interfaces.

Components, Services, and Modules

Components are the heart of every Angular application. A component controls a patch of the screen; it contains the template (the HTML to render) and the logic that supports interaction with that template. By designing applications as collections of reusable components, developers break down complex UIs into manageable pieces.

Services encapsulate shared logic that does not belong in a component's view or local state. Services handle tasks like retrieving data from an API, managing user authentication, or storing shared application state. Angular's dependency injection system makes it easy to provide services wherever they're needed, promoting reusability and testability.

Modules, historically, have been Angular's way of organizing related components, services, and other features into cohesive units. While many modern applications now use **standalone components** to reduce boilerplate and simplify project structure, understanding both approaches remains valuable. Standalone components allow developers to declare individual components without wrapping them in a module, streamlining smaller applications or features while still supporting modular design when needed.

Key Point: Whether using modules, standalone components, or a hybrid, the goal remains the same: to keep the codebase organized, maintainable, and easy to reason about as it grows.

Routing and Navigation

Single-page applications rely on client-side routing to display different views without reloading the page. Angular's **Router** provides a flexible way to define application routes, associate them with components, and manage navigation.

Routes are typically defined in a configuration object that maps URL paths to the components that should render for each path. The *<router-outlet>* directive acts as a placeholder in the template where the matched component appears.

In larger applications, the router also supports advanced features like **lazy loading**, which loads feature areas only when needed, improving initial load time and overall performance.

Change Detection

Angular's change detection mechanism keeps the application's view in sync with its underlying data model. When data changes, Angular automatically updates the DOM to reflect those changes.

Traditionally, Angular has relied on a mechanism known as Zone.js to track when changes occur. However, modern approaches increasingly favor **zoneless change detection**, where explicit signals track reactivity and developers can control when updates propagate through the component tree. This fine-grained reactivity reduces unnecessary work and can significantly improve performance in complex applications.

Forms: Template-Driven vs. Reactive

Forms are central to most web applications. Angular offers two complementary approaches for building forms:

- **Template-driven forms** use directives in the template to bind input elements to model data. They are straightforward and suitable for simple forms with minimal logic.

- **Reactive forms** use explicit form control objects in the component's TypeScript code to model the form's structure and validation rules. This approach provides greater control, making it ideal for dynamic, complex forms with robust validation requirements.

Both approaches leverage Angular's binding system and validators to ensure user input is collected, verified, and processed efficiently.

Directives and Pipes

Directives and pipes extend templates with dynamic behavior and transformations.

Directives come in two forms:

- *Attribute directives* modify the appearance or behavior of an existing element (e.g., changing styles or listening for events).

- *Structural directives* change the structure of the DOM by adding or removing elements. Examples include conditional rendering and iteration.

Modern Angular introduces a more expressive control flow syntax for structural directives, offering a clearer, more maintainable way to handle common patterns like if conditions and loops.

Pipes transform displayed data within templates. Common uses include formatting dates and currencies or filtering lists. Pipes keep templates declarative and concise.

Component Lifecycle Hooks

Angular provides a set of **lifecycle hooks** that let developers tap into key moments in a component's life, from creation through rendering to destruction. These hooks allow for initialization logic, responding to input changes, subscribing to streams, and performing cleanup.

Examples include

- *ngOnInit*: runs after the component's data-bound properties are initialized.

- *ngOnChanges*: responds when input properties change.

- *ngOnDestroy*: handles teardown tasks like unsubscribing from observables.

Putting It All Together

The interplay of components, services, routing, forms, directives, and lifecycle hooks shapes how an Angular application works. Together, these core concepts create a clear separation of concerns, encourage reuse, and make applications easier to test and maintain. Figure 9-1 illustrates the layered architecture of a modern Angular application.

CHAPTER 9 WEB DEVELOPMENT WITH ANGULAR

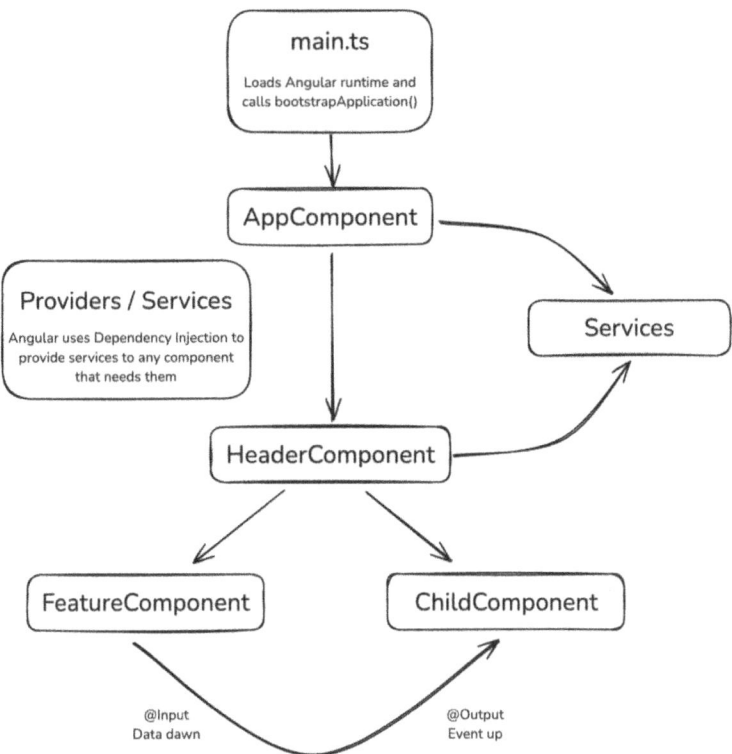

Figure 9-1. *Angular Application Architecture*

Angular CLI and Project Setup

A robust framework is only as good as its tooling. Angular's command-line interface (CLI) is an integral part of its ecosystem, designed to streamline every stage of development, from project scaffolding to building, testing, and deployment.

Understanding how to set up a project and navigate its structure lays the groundwork for building reliable, maintainable applications.

Installing the Angular CLI

The Angular CLI is installed globally using a Node package manager. Once installed, it provides a suite of commands to generate code, manage dependencies, run a local development server, and optimize builds.

1. npm install -g @angular/cli

After installation, the version can be verified to ensure the development environment is correctly set up:

1. `ng version`

Creating a New Project

A new project is initialized with the ng new command. The CLI prompts developers to make choices such as

- Whether to include routing for client-side navigation.
- Which stylesheet format to use (CSS, SCSS, etc.).
- Whether to generate the project structure using standalone components or traditional modules.

For example:

1. `ng new my-app`

This command creates a ready-to-run application with all dependencies configured. The project can be served locally with:

1. `cd my-app`
2. `ng serve`

By default, the application runs on http://localhost:4200/, providing instant feedback for any changes made during development.

Project Structure

A typical Angular project follows a clear and predictable folder structure. At the root, several key files define how the project behaves:

- *angular.json*: The workspace configuration file that manages build options, project targets, and assets.
- *package.json*: Lists project dependencies, scripts, and metadata.

- *package-lock.json*: Automatically generated file that locks the dependency tree to specific versions, ensuring consistent installs across environments.

- *tsconfig.json*: Configures TypeScript options for compilation.

- *src/*: The source folder, containing the application code, assets, and styles.

Inside *src/*, the core files include

- *main.ts*: The entry point of the application, which bootstraps the root component.

- *index.html*: The single HTML page that hosts the app.

- *styles.**: Global stylesheets.

- *app/*: The root folder for components, services, and feature modules or standalone components.

Note Many modern applications favor standalone components as the default. This approach reduces boilerplate and allows developers to bootstrap applications directly from a single root component without wrapping it in a module.

Standalone vs. Module-Based Structure

In a standalone structure, the main.ts file typically bootstraps the application using a direct call to bootstrapApplication, specifying the root component and any providers:

```
1. import { bootstrapApplication } from '@angular/platform-browser';
2. import { AppComponent } from './app/app.component';
3.
4. bootstrapApplication(AppComponent);
```

CHAPTER 9   WEB DEVELOPMENT WITH ANGULAR

For module-based setups, an AppModule would first be defined and then bootstrapped instead:

```
1. import { platformBrowserDynamic } from '@angular/platform-browser-
   dynamic';
2. import { AppModule } from './app/app.module';
3.
4. platformBrowserDynamic().bootstrapModule(AppModule);
```

Both structures are fully supported. Choosing between them depends on team preferences and project requirements.

Environmental Management

Angular projects often require different configurations for development, staging, and production environments. Environment files (*environment.ts*) provide a clean way to define variables specific to each context.

The build system automatically replaces these files during compilation, ensuring that sensitive production settings, like API endpoints and feature flags, remain isolated from development values.

Common naming conventions for environment files include:

- *Environment.ts*: Default development environment
- *Environment.prod.ts*: Production environment
- *environment.staging.ts*: Staging or pre-production environment

Modern Build System

Angular's build process has steadily improved to provide faster development servers and optimized production bundles. Modern projects benefit from high-performance build tools that leverage technologies like **esbuild** and **Vite** under the hood, delivering rapid rebuilds, hot module replacement (HMR), and smaller output bundles.

These optimizations result in quicker feedback during development and faster page loads for end users in production.

Extending the Project with Schematics

Beyond project creation, the CLI supports **schematics**, which are templates for generating code snippets like components, directives, services, or entire features. This reduces repetitive boilerplate and enforces consistent conventions across teams.

For example, to generate a new component:

1. `ng generate component dashboard`

This command creates the component's TypeScript, template, stylesheet and test files, updating any necessary declarations automatically.

Putting It into Practice

A well-structured project setup, supported by clear configuration and a powerful CLI, forms the backbone of a maintainable Angular application. Understanding how to navigate this setup ensures that developers can spend more time solving business problems and less time wrestling with configuration.

Practical Tip   Consider adding linters, formatting tools, or monorepo support early in a project's lifecycle. Integrating these tools through the CLI ensures consistent quality and productivity as the codebase grows.

A solid foundation starts here. With the project structure in place, the next step is learning how to handle application state effectively, balancing local reactivity and shared state for modern single-page applications.

State Management in Angular

State management is at the heart of every dynamic web application. It determines how user interactions, API responses, and component updates are handled and kept in sync. Poor state handling can lead to unpredictable bugs, inconsistent data, and performance bottlenecks, so it is vital to adopt patterns that match your application's scale and complexity.

Why State Management Matters

In a single-page application, state can come from various sources:

- **Local Component State**: Data that belongs to a single component, such as form input or a toggle.

- **Shared Application State**: Data that multiple components depend on, such as user authentication status, theme preferences, or cached API results.

Managing this flow of data cleanly ensures that views stay in sync with logic and that changes propagate predictably throughout the application.

Local State with Components

For many use cases, local state is sufficient. This might include form inputs, UI toggles, or temporary data only relevant to a single component. Local state is often handled using standard class properties, template bindings, and built-in lifecycle hooks.

For example, a simple toggle for showing or hiding a section:

```
1. export class ExampleComponent {
2.   showDetails = false;
3.
4.   toggleDetails() {
5.     this.showDetails = !this.showDetails;
6.   }
7. }
```

The template reacts automatically:

```
1. <button (click)="toggleDetails()">Toggle Details</button>
2.
3. @if (showDetails) {
4.   <div>
5.     Additional content here.
6.   </div>
7. }
```

Reactive State with RxJS

When dealing with asynchronous data (e.g., data fetched from an API), Angular developers commonly use **RxJS**, a library for reactive programming with observables.

Observables allow components and services to emit streams of data that other parts of the application can subscribe to and react to in real time.

A simple service using RxJS:

```
1.  import { Injectable } from '@angular/core';
2.  import { HttpClient } from '@angular/common/http';
3.  import { BehaviorSubject } from 'rxjs';
4.
5.  @Injectable({ providedIn: 'root' })
6.  export class UserService {
7.    private userSubject = new BehaviorSubject<User | null>(null);
8.    user$ = this.userSubject.asObservable();
9.
10.   constructor(private http: HttpClient) {}
11.
12.   loadUser() {
13.     this.http.get<User>('/api/user').subscribe(user => this.userSubject.next(user));
14.   }
15. }
```

A component can subscribe to this observable using the async pipe:

```
1.  @if (userService.user$ | async as user) {
2.    <div>
3.      Welcome, {{ user.name }}!
4.    </div>
5.  }
```

This pattern keeps components declarative and reactive without manual subscription management in most cases.

Global State with Store Patterns

As applications grow larger, developers often adopt centralized state management patterns. These patterns help coordinate state shared across multiple areas of the application in a predictable and testable way.

One popular approach is the **Redux-inspired Store pattern**, commonly implemented with libraries that integrate naturally with Angular. The store acts as a single source of truth for the application state. Actions are dispatched to update state, and selectors allow components to read specific pieces of that state.

A centralized store is especially useful for

- Applications with complex workflows
- Features that require undo/redo
- Scenarios where multiple parts of the UI depend on the same data

While powerful, store patterns can introduce additional boilerplate. For smaller or medium applications, simpler state management may be more practical.

Fine-Grained Reactivity with Signals

Modern Angular applications can take advantage of **signals**, a primitive for fine-grained reactivity. Signals provide a simple, declarative way to manage local state that automatically triggers updates when the underlying value changes.

A signal example:

```
1. import { signal } from '@angular/core';
2.
3. export class CounterComponent {
4.   count = signal(0);
5.
6.   increment() {
7.     this.count.update(v => v + 1);
8.   }
9. }
```

CHAPTER 9   WEB DEVELOPMENT WITH ANGULAR

In the template:

1. `<button (click)="increment()">Increment</button>`
2. `<p>Count: {{ count() }}</p>`

Signals reduce the need for manual subscriptions and can be combined with observables and other reactive patterns for more advanced scenarios.

When to Avoid Overengineering

Not every project needs a heavy state management solution. For simple or medium-sized applications, well-organized local state and reactive services are often enough. Overly complex stores can add unnecessary overhead, slow onboarding for new developers, and increase maintenance costs.

A practical rule:

- Use local component state for isolated features.
- Use services and observables for shared or asynchronous data.
- Introduce a store pattern only when the complexity of data flow and interactions justifies it.

Putting It into Practice

Choosing the right state management strategy is not about selecting a single tool but about combining multiple patterns that complement each other. A well-designed application uses local state, services, reactive streams, and modern primitives like signals together to balance simplicity and power. As shown in Figure 9-2, Angular offers multiple approaches for handling application state.

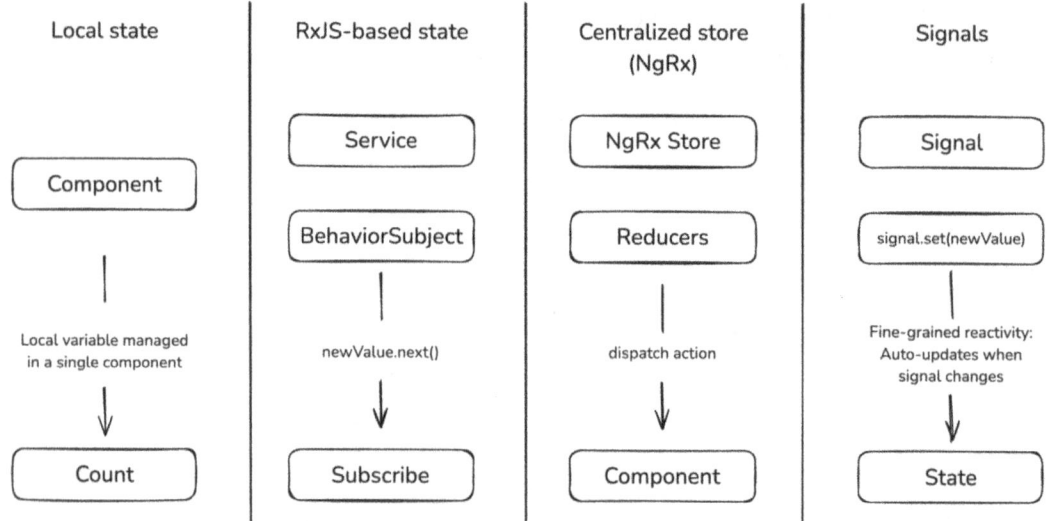

Figure 9-2. Comparing State Management Approaches in Angular

By understanding and applying these patterns wisely, developers can ensure their Angular applications remain predictable, responsive, and maintainable as they grow.

Working with HTTP and APIs

Modern web applications rarely operate in isolation. They interact constantly with remote servers, third-party services, and real-time data streams. Angular provides powerful tools and patterns for handling HTTP requests and managing external data in a clean, testable way.

The HttpClient

At the core of Angular's networking capabilities is the HttpClient. It offers a streamlined API for making HTTP calls and handling request headers, query parameters, and response types with ease.

To enable HTTP communication, the relevant provider is added to the application's configuration. In projects using standalone components, this is typically done during bootstrap:

```
1. import { provideHttpClient } from '@angular/common/http';
2. import { bootstrapApplication } from '@angular/platform-browser';
3. import { AppComponent } from './app/app.component';
4.
5. bootstrapApplication(AppComponent, {
6.   providers: [provideHttpClient()]
7. });
```

Once configured, the HttpClient can be injected into services or components to send requests.

Creating a Service for API Calls

A best practice in Angular is to isolate data-fetching logic in dedicated services. This keeps components focused on presentation and interaction while services handle communication with external systems.

A simple example:

```
1.  import { Injectable } from '@angular/core';
2.  import { HttpClient } from '@angular/common/http';
3.  import { Observable } from 'rxjs';
4.
5.  export interface Post {
6.    id: number;
7.    title: string;
8.    body: string;
9.  }
10.
11. @Injectable({ providedIn: 'root' })
12. export class ApiService {
13.   constructor(private http: HttpClient) {}
14.
15.   getPosts(): Observable<Post[]> {
16.     return this.http.get<Post[]>('https://jsonplaceholder.typicode.com/posts');
17.   }
18. }
```

Chapter 9 Web Development with Angular

By exposing an observable, this service allows consuming components to subscribe reactively and handle data as it arrives.

Consuming Data in a Component

A component uses the service by subscribing to its method or by binding the observable directly in the template with the async pipe:

```
1. import { Component, OnInit } from '@angular/core';
2. import { ApiService, Post } from './api.service';
3.
4. @Component({
5.   selector: 'app-posts',
6.   templateUrl: './posts.component.html'
7. })
8. export class PostsComponent implements OnInit {
9.   posts$ = this.apiService.getPosts();
10.
11.   constructor(private apiService: ApiService) {}
12.
13.   ngOnInit(): void {}
14. }
```

Template:

```
1. <ul>
2.   @for (post of posts$ | async) {
3.     <li>
4.       {{ post.title }}
5.     </li>
6.   }
7. </ul>
```

This pattern ensures the UI stays reactive without manual subscriptions or unsubscriptions.

Handling Errors and Retries

Robust applications anticipate network failures. Using RxJS operators, developers can handle errors, retry requests, or cancel them cleanly.

Example with catchError and retry:

```
1. import { catchError, retry } from 'rxjs/operators';
2. import { throwError } from 'rxjs';
3.
4. getPosts(): Observable<Post[]> {
5.   return this.http.get<Post[]>('https://jsonplaceholder.typicode.com/posts').pipe(
6.     retry(2), // Retry up to 2 times before failing
7.     catchError(error => {
8.       console.error('Request failed', error);
9.       return throwError(() => new Error('Something went wrong'));
10.    })
11.  );
12. }
```

Working with REST and GraphQL APIs

Angular's HttpClient works naturally with RESTful APIs, supporting all HTTP verbs – GET, POST, PUT, PATCH, and DELETE – and custom headers.

For GraphQL, a common practice is to use dedicated client libraries. These libraries integrate with Angular services to send queries and mutations, cache responses, and manage updates efficiently.

Example: Using a GraphQL client in a service to query data could follow the same pattern, keeping the GraphQL logic in the service and exposing observables to the component.

Real-Time Data with WebSockets

For applications that require real-time updates, such as chat apps, dashboards, or live feeds, Angular can integrate with **WebSockets** or **Server-Sent Events (SSE)**.

WebSocket connections can be managed inside a service using RxJS subjects or observables to push new data to subscribers:

```typescript
1. import { Injectable } from '@angular/core';
2. import { webSocket, WebSocketSubject } from 'rxjs/webSocket';
3.
4. @Injectable({ providedIn: 'root' })
5. export class LiveUpdatesService {
6.   private socket$: WebSocketSubject<any> = webSocket('ws://example.com/socket');
7.
8.   getMessages() {
9.     return this.socket$;
10.  }
11.
12.  sendMessage(msg: any) {
13.    this.socket$.next(msg);
14.  }
15. }
```

This service streams live data to components in real time, keeping the user interface reactive and up-to-date.

Example: API Service with Pagination

In a real-world scenario, a service might fetch paginated results from an API. Here's a simplified version:

```typescript
1. getPaginatedPosts(page: number, limit: number): Observable<Post[]> {
2.   return this.http.get<Post[]>(
3.     `https://jsonplaceholder.typicode.com/posts?_page=${page}&_limit=${limit}`
4.   );
5. }
```

A component can expose the current page state and update it with user interaction, fetching new data when needed.

Putting It into Practice

By separating API logic into services, using observables to handle asynchronous flows, and taking advantage of built-in tools for error handling and real-time communication, Angular developers build applications that stay responsive and resilient under changing conditions.

Practical Example: Try building a simple dashboard that loads a list of items from a public API, shows a loading state, handles errors gracefully, and supports basic pagination.

With data retrieval in place, the next step is ensuring that applications look polished and provide a great user experience, often using reusable UI components and design systems.

Building Reusable UI with Angular Material

A professional user interface is more than just a collection of HTML elements; it's a system of consistent, accessible, and reusable components. To help developers deliver polished, production-ready UIs efficiently, Angular provides integration with **Angular Material**, a comprehensive component library based on Google's Material Design system.

What Is Angular Material?

Angular Material offers a wide range of prebuilt UI components (buttons, form fields, navigation elements, tables, dialogs, and more), all following modern design guidelines and built to integrate seamlessly into Angular applications.

The library emphasizes accessibility, responsiveness, and theming out of the box, allowing teams to maintain visual consistency across their applications while focusing on business logic rather than low-level UI implementation.

In addition to the main components, the **Component Dev Kit (CDK)** provides low-level building blocks for creating custom behaviors, like overlays, drag-and-drop, and virtual scrolling.

Adding Angular Material to a Project

Angular Material is installed via the CLI, which helps developers configure themes, typography, and animations automatically:

1. `ng add @angular/material`

The CLI prompts for theme choices and sets up global styles and animations modules, ensuring the project is ready to use Material components immediately.

Theming and Customization

A key strength of Angular Material is its theming system. Developers can define custom color palettes, typography, and design tokens to match brand guidelines.

A typical theme uses primary, accent, and warn palettes, plus background and surface colors. Themes can be extended with custom design tokens for finer control.

Example: setting up a custom theme using SCSS:

```scss
1.  @use '@angular/material' as mat;
2.
3.  $my-primary: mat.define-palette(mat.$indigo-palette);
4.  $my-accent: mat.define-palette(mat.$pink-palette, A200, A100, A400);
5.  $my-theme: mat.define-light-theme((
6.    color: (
7.      primary: $my-primary,
8.      accent: $my-accent,
9.    )
10. ));
11.
12. @include mat.all-component-themes($my-theme);
```

This approach ensures a consistent look while allowing full control over branding.

Commonly Used Components

Angular Material provides ready-made solutions for many everyday UI needs. Some typical examples include:

- **Navigation Toolbar:** Provides headers, side navigation, and menus.
- **Form Controls:** Includes text fields, checkboxes, radio buttons, and sliders with built-in validation states.
- **Data Tables:** Offer sorting, pagination, and filtering for large data sets.
- **Dialogs and Overlays:** Support modal dialogs and popups for user interactions.
- **Snackbars and Toasts:** Display brief notifications.

Example: A simple form field with validation:

```
1.  <mat-form-field appearance="fill">
2.    <mat-label>Email</mat-label>
3.    <input matInput placeholder="example@example.com"
         [formControl]="emailControl">
4.  
5.    @if (emailControl.hasError('email')) {
6.      <mat-error>
7.        Please enter a valid email address
8.      </mat-error>
9.    }
10. </mat-form-field>
```

The mat-form-field component wraps the input, label, and error state, providing a consistent style and behavior.

Creating Custom Components with the CDK

Sometimes, applications require custom UI elements not covered by the core library. The **Angular CDK** helps developers build these elements by providing reusable behaviors.

For example:

- **Overlay**: Create floating panels like tooltips or custom dropdowns.

CHAPTER 9   WEB DEVELOPMENT WITH ANGULAR

- **Drag and Drop**: Add reorderable lists or draggable items.
- **Portal**: Dynamically render templates or components in different parts of the DOM.

By combining the CDK's low-level tools with Angular's component architecture, developers can create reusable custom UI elements while maintaining consistency with the rest of the application.

Combining Components into a Layout

A typical Angular Material application uses multiple components together to build a cohesive layout.

Example: A basic app shell with a toolbar, side navigation, and content area:

```
1.  <mat-sidenav-container class="example-container">
2.    <mat-sidenav mode="side" opened>
3.      <p>Navigation Links</p>
4.    </mat-sidenav>
5.
6.    <mat-sidenav-content>
7.      <mat-toolbar color="primary">
8.        My Application
9.      </mat-toolbar>
10.     <div class="content">
11.       <!-- Routed views render here -->
12.       <router-outlet></router-outlet>
13.     </div>
14.   </mat-sidenav-content>
15. </mat-sidenav-container>
```

The layout ensures that navigation, headers, and content work together responsively.

Putting It into Practice

By combining Angular Material's prebuilt components with custom elements built using the CDK, teams can deliver UIs that are beautiful, accessible, and maintainable. The theming system makes it easy to adapt the look and feel to match any brand, while reusable patterns speed up development. Figure 9-3 demonstrates how Angular Material provides ready-to-use components for building cohesive interfaces.

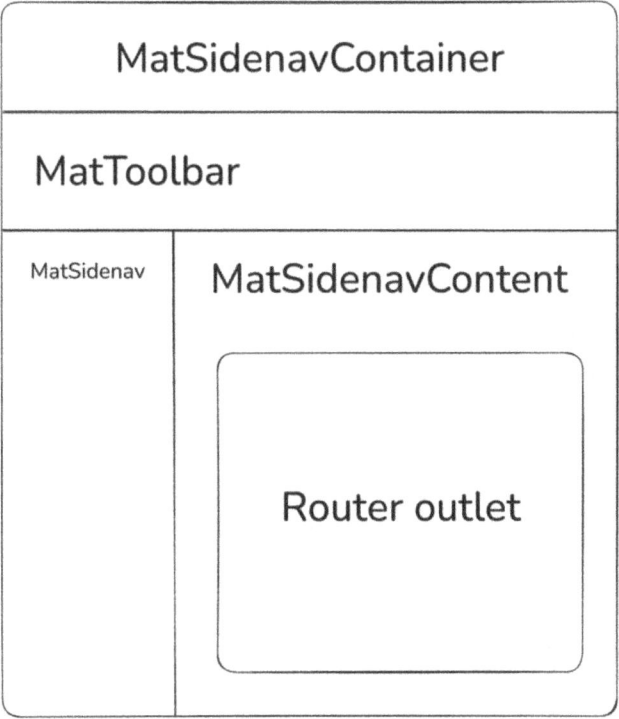

Figure 9-3. *Angular Material UI Components for Consistent Design*

With the UI in place, the next step is handling navigation, route security, and performance optimizations through routing, guards, and lazy loading.

Routing, Guards, and Lazy Loading

Routing is a fundamental part of building a single-page application (SPA) with Angular. It determines how users navigate between different views without reloading the entire page, how data is fetched before navigation occurs, and how developers optimize application performance by loading only what's needed, when it's needed.

CHAPTER 9　WEB DEVELOPMENT WITH ANGULAR

Angular Router Fundamentals

The **Angular Router** is a powerful module that maps URL paths to specific components. This allows users to navigate through an application's different features while staying on the same page.

A simple route configuration maps a URL path to a component:

```
1. import { Routes } from '@angular/router';
2.
3. export const routes: Routes = [
4.   { path: '', component: HomeComponent },
5.   { path: 'about', component: AboutComponent },
6.   { path: '**', component: NotFoundComponent }
7. ];
```

The ** wildcard matches any unmatched paths, helping handle 404 scenarios.

In the root template, the *<router-outlet>* directive marks where the routed component should render:

```
1. <nav>
2.   <a routerLink="/">Home</a>
3.   <a routerLink="/about">About</a>
4. </nav>
5.
6. <router-outlet></router-outlet>
```

Links use routerLink to enable client-side navigation without a page reload.

Nested Routes and Route Parameters

Applications often require nested routes or dynamic segments. Child routes allow developers to define sub-sections within a parent view. For example, an admin section might have routes for users, settings, and logs:

```
1. {
2.   path: 'admin',
3.   component: AdminComponent,
4.   children: [
```

5.   { path: 'users', component: UserListComponent },
6.   { path: 'settings', component: SettingsComponent }
7.   ]
8. }

Dynamic segments use *:param* syntax to capture variable values:

1. { path: 'post/:id', component: PostDetailComponent }

A component can then access route parameters to fetch specific data:

1. constructor(private route: ActivatedRoute) {}
2.
3. ngOnInit() {
4.   const id = this.route.snapshot.paramMap.get('id');
5.   // Use id to fetch post details
6. }

Route Guards

Route guards protect routes by controlling whether navigation can proceed. They can check permissions, prompt users to save changes, or pre-fetch data.

Common guard interfaces include:

- *CanActivate*: decides if a route can be activated.
- *CanDeactivate*: checks if it's safe to leave a route.
- *Resolve*: fetches data before the route loads.

Example CanActivate guard:

1. import { Injectable } from '@angular/core';
2. import { CanActivate, Router } from '@angular/router';
3.
4. @Injectable({ providedIn: 'root' })
5. export class AuthGuard implements CanActivate {
6.   constructor(private router: Router) {}
7.
8.   canActivate(): boolean {

```
 9.     const isAuthenticated = /* check user authentication */;
10.     if (!isAuthenticated) {
11.       this.router.navigate(['/login']);
12.       return false;
13.     }
14.     return true;
15.   }
16. }
```

The guard is applied in the route config:

```
1. { path: 'admin', component: AdminComponent, canActivate: [AuthGuard] }
```

Lazy Loading

One of the key performance strategies in Angular is **lazy loading**, the practice of splitting the application into feature areas that load only when the user needs them. This reduces the initial bundle size and speeds up the time to first meaningful paint.

To lazy load a feature area, the router configuration uses the loadChildren property:

```
1. {
2.   path: 'admin',
3.   loadChildren: () => import('./admin/admin.routes').then(m => m.routes)
4. }
```

In this setup, the admin section and its child routes load only when a user navigates to */admin*.

Lazy loading is especially useful for large applications with many independent sections.

Advanced Routing Features

Modern routing configurations can handle additional concerns:

- **Preloading Strategies:** Load some feature areas in the background to balance performance and responsiveness.
- **Scroll Position Restoration:** Control whether the scroll position resets or restores when navigating back and forth.

- **Custom Route Reuse Strategies:** Configure Angular to precisely manage component reuse during route transitions.

These features ensure that navigation feels fast, intuitive, and smooth for the user.

Putting It into Practice

A secure admin panel is a common scenario that demonstrates routing, guards, and lazy loading in action:

- Routes for admin features are defined in a separate module or standalone route file.
- Access is protected with a guard that verifies user roles.
- The admin section is lazy loaded to keep the main bundle lightweight for public users.

Practical Tip For public-facing applications, lazy loading rarely accessed areas (like analytics dashboards, settings panels, or admin tools) helps keep the core experience fast and responsive.

Angular's router provides the tools needed to create seamless navigation experiences, protect routes, and optimize performance through code splitting. Combined with good state management and a polished UI, routing ties together the structure of a modern, robust application.

Testing Angular Applications

Testing is an essential part of any serious web development workflow. Well-tested applications are more reliable, easier to maintain, and simpler to extend as requirements evolve. Angular's tooling and conventions make testing a first-class citizen, providing robust support for unit tests, integration tests, and end-to-end (E2E) tests.

Why Test?

Testing ensures that

- Features work as intended.
- Future changes don't introduce unexpected bugs.
- Code is easier to refactor with confidence.
- Edge cases and failure conditions are handled gracefully.

A thoughtful testing strategy balances different levels of tests: small and fast unit tests, meaningful integration tests, and a few high-level E2E tests that simulate real user behavior.

Unit Testing Components and Services

Unit tests validate the smallest pieces of code in isolation. In Angular, unit tests typically cover:

- Components and their bindings
- Services and their business logic
- Pipes, directives, and utility functions

Angular applications commonly use testing utilities like TestBed to create test modules that replicate the real runtime environment.

Example: Testing a simple service.

```
1.  import { TestBed } from '@angular/core/testing';
2.  import { AuthService } from './auth.service';
3.
4.  describe('AuthService', () => {
5.    let service: AuthService;
6.
7.    beforeEach(() => {
8.      TestBed.configureTestingModule({});
9.      service = TestBed.inject(AuthService);
10.   });
11.
```

```
12.   it('should be created', () => {
13.     expect(service).toBeTruthy();
14.   });
15.
16.   it('should authenticate a user', () => {
17.     const result = service.login('user', 'password');
18.     expect(result).toBeTrue();
19.   });
20. });
```

Note The *toBeTrue()* assertion checks that the value is strictly the **boolean** *true*, while *toBeTruthy()* passes for any truthy value (not just *true*) in Angular tests using TestBed.

Testing Components with TestBed

Components often depend on templates, bindings, inputs, and outputs. TestBed helps create an isolated testing module where a component can be rendered and interacted with as if it were part of a real application.

Example: Testing a simple counter component.

```
1. import { ComponentFixture, TestBed } from '@angular/core/testing';
2. import { CounterComponent } from './counter.component';
3. import { By } from '@angular/platform-browser';
4.
5. describe('CounterComponent', () => {
6.   let fixture: ComponentFixture<CounterComponent>;
7.   let component: CounterComponent;
8.
9.   beforeEach(() => {
10.     TestBed.configureTestingModule({
11.       declarations: [CounterComponent]
12.     });
13.
```

```
14.     fixture = TestBed.createComponent(CounterComponent);
15.     component = fixture.componentInstance;
16.     fixture.detectChanges();
17.   });
18.
19.   it('should increment count when button clicked', () => {
20.     const button = fixture.debugElement.query(By.css('button'));
21.     button.triggerEventHandler('click');
22.     fixture.detectChanges();
23.     expect(component.count).toBe(1);
24.   });
25. });
```

Modern Test Runners

Angular projects typically use Jasmine and Karma for unit tests. However, modern teams often choose faster alternatives like Jest or Vitest, which run tests outside the browser and provide simpler configuration, faster feedback loops, and improved developer experience.

Switching to a modern test runner can reduce flakiness and speed up development.

Mocking HTTP Requests

Services that make HTTP calls are tested by mocking backend responses. Angular provides the HttpTestingController to intercept requests in unit tests and verify that expected calls are made.

Example:

```
1. import { TestBed } from '@angular/core/testing';
2. import { HttpClientTestingModule, HttpTestingController } from
   '@angular/common/http/testing';
3. import { ApiService } from './api.service';
4.
5. describe('ApiService', () => {
6.   let service: ApiService;
7.   let httpMock: HttpTestingController;
```

```
 8.
 9.    beforeEach(() => {
10.      TestBed.configureTestingModule({
11.        imports: [HttpClientTestingModule],
12.        providers: [ApiService]
13.      });
14.
15.      service = TestBed.inject(ApiService);
16.      httpMock = TestBed.inject(HttpTestingController);
17.    });
18.
19.    it('should fetch posts', () => {
20.      const mockPosts = [{ id: 1, title: 'Post' }];
21.      service.getPosts().subscribe(posts => {
22.        expect(posts).toEqual(mockPosts);
23.      });
24.
25.      const req = httpMock.expectOne('https://jsonplaceholder.typicode.com/posts');
26.      expect(req.request.method).toBe('GET');
27.      req.flush(mockPosts);
28.    });
29.
30.    afterEach(() => {
31.      httpMock.verify();
32.    });
33. });
```

End-to-End (E2E) Testing

E2E tests simulate real user interactions. They verify that multiple parts of the application work together correctly, covering routing, forms, state changes, and backend integration.

Modern Angular projects use tools like **Playwright** or **Cypress** for E2E testing. These tools control a real browser, interact with elements, and assert outcomes as a user would.

Example: A simple E2E test using Cypress.

```
1.  describe('Login Flow', () => {
2.    it('should allow a user to log in', () => {
3.      cy.visit('/login');
4.      cy.get('input[name="username"]').type('testuser');
5.      cy.get('input[name="password"]').type('password123');
6.      cy.get('button[type="submit"]').click();
7.      cy.url().should('include', '/dashboard');
8.    });
9.  });
```

A Balanced Testing Strategy

A healthy angular project balances:

- **Unit Tests:** Fast, plentiful, covering small units of logic.

- **Integration Tests:** Ensure components and services work together as expected.

- **E2E Tests:** A few key flows that catch critical breakages and verify the user experience.

A common approach is the **testing pyramid**, which emphasizes writing many unit tests, fewer integration tests, and a small set of E2E scenarios. Figure 9-4 depicts the recommended Angular testing pyramid, highlighting the balance of unit, integration, and end-to-end tests.

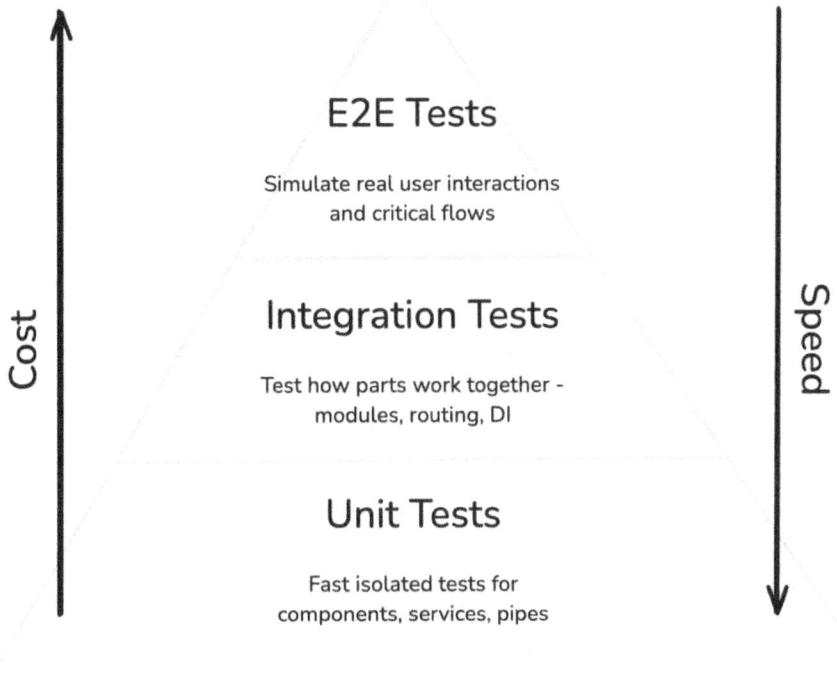

Figure 9-4. Angular Testing Pyramid Showing Unit, Integration, and E2E Layers

With testing in place, developers can maintain high confidence in their work, refactor freely, and deliver robust features, all while catching bugs early, before they reach users.

Performance Optimization

Performance is a critical measure of user experience. Even the most feature-rich applications risk losing users if pages load slowly, interactions lag, or resources are wasted. Angular equips developers with powerful techniques to build applications that are efficient, responsive, and maintainable at scale.

Tree-Shaking and Ahead-of-Time (AOT) Compilation

Angular's build system optimizes production bundles by eliminating unused code, a process called **tree-shaking**. This reduces bundle size, delivering only the JavaScript that the application actually uses.

Ahead-of-Time (AOT) compilation transforms Angular templates and components into highly efficient JavaScript during the build process, rather than at runtime. This results in faster rendering, smaller payloads, and fewer framework-related computations in the browser.

Change Detection Strategies

Angular's change detection system automatically checks for updates when data changes. While powerful, it can be costly if not configured carefully, especially in large applications with many bindings.

By default, Angular checks every component when any event occurs. Developers can optimize this by using the **OnPush** change detection strategy, which tells Angular to update a component only when its inputs change.

Example: Using OnPush in a component:

```
1. import { ChangeDetectionStrategy, Component } from '@angular/core';
2.
3. @Component({
4.   selector: 'app-card',
5.   templateUrl: './card.component.html',
6.   changeDetection: ChangeDetectionStrategy.OnPush
7. })
8. export class CardComponent {
9.   // Component logic here
10. }
```

Using OnPush encourages the use of immutable data patterns, which makes the application's data flow more predictable and efficient.

Fine-Grained Reactivity and Zoneless Change Detection

Modern Angular projects often adopt fine-grained reactivity through **signals**. Signals let developers explicitly track when data changes and which parts of the UI depend on it. This minimizes unnecessary checks and updates.

Alongside signals, developers can opt for **zoneless change detection**, removing the traditional reliance on automatic patching of asynchronous operations. Instead, updates are triggered directly through signals or explicit calls, giving full control over when and how the UI refreshes.

This approach reduces overhead, leading to faster runtime performance in large or highly interactive applications.

Component-Level Optimizations

Small improvements add up. Practical techniques at the component level include:

- Using trackBy with @for to prevent unnecessary DOM re-renders when iterating over lists.

  ```
  1. @for (item of items; track trackById) {
  2.   {{ item.name }}
  3. }
  ```

  ```
  1. trackById(index: number, item: Item) {
  2.   return item.id;
  3. }
  ```

- Detaching or manually reattaching change detectors for parts of the UI that update infrequently.

- Breaking down large components into smaller, focused ones to reduce rendering work.

Lazy Loading and Route-Level Code Splitting

Large applications benefit greatly from splitting the application into multiple bundles that load only when needed. Angular's router supports **lazy loading**, which loads feature areas on demand rather than bundling them all into the initial download.

This reduces the amount of JavaScript the browser has to parse and execute up front, improving time to first paint and user-perceived performance.

Server-Side Rendering (SSR) and Hydration

Server-side rendering generates HTML on the server and sends it to the client fully formed, enabling content to appear quickly. The browser then "hydrates" this static markup into an interactive application.

Modern Angular supports **incremental hydration**, which hydrates only the parts of the page that require interactivity, deferring non-critical scripts until needed. This results in faster load times and a smoother user experience, especially on slower networks or devices.

Putting It into Practice

Optimizing performance is not about a single trick but about thoughtful choices at every level:

- Build smaller bundles with tree-shaking and AOT.
- Use efficient change detection strategies and signals.
- Optimize rendering with trackBy, smart component design, and lazy loading.
- Consider SSR and hydration for faster initial loads.

Practical Tip Use performance auditing tools like Lighthouse and Angular's profiling tools to spot slow change detection cycles, large bundles, or unoptimized templates early in development.

A performant application respects the user's time and device capabilities, whether they're on a fast desktop or a limited mobile connection. With careful architecture, Angular developers can deliver consistently fast, reliable experiences.

Angular in the Real World

Building robust applications requires more than knowing syntax and patterns; it demands practices that scale well in production, support large teams, and adapt to future requirements. This section explores how Angular fits into real-world projects, why it remains a trusted choice for demanding environments and how to prepare applications for modern needs, including future integration with decentralized technologies.

Angular vs. Other Frontend Approaches

In the broader landscape of web frameworks, Angular is often compared with libraries like React or Vue.

Unlike libraries that focus on the view layer alone, Angular provides an integrated solution for routing, forms, HTTP communication, state management patterns, and more. This full-framework approach reduces the need for piecing together disparate tools and ensures that teams follow proven architectural guidelines.

In recent years, innovations like fine-grained reactivity, standalone components, and flexible rendering modes have modernized Angular's core to stay competitive while preserving its strengths.

The trade-off is that Angular can feel more opinionated and heavier upfront than a lightweight library, but for large, long-lived applications, its structure often saves time and effort in the long run.

Best Practices from Large Projects

Angular's flexibility makes it adaptable to projects of all sizes. For complex applications, some proven best practices include:

- **Modular Design:** Break large features into self-contained areas, whether through traditional modules or standalone components. This keeps the application maintainable and testable.

- **Monorepo Setups:** Tools like Nx help manage large Angular projects with multiple apps or libraries in a single workspace, improving consistency and code sharing.

CHAPTER 9   WEB DEVELOPMENT WITH ANGULAR

- **Consistent Coding Standards:** Use linters, formatters, and strict TypeScript configurations to enforce quality and catch problems early.

- **Micro-frontend Strategies:** For organizations with multiple teams delivering parts of the same product, splitting a large app into independently developed, deployable pieces can help scale development.

Preparing for Modern Integrations

Well-structured Angular applications are well suited to integrate with modern trends, such as decentralized technologies or blockchain networks. Many best practices that apply to traditional apps (like clear state management, modular design, and reactive data handling) make it easier to layer in Web3 libraries and connect to smart contracts or decentralized APIs.

For example:

- **State Management Patterns** support handling wallet connections or blockchain events.

- **Reactive Services** keep UIs in sync with real-time data from distributed networks.

- **Secure Routing and Guards** help control access to features that depend on user authentication or blockchain account verification.

A solid architectural foundation makes it easier to extend an app into new domains without major rewrites.

Case Study: Evolving an Enterprise Dashboard

Imagine a company that starts with a traditional analytics dashboard built with Angular, displaying reports and charts for internal teams. As business needs grow:

- They refactor the dashboard into clearly separated feature areas using standalone components.

- They optimize load performance with server-side rendering and incremental hydration.

- They scale the app's state handling with reactive services and selective store patterns.

- They later integrate a decentralized data source (e.g., pulling blockchain-based audit trails) without rewriting the core architecture.

Such an evolution highlights why good architectural decisions and modern Angular features pay dividends over time.

Putting It All Together

Angular remains a reliable foundation for real-world web applications. Its strong ecosystem, solid conventions, and continual evolution make it an excellent choice for teams who value maintainability, productivity, and long-term support.

When built on clear principles and current best practices, an Angular application is ready to meet the challenges of modern web development, including the integration of emerging technologies.

Practical Example: Explore a complete demo app that combines routing, reusable UI components, lazy loading, state management, and API integration. Then adapt its structure for future decentralized features (e.g., connecting a wallet or displaying blockchain data) using the same clean architecture.

With this knowledge, developers can confidently move forward to build advanced applications that combine Angular's strengths with innovative domains, such as decentralized applications and smart contract integrations.

Conclusion

Angular remains a leading choice for building dynamic and large-scale applications thanks to its strong architectural foundations, reactive programming model, and continuous improvements in performance and developer experience.

CHAPTER 9   WEB DEVELOPMENT WITH ANGULAR

By mastering Angular's component-based architecture, routing, testing practices, and advanced optimizations introduced in Angular 20, developers can create applications that are not only efficient but also ready to integrate decentralized technologies.

In the next chapter, we'll build on these fundamentals to explore how Angular can be combined with blockchain and Web3 concepts to develop decentralized applications (dApps) with secure, scalable frontends.

Chapter Summary

Section	Key Takeaways
Introduction to Angular	Overview of Angular's ecosystem, modular design, and evolution to Angular 20.
Core Building Blocks	Understanding modules, components, services, directives, and dependency injection.
Reactive Programming	Signals, observables, and state management in Angular applications.
Server-Side Rendering (SSR)	Benefits of SSR and hydration, incremental rendering for performance.
Routing and Lifecycle Hooks	Navigation flows and component lifecycle for robust app design.
Testing in Angular	Unit, integration, and E2E testing best practices.
Performance Optimization	Techniques and tools to enhance app responsiveness and scalability.

CHAPTER 10

Web3 Development with Angular

Introduction

The web is evolving from centralized servers and trusted intermediaries toward decentralized systems that empower users to own their data, assets, and identities. Decentralized applications connect familiar frontend interfaces to blockchains and smart contracts, shifting trust from corporations to transparent, self-executing code.

In this chapter, you'll learn how to extend your Angular knowledge to build real-world dApps. You'll see how to connect a modern frontend to blockchain networks, integrate secure wallet interactions, interact with smart contracts, and manage blockchain state reactively. Each section builds on the same principles you've already mastered: modular design, clear separation of concerns, reactive patterns, and secure best practices.

By the end of this chapter, you'll not only understand how to build a functional dApp but also how to approach the unique challenges of decentralization, ensuring your applications are secure, resilient, and ready for the next era of the web.

Introduction to Decentralized Applications (dApps)

In recent years, the rise of decentralized technologies has transformed how applications are built, deployed, and used. At the heart of this shift is the **decentralized application**, or **dApp**, an application that combines familiar web interfaces with blockchain-based backends to enable trustless, transparent, and user-empowered interactions.

CHAPTER 10   WEB3 DEVELOPMENT WITH ANGULAR

What Defines a dApp?

A decentralized application looks similar to any other modern web application on the surface. Users interact through a web interface, perform actions, and see data rendered in the browser. The key difference lies in where critical logic and data storage reside.

Unlike traditional apps, which rely on centralized servers to handle data and business logic, dApps offload critical operations to a **blockchain network**. Smart contracts (self-executing pieces of code deployed to the blockchain) handle core functions like token transfers, voting, digital asset management, or ownership verification. Once deployed, these contracts operate autonomously, enforcing rules exactly as written without requiring a centralized authority to maintain or execute them.

This design makes dApps:

- **Trustless:** Users interact directly with the blockchain; no central party can arbitrarily alter rules.

- **Transparent:** Smart contracts are typically open source, allowing anyone to audit the code and see how decisions are made.

- **Immutable:** Once deployed, smart contract logic cannot be changed easily, which protects data integrity and rules enforcement.

- **Censorship-Resistant:** Applications remain accessible as long as the underlying blockchain network is active.

The Role of the Frontend

The blockchain alone is not user-friendly. Smart contracts expose programmatic functions, but interacting directly with raw contract calls is impractical for most people. This is where the web frontend comes in: it acts as a familiar bridge between users and the decentralized backend.

A well-designed dApp frontend handles

- Displaying data read from the blockchain

- Helping users connect a wallet securely

CHAPTER 10   WEB3 DEVELOPMENT WITH ANGULAR

- Preparing and sending transactions to smart contracts
- Providing clear feedback: transaction progress, confirmations, or errors
- Reacting to on-chain events and updating the UI in real time

Typical dApp Architecture

Most dApps follow a three-layer pattern (Figure 10-1):

1. **Smart Contracts:** Deployed to a blockchain network (e.g., Ethereum). They contain the core rules and store critical state.

2. **Blockchain Node or RPC Provider:** Connects the frontend to the blockchain network, allowing the app to read chain data and send signed transactions.

3. **Frontend Application:** A web app (often built with Angular, React, or similar frameworks) that uses libraries like ethers.js or web3.js to interact with the blockchain through the provider.

The **wallet** sits between the frontend and the blockchain, managing the user's private keys. When a transaction is created in the frontend, the wallet signs it securely before sending it to the network.

CHAPTER 10   WEB3 DEVELOPMENT WITH ANGULAR

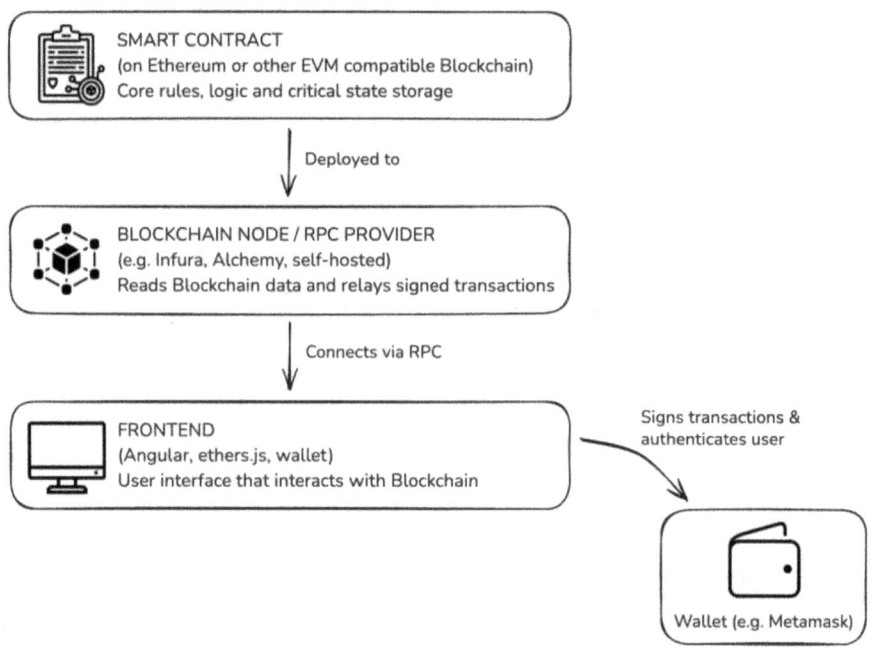

Figure 10-1.   Typical dApp Architecture

Why Use Angular for dApps?

Modern dApps require the same solid design principles as any other sophisticated web application: component-based architecture, modular design, strong reactivity, predictable state management, and reliable routing. These are all strengths that Angular provides natively.

By building the frontend with Angular,

- Teams can leverage clear patterns for state handling, forms, and validation.

- The structure supports larger, maintainable projects.

- Reactive patterns help manage real-time data updates from blockchain events.

- Robust tooling simplifies testing and debugging interactions with decentralized systems.

What Comes Next

This section sets the foundation for the practical integration to follow. In the next sections, you'll see how to

- Connect your Angular application securely to blockchain networks.
- Manage wallet connections and signing.
- Interact with smart contracts by reading and writing data.
- Handle events, feedback, and errors in a user-friendly way.

Together, these practices extend your Angular skills into the emerging world of decentralized web applications.

Connecting Angular with Blockchain Networks

Setting Up the Development Environment

Before you build a real-world dApp with Angular, it helps to set up a local blockchain development environment. This gives you a safe playground to test smart contracts and simulate transactions without spending real tokens.

Required Tools and Versions

To follow along, you'll need

- **Node.js** (LTS version recommended)
- **npm** or **yarn** for package management
- **Angular CLI** for scaffolding and building your frontend:
    1. ```npm install -g @angular/cli```
- **Hardhat** for writing, compiling, and deploying smart contracts:
    1. ```npm install --save-dev hardhat```

Hardhat provides a local blockchain node for fast testing and debugging. It's also widely used for deploying to public testnets like Sepolia or Polygon Mumbai.

Creating the Project Structure

A practical setup might look like this:

1. my-dapp/
2. ├── angular-app/   # Your Angular frontend
3. ├── smart-contracts/   # Hardhat project for Solidity contracts
4. ├── README.md

Inside smart-contracts/:

1. npx hardhat

Choose *Create a basic sample project*. Hardhat will scaffold:

- *contracts/* folder with a sample contract.
- *scripts/* for deploy scripts.
- *hardhat.config.js*.

Running a Local Blockchain

Start a local Hardhat node to simulate a blockchain:

1. npx hardhat node

This runs on http://localhost:8545 by default and provides test accounts with private keys and balances.

Compiling and Deploying

Compile your contracts:

1. npx hardhat compile

Deploy them to your local network:

1. npx hardhat run scripts/deploy.js --network localhost

The output gives you the deployed contract address; you'll paste this into your Angular service to interact with the contract.

Connecting the Angular App

Your Angular service uses the local RPC URL:

1. `const provider = new ethers.JsonRpcProvider('http://localhost:8545');`

For production, switch this to a testnet provider (e.g., Infura or Alchemy).

Using a Wallet

For local development, you can import one of the private keys from the Hardhat output into MetaMask. This lets your frontend sign transactions on the local blockchain exactly like it would on a testnet or mainnet.

With this environment ready, you can now write, deploy, and interact with real smart contracts directly from your Angular application, all without spending real tokens.

A decentralized application relies on a reliable connection to a blockchain network to read on-chain data and submit transactions. Unlike traditional APIs, which rely on a centralized server, dApps use **blockchain nodes**, often accessed through RPC (Remote Procedure Call) providers, to interact with distributed ledgers securely.

Understanding Blockchain RPC Providers

A blockchain network, like Ethereum or Polygon, is made up of thousands of nodes that maintain consensus and store the blockchain's state. To read data or send transactions, a dApp must communicate with one of these nodes through a **provider**.

Public RPC providers and infrastructure services, such as Infura, Alchemy, or QuickNode, offer reliable access to the blockchain without requiring every dApp to run its own node. These providers expose standard APIs that frontend applications can call to

- Query the latest blockchain data.
- Broadcast signed transactions.
- Subscribe to blockchain events, like new blocks or emitted contract logs.

Using Libraries for Blockchain Access

In an Angular context, developers typically use JavaScript libraries like **ethers.js** or **web3.js** to handle blockchain communication. These libraries simplify tasks such as

- Connecting to a node via RPC.
- Building transactions.
- Reading smart contract ABIs.
- Managing unit conversions (e.g., from Ether to Wei).

Example: Setting up an ethers provider.

```
1.  import { Injectable } from '@angular/core';
2.  import { ethers } from 'ethers';
3.
4.  @Injectable({ providedIn: 'root' })
5.  export class BlockchainService {
6.    provider: ethers.JsonRpcProvider;
7.
8.    constructor() {
9.      this.provider = new ethers.JsonRpcProvider('https://mainnet.infura.io/v3/YOUR_PROJECT_ID');
10.   }
11.
12.   async getBlockNumber(): Promise<number> {
13.     return await this.provider.getBlockNumber();
14.   }
15. }
```

This service connects the Angular app to the blockchain and exposes methods for reading data.

Managing Provider Connections in Angular Services

A good practice is to encapsulate blockchain logic in Angular **services**, separating it from UI components. This makes the application more testable, maintainable, and secure.

A provider service might handle

- Establishing the RPC connection
- Switching networks if the user chooses a different chain
- Handling fallback providers for redundancy
- Exposing observables or signals to keep the UI reactive when new data arrives

For example:

```
1.  import { signal } from '@angular/core';
2.
3.  export class BlockchainService {
4.    provider = new ethers.JsonRpcProvider('https://...');
5.    blockNumber = signal<number | null>(null);
6.
7.    constructor() {
8.      this.watchBlockNumber();
9.    }
10.
11.   watchBlockNumber() {
12.     this.provider.on('block', (blockNumber) => {
13.       this.blockNumber.set(blockNumber);
14.     });
15.   }
16. }
```

This keeps the latest block number up-to-date in real time, so components can react automatically.

Network Switching and Fallbacks

Users may connect with wallets that support multiple blockchains. Modern dApps often detect the active network and adjust their RPC provider dynamically to match.

A well-designed provider service:

- Detects which network the user's wallet is connected to.
- Switches RPC endpoints automatically.
- Provides fallback nodes in case the primary RPC fails.

This prevents disruptions and keeps the user experience smooth, even when networks are congested or a provider is unavailable.

Security Considerations

The provider only **reads** or **broadcasts signed transactions**; it does not store private keys. Signing is handled by the user's wallet, an essential security feature that prevents the dApp from managing sensitive credentials directly.

Always ensure that:

- RPC endpoints are reliable and reputable.
- Sensitive operations are signed in the wallet, not the frontend.
- User data is never mixed with server-side state unnecessarily.

Putting It into Practice

A robust provider service is the backbone of any dApp's frontend. By organizing provider logic in Angular services, developers keep components focused on presentation and interaction, while the backend connection remains secure and modular.

Practical Tip Start with a single network and provider. As your application grows, add support for multiple chains, fallback nodes, and automatic network detection for wallets.

Next, you'll see how to add **wallet integration** to your Angular app, connecting the user's identity to the blockchain securely and interactively.

Managing Wallet Integration

A decentralized application's most important connection point is the **wallet**, the user's secure key manager that controls access to blockchain accounts and signs transactions. Integrating wallet functionality into an Angular application bridges the gap between the user's identity and the decentralized network.

What Is a Wallet?

A blockchain wallet is more than a place to store tokens. It securely manages private keys that prove ownership of an address and signs transactions to authorize changes on the blockchain.

Popular wallets include

- **Browser extensions** (e.g., MetaMask and Phantom)
- **Hardware wallets** (e.g., Ledger and Trezor)
- **Mobile wallets** (e.g., Trust Wallet and Rainbow)

These wallets connect to the browser or app through standardized APIs, allowing users to interact with smart contracts and dApps securely.

Connecting to a Wallet in an Angular App

A typical dApp needs to

1. Detect whether a wallet is available.
2. Request permission to connect.
3. Read the connected account's address.
4. Use the wallet to sign transactions or messages.

This is usually handled in a dedicated Angular **wallet service** that interacts with *window.ethereum* (for MetaMask and similar wallets) or a wallet SDK.

Example: Simple wallet connection service.

```
1. import { Injectable } from '@angular/core';
2.
3. declare global {
```

```
4.   interface Window {
5.     ethereum?: any;
6.   }
7. }
8.
9. @Injectable({ providedIn: 'root' })
10. export class WalletService {
11.   account: string | null = null;
12.
13.   async connectWallet(): Promise<void> {
14.     if (window.ethereum) {
15.       const accounts = await window.ethereum.request({ method: 'eth_requestAccounts' });
16.       this.account = accounts[0];
17.     } else {
18.       throw new Error('No wallet found');
19.     }
20.   }
21. }
```

Handling Wallet State Reactively

Because wallet state can change at any time (e.g., when a user switches accounts or networks), a robust integration must react to these changes.

Modern Angular applications often use signals or observables to update the UI automatically.

Example with a signal:

```
1. import { signal } from '@angular/core';
2.
3. export class WalletService {
4.   account = signal<string | null>(null);
5.
6.   async connectWallet(): Promise<void> {
7.     if (window.ethereum) {
```

```
8.      const accounts = await window.ethereum.request({ method: 'eth_
        requestAccounts' });
9.      this.account.set(accounts[0]);
10.   }
11. }
12.
13. constructor() {
14.   this.watchAccountChanges();
15. }
16.
17. private watchAccountChanges() {
18.   if (window.ethereum) {
19.     window.ethereum.on('accountsChanged', (accounts: string[]) => {
20.       this.account.set(accounts[0] || null);
21.     });
22.     window.ethereum.on('chainChanged', (_chainId: string) => {
23.       window.location.reload();
24.     });
25.   }
26. }
27. }
```

Requesting Permissions and Signing

When a user wants to perform a blockchain action, like sending tokens or interacting with a smart contract, the transaction must be signed by the wallet. The dApp prepares the transaction and asks the wallet to sign it. The wallet prompts the user to confirm, ensuring they have full control.

Example: Signing a message.

```
1. async signMessage(message: string): Promise<string> {
2.   if (!window.ethereum || !this.account()) {
3.     throw new Error('Wallet not connected');
4.   }
5.
6.   const signature = await window.ethereum.request({
```

```
 7.      method: 'personal_sign',
 8.      params: [message, this.account()],
 9.    });
10.
11.    return signature;
12. }
```

The signature can then be verified on-chain or off-chain, depending on the use case.

Security Best Practices

Good wallet integrations respect user security:

- Never store private keys in the frontend.
- Always require explicit user confirmation for actions.
- Validate connected accounts before performing sensitive operations.
- Handle errors gracefully (e.g., user rejection, network issues).

Putting It into Practice

A well-designed wallet service integrates seamlessly with Angular's reactive architecture:

- Use signals or observables to keep components in sync with connection status.
- Display clear prompts: connect, disconnect, and change network.
- Protect routes or features that depend on wallet access.

Practical Tip   Test wallet interactions in multiple scenarios (switching accounts, rejecting transactions, or disconnecting) to ensure the app handles edge cases gracefully.

Next, you'll see how to connect this wallet functionality with **smart contracts**, reading blockchain state and submitting transactions securely from your Angular application.

Smart Contracts: Reading and Writing Data

As already mentioned in Chapter 8, smart contracts are the backbone of any decentralized application. They define the business rules that run on a blockchain, handling tasks like transferring tokens, verifying ownership, or executing logic without relying on centralized servers.

Connecting your Angular frontend to smart contracts unlocks the real potential of a dApp, giving users the power to read blockchain data and execute secure transactions directly from the browser.

A smart contract is self-executing code deployed to the blockchain. Once deployed, its logic is immutable and publicly accessible. Users and applications interact with smart contracts by calling their exposed functions.

Smart contracts often expose two kinds of functions:

- **Read-Only Functions**: Retrieve data from the blockchain without modifying state. These calls are free and don't require gas.

- **State-Changing Functions**: Modify on-chain data. These require a signed transaction and consume gas.

Interacting with Smart Contracts in Angular

In an Angular dApp, the usual workflow is the following:

1. Connect the frontend to the blockchain using a provider.
2. Connect the user's wallet to sign transactions.
3. Use a library like **ethers.js** to call contract functions.

A contract is represented in the frontend by its **ABI (Application Binary Interface)**, a JSON file that defines available functions and data structures.

Reading Contract State

Read-only interactions use the provider directly. For example, suppose you have a simple contract that stores a greeting:

```
1. function greet() public view returns (string memory)
```

The Angular service might look like this:

```
1. import { Injectable } from '@angular/core';
2. import { ethers } from 'ethers';
3. import GreeterABI from './GreeterABI.json';
4.
5. @Injectable({ providedIn: 'root' })
6. export class ContractService {
7.   private provider = new ethers.JsonRpcProvider('https://...');
8.   private contract = new ethers.Contract(
9.     '0xYourContractAddress',
10.     GreeterABI,
11.     this.provider
12.   );
13.
14.   async getGreeting(): Promise<string> {
15.     return await this.contract.greet();
16.   }
17. }
```

This call is free and does not require the user's wallet to sign anything.

Writing Data and Sending Transactions

To change state, the dApp needs the user's wallet to sign and broadcast a transaction. This uses a **signer**, which is connected to the wallet.

Example: Updating a greeting.

```
1. import { ethers } from 'ethers';
2.
3. async updateGreeting(newGreeting: string) {
4.   if (!window.ethereum) throw new Error('No wallet found');
5.
6.   const provider = new ethers.BrowserProvider(window.ethereum);
7.   const signer = await provider.getSigner();
```

CHAPTER 10   WEB3 DEVELOPMENT WITH ANGULAR

```
 8.   const contract = new ethers.Contract('0xYourContractAddress',
      GreeterABI, signer);
 9.
10.   const tx = await contract.setGreeting(newGreeting);
11.   await tx.wait(); // Wait for transaction confirmation
12. }
```

This pattern ensures

- The wallet prompts the user to approve the action.
- The transaction is signed securely by the user's private key.
- The frontend can wait for confirmations and provide feedback.

Handling Gas and Fees

State-changing transactions consume **gas**, which users pay to incentivize miners or validators to process them. A good dApp

- Clearly displays expected gas costs.
- Estimates gas limits before sending.
- Handles failed transactions gracefully.

For advanced scenarios, developers may integrate features like

- Adjustable gas fees
- Batch transactions
- Meta-transactions or relayers for gasless experiences

Handling Errors and Edge Cases

Blockchain transactions can fail for many reasons: insufficient funds, user rejection, or unexpected smart contract logic. Always

- Wrap calls in try/catch blocks.
- Provide clear error messages.
- Allow users to retry or cancel safely.

Example:

```
1. try {
2.   const tx = await contract.doSomething();
3.   await tx.wait();
4. } catch (error) {
5.   console.error('Transaction failed:', error);
6. }
```

Putting It into Practice

A robust contract service in Angular:

- Keeps contract logic separate from components.
- Uses observables or signals to reflect on-chain changes in real time.
- Ensures secure signing through the user's wallet.
- Provides clear feedback during pending, confirmed, or failed transactions.

Practical Tip Use tools like block explorers (e.g., Etherscan) to debug transactions and monitor contract events during development.

With contract interactions in place, the next step is designing **real-world patterns** that handle routing, state updates, and user feedback smoothly, ensuring your Angular dApp feels polished and trustworthy.

Full Smart Contract Example with Hardhat

To see how all the parts fit together, let's walk through a complete example: deploying a simple Solidity contract and integrating it into an Angular service.

Writing the Contract

First, create a file called SimpleStorage.sol inside your contracts/ folder in your Hardhat project:

```
1. // SPDX-License-Identifier: MIT
2. pragma solidity ^0.8.20;
3.
4. contract SimpleStorage {
5.     uint256 private data;
6.
7.     event DataUpdated(uint256 oldValue, uint256 newValue);
8.
9.     function set(uint256 _data) public {
10.         uint256 old = data;
11.         data = _data;
12.         emit DataUpdated(old, _data);
13.     }
14.
15.     function get() public view returns (uint256) {
16.         return data;
17.     }
18. }
```

This contract

- Stores a single unsigned integer
- Lets anyone set or get the value
- Emits an event when the value changes

Compiling the Contract

Run:

1. npx hardhat compile

Hardhat will generate the compiled contract artifacts in artifacts/.

Deploying the Contract Locally

Create a deploy script in scripts/deploy.js:

```js
async function main() {
  const SimpleStorage = await ethers.getContractFactory("SimpleStorage");
  const storage = await SimpleStorage.deploy();
  await storage.deployed();
  console.log(`SimpleStorage deployed to: ${storage.address}`);
}

main().catch((error) => {
  console.error(error);
  process.exitCode = 1;
});
```

Run the local Hardhat node if you haven't yet:

```
npx hardhat node
```

Deploy the contract:

```
npx hardhat run scripts/deploy.js --network localhost
```

Note the deployed address; you'll use this in your Angular service.

Copy the ABI

In *artifacts/contracts/SimpleStorage.sol/SimpleStorage.json*, copy the *ABI* section. You can save it as *src/assets/abi/SimpleStorage.json* in your Angular project.

Creating the Angular Contract Service

In your Angular app, create a *contract.service.ts*:

```ts
import { Injectable, signal } from '@angular/core';
import { ethers } from 'ethers';
import SimpleStorage from '../assets/abi/SimpleStorage.json';
```

```
 4.
 5. declare global {
 6.   interface Window {
 7.     ethereum?: any;
 8.   }
 9. }
10.
11. @Injectable({ providedIn: 'root' })
12. export class ContractService {
13.   private provider: ethers.JsonRpcProvider;
14.   private contract: ethers.Contract;
15.
16.   value = signal<number | null>(null);
17.
18.   constructor() {
19.     this.provider = new ethers.JsonRpcProvider('http://
       localhost:8545');
20.
21.     const contractAddress = '0xYourDeployedAddressHere'; // replace
       with your deployed address
22.     this.contract = new ethers.Contract(contractAddress, SimpleStorage.
       abi, this.provider);
23.
24.     this.listenToEvents();
25.     this.loadValue();
26.   }
27.
28.   async loadValue() {
29.     const data = await this.contract.get();
30.     this.value.set(data);
31.   }
32.
33.   async setValue(newValue: number) {
34.     if (!window.ethereum) throw new Error('Wallet not detected');
35.
```

```
36.     const provider = new ethers.BrowserProvider(window.ethereum);
37.     const signer = await provider.getSigner();
38.     const contractWithSigner = this.contract.connect(signer);
39.
40.     try {
41.       const tx = await contractWithSigner.set(newValue);
42.       await tx.wait();
43.     } catch (error) {
44.       console.error('Transaction failed:', error);
45.     }
46.   }
47.
48.   listenToEvents() {
49.     this.contract.on('DataUpdated', (oldValue, newValue) => {
50.       console.log(`Value updated: ${oldValue} → ${newValue}`);
51.       this.value.set(newValue);
52.     });
53.   }
54. }
```

Using the Service in a Component

Example SimpleStorageComponent:

```
1.  @Component({
2.    selector: 'app-simple-storage',
3.    template: `
4.      <div>
5.        <p>Current Value: {{ contractService.value() }}</p>
6.        <input [(ngModel)]="inputValue" type="number" />
7.        <button (click)="updateValue()">Update Value</button>
8.      </div>
9.    `
10. })
11. export class SimpleStorageComponent {
12.   inputValue = 0;
```

```
13.
14.     constructor(public contractService: ContractService) {}
15.
16.     updateValue() {
17.         this.contractService.setValue(this.inputValue);
18.     }
19. }
```

Recap

With this full example you now have

- A real smart contract.
- Local deployment.
- A connected Angular service that
  - Reads the value
  - Sends transactions through the user's wallet
  - Reacts to on-chain events

This shows exactly how a real dApp integration works from Solidity to Angular.

Handling Real Errors and Gas Estimation Problems

Building real dApps means handling real errors. Unlike a simple API call, blockchain transactions involve multiple moving parts: gas fees, wallet signatures, network delays, and contract edge cases.

A common stumbling block for new developers is the infamous **"cannot estimate gas"** error. Understanding why it happens (and how to handle it) makes your dApp more robust and user-friendly.

Why "Cannot Estimate Gas" Happens

When you send a transaction, your wallet or provider first tries to **simulate** the transaction locally to estimate how much gas it will cost.

If the simulation fails, you'll see an error like:

`Error: cannot estimate gas; transaction may fail or may require manual gas limit`

This usually means

- The function call would **revert** if actually executed (e.g., a require condition fails).
- The call depends on a dynamic on-chain state that the local simulation can't resolve.
- The wallet or provider can't find enough context to estimate gas accurately.

Practical Strategies to Handle It

1. **Test the Logic with *callStatic***

    Before sending a real transaction, you can dry-run it with *callStatic*. This simulates the transaction **without executing it**, letting you catch errors early.

    Example:

    ```
    try {
      await contract.callStatic.set(42);
    } catch (error) {
      console.error('Transaction would fail:', error);
      return;
    }

    const tx = await contract.set(42);
    await tx.wait();
    ```

2. **Provide a Manual Gas Limit**

    If the simulation fails but you know the function should succeed (e.g., you validated input client-side), you can supply a conservative *gasLimit* override:

    ```
    const tx = await contract.set(42, { gasLimit: 200000 });
    ```

Pick a limit based on typical runs plus some buffer. Avoid excessive values to save user fees.

3. **Handle User Rejection Gracefully**

   Users may decline a transaction in their wallet. Always wrap your transaction in try/catch to handle rejections or other issues:

   ```
   try {
     const tx = await contract.set(42);
     await tx.wait();
   } catch (error: any) {
     if (error.code === 4001) {
       console.log('User rejected the transaction');
     } else {
       console.error('Transaction failed:', error);
     }
   }
   ```

   Most wallet libraries use error codes like 4001 for user rejection.

4. **Show Clear Feedback**

   When estimation fails, tell the user **why**:

   - Is the input invalid?
   - Are they missing a required balance?
   - Is the network congested?

Transparent feedback builds trust.

Defensive Patterns

- Validate **all inputs** on the frontend. For example, check that token amounts are positive, the user has enough balance, or preconditions are met.
- Use clear UI states: **pending**, **confirmed**, **failed**, and **rejected**.
- Log errors during development. For production, handle them gracefully and consider logging to a secure backend if needed for support.

Putting It into Practice

Updating your smart contract calls to handle estimation issues makes your app more resilient:

```
1.  async setValue(newValue: number) {
2.    if (!window.ethereum) throw new Error('Wallet not found');
3.
4.    const provider = new ethers.BrowserProvider(window.ethereum);
5.    const signer = await provider.getSigner();
6.    const contractWithSigner = this.contract.connect(signer);
7.
8.    try {
9.      await contractWithSigner.callStatic.set(newValue);
10.
11.     const tx = await contractWithSigner.set(newValue, { gasLimit: 200000 });
12.     await tx.wait();
13.   } catch (error: any) {
14.     if (error.code === 4001) {
15.       console.log('User rejected the transaction');
16.     } else {
17.       console.error('Error sending transaction:', error);
18.     }
19.   }
20. }
```

By combining **callStatic**, manual gas limits, strong validation, and clear error messages, you protect your users from confusion and build trust in your dApp's reliability.

Real-World Patterns for Web3 Frontends

Integrating blockchain logic into an Angular application goes beyond just connecting a wallet or calling a smart contract. Real-world dApps must handle changing blockchain states, manage secure routes, give clear user feedback, and recover gracefully from unexpected errors.

This section explores practical patterns that make Web3 frontends reliable, secure, and user-friendly.

Protecting Routes and Features

In many dApps, certain features depend on wallet authentication or a verified blockchain state, for example, showing a dashboard only to token holders or restricting access to admin functionality.

Angular's routing system makes it easy to secure routes using **route guards**. A guard can check whether the wallet is connected, whether the user is on the correct network, or whether the user's address meets specific conditions (like holding a role or a token).

Example: A simple CanActivate guard for wallet connection.

```
1.  import { Injectable } from '@angular/core';
2.  import { CanActivate, Router } from '@angular/router';
3.  import { WalletService } from './wallet.service';
4.
5.  @Injectable({ providedIn: 'root' })
6.  export class WalletGuard implements CanActivate {
7.    constructor(private walletService: WalletService, private router: Router) {}
8.
9.    canActivate(): boolean {
10.     if (!this.walletService.account()) {
11.       this.router.navigate(['/connect']);
12.       return false;
13.     }
14.     return true;
15.   }
16. }
```

Listening for Blockchain Events

Smart contracts often emit events when something important happens: a token transfer, a vote cast, or a new NFT minted. A responsive dApp listens for these events and updates the UI in real time.

In Angular, you can use observables, signals, or behavior subjects to stream contract events into your components.

Example: Listening for events with *ethers.js*.

```
1. this.contract.on('Transfer', (from, to, value) => {
2.   console.log(`Token transferred from ${from} to ${to}: ${value}`);
3. });
```

Always unsubscribe or remove listeners properly when the component is destroyed to prevent memory leaks.

Keeping UX Responsive

Blockchain operations can take time, especially transactions waiting to be mined. A good dApp keeps users informed at every step:

- Show a pending state when a transaction is submitted.
- Display the transaction hash and a link to a block explorer.
- Notify when the transaction is confirmed or if it fails.
- Handle rejection gracefully if the user cancels.

Example: Transaction status pattern.

```
1. this.contract.doSomething().then((tx) => {
2.   this.status = 'pending';
3.   return tx.wait();
4. }).then(() => {
5.   this.status = 'confirmed';
6. }).catch((error) => {
7.   this.status = 'failed';
8. });
```

Security Best Practices

In decentralized apps, the frontend must never be trusted as the sole source of truth. Smart contracts enforce the final rules, but the frontend must be defensive:

- Validate user inputs thoroughly before sending transactions.

CHAPTER 10   WEB3 DEVELOPMENT WITH ANGULAR

- Do not store sensitive data like private keys in the browser.
- Keep contracts audited and ABIs up to date.
- Clearly show the user what they are signing.

Handling Network Changes

Users might switch networks in their wallet while using the app. Detecting these changes and responding appropriately prevents user confusion or accidental transactions on the wrong chain.

Example: Reacting to chain changes.

```
1. if (window.ethereum) {
2.   window.ethereum.on('chainChanged', (_chainId: string) => {
3.     window.location.reload();
4.   });
5. }
```

This ensures the app resets its state to match the new network.

Resilient Error Handling

Web3 interactions introduce edge cases:

- Users may reject a signature prompt.
- Transactions may be dropped or replaced.
- RPC nodes may fail or return incomplete data.

A robust Angular dApp:

- Wraps blockchain calls in try/catch blocks.
- Shows meaningful error messages.
- Provides fallback strategies (e.g., multiple providers).

Putting It into Practice

Bringing these patterns together helps turn a basic prototype into a real product:

- Use route guards for secure access.
- React to wallet and network changes.
- Stream contract events to the UI reactively.
- Give users clear feedback for every action.
- Always assume the blockchain is the source of truth.

Practical Tip Test your dApp with multiple wallets and network conditions to ensure your patterns hold up under real-world scenarios.

Next, you'll tie all of this together by building a **mini Angular dApp**, combining wallet connection, provider setup, contract interactions, and real-world UX patterns into one working example.

Putting It All Together: A Mini Angular dApp

Building blocks are only truly useful when combined into a complete, working example. In this section, you'll see how to combine Angular's modern features, wallet integration, blockchain connections, and smart contract interactions to create a simple yet realistic decentralized application.

A Practical Example: Decentralized Voting App

As an illustrative case, imagine a **decentralized voting app**. This dApp lets connected wallet users vote on a proposal, view live results, and verify that votes are counted transparently on the blockchain.

Project Structure

A practical Angular dApp follows a clear, modular structure:

CHAPTER 10   WEB3 DEVELOPMENT WITH ANGULAR

```
1.  src/
2.  ├── app/
3.  │   ├── services/
4.  │   │   ├── blockchain.service.ts
5.  │   │   ├── wallet.service.ts
6.  │   │   └── contract.service.ts
7.  │   ├── components/
8.  │   │   ├── connect-wallet/
9.  │   │   ├── voting-form/
10. │   │   └── results-display/
11. │   ├── guards/
12. │   │   └── wallet.guard.ts
13. │   ├── app.routes.ts
14. │   ├── app.component.ts
15. │   └── app.config.ts
```

Each piece is focused:

- **Services** handle connections, wallet state, and contract calls.
- **Components** handle UI and user interaction.
- **Guards** protect routes that require a connected wallet.

Connecting the Wallet

The user first lands on a **Connect Wallet** page. This component calls the wallet service to request a wallet connection:

```
1. async connect() {
2.   try {
3.     await this.walletService.connectWallet();
4.   } catch (error) {
5.     console.error('Connection failed:', error);
6.   }
7. }
```

The service uses a signal or observable to store the user's address, keeping the rest of the app reactive.

Reading On-Chain Data

Once connected, the user navigates to the voting form. The contract service reads whether the user has voted, retrieves the current tally, and subscribes to contract events for real-time updates.

Example: Getting the current vote count.

```
1. async getVotes(): Promise<number> {
2.   return await this.contract.totalVotes();
3. }
```

Writing a Transaction

When a user casts a vote, the transaction must be signed and sent. The contract service prepares the transaction and prompts the wallet to sign:

```
1. async vote(option: number) {
2.   const provider = new ethers.BrowserProvider(window.ethereum);
3.   const signer = await provider.getSigner();
4.   const contractWithSigner = this.contract.connect(signer);
5.
6.   const tx = await contractWithSigner.vote(option);
7.   await tx.wait();
8. }
```

The UI should reflect:

- Pending status while waiting for confirmation.
- A link to the transaction on a block explorer.
- An updated tally when the vote is mined.

Protecting Voting Routes

The voting form route is protected by a guard to ensure only connected users can access it:

1. { path: 'vote', component: VotingFormComponent, canActivate: [WalletGuard] }

Reactive Feedback

As votes come in, the frontend listens to smart contract events and updates the results display:

1. this.contract.on('VoteCast', (voter, option) => {
2.   this.refreshResults();
3. });

The UI remains in sync with the blockchain state without needing manual refreshes.

Full Example: Combining It All

Putting these parts together shows the full lifecycle:

- The wallet service manages account state.
- The blockchain service provides a reliable RPC connection.
- The contract service handles ABI calls and transactions.
- Components use Angular's signals or observables to react to state changes.
- Routing guards ensure only eligible users access protected views.
- The UI shows clear progress, confirmations, and on-chain data.

Final Tips

A real dApp should also

- Handle errors if the user rejects a transaction.

- Prompt the user to switch networks if needed.
- Display a fallback message if the wallet is disconnected.
- Keep contract ABIs updated and verified.

Practical Tip Start simple: a single contract and wallet connection. Expand gradually to multiple contracts, networks, and advanced UX once the core is stable.

With these pieces working together, you now have a blueprint for a production-ready Angular dApp: modular, secure, reactive, and aligned with best practices for decentralized applications.

Testing and Deployment Strategies for Angular dApps

A professional dApp isn't just about deploying a smart contract and wiring up a UI; it's about verifying that every part works reliably and stays secure as you make changes over time. Testing and thoughtful deployment practices ensure your decentralized application can grow without surprises.

Testing Smart Contracts

Smart contract logic should always be tested thoroughly before you deploy to any network. Bugs in smart contracts are expensive; they can't be patched as easily as backend servers.

Tools like **Hardhat** or **Foundry** let you write repeatable unit tests for your Solidity contracts:

```
1. const { expect } = require("chai");
2.
3. describe("SimpleStorage", function () {
4.   it("Should store and retrieve a value", async function () {
5.     const SimpleStorage = await ethers.getContractFactory("Simple
       Storage");
```

```
6.      const storage = await SimpleStorage.deploy();
7.      await storage.deployed();
8.
9.      await storage.set(42);
10.     expect(await storage.get()).to.equal(42);
11.   });
12. });
```

Run your tests with:

1. npx hardhat test

Testing covers:

- Normal paths (expected values).

- Edge cases (zero values, large numbers).

- Failure conditions (e.g., unauthorized calls).

Testing Angular Wallet Logic

On the frontend, test your wallet integration and contract services like any other Angular service:

- Use dependency injection and mocks.

- Simulate wallet connections and disconnections.

- Mock blockchain calls with fake data or use local Hardhat nodes for integration tests.

Example test outline:

```
1. import { TestBed } from '@angular/core/testing';
2. import { WalletService } from './wallet.service';
3.
4. describe('WalletService', () => {
5.   let service: WalletService;
6.
7.   beforeEach(() => {
```

```
8.      TestBed.configureTestingModule({});
9.      service = TestBed.inject(WalletService);
10.   });
11.
12.   it('should create', () => {
13.     expect(service).toBeTruthy();
14.   });
15.
16.   // Add more tests to simulate wallet connection logic
17. });
```

For E2E tests, you can automate wallet flows using tools like **Playwright** or **Cypress**, though real signing steps often require manual interaction or custom stubbing for full automation.

Using Testnets

Before deploying to a live network:

- Always deploy to a testnet like **Sepolia, Goerli,** or **Polygon Mumbai**.
- Use faucets to get free test tokens.
- Verify your contract works with real wallets and real blocks.
- Share your testnet app with users to get early feedback.

Deployment Best Practices

When you're ready to go live:

- **Verify your contract** on a block explorer (like Etherscan) so others can audit it.
- Use secure deployment tools, such as Hardhat or third-party deployment managers.
- Keep your private keys out of version control.
- Host your Angular app using a static site host (Netlify, Vercel) or deploy to decentralized storage (IPFS) for fully decentralized delivery.

Maintainability

Good deployment doesn't end at go-live. Keep track of:

- Contract addresses for each network.
- ABI versions: update your Angular app when you update your contracts.
- New features or bug fixes that may require migrating state or upgrading contracts (with proxies or new deployments).

Practical Tip Create an environment file to manage sensitive keys and network URLs securely, and use environment variables to switch between local, testnet, and mainnet providers.

A well-tested, securely deployed Angular dApp shows users that your project respects their trust and that it's built to last.

Conclusion

In this chapter, we put theory into action by building a complete decentralized application from scratch. You saw how to integrate Angular with a blockchain backend, connect and manage user wallets, interact with smart contracts securely, and handle data updates in real time.

We explored patterns for routing, state management, and event handling tailored to dApps, along with testing and deployment steps that ensure both reliability and security. By walking through a working example, you've learned not only the individual techniques but also how they fit together into a cohesive development workflow.

These skills equip you to design and deliver functional, user-friendly Web3 applications.

Chapter Summary

Topic	Key Takeaways
Decentralized Applications (dApps)	Combine blockchain logic with familiar web frontends for trustless interactions.
Angular for dApps	Modular design, strong reactivity, and tooling make Angular ideal for Web3 apps.
Wallet Integration	Securely connects users to dApps, manages accounts, and signs transactions.
Smart Contract Interaction	Read/write blockchain state via ethers.js and secure wallet signing.
Real-World Frontend Patterns	Protect routes, handle events reactively, and provide robust error handling.
Full Angular dApp Example	Demonstrated contract deployment, service integration, and live UI updates.
Testing and Deployment	Covers smart contract testing, frontend integration tests, and secure deployment.
Final Thoughts	Principles and skills learned here extend to future decentralized innovations.

Final Words and Further Learning

Throughout this book, you've explored how to build modern, scalable web applications with Angular and how to extend them into the emerging world of decentralized applications. You've seen how clear architecture, reactivity, strong typing, and thoughtful design empower you to tackle new technical frontiers like blockchain and Web3.

No single tool or framework guarantees success. What makes your work stand out is how you combine these tools with secure patterns, user-first experiences, and the discipline to keep learning.

As technology continues to evolve, the core ideas remain:

- Keep your code maintainable and readable.
- Test thoroughly and adapt best practices for new contexts.
- Stay curious and open to new tools and patterns.
- Build with trust, security, and usability in mind.

Above all, keep sharing your knowledge and experimenting, because the next generation of the web will be built by developers like you, ready to adapt, collaborate, and lead.

Suggested Resources for Continued Learning

To go deeper:

- **Angular Official Docs**: angular.io
- **Ethers.js Documentation**: docs.ethers.io
- **Web3.js Documentation**: web3js.readthedocs.io
- **Hardhat (Smart Contract Development)**: hardhat.org
- **OpenZeppelin Guides**: docs.openzeppelin.com
- **Block Explorers**: Use tools like Etherscan or Polygonscan to verify contracts and monitor transactions.
- **Testnets and Faucets**: Practice safely before deploying on mainnet.
- **Community and Standards**: Follow EIPs, forums, and developer groups to stay updated.

Keep Building

The foundations you've laid (clear structure, robust state management, strong testing, secure blockchain integration) will serve you well as you tackle new ideas and build solutions that push the web forward.

Your curiosity, discipline, and willingness to experiment are your best tools. Use them well; the decentralized future is yours to shape.

Index

A

ABI, *see* Application binary interface (ABI)
Ahead-of-Time (AOT) compilation, 386
AI, *see* Artificial intelligence (AI)
AML, *see* Anti-money laundering (AML)
AMMs, *see* Automated market
      makers (AMMs)
Angular application
    architecture, 354, 357
    benefits, 353
    blockchain networks, 397–402
        compile/deployment, 398
        components, 402
        development environment, 397
        libraries, 400
        local Hardhat node, 398
        network switching/fallbacks, 401
        project structure, 398
        required tools/versions, 397
        RPC providers, 399
        security considerations, 402
        service, 399–401
        wallet, 399
    change detection, 355
    CLI (*see* Command-line
        interface (CLI))
    components, 354
    concepts, 352, 354
    continuous learning/innovation, 353
    decentralized application, 393–397
    definition, 351
    design principles, 352
    directives and pipes, 356
    HTTP/APIs, 366–371
    lifecycle hooks, 356
    mini angular dApp
        decentralized voting app, 422
        lifecycle, 425
        modular structure, 422, 423
        reactive feedback, 425
        reading on-chain data, 424
        real-life application, 425
        transaction, 424
        voting form route, 425
        wallet connection, 423
    modernization, 352
    modular design, 352
    modules, 354
    performance optimization, 385
        change detection system, 386
        component level, 387
        fine-grained reactivity, 387
        incremental hydration, 388
        lazy loading, 387
        server-side rendering, 388
        time/device capabilities, 388
        tree-shaking/AOT compilation, 386
        zoneless change detection, 387
    reactive forms, 355
    real-world projects, 389
        consistent coding standards, 390
        emerging technologies, 391
        frontend approaches, 389
        libraries, 389

INDEX

Angular application (*cont.*)
    micro-frontend strategies, 390
    modern integration, 390
    modular design, 389
    Monorepo setups, 389
    traditional analytics, 390
  reinvention, 352
  resources, 431
  routes/navigation, 355
  routing/guards/lazy loading, 375–379
  services, 354
  smart contracts, 407–422
  standalone components, 354
  state management, 361–366
  template-driven forms, 355
  testing
    components/services, 380
    concepts, 379
    end-of-end (E2E), 383
    features, 380
    HTTP requests, 382, 383
    modern test runners, 382
    Playwright/Cypress, 383
    pyramid, 384, 385
    strategies, 384
    TestBed, 381
    unit tests, 380, 381
  testing/deployment strategies, 426
    deployment, 428
    Hardhat/Foundry, 426
    maintainability, 429
    smart contract, 426
    Testnets, 428
    wallet integration/contract
      services, 427
  user interface, 371–375
Angular, lazy loading, 355
Anti-money laundering (AML), 110

API, *see* Application programming
    interfaces (APIs)
Application binary interface (ABI),
    303, 346
Application programming
    interfaces (APIs)
  GraphQL client, 369
  handling errors/retries, 369
  HTTP (*see* Hypertext transfer
    protocol (HTTP))
  pagination, 370
  remote procedure call, 274, 275
  services, 367, 368
Applications
  comparison, 188
  currency, 110–118
  decentralization, 186
  decision-making framework, 189, 190
  developer ecosystem, 186
  fees comparison, 187
  financial sector, 105–110
  framework priorities, 190
  interoperability, 188
  key factors, 184
  key industries, 104, 105
  long-term evolution, 190
  Minimum Viable Product (MVP), 189
  project priorities, 189
  property record management, 118–123
  regulatory environment, 187
  scalability, 185, 186
  security, 185
  smart contract, 129–134
  supply chain management, 130–136
  transactions per Second (TPS), 184
  voting system, 136–143
Artificial intelligence (AI), 135, 143
  cost considerations, 165

INDEX

regulatory approaches, 174
transaction speed, 169
Automated market makers (AMMs), 59

B

BaaS, *see* Blockchain-as-a-Service (BaaS)
BFT, *see* Byzantine Fault Tolerance (BFT)
Binance Smart Chain (BSC), 84
Bitcoin (BTC), 28, 68, 69
    cross-border payments, 108
    cryptocurrencies, 111
    network security mechanisms, 101
    transaction fees, 83
Blockchain-as-a-Service (BaaS), 169
Blockchain technology, 103, 177
    applications (*see* Applications)
    architecture, 43, 72
    Bitcoin, 68
    components, 72
    concepts, 65, 66
    consensus mechanisms, 44, 45, 74–77
    cost structure, 159–165
    decentralization (*see* Decentralization)
    decentralized ledger, 43, 44
    definition, 66
    distributed ledger, 74
    efficient transactions, 149–154
    Ethereum (*see* Ethereum (ETH))
    evolution, 69
    features, 66, 67
    fee market dynamics, 85, 86
    genesis block, 73
    historical background/evolution, 67
    immutable ledger, 39
    key players/projects, 69–71
    layer 2 solutions, 45, 46
    Merkle tree structure, 73, 74
    multiple layers and components, 71
    nodes/network structure
        full nodes, 77
        hard fork *vs.* soft fork, 80
        light nodes (SPV nodes), 78
        mining/validator nodes, 78
        P2P network, 78, 79
        structure/funtion, 77
        types, 78
    platforms, 71
    PoS, 44
    PoW, 44, 72
    pros and cons, 149
    providers (*see* Providers)
    regulatory approaches, 170–175
        adoption/scalability, 170
        China, 172
        consumer protection, 173
        cross-border collaboration, 172
        digital identity systems, 174
        El Salvador, 172
        environmental considerations, 174
        European Union, 171
        India, 172
        innovation control, 172
        intellectual property, 174
        legal/compliance issues, 170, 171
        perspectives, 170
        sandboxes, 173
        self-regulation, 173
        smart contracts, 171
        South Korea, 172
        taxation, 174
        technical expertise, 172
        tokens, 173
        United States, 171
        voting/governance, 174

INDEX

Blockchain technology (*cont.*)
    rollups, 46
    scalability, 68
    scalability requirements, 76
    scaling solutions, 86
    sidechains, 45
    smart contracts, 46–49, 68
    state channels, 45
    structure of, 66
    technical architecture, 44
    transactions, 80
        broadcasting network, 81
        components, 81
        creation, 81
        double-spending, 82
        fees/incentives, 83–86
        finality, 83
        inclusion, 82
        lifecycle, 81, 83
        miners/validators, 84
        signature validity, 82
        validation/verification, 82
    transparency, 155–159
BSC, *see* Binance Smart Chain (BSC)
Byzantine Fault Tolerance (BFT), 44, 76, 77, 147
    network security mechanisms, 97

C

Cardano (ADA), 70
CBDCs, *see* Central bank digital currencies (CBDCs)
Central bank digital currencies (CBDCs), 110
    benefits, 114
    competition, 115
    definition, 114
    implementation costs, 115
    implementation initiatives, 115
    key features, 114
    privacy concerns, 115
Chainlink (LINK), 70
CLI, *see* Command-line interface (CLI)
Command-line interface (CLI)
    build process, 360
    creation, 358
    environment files, 360
    folder structure, 358
    hot module replacement (HMR), 360
    installation, 358
    module-based setups, 360
    schematics, 361
    setup, 357
    solid foundation, 361
    standalone *vs.* module structure, 359
    well-structured project, 361
Component Dev Kit (CDK), 371, 373
Cost considerations
    architecture, 160
    cost-saving opportunities, 162
    development, 161
    energy consumption, 161
    energy-intensive, 163
    energy requirements, 163
    environmental impact, 163
    fraud mitigation, 162
    hardware/software infrastructure, 160
    implementation, 164
    industries, 163
    integration costs, 161
    intermediaries, 162
    mining operations, 163
    open-source frameworks, 164
    operational efficiency, 162
    scalability, 163

smart contracts, 162
token incentives, 164
Cryptocurrencies
    Altcoins/tokens, 28
    Bitcoin, 28, 68, 103
    cross-border remittances, 35
    definition, 111
    ETH, 28
    features, 111
    financial inclusion, 33
    Litecoin (LTC), 111
    native payments, 26
    smart contracts, 29, 30
    stablecoins, 28, 60
    traditional online payments, 27
    types of, 29
    wallets (*see* Wallets)
Currencies
    central bank digital currencies, 114, 115
    concepts, 110
    cryptocurrencies, 111
    stablecoins, 111–113
    use cases/adoption, 115
        adoption trends, 116
        cross-border trade, 116
        digital payments, 116
        regulatory uncertainty, 116
        scalability, 116
        technological accessibility, 116
        timeline, 117, 118
        tokenized ecosystems, 116

D

DAOs, *see* Decentralized Autonomous Organizations (DAOs)
dApps, *see* Decentralized applications (dApps)
DDOs, *see* Distributed Denial of Service (DDoS)
Decentralization, 6
    advantages/trade-offs, 148
    benefits, 88, 91, 146
    censorship, 147
    censorship resistance, 89
    central authority, 87
    centralized *vs.* distributed architecture, 146
    centralized *vs.* distributed networks, 87
    challenges, 93, 148, 149
    computational power and electricity, 92
    consensus mechanisms, 87
    cryptography, 94–96
        digital signature, 95
        hash function, 94
        private key, 96
        public-key, 96
    definition, 86
    features, 87
    financial inclusion, 148
    governance models, 92
    health data platforms, 148
    integrity, 146
    intermediaries, 90
    key advantages, 88
    levels of, 279
    network security mechanisms, 96
        architecture, 97
        51% attack, 98
        attack vectors, 98–100
        consensus mechanisms, 97
        fault tolerance, 98
        security breaches, 100, 101
        smart contracts, 98
        Sybil attack, 98

INDEX

Decentralization (*cont.*)
    practical principle, 186
    providers, 279
    regulation/compliance, 93
    scalability, 91
    sectors, 148
    security, 94
    security and resilience, 88, 89, 147
    security/transparency, 87
    self-hosting, 284
    single point failure, 146
    supply chains, 148
    trade-offs, 91
    transparency/trust, 90
    user control/ownership, 89
    user experience (UX), 93
Decentralized applications (dApps), 27, 295, 422
    angular, 393, 396
    architecture, 55
    architecture layers, 345
    blockchain network, 394
    calling view functions, 346
    characteristics, 55
    components, 54
    computing, 51
    definition, 54, 394
    ETH, 191
    ethers.js, 346
    events/real-time feedback, 346
    features, 56
    finance, 57
    frontend libraries/frameworks, 348
    gaming, 57
    governance, 57
    handling gas/errors/confirmation, 346
    integration, 344, 397
    network management, 347
    sector, 56, 58
    sending transactions, 346
    smart contracts (*see* Smart contracts)
    social media, 57
    srchitecture, 396, 397
    testnets, 347
    UI/UX patterns, 348
    wallets, 211, 345
    web frontend, 394
Decentralized Autonomous Organizations (DAOs), 13, 37, 169
    DApps, 57
    decentralization, 92
    ETH, 204, 205
    smart contracts, 311
Decentralized computing
    challenges, 52, 53
    definition, 51
    Golem and Filecoin, 52
    ongoing developments, 52
    platforms, 51
    solutions, 53
Decentralized exchanges (DEXs), 48, 59, 105
Decentralized finance (DeFi), 11, 105–107, 173
    advantages, 60, 106
    applications, 103
    automated market makers, 309
    benefits and risks, 62
    challenges, 106
    components, 59
    Curve Finance, 63
    DAO contracts, 311
    derivatives/synthetic assets, 60
    DEXs, 105
    ecosystem, 59, 107
    ETH, 202, 203

features, 105
financial applications, 59
financial system, 40
interest/borrow assets, 60
lending and borrowing, 106
lending protocols, 309
liquidity invariant, 309
MakerDAO, 63
marketplace contracts, 311
native payment systems, 33, 34
NFT smart contracts, 310
open-source protocols, 308
platforms, 58, 62, 63
responsibility, 61
risks/challenges, 61
smart contracts, 48, 106, 125
stablecoins, 60, 106, 113
transaction efficiency, 153
Uniswap/Aave, 62
vulnerabilities, 61
Web2/Web3 application, 182
yield farming and aggregators, 310
yield farming and liquidity mining, 60
Decentralized identifiers (DIDs), 158, 173
Decentralized identity (DID), 11, 12
DeFi, *see* Decentralized finance (DeFi)
Delegated Proof of Stake (DPoS), 44, 166
    comparison, 77
    consensus mechanism, 75
DEXs, *see* Decentralized
    exchanges (DEXs)
DIDs, *see* Decentralized identifiers (DIDs)
Digital ownership
    central concept, 19
    centralized *vs.* decentralized
        systems, 19, 20
    concept, 19, 26
    consumers, 25

content creators, 24–26
direct and exclusive control, 20, 21
integration, 26
non-fungible tokens, 21–24
Distributed Denial of Service (DDoS), 146
    network security mechanisms, 98
DLD, *see* Dubai Land Department (DLD)
Dubai Land Department (DLD), 122

E

ECC, *see* Elliptic Curve
    Cryptography (ECC)
EEA, *see* Enterprise Ethereum
    Alliance (EEA)
Elliptic Curve Cryptography (ECC), 96
Enterprise Ethereum Alliance (EEA), 173
Ethereum (ETH), 28, 69, 197, 198
    Bitcoin development, 191
    Blockchain, 68
    community-driven approach, 201
    concepts, 190
    core components, 194, 195
    creation of, 192
    cross-border payments, 108
    cryptocurrencies, 111
    DAO governance process, 205, 206
    DAO hack, 100
    DeFi ecosystem, 203, 204
    developer ecosystem, 205
    developer tools, 201
    EVM concepts, 195–197
    features, 193
    financial paradigm, 202
    Frontier, 191
    Gas System, 198
    global computer, 196
    JSON-RPC methods, 274

INDEX

Ethereum (ETH) (*cont.*)
    NFT revolution, 203, 204
    nodes/network structure, 80
    PoS, 198, 199
    roadmap phases, 205
    scaling solutions, 199, 200
    smart contracts, 129, 194, 195, 197
    token standards, 200, 201
    transaction fees, 83
    vision, 192, 193
Ethereum Classic (ETC), 80
Ethereum Virtual Machine (EVM), 195–197
    compilation process, 334
    gas/costs/efficiency, 318
    providers, 254
    smart contracts, 299, 300
EVM, *see* Ethereum Virtual Machine (EVM)

F

FATF, *see* Financial Action Task Force (FATF)
Financial Action Task Force (FATF), 173
Financial sector
    cross-border payments, 107, 108
        Bitcoin/Ethereum, 108
        intermediaries, 107
        international trade, 108
        regulations, 108
        Ripple (XRP), 107
        Stellar (XLM), 107
        traditional *vs.* blockchain, 108
        transfer services, 108
        transparency/security, 107
        volatility, 108
    decentralized finance, 105–107
    definition, 105
    P2P lending platforms, 109, 110

G

Gas System, 198, 199

H

Honduras Land Title Pilot Project, 122
HTTP, *see* Hypertext transfer protocol (HTTP)
Hypertext transfer protocol (HTTP)
    data consuming, 368
    error handling, 371
    GraphQL client, 369
    handle errors/retry requests/cancel, 369
    HttpClient, 367
    pagination, 370
    real-time data, 369
    service creation, 367, 368
    WebSockets, 369
    working process, 366

I, J

India's Land Registry Projects, 122
Internet of Things (IoT), 135
InterPlanetary File System (IPFS), 50
IoT, *see* Internet of Things (IoT)
IPFS, *see* InterPlanetary File System (IPFS)

K

Key performance indicators (KPIs), 278
KPIs, *see* Key performance indicators (KPIs)

L

Litecoin (LTC), cryptocurrencies, 111

M

Man-in-the-Middle (MITM), 267
MITM, *see* Man-in-the-Middle (MITM)
Mnemonic phrase
    advanced security strategies, 224
    backups, 222
    benefits, 221
    cold storage solutions, 225
    creation, 216
    crypto community, 223, 224
    encryption, 225
    financial sovereignty, 219
    flow process, 217
    geopolitical risk, 220
    hidden wallets, 225
    key management
        air-gapped devices, 232
        concepts, 229
        crypto world, 230
        hardware wallets, 231
        hierarchical deterministic (HD), 232
        multi-signature wallets, 231
        strategies and risks, 230
        Web3, 232
    master key, 217, 218
    multiple signature, 225
    online risks, 219
    physical/digital/procedural protection, 219
    physical gold/bearer bonds, 218
    public/private keys, 226
        definition, 226
        differences, 228
        key management, 229–232
        master password, 226
        properties, 227
        public keys, 227, 228
        technical details, 227
        trustless security model, 228
    radical empowerment, 218
    safe locations, 220
    security, 216, 219, 223
    seed phrase, 220
    sharding process, 221

N

NAPR, *see* National Agency of Public Registry (NAPR)
National Agency of Public Registry (NAPR), 122
Native payment systems
    benefits, 31
    concepts, 26
    cross-border remittances, 35, 36
    cryptocurrencies, 26, 28, 29
    DeFi platforms, 33, 34
    e-commerce platforms, 34, 35
    financial inclusion, 33
    OpenSea payment flow, 35
    privacy, 32
    security, 32
    smart contract, 29, 30
    speed and efficiency, 31
    vs. traditional payments, 27
    vs. traditional systems, 30–33
    transaction fees, 32
Network considerations
    automatic retries, 264
    circuit breakers, 264
    data injection attacks, 267

INDEX

Network considerations (*cont.*)
    definition, 258
    failures, 263
    fallback systems, 265, 266
    global geographic coverage, 263, 264
    IP address, 268
    key management, 268
    latency, 258, 259
    man-in-the-middle attack, 267
    multi-region setup, 264
    performance metrics, 258
    privacy, 268
    privacy-preserving approach, 269
    reliability, 263
    security risks, 266
    server deployment, 263
    throughput, 260, 261
    uptime tiers, 261, 262
NFTs, *see* Non-fungible tokens (NFTs)
Non-fungible tokens (NFTs), 6, 310
    definition, 21
    digital ownership, 19
    ETH, 203, 204
    fungible *vs.* non-fungible tokens, 22
    gaming industry, 23
    impact of, 23, 24
    lifecycle overview, 22, 23
    smart contracts, 48, 126

O

Open-source software (OSS)
    community-driven development, 37
    concepts, 36
    governance decisions, 37
    security audits, 38
OSS, *see* Open-source software (OSS)

P, Q

Peer-to-peer (P2P), 13
    financial sector
        advantages, 109
        Celsius, 109
        challenges, 110
        global access, 109
        lending platforms, 109
        MakerDAO, 109
        smart contracts, 109
        tokenization, 109
Polkadot (DOT), 70
PoS, *see* Proof of Stake (PoS)
PoW, *see* Proof of Work (PoW)
P2P, *see* Peer-to-peer (P2P)
Proof of Authority (PoA)
    comparison, 77
    consensus mechanism, 44, 76
Proof of History (PoH), 70, 76, 77
Proof of Stake (PoS), 69
    block rewards/transaction fees, 85–88
    comparison, 76
    consensus mechanism, 44, 75
    decentralization, 92
    energy consumption, 154
    ETH, 198, 199
    network security mechanisms, 97
    transaction speed, 166
Proof of Work (PoW)
    block rewards/transaction fees, 85–88
    comparison, 76
    consensus mechanism, 44, 75
    decentralization, 92
    energy consumption, 154
    network security mechanisms, 97
    transaction speed, 166

INDEX

Property record management
  case studies/
      implementations, 121–124
  concepts, 118
  digital land registries, 118
    architecture, 120
    benefits, 119
    challenges, 118
    integration, 119
    key features, 118
    legal and regulatory
      frameworks, 119
    working process, 119
  ownership verification, 120
    disasters, 121
    immutable records, 121
    mortgages and loans, 121
    ownership verification, 121
    smart contracts, 120
    title insurance, 121
    tokenization, 120
Providers
  accessibility, 258
  aggregation strategies, 289
  architectural decisions, 277
  characteristics, 279
  complex systems, 251
  decentralization, 279
  decentralized RPC networks, 287, 288
  developer experience (DX), 282
  emerging technologies, 283
  evolution, 252
  factors, 280, 282, 286
  fallback systems, 288
  full node, 251, 253, 254, 285
  gateway, 256
  hardware requirements, 284
  historical evolution, 251, 252
  hybrid architecture, 287, 288
  hybridization, 257
  indexing, 256
  Infura outage, 280
  key trends shaping, 291
  KPIs, 278
  libraries, 289
  metadata, 268
  multichain applications, 290
  multichain development, 283
  multichain orchestration, 292
  network (*see* Network considerations)
  NFT minting test, 278
  operational challenges, 285, 286
  optimization, 282
  pocket network growth, 288
  pricing models, 282
  privacy-preserving interactions, 291
  production-ready applications,
    290, 291
  protocols, 250
  querying, 256
  regional optimization, 278
  regulations, 281
  resilience, 258
  responsibilities, 290
  role of, 249
  RPC methods, 253, 254
  RPC/wallet providers, 269–277
  scalability, 258
  seamless multichain orchestration, 292
  security/compliance, 280
  self-hosting, 284, 286
  service/software component, 250
  software, 284
  speed/performance, 277
  synchronization, 285
  Tornado Cash Sanctions, 281

INDEX

Providers (*cont.*)
  transaction signing process, 255
  trust models, 279
  types of, 252
  users/applications, 250
  wallet, 254, 255
  zero-knowledge proofs, 291

R

Remote procedure call (RPC)
  Alchemy/QuickNode, 275
  API exposure, 274, 275
  blockchain networks, 399
  centralized/decentralized model, 279
  data access/transaction, 274
  decentralized networks, 287, 288
  Infura, 275
  JSON-RPC methods, 274
  node management/scaling, 275
  providers, 253, 254
  wallet providers, 276
Representational State Transfer (REST), 369
REST, *see* Representational State Transfer (REST)
Ripple (XRP), 70, 107
Ripple Protocol Consensus Algorithm (RPCA), 71
Routing system
  CanActivate guard, 377
  configuration, 376, 378
  features, 379
  guard interfaces, 377
  lazy loading, 378
  nested routes/dynamic segments, 376, 377
  parameters, 377
  public-facing applications, 379
  scenario, 379
RPCA, *see* Ripple Protocol Consensus Algorithm (RPCA)

S

Security mechanisms
  challenges/solutions, 15
  cryptographic principles, 9–12
  decentralized governance, 13, 14
  decentralized identity, 11, 12
  encryption, 10
  global regulatory considerations, 18
  homomorphic encryption, 15
  key management, 16
  legal/regulatory challenges, 18
  mixing services, 15
  P2P networks, 13
  phishing attack vectors, 17
  privacy-enhancing technologies, 15
  privacy via mixing services, 15
  public and private key, 10
  responsibility/education, 16
  social engineering/phishing attacks, 17
  zero-knowledge proofs, 10
Server-Sent Events (SSE), 369
Server-side rendering (SSR), 388
Single-page application (SPA), 375
Smart contracts, 29, 30
  angular application
    contract service, 410
    error handling/edge cases, 409
    gas/fees, 409
    interaction, 407
    read-only functions, 407, 408
    real-world patterns, 410
    state-changing functions, 407

INDEX

writing data/sending transaction, 408, 409
architecture, 302
Axie Infinity, 129
blockchain, 46–49
bytecode, 298
close voting, 333
coding errors, 128
compilation process
    Foundry, 336, 337
    Hardhat, 334, 335
    Remix, 337
    solidity, 334
    tool generation, 334
compiler, 316
compiling/deployment, 334
compliance, 127
composability, 308
concepts, 310
constructor, 332
core building blocks, 295
core properties, 296
definition, 47, 124, 296, 329
DeFi platforms, 48
delegation, 306
deployment, 316, 338, 343
design constraints/limitations, 300
development lifecycle, 314
development tools, 323
error handling, 421
escrow/conditional payments, 312
escrow services, 125
ETH, 194, 195
ethical concerns, 128
events, 306, 331, 419
EVM, 299, 300
EVM bytecode, 316
execution, 124

flow, 47
stack, 300
features, 124
flowchart/state machine, 315
formal audits, 343
foundation, 302
Foundry, 325, 326, 328, 343
full code (solidity 0.8+), 329, 330
gaming and NFTs, 126
gaming/virtual economies, 313
gas
    costs/efficiency, 318
    data types, 321
    developers, 319
    limits/out-of-errors, 322
    logging, 321
    operation, 319, 320
    optimization techniques, 323
    pack structs and mappings, 321
    protocol design, 320
    storage operations, 320
    temporary variables, 321
    testing/profile, 322
    tools, 322
    transaction fee breakdown, 319
handling networks, 421
Hardhat, 325, 326, 328
Hardhat project, 410
    ABI section, 412
    angular contract services, 412–414
    compiling contract, 411
    defensive patterns, 417
    estimation issues, 418
    gas problems, 415
    handling real errors, 415
    script deployment, 412
    SimpleStorageComponent, 414
    SimpleStorage.sol, 411

INDEX

Smart contracts (*cont.*)
    simulation fails, 416
    strategies, 416, 417
healthcare, 126
high-value protocols, 308
identity and reputation systems, 312, 313
industries, 125
inheritance, 305
insurance, 126
interaction, 317
key applications, 47
legal and regulatory challenges, 127–129
liability, 128
lifecycle, 125
line by line contract, 328
logic errors, 343
maintenance strategy, 318
marketplaces, 48
modifiers, 332
monitoring tools, 318
MythX, 343
Nexus Mutual, 129
on-chain *vs.* off-chain logic, 303, 304
patterns, 343, 422
payments, 126
plugins/custom scripts, 328
pragma/license, 331
programming languages, 124
Propy, 129
proxy pattern, 306
public functions/events, 303, 304
real-world application, 129
real-world asset tracking, 313
real-world management, 49
real-world patterns, 418
real-world use cases, 301
reentrancy/call context, 307
Remix IDE, 327
rental agreements, 125
route guards, 419
sector, 127
security, 420
slither, 343
solidity, 305, 306, 315
source code, 298
state variables, 331
supply chain, 48
testing, 333
    Foundry, 341
    fuzz flow, 342, 343
    goals, 339
    invariant, 342
    security, 339
    strategies, 344
    traditional applications, 339
    types/tools, 340
    unit testing (Hardhat), 340
tool comparison table, 327
traceability, 126
vs. traditional contracts, 297, 298
transaction status pattern, 420
Truffle, 326
validity, 127
verification, 125
verification links, 317
vote function, 333
vulnerabilities, 342
workflow recommendation, 328
Solana (SOL), 70, 84
SPA, *see* Single-page application (SPA)
SSE, *see* Server-Sent Events (SSE)
SSR, *see* Server-side rendering (SSR)
Stablecoins, 28
    adoption barriers, 113

algorithmic adjustments, 113
commodity, 112
comparison, 112
E-Commerce, 113
fiat currency, 112
key features, 111
remittances, 113
types of, 113
use cases, 113
volatility, 113
State management
    approaches, 366
    components, 361, 362
    fine-grained reactivity, 364, 365
    overengineering, 365
    reactive state (RxJS), 363
    signals, 364
    single-page application, 362
    store patterns, 364
Stellar (XLM), 107
Storage decentralization
    architecture, 51
    censorship resistance, 50
    components, 49
    data integrity, 50
    networks, 50
    security and privacy, 50
    vulnerabilities, 49
Supply chain management
    advantages, 134, 135
    benefits, 133, 134
    emerging technologies, 135, 136
    Everledger, 132
    future trends, 136
    key application, 130
    logistics and retail companies, 131
    Maersk/TradeLans, 132
    real-world application, 133
    smart contracts, 135
    standards, 135
    transparency/traceability
        features, 130
        food items, 130
        high-value items, 131
        IBM Food Trust, 131
        pharmaceutical industry, 131
        provenance verification, 130
        real-time tracking, 130
    trust/efficiency, 133
    VeChain, 132
Supply chains, 156
Sweden's Lantmäteriet, 123

T

Traditional transaction systems
    batch processing, 151
    challenges, 154
    consensus protocols, 154
    cost/speed benefits, 150, 151
    cross-border payments, 151
    cross-chain solutions, 154
    DeFi platforms, 153
    e-governments, 153
    gaming industry, 153
    healthcare billing, 153
    improvements, 149
    instant settlements, 150
    integration, 154
    IoT devices, 153
    key comparisons, 151
    microtransactions, 152
    reliability and accessibility, 152
    remittance services, 152
    settlement, 151
    speed information, 165

Traditional transaction systems (*cont.*)
  Avalanche, 167
  banking systems, 167
  block size/time, 166
  comparisons, 165
  consensus protocol, 165
  cross-chain communication, 169
  energy consumption, 168
  hardware acceleration, 169
  interoperability, 168
  multi-tiered system, 169
  network congestion, 166
  network scalability, 166
  optimistic rollups/zk-Rollups, 168
  Polygon processes, 167
  real-time processing, 167
  Ripple (XRP), 167
  settlement times, 167
  sharding techniques, 168
  Solana, 167
  technical complexity, 168
  trade-offs, 168
  supply chains, 153
Transparency
  academic institutions, 156
  auditability, 155
  challenges, 157
  charitable donations, 157
  collaboration, 155
  consensus mechanisms, 155
  corporate governance, 156
  DIDs, 158
  food products, 157
  hybrid models, 159
  industries, 156
  integration, 158
  intellectual property, 157
  interoperability, 159
  medical records, 156
  misinterpretation, 158
  participants, 155
  principles, 155
  privacy concerns, 157
  public records, 156
  recordkeeping, 155
  security, 158
  sustainability, 157
  tokenization, 159
Transparent transaction records
  accountability/security, 41
  driving technologies, 43–53
  features, 38
  financial system, 40
  fundamental principle, 36
  immutable ledgers, 38
  open-source development, 36–38
  supply chain management, 39, 40
  trust mechanisms, 42
  user empowerment, 41
  users/developers, 41–43

U

UI, *see* User interface (UI)
User interface (UI)
  angular materials, 371
  components, 371, 374, 375
  consistent design, 375
  customization, 372
  layout components, 374
  material components, 372
  navigation, 373
  theming system, 372
  validation, 373

V

Voting system
  accessibility, 137
  authentication, 136, 139
  benefits, 137, 139
  casting, 136
  challenges, 136, 141
  decentralized storage, 137
  developments, 143
  emerging technologies, 143
  Estonia, 141
  features, 136, 137
  immutable record, 137
  initiatives, 142
  privacy concerns, 140
  public perception, 140
  real-time auditing, 137
  regulations/legal frameworks, 140
  scalability, 139
  security, 137
  Sierra Leone, 142
  Switzerland, 142
  transparency, 137
  Voatz, 142
  West Virginia, 141
  working process, 137
  zero-knowledge proofs, 143

W, X, Y

Wallets
  angular applications, 423
  asymmetric cryptography, 211, 212
  backup recovery phrase, 215
  custodial, 214
  dApps, 345
  fundamental concepts, 209
  hardware devices
    advantages, 239
    browser extension, 241
    disadvantages, 240
    private keys, 239
    transaction, 239
    use of, 240
  hot/cold wallets, 213, 214
  indispensable roles, 210
  integration
    blockchain, 403
    connection, 403
    reactive architecture, 406
    requesting permissions/signing, 405, 406
    service, 403
    signals/observables, 404
    state reaction, 404, 405
    user security, 406
  mnemonic phrase (*see* Mnemonic phrase)
  non-custodial, 214
  paper
    advantages, 244
    comparison, 246
    disadvantages, 244
    physical printout, 243
    real-world application, 245
    use of, 245
    working process, 244
  private and public keys, 210
  providers
    authentication, 254, 255
    categories, 273
    critical differences, 269
    key management, 254, 255, 270
    keys/identities/signatures, 270

INDEX

Wallets (*cont.*)
    MetaMask, 273
    pluggable modules, 277
    private key, 270
    RPC comparison, 276
    session management/
      permissions, 272
    signing flow process, 272, 273
    technical approaches, 270
    types of, 276
  real-world application, 215
  security, 215
  setup process
    comparison, 233
    convenience/control, 233
    creation, 233, 234
    customization, 236
    mnemonic phrase, 234
    password protection, 235
    physical device, 239
    pitfalls/solutions, 236, 237
    principles, 233
    self-empowerment, 238
    software/hardware wallets, 233, 234
    testing process, 236
    types of, 238
  software devices
    advantages, 242
    disadvantages, 242
    program/application, 241
    real-world application, 243
    users protocols, 243
    working process, 241
  transaction process, 212, 213
Web2 application *vs.* Web3 application
  architectural differences, 177
  cloud storage, 182
  content ownership, 180, 181
  DeFi platforms, 182
  financial interactions, 180
  identities, 179, 180
  industry transitions, 183
  login flow, 179
  social media, 181
  social web, 177
  transformation, 178
  user experience, 179
Web3 application
  application types, 53–63
  benefits/features, 5–7
  Blockchain (*see* Blockchain
    technology)
  centralized *vs.* decentralized
    network, 3
  digital ownership/identity, 6
  dynamic/interactive/social web, 4
  evolution, 2, 3
  foundational transformation, 1
  frontends, 419
  incentivization, 7
  interoperability, 6
  migration, 5
  native payments, 26–36
  ownership, 19–26
  security, 7, 9–18
  social impact, 9, 10
  societal implications, 8
  static web pages, 4
  technologies, 2
  tokenomics, 7
  transition, 4
  transparency, 36–42
  transparency/open source, 7
  trustless/permissionless, 6
  UI/UX patterns, 348
  Web2 architecture, 8

Web development *(see* Angular application*)*
WebSockets, 369

Z

Zero-knowledge proofs (ZKPs), 10
ZKPs, *see* Zero-knowledge proofs (ZKPs)

GPSR Compliance

The European Union's (EU) General Product Safety Regulation (GPSR) is a set of rules that requires consumer products to be safe and our obligations to ensure this.

If you have any concerns about our products, you can contact us on

ProductSafety@springernature.com

In case Publisher is established outside the EU, the EU authorized representative is:

Springer Nature Customer Service Center GmbH
Europaplatz 3
69115 Heidelberg, Germany